h o s t e l s   s e r i e s

hostels
european cities

the only comprehensive, unofficial, opinionated guide

fourth edition

Text for Brussels, Paris, Marseille, Lyon, Dublin, Rome, Milan, Florence, Pisa, Venice, Luxembourg City, Amsterdam, Edinburgh, London, Cardiff, Glasgow, and Manchester copyright © 2002, 2004, 2006, 2008 by Paul Karr

Text for Vienna, Prague, Copenhagen, Berlin, Munich, Athens, Budapest, Oslo, Lisbon, Barcelona, Madrid, Seville, Stockholm, Geneva, and Zürich copyright © 2002, 2004, 2006, 2008 Morris Book Publishing, LLC

Text design: M. A. Dubé
Maps created by XNR Productions, Inc., © Morris Book Publishing, LLC
Freelance contributors: Ashlee Arling, Scott Goodell, Klaus Heindl, Wes Ingwersen, Dyveke Kanth, Oliver Krausz, Yasmin Mistry, Piran Montford, Hiro Nakajima, Michael Roth, Dawn Severenuk
Co-concept and other editorial assistance: Evan Halper

ISSN 1541-8065
ISBN 978-0-7627-4778-8

Printed in the United States of America
10 9 8 7 6 5 4 3 2 1

contents

acknowledgments

Many people have contributed to this book. Thanks to Betsy Wright and Klaus Heindl for helping recruit freelance help. Thanks, too, to all the independent and official hostel associations of Europe—especially those who went beyond the call of duty for this and previous editions: Danhostel in Copenhagen, NHJC in Amsterdam, LAJ in Belgium, AIG in Rome, FUAJ in Paris, YHA in London, and American Youth Hostels. All supplied a world of help as well as continuous encouragement and assistance.

Thanks again to friends and family in New England, Europe, Georgia, Canada, and Japan for bringing light and joy to travel and for providing a home away from home.

Thanks to the editors at Globe Pequot for continuing to champion this series, edit it well, and allow us to remain ourselves. Well done! Rail Europe and DER Travel (now part of the same company) assisted once again with expertise and customer service. And thanks to our fearless freelancers for deciphering the various hostel systems and contributing some wickedly funny write-ups.

And thanks, finally, to a world (literally) of new friends met or made on the road. So many of you have taught us about your corner of the world or otherwise made this work enjoyable and useful.

thank you all.

how to use
this book

What you're holding in your hands is the first-ever attempt of its kind: a fairly complete listing and rating of the most popular hostels in Europe. Dozens of hostellers from countries all over the globe were interviewed in the course of putting this guide together, and their comments and thoughts run throughout its pages. Who knows? You, yourself, might be quoted somewhere inside.

We wrote this guide for two pretty simple reasons: First, we wanted to bring hostelling to a wider audience. Hostels continue to grow in popularity, but many North American travelers still don't think of them as options when planning a trip. We wanted to encourage that because—at its best—the hostelling experience brings people of greatly differing origins, faiths, and points of view together in a convivial setting. You learn about these people, and also about the place in which the hostel is situated, in a very personal way that no textbook could ever provide.

Second, we wanted very much to give people our honest opinions of the hostels. You wouldn't send your best friend to a fleabag, and we don't want readers traveling great distances only to be confronted with filthy kitchens, nasty managers, or dangerous neighborhoods. At least, we thought, we could warn them about unsafe or unpleasant situations ahead of time.

Of course we would also tip our friends off to the truly wonderful hostels—the ones with treehouses, cafes, free breakfasts, and real family spirit. So that's what we've done. Time after time on the road, we have heard fellow travelers complaining that the guidebooks they bought simply listed places to stay but didn't rate them. Well, now we've done it—and we haven't pulled a single punch or held back a bit of praise.

how we wrote this book

The author, along with a cadre of assistants, fanned out across Europe with notebooks and laptops in hand. Sometimes we identified ourselves in advance as authors; sometimes we just popped in for surprise visits. We counted rooms, turned taps, tested beds. And then we talked with managers and staff.

Before we left we also took the time to interview plenty of hostellers in private and get their honest opinions about the places they were staying or had already stayed.

The results are contained within this book: actual hosteller quotes, opinions, ratings, and more.

what is a hostel?

If you've picked up this book, you probably know what a hostel is. A surprising number of people interviewed for this book, however, weren't sure at all what it means.

So let's check your knowledge with a little pop quiz. Sharpen up your pencils, put on your thinking caps, then dive in.

1. A hostel is:
   A. A hospital.
   B. A hospice.
   C. A hotel.
   D. A drunk tank.
   E. None of the above.

   (correct answer worth 20 points)

2. A hostel is:
   A. A place where international travelers bunk up.
   B. A cheap sleep.
   C. A place primarily dedicated to bunks.
   D. All of the above.

   (correct answer worth 20 points)

3. You just turned thirty. Word on the street has it that you'll get turned away for being that age. Do you tell the person at the hostel desk the grim news?
   A. No, because a hostel is restricted to students under twenty-seven.
   B. No, because a hostel is restricted to folks over sixty-five.
   C. No, because they don't care about your midlife crisis.
   D. Yes.

   (correct answer worth 10 points)

4. You spy a shelf labeled FREE FOOD! in the hostel kitchen. What do you do?
   A. Begin stuffing pomegranates in your pockets.
   B. Ask the manager how food ended up in jail.
   C. Run for your life.

   (correct answer worth 5 points)

5. Essay question. Why do you want to stay in a hostel?

(extra credit; worth up to 45 points)

Done? Great! And the envelope, please . . .

1. E. None of the above. The word *hostel* has German origins, and it means "country inn for youngsters" or something like that.

2. D. All of the above. You got that one, right?

3. D. Normally, there are no age limits or restrictions at a hostel. However, in Bavaria—the south of Germany—there is an age limit; if you're twenty-seven or older, you can stay only under special conditions. Some hostels in Berlin also enforce this restriction. Many other places tack on a surcharge for persons over age twenty-six, but you can still stay.

4. A. Free means free.

5. Give yourself 15 points for every use of the word "friends," "international," or "cool," okay? But don't give yourself more than 45. Yes, we mean it. Don't make us turn this car around right now. We will. We mean it.

What? All you wrote was "It's cheap"? Okay, okay, give yourself 20 points.

So how did you do?

100 points:	Born to be wild
80–99:	Get your motor runnin'
40–79:	Head out on the highway
20–39:	Lookin' for adventure
0–19:	Hope you don't come my way

Don't be embarrassed if you flunked this little quiz, though. Hostel operators get confused and blur the lines, too. You'll sometimes find a campground or retreat center or college setting aside a couple bunks—and calling itself a hostel anyway. In those cases we've used our best judgment about whether a place is or isn't a hostel.

Also, we excluded some joints—no matter how well-meaning—if they (a) exclude men or women, (b) serve primarily as a university residence hall (with a few, very special exceptions), or (c) serve you a heavy side of religious doctrine with the eggs in the morning.

In a few cases our visits didn't satisfy us either way; those places were either left out, set aside for a future edition, or briefly described here but not rated.

The bottom line? If it's in this book, it probably is a hostel. If it isn't, it's not, and don't let anyone tell you otherwise. There. 'Nuff said.

understanding the ratings

All the listings information in this book was current as of press time. Here's the beginning of an entry in the book, from a hostel in Denmark.

bellahøj hostel

Herbergvejen 8, 2700 Brønshøj (Copenhagen)
Phone: 038–289–715

Fax: 038–890–210
E-mail: bellahoej@danhostel.dk
Rates: 120 DKK (about $24 US) per Hostelling International member; doubles 350 DKK (about $70 US)
Credit cards: No
Beds: 248
Private/family rooms: Yes
Kitchen available: Yes
Season: February 1–December 2
Office hours: Twenty-four hours
Affiliation: HI-Danhostel
Extras: Parking, TV lounge, Internet access, luggage storage, laundry, grill, snacks

First things first. See those little pictures immediately above? Those are icons, and they signify something important we wanted you to know about the hostel. We've printed a key to these icons on page 6.

The overall hostel rating consists of those hip-looking thumbs sitting atop most entries. It's pretty simple: Thumbs up means good. Thumbs down means bad.

We've used these thumbs to compare the hostels with one another. Only a select number of hostels earned the top rating of two thumbs up, and a few were considered unpleasant enough to merit a thumb down.

You can use this rating as a general assessment of a hostel.

Often we didn't give any thumbs at all to a hostel that was a mixed-bag experience. Or maybe, for one reason or another—bad weather, bad luck, bad timing, remoteness, an inability to get a hold of the staff, or our own confusion about the place—we just didn't feel we collected enough information to properly rate that hostel for you.

That said, here's a key to what these ratings mean:

🖐🖐	Cream of the crop; recommended
🖐	Pretty good
No thumbs	OK; average; jury's still out
👎	Only if you're desperate
😣	Bad news; don't even THINK of calling

Note that hostels in our "at-a-glance" charts are ranked according to quality—that is, if there are eight hostels all with a one-thumb-up rating, we consider the one listed at the top of the pile to be the best (and the one at the bottom to be the, er, least) of the bunch.

The rest of the information is pretty much self-explanatory:

Address is usually the hostel's street address; occasionally we add the mailing address if different from the physical address.

Phone is the primary telephone number.

Fax is the primary fax number.

E-mail is the staff's e-mail address, for those who want to get information or (sometimes) book a room by computer.

Web site indicates a hostel's World Wide Web address.

Rates are the cost per person to stay at the hostel—when all the currency converting's said and done, expect to pay somewhere around $15 US per person, more (sometimes considerably more) in cities or popular tourist areas. For private or family rooms, we've listed the total price for two people to stay in the room; usually it's higher than the cost of two singles, sometimes considerably so. Single or triple room rates will vary; ask ahead if you're unsure what you'll pay.

Note that these rates sometimes vary by season or by membership in a hostelling group such as Hostelling International (HI); we have tried to include a range of prices where applicable. Most HI member hostels, for instance, charge $2 to $4 extra per day if you don't belong to one of Hostelling International's worldwide affiliates.

Also, many European hostels might charge you the equivalent of $1 to $5 US to supply sheets and/or towels if you haven't brought your own, a charge that can add up fast over time. (Sleeping bags, no matter how clean you think they are, are often frowned upon.) Finally, various local, municipal, or other taxes might add slightly to the rates quoted here.

key to icons

Attractive natural setting

Ecologically aware hostel

Superior kitchen facilities or great cafe/restaurant

Offbeat or eccentric place

Superior bathroom facilities

Romantic private rooms

Comfortable beds

A particularly good value

Wheelchair-accessible

Good for business travelers

Especially well suited for families

Good for active travelers

Visual arts at hostel or nearby

Music at hostel or nearby

Great hostel for skiers

Bar or pub at hostel or nearby

Editors' choice: among our very favorite hostels

Credit cards can be a good way to pay for a bed in a foreign country (you get the fairest exchange rates on your home currency); here we have mentioned whether cards are accepted by the hostels. More and more hostels are taking them, and even if we haven't listed a hostel as accepting credit cards, things may have changed. When in doubt, call ahead and ask.

Beds indicates the number of beds available at the hostel.

Private/family rooms are rooms for a couple, a family with children, or (sometimes) a single traveler. Sometimes it's nice to have your own room on the road: It's more private, more secure, and your snoring won't bother anyone. They're becoming more common in Europe but are still hard to snag during the busy season. So book months ahead for one if you're going to a popular place like Berlin or London. Really.

Kitchen available indicates whether the hostel allows hostellers to cook in a kitchen or not. In North America and the U.K., almost every hostel has a kitchen—but the situation changes in the rest of Europe. Very few of these hostels have a kitchen setup. Almost all, however, serve a delicious meal instead, so take advantage and fill 'er up. Breakfast is often included with the price of your bed; if it is, we have noted this under "Extras" (see next page).

Season indicates what part of the year a hostel is open—if it's closed part of the year. We've made our best effort at listing the seasons of each hostel, but schedules sometimes change according to weather or a manager's vacation plans. Call if you're unsure whether a hostel will be open when you want to stay there.

Office hours indicates the hours when staff are at the front desk and answer the phones, or at least would consider answering the phones. Although European custom is to use military time (23:30 for 11:30 P.M.), we've used "American" time throughout this book.

Keep in mind that nothing is fixed in stone, however; some hostel staffs will happily field calls in the middle of the night if you're reasonable, while others can't stand it. Try to call within the listed hours if possible.

A good rule to follow: The smaller a place, the harder it is for the owner/manager to drag him/herself out of bed at four in the morning just because you lost your way. Big-city hostels, however, frequently operate just like hotels—somebody's always on duty, or at least on call.

Do keep in mind that some Europeans are notorious for their strict attitudes toward time and punctuality. Don't expect the front desk to stay open a few minutes late or end the lockout ten minutes early. Don't knock it; adapt and deal. It's just their way.

Lockout and **Curfew.** Some hostels have hours during which you are locked out of the place (in other words, you're not permitted on the premises). Some also have a curfew; be back inside before this time, or you'll be locked out for the night.

Affiliation indicates whether a hostel is affiliated with Hostelling International. For more information about what these organizations do, see "A Word About Affiliations" (page 11).

Extras lists some of the other amenities that come with a stay at the hostel. Some—but not all—will be free. There's an amazing variety of services, and almost as big a variety in managers' willingness to do nice things for free. Laundries, for instance, are never free, and there's almost always a charge for meals, lockers, bicycle or other equipment rentals, and other odds and ends. On the other hand, some hostels maintain free information desks, and a few will pick you up at rail stations and the like.

With each entry, we've also given you a little more information about the hostel, to make your stay a little more informed—and fun. The sidebar to the left is part of the hostel entry that began above.

What does all that stuff mean?

Best bet for a bite:
Better eat here

What hostellers say:
"Fun place."

Gestalt:
Great Dane

Safety:

Hospitality:

Cleanliness:

Party index:

Best bet for a bite tells you where to find food in the area; usually we'll direct you to the cheapest and closest supermarket. But sometimes, in the interest of variety—and good eatin'—we'll point you toward a surprising health food store, a farmers' market, a place rich with local color, or even a fancy place well worth the splurge.

Insiders' tip is a juicy secret about the area, something we didn't know until we got to the hostel ourselves.

What hostellers say relates what hostellers told us about a hostel—or what we imagine they would say.

Gestalt is the general feeling of a place, our (sometimes humorous) way of describing what it's about.

Safety rates urban hostels only. This grade is normally based on both the quality of the neighborhood and the security precautions taken by the hostel staff.

     No worries

     Dial 911

Hospitality rates the hostel staff's friendliness toward hostellers (and travel writers).

Smile city

Very hostile hostel

Cleanliness rates, what else, the general cleanliness of a place. Bear in mind that this can change—rapidly—depending on the time of year, turnover in staff, and so forth. Use it only as a general guide.

Spic-and-span

Don't let the bedbugs bite

The **party index** is our way of tipping you off about the general scene at the hostel:

Rage all night

Party hearty

Lively

Mellow

Downright quiet

Finally, **How to get there** includes directions for how to get to many of the hostels—by car, bus, train, plane, or, in some cases, even ferry. Subway directions are given in big cities if applicable. Often these directions are complicated, however. In those cases, managers have asked (or we recommend) that you call the hostel for more precise directions.

a short history
of hostelling

Hostelling as we know it started around 1907 when Richard Schirmann, an assistant schoolteacher in the hill town of Altena, Germany, decided to make one of the empty classrooms a space for visiting students to sleep. That was not a completely unique idea, as Austrian inns and taverns had been offering reduced rates and bunk space to students since 1885. But Schirmann would develop much grander plans. He was about to start a movement.

His idea was to get students out of the industrial cities and into the countryside. Schirmann was a strong believer that walking and bicycling tours in the fresh air were essential to adolescent development and learning. But such excursions were impossible without a place to spend the night. His logic was simple: Since rural schoolhouses were deserted during weekends and holidays, why not make use of those spaces?

The caretakers of the school he chose agreed to serve as houseparents, and some fast ground rules were established. Students were responsible for piling up the tables and benches in the classroom and laying out thin straw mats on the floor. At some ungodly early-morning hour, the students were to stack the straw mats back up and organize the classroom back as they found it. Boys and girls slept in separate rooms but were treated as equals. Detractors cried scandal, wondering aloud what was going on in these schoolrooms after dark.

The experiment worked, sort of. Altena became a haven for student excursions into the countryside, but finding shelter in other communities proved difficult. Sometimes the situation would become dire. Late one night in the summer of 1909, Schirmann decided it was time to expand his movement beyond Altena. His goal was to establish a network of hostels within walking distance of one another; beginning in a schoolhouse with straw mats, Schirmann eventually acquired the use of a castle. It still stands—the Ur-hostel, if you will—in Altena, and it's still used as a hostel.

After World War I the movement really began to spread. By 1928 there were more than 2,000 hostels worldwide. Today tens of thousands of hostellers stay at HI-affiliated hostels each year, hailing from everywhere from Alaska to Zaire. Thousands more stay at independent hostels. The goal of a single association of hostels located within a day's walk of one another will probably never be realized in the United States. But it is reality in many places in Europe.

You may never get to every hostel in Europe; we certainly didn't. But wherever you do end up, you're likely to find a promising brew of cultural exchange and friendship over pots of ramen noodles and instant coffee almost anywhere you go.

In that sense, perhaps, Richard Schirmann's dream has been realized after all.

a word about affiliations

A majority of hostels in this book are affiliated with Hostelling International (HI); the rest, we've labeled independent hostels.

Hostelling International (HI)-affiliated hostels are part of the International Youth Hostel Federation, which has 5,000 member hostels in seventy countries worldwide. Member hostels are held to a number of regulations, such as maximum number of beds per shower, even a minimum amount of space that must exist between top bunks and the ceiling. To get into an HI hostel you must sometimes have an HI membership card (see next section).

Overall, these HI hostels tend to earn higher marks from our reviewers than independent hostels. They regularly own the nicest buildings and keep the floors cleanest. On the other hand, the organization's mission statement trumpets its contribution to "the education of young people," so be warned that some of its most popular hostels attract youth groups like molasses does flies. These places are also kind of strict with the rules (what did you expect?), and some big-city joints (in huge concrete tenement-like blocks) seem to thrive on packing in busloads of schoolkids or tourists. That said, they also are uniformly clean, safe, informative—and a little blah.

English isn't always spoken well, but it is usually spoken by at least one staff member. HI-affiliated city hostels in Europe are generally open twenty-four hours and year-round. Also take note that some kick you out for part of the day to clean. (There are some exceptions for couples paying more for a double room.) At least a breakfast is often included in the rate, and dinner—which you pay for—is usually cheap and filling.

Independents (no affiliation) are what we call all the rest. Some independent owners have opted not to join Hostelling International because membership costs are high and the rules are strict. Such a decision—in and of itself—does not reflect on the quality of the hostel. It would be foolish to write a hostel off simply because it is not affiliated.

However, you need to know that things in an independent hostel are more laid-back—and that's not always a good thing. Some of them are just Party Central twenty-four hours a day—and night. Liquor isn't always officially off-limits at these places. (In HI joints, you usually must either buy it at the hostel bar or restaurant or forget about it.) Some independent hostels do the lockout thing, but it's not as common or long-lasting as the one at HI hostels. Rooms are probably homier, but they're also more crowded and smoky. There's no guarantee of quality, and the standards, upkeep, noise level, and beer flow tend to vary wildly from place to place. Some are outstandingly fun; some are grungy beyond belief.

A few independent hostels are run by church organizations such as convents. These obviously have stricter lockouts, curfews, and alcohol rules than anyone else in this book. Some also ban unmarried couples from sharing a bed. If they do, we have banned THEM from this book.

hostel memberships and
international booking

First things first. We advise you to get a Hostelling International membership *before* you set out on your trip.

How do you do that? Easy. Contact the home office of your country's Hostelling International chapter and get a membership card plus other goodies, like individual country hostelling guides. Membership costs about $28 US for an adult—it varies according to country—and is good for one year. If there's a Hostelling International hostel in your neck of the woods, ask about buying the card there instead. (You can also order online at www.hiusa.org.)

If you want to try some hostels before committing to the responsibility of owning a card, you can also obtain a guest membership. Just pay a small supplement of about $3 US at an "official" hostel, which stamps your "guest card" each night you pay it. After six stamps, presto! You're a member. As a bonus, many hostels have established discounts for hostellers at businesses in the towns where hostels are located; you might get 10 percent off a meal at a restaurant, discounted train tickets or museum entrance fees, or other perks.

If you're the type who needs the security of knowing where you're staying each night of your trip, you might also want to participate in the International Booking Network (IBN). Participating hostels (usually located in big cities or major tourist areas) call ahead to another IBN hostel (located in the same sorts of areas) and secure your bunk, even in high season if it's humanly possible. Most ask for an advance notice of three to seven days. If there's any room, you'll get priority—you need only pre-pay for your bed with a VISA, MasterCard, or Discover card (plus a $5 US booking fee) and you're in. The system is fairly straight-forward. However, *be prepared to eat the whole cost of the bed if you need to cancel* on short notice.

how to hostel

Hostelling is, generally speaking, easy as pie. Plan ahead a bit and use a little common sense, and you'll find that check-in goes pretty smoothly.

reserving a bed

Getting a good bunk will often be your first and biggest challenge, especially if it's high season. Summer is usually high season in Europe, thanks to loads of college students on summer break; Christmas can be tough, too, even in cold cities like Copenhagen and Stockholm. Popular places like London, Paris, Rome, and Berlin seem to be busy almost year-round, so book early. And to hit Oktoberfest in Munich, well, you might have to book a year in advance. No kidding. Hostellers often have an amazingly laissez-faire attitude about reservations; many simply waltz in at midnight expecting that a bed will be available.

Sometimes it is. Sometimes it isn't.

Almost every Hostelling International abode takes advance reservations of some form or another, so if you know where you're going to be, use this service. Be aware that you might need a credit card number to hold a bed, and some hostels require you to send a deposit check in the mail. You might also need to show up by a certain hour, like 6:00 P.M., to get in.

The larger and busier HI hostels in Europe are also affiliated with the worldwide International Booking Network (IBN, for short), whereby you can buy a bunk at your next HI stop while sleeping in another one.

Independent hostels are sometimes stricter and sometimes more lax about taking solid reservations. Note that they're often much faster to fill up than HI joints because of the wild popularity of no-rules places, so check into their policies. A growing number of these independent joints now take online reservations via the Internet.

If you can't or won't reserve, the best thing to do is get there super-early. Office opens at 8:00 A.M.? Get there at 7:00. No room, but checkout ends at 11:00? Be back at 11:05 in case of cancellations or unexpected checkouts. The doors are closed again till 4:30 in the afternoon? No problem. Come back around 4:00 with a paperback and camp out on the porch. That's your only shot if you couldn't or wouldn't reserve ahead, and hostellers are somewhat respectful of the pecking order: It really is first come, first served. So come first.

paying the piper

Once you're in, be prepared to pay for your night's stay immediately—before you're even assigned a bunk. Take note ahead of time which hostels take credit cards, checks, and so forth. Learn the local currency, and don't expect every little hostel to change your big bill for a couple bucks' worth of laundry.

You will almost always be required to give up your passport and (if you have one) Hostelling International card for the night. Don't sweat it; it's just the way it's done over there, and in fact they have good reasons. Sometimes it's a police requirement. Also, if an emergency happens (nah, no chance), the passport might help hostel staff locate your significant others.

Remember to pay ahead if you want a weekly stay. Often you can get deep discounts, though the downside is that you'll almost never get even a partial refund if you decide you can't stand the place and leave before the week is up.

If you're paying by the day, rebook promptly each morning; hostel managers are very busy during the morning hours, keeping track of check-ins, checkouts, cleaning duties, and cash. You'll make a friend if you're early about notifying them of your plans for the next day. Managers hate bugging guests all morning or all day about whether they'll be staying on. Don't put the staff through this.

All right, so you've secured a bed and paid up. Now you have to get to it. This may be no easy task at some hostels, where staff and customers look and act like one and the same. A kindly manager will probably notice you bumbling around and take pity. As you're being shown to your room, you're also likely get a short tour of the facilities and a briefing on the ground rules.

On checkout you'll get your card and passport back. You might need to pay a small amount if you lose your room key—usually about $5 but sometimes as much as $25 US.

knowing the ground rules

There's one universal ground rule at every hostel: You are responsible for serving and cleaning up after yourself. And there's a corollary rule:

Be courteous. So while you're welcome to use the kitchen facilities (if a kitchen's available), share the space with your fellow guests—don't spread your five-course meal all over the counter space and rangetop burners if other hungry folk are waiting. And never, ever, leave a sink full of dirty pots and pans behind. That's bad form.

Hostel guests are almost always asked to mark their name and check-in date on all the food they put in the refrigerator. Only a shelf marked FREE FOOD is truly up for grabs; everything else belongs to other hostellers, so don't touch it. (Hostellers get very touchy about people stealing their grub.) Some of the better-run hostels have a spice rack and other kitchen essentials on hand. If you're not sure whether something is communal, ask. Don't assume anything is up for grabs unless it is clearly marked as such.

Then there's the lockout, a source of bitter frustration among non-European hostellers. A few hostels kick everybody out in the morning and don't let them back in until the afternoon or early evening; big-city joints are usually but not always immune to this rule. Lockouts tend to run from around 9:30 A.M. (which is ungodly, we say, but pretty typical) to 5:00 or 6:00 P.M., during which time your bags might be inside your room—but you won't be. A few places let you back in around 2:00 or 3:00 P.M. Oooooooh, the generosity.

The practice has its pros and cons; managers usually justify a lockout by noting that it forces travelers to interact with the locals and also allows their staff to "meticulously clean" the rooms. The real reason is usually that the hostel can't or won't pay staff to hang around and baby-sit you all day. On the other hand, these hostels never become semiresidential situations stuffed with couch potatoes, like many U.S. hostels do, so maybe the lockouts do solve that problem.

Curfews are very common; usually the front doors lock between 11:00 P.M. and midnight, and they won't give you a key. Big-city joints generally have some system in place to let you get in twenty-four hours: a guard, a numbered keypad, or a room key that also opens the main door. But check first.

In the reviews we've tried to identify those hostels that enforce lockouts. Usually you wouldn't want to be hanging out in the hostel in the middle of the day anyway, but after several sleepless nights of travel—or when you're under the weather—daytime downtime sure is appreciated. So beware. Note that even if we haven't listed a lockout or a curfew, it might exist. These things change. Assume that you WILL get kicked out at 9:00 A.M. for the day and—except in big cities—will need to be back by midnight.

Finally, some hostels also enforce a limit on your stay—anywhere from three days, if the hostel is really popular, to about two weeks.

Savvy budget travelers have learned how to get around this unfortunate situation, of course: They simply suck it up and spend a night at
the "Y" or a convenient motel—then check back into the cheaper hostel
first thing in the morning. But we didn't tell you to do that. Uh-uh.

etiquette and smarts

Again, to put it simply, use common sense. Hostellers are a refreshingly
flexible bunch. All these people are able to make this system work by
looking after one another; remember, in a hostel you're a community
member first and a consumer second. With that in mind, here are some
guidelines for how to act:

- The first thing you should do after check-in is get your bed made.
  When you're assigned a bed, stick to it. Don't spread your stuff
  out on nearby bunks, even if they are empty. Someone's going to
  be coming in late-night for one of them, you can bet the backpack on it.
- Be sure to lock your valuables in a locker or safe if they've got
  one or in the trunk of your car. Good hostels offer lockers as a
  service; it might cost a little, but it's worth it. Bring a padlock in
  case the hostel has run out or charges an arm and a leg.
- Set toiletries and anything else you need in a place where they
  are easily accessible. This avoids your having to paw through
  your bag late at night, potentially disturbing other guests from
  their slumber. The same goes for early-morning departures: If
  you're taking off at the crack of dawn, take precautions not to
  wake the whole place.
- If you're leaving early in the morning, try to make all arrangements with the manager before going to bed the night before.
  Managers are usually accommodating and pleasant folk, but
  guests are expected to respect their privacy and peace of mind
  by not pushing things too far. Dragging a manager out of bed
  at four in the morning to check out—or for some other trivial
  matter—is really pushing it.
- Be sure to mind the bathroom. A quick wiping of the shower floor
  with a towel after you use it is common courtesy.
- Finally, be sure to mind the quiet hours. Some hostels have
  curfews, but very few force lights-out. If you are up after hours,
  be respectful. Don't crank the television or radio too loud; don't
  scream in the hallways late at night. (Save that for the beach—
  and for annoying people staying in much nicer digs.)

packing

Those dainty hand towels and dapper shaving kits and free soaps you get at a hotel won't be anywhere in sight at the hostel. In fact, even some of the base essentials may not be available—kitchens are NOT a given in Europe, for instance, so check our listings carefully. You're on your own, so bring everything you need to be comfortable.

There are only a few things you can expect the hostel to supply:

- a bed frame with a mattress and pillow
- shower and toilet facilities
- a common room with some spartan furniture
- maybe a few heavy blankets.

Some of the more chic hostels we've identified in this guide may be full-service. But they are the exception to the rule.

Bring stuff like this to keep your journey through hostel territory comfortable:

- If you're traveling abroad from the United States, you obviously need a passport. Unlike U.S. hostels, a European hostel will often take your passport as collateral when you check in. Don't get nervous; this is extremely common. It's the European equivalent of taking down your driver's license number when you write a check. However, in the unlikely event that someone loses your passport, make sure you've got backup copies of the issuing office, date, and passport number in your luggage and also back home.
- Hostelling International membership cards are a good thing to have on hand—most of the official European hostels require one just to stay. They can be purchased at many foreign HI hostels for about $28 annually per person; you can also buy cards at HI-affiliated U.S. hostels ahead of time, or from the American Youth Hostels headquarters in Washington, D.C. Log onto www .hiusa.org for more information. If you can't get a card before you arrive in Europe and you'll be there at least a week, don't panic: You can buy an HI "guest stamp" for about €3.00 (about $3.75 US), and when you collect six of those, you get a free card.

This card identifies you as a certified superhosteller and gets you the very cheapest rate for your bed in all HI (and also some unaffiliated) hostels. At $2 to $4 US per night, the savings can add up fast.

Sometimes that membership card also gets you deals at local restaurants, bike shops, and tours. Again, it will be easier to deal with the front desk at some of the more cautious hostels (even nonmember ones) if you can flash one of these cards.

- Red Alert! Do not plan on using a sleeping bag in every hostel. A good number of places simply won't allow it—problems with ticks and other creatures dragged in from the great outdoors have propelled this prohibition. The alternative is a sleepsack, which is basically two sheets sewn together with a makeshift pillowcase. You can find them at most budget travel stores, or make your own. Personally we hate these confining wraps, and we rarely get through the night in one without having it twist around our bodies so tight that we wake up wanting to charge it with attempted manslaughter. Our preferred method is to bring our own set of sheets, though that might be too much extra stuff to carry if you're backpacking.

  Some hostels give you free linen; most that don't will rent sheets for about $1 to $3 US per night. You don't get charged for use of the standard army surplus blankets or the musty charm that comes with them.

- Some people bring their own pillows, as those supplied tend to be on the frumpy side. This is a good idea if you're traveling by car and can afford the space. Small pillows are also useful for sleeping on trains and buses.

- We definitely suggest earplugs for light sleepers, especially for urban hostels—but also in case you get caught in a room with a heavy snorer.

- A small flashlight is a must—not only for late-night reading but also to find your bed without waking the entire dorm.

- A little bit of spice is always nice, especially when you have had one too many plates of bland pasta. You'll find the cost of basil, oregano, and the like in convenience stores way too high to stomach once you're on the road. Buy it cheap before you leave and pack it in jars or small plastic bags.

- Check which hostels have laundry facilities. Most won't, and you'll need to schlep your stuff to the local Laundromat. It'll be expensive, so bring lotsa money.

- Wearing flip-flops or other plastic sandals in the shower might help you avoid a case of athlete's foot.

- Be sure your towel is a quick-drying type. Otherwise you'll wind up with mildew in your pack—and your food.

traveling in europe

getting there

Take a careful look at your transportation options when planning a hostel journey. You should be able to hop from city to city by bus or train without a problem, but you could have trouble getting to rural hostels without a car.

FROM NORTH AMERICA BY PLANE The airline business is crazy: Great deals and rip-off fares come and go with a regularity that is frightening to behold—supply, demand, season, the stock market, and random acts of cruelty or kindness all appear to contribute to the quixotic nature of fares.

As a result, there is no one simple piece of advice we can give you, other than this one: Find a darned good travel agent who cares about budget travelers, and trust him/her with all the planning. You can cruise the Internet if you like, and you might find an occasional great deal your agent doesn't know about. Just make sure the sellers are reputable before giving out that credit-card number.

A couple tips:

- **Charters** are often the cheapest way to go, though it's no-frills all the way. You'll need to do some serious Web cruising and calling and Sunday newspaper reading to find the best deals, though.
- **Phoning a student travel agency** in your hometown or city isn't a bad idea—they know lots about cheap flights.
- **Cheap-ticket brokers** (also called consolidators or bucket shops) are a great bet for saving money, but you have to be fast on your feet to keep up, as the deals appear and disappear literally daily. London and New York are major centers for bucket shops.
- **Flying as a courier** comes highly recommended by some folk who've tried it. Others are nervous about it. It works this way: You agree to carry luggage for a company in exchange for a very cheap round-trip ticket abroad. You must be flexible about your departure and return dates, you can't change those dates once assigned to you—and you usually can bring only carry-on luggage.

There isn't nearly as much demand for couriers from smaller destinations to Europe as there is from places like New York or Los Angeles, but it's still worth a shot. Check out guidebooks and Web sites on the subject.

FROM EUROPE BY PLANE Flights within Europe used to be fantastically expensive. However, times are changing: A raft of cut-rate short-hop airlines have sprung up, such as Go!, Easyjet, British Midland, Ryanair, and Virgin Express. Check out the papers and travel agents for the latest-breaking deals, and be prepared to sometimes fly into or out of a weird airport to save the dough.

FROM EUROPE BY TRAIN Most folks travel by train around Europe, and it's a sensible choice. Services and connections are generally good, so getting around by rail is normally a straightforward matter of booking and then taking a long-distance journey, possibly with a change or two en route. You've got two choices: (1) Buy point-to-point tickets for every leg of the journey, or (2) buy a Europe-wide pass.

If you're math-and-map friendly, definitely buy a copy of the *Thomas Cook European Rail Timetable* before you go—or in an English-language bookstore in London, Paris, or elsewhere in Europe after you arrive. It's an invaluable reference to the changing train schedules of Great Britain and Eastern and Western Europe.

FROM ENGLAND BY TRAIN There's only one way to get to Europe from England by train: Begin with **Eurostar** (www.eurostar.com). They've got a monopoly on the sub-Chunnel service that takes you from England to Brussels or Paris in under three hours, but they run it well: You'll never get onto a faster or more efficiently run train. You can have breakfast in SoHo and lunch in Paris—without the delays of airport check-in and checkout and with pretty minimal customs and immigration formalities. From either Paris or Brussels, you can take a daytime or overnight train directly to most other European capitals.

Of course you pay extra for the privilege. Round-trip tickets run from as little as £59 (about $118 US) off-season, booking three weeks in advance, up to much more if you book on short notice or travel during a summer weekend. And—bummer—buying a single one-way ticket isn't much cheaper than purchasing a round-tripper. So you might as well go whole hog.

At least there are big discounts for Eurail and BritRail pass holders and for young travelers: It costs £40 to £250 (about $80 to $100 US) one-way if you're under twenty-six—or have a pass.

Always check ahead for price information. It's easiest to book ahead through your travel agent at home, but Eurostar also has offices in London's Waterloo Station, Paris's Gare du Nord, and Brussels's Gare du Midi. Or, of course, you can book online.

One additional plus with Eurostar: If you somehow manage to miss your train (you oaf), they will let you reschedule your ride for another convenient and available time—within certain limits—at no extra penalty! Wouldn't it be nice if the airlines worked that way? Yep. It sure would.

GETTING AROUND EUROPE BY TRAIN Using trains in Europe is an absolute snap. You've got three choices: (1) Buy point-to-point tickets for every leg of the journey, (2) get a regional pass, or (3) buy a Europe-wide pass.

- **Eurail passes** can be key if you're touring the continent. In our experience these passes are a great deal for covering big distances. Rail Europe (www.raileurope.com; 888–382–7245 or 877–257–2887 in the United States; 800–361–7245 in Canada) sells the passes via phone and the Internet.

  Sure, they're not cheap, but they're superconvenient and cover almost everything. If you do get the Eurail pass, you've gotta play by the rules: Wait until the first day you're going to use it, then go to the station early and have the pass validated (stamped) by a ticket agent. Write the current date into the first square (it should have a "1" beneath it)—and remember to put the day first (on top), European-style.

  Now it gets easier. Just show your pass to ticket agents when you want to reserve a seat on a train (which is crucial in summer season, on weekends, and during rush hours); that smiling person will print you out a seat reservation, which you show to the conductor. You must reserve seats before the train arrives, and since you'll have no idea where or when that is, it's best to reserve a day or two ahead as you're getting off the train.

  If you can't or won't get a reservation, just show your pass to the conductor. Sometimes he'll let you get on anyway.

  Finally, don't fold, bend, or otherwise mangle the long cardboard pass (and that can be difficult to achieve while fumbling for your money belt at the station as the train whips in). For some reason, that might invalidate the whole thing.

  The cost of these passes depends on a few things, including how long you're traveling and how much comfort you want. First-class passes, *which anyone over twenty-seven is required to buy,* cost more and give you a little more legroom. Call one of the railpass vendors listed above for the very latest pricing information.

The full pass costs $675 US for fifteen consecutive days of travel, with prices going up from there for twenty-one-day, one-month, two-month, and three-month passes. Those under twenty-six pay just $440 US for the same pass, but you've gotta ride second-class on all trains. Children ages four to eleven get half-off the regular adult prices, while children under four ride free. The "Flexi" pass gives you ten to fifteen days in a two-month period for $789 to $1,049 US. Those under age twenty-six pay $519 to $681 US for the Flexipass, but again it's all second-class, not first-class. (Don't sweat it: Usually you can't tell the difference anyway.)

- **Point-to-Point Tickets** might be the best route to go if you're just blowing through a single country in a hurry. Get them at stations at ticket windows or—if you have cash or credit cards—automatic machines.

- **Combo Passes:** Eurail also offers three- to five-country and one- to two-country combo passes; check the Web site.

A few more tips on cross-European train travel:

- If you're just buying point-to-point tickets, go for second-class.

- For long distances you can sometimes take a sleeper car (also known as a couchette). At around $20 US per person (usually), it saves you a night in a hotel or hostel and gets you closer to where you want to go. The drawback is that you sleep four or, more likely, six to a room. You can also pay a lot more (usually $100 to $200 US) for a private double compartment.

- Remember that trains don't run as frequently on weekends; Saturday is usually the worst day to travel. International trains and sleeper cars usually run seven days a week, and Fridays and Sundays are feast or famine; check schedules and think like a local.

FROM EUROPE BY BUS **Eurolines** (www.eurolines.com) is a Europe-wide company running comfortable long-distance buses around Europe for very competitive rates, certainly cheaper than trains and cheaper than planes if you're booking on short notice. They serve quite a network of cities.

getting around

BY TRAIN Trains are still king in Europe. Sure, the car dominates everyday life for locals, but when you're a tourist you just can't beat the iron horse.

While these rail systems cross an incredible variety of landscapes, even the iron horse can't get everywhere. It's likely, at some point, that you might need to supplement your train travel with some form of gondola, lift, bus, cog railway, or steam train—all part of the fun.

tickets and passes What to buy? If you're going to be doing lots of short city-to-city hops, just buy tickets each day; it's cheaper. If you'll be in the area for a week or two, get a pass.

Always remember to punch your train ticket before you get on the train; there will be a machine in every station that stamps the current date and time on the ticket, showing the conductor that it has been "used up."

BY BUS Buses can be a cheaper ride than the train or more expensive, depending on local whims. They're extremely useful in places where trains simply don't go—reasonably on time, scenic, and with lots of locals riding alongside you happy to give advice or opinions or soccer scores.

It might take you all day to make connections, but most bus drivers are helpful and knowledgeable. As a bonus, they'll sometimes let you off where you want to go even if there isn't an actual scheduled bus stop there. They are also quite accustomed to hostellers asking "where's my stop?" and handle the situation calmly and professionally. Usually. (In small towns, though, anything goes.)

In many cities, you often buy tickets in transit stations, at newsstands, or right on the bus—it's more expensive to buy 'em from the driver, however.

Always remember to punch your ticket for local bus rides; there will be a machine either at the bus stop or on the bus. Most single tickets are good for one hour; most passes are good for a day or more.

You can purchase Eurolines bus passes allowing free travel among thirty-five European cities served by the line; at press time, these were available for periods of fifteen or thirty days and cost from €199 (about $400 US) per person—for a fifteen-day pass in the low season—up to €439 (about $878 US) for a thirty-day pass in the high season. Buy the passes online at www.eurolines-pass.com. Travelers under age twenty-six get a further 15–25% discount on those rates.

BY BOAT On a few occasions you might be cruising lakes or rivers; your Eurail pass covers some (though not all) of these journeys.

A tongue-twisting transport organization in Germany called Donaudampfschiffahrtsgesellschaft (DDSG), for instance, runs cruises up and down the scenic Rhine River, including a bunch of pokey regular boats, a fast hydrofoil (which is more expensive, of course), and even the occasional steamer. The best part? Rides on this line are discounted 20 percent with a Eurail pass.

Other ferries run around Lake Konstanz (also known as Lake Constance or the Bodensee) between Switzerland, Austria, and Germany. There are also ferries between the U.K., France, Ireland, Scotland, Italy, and Greece. And between Denmark, Sweden, Norway, and Germany. Some of them are discounted or even free with a Eurail pass.

BY CAR Renting a car is definitely the most expensive way to see Europe, and yet it has advantages: You can cover the hamlets a whole lot quicker, you have complete freedom of movement, and you get that cool feeling of the wind and rain rushing past your ears.

Germany is by far the cheapest country in Europe in which to rent a car, with plenty of opportunities to rent in one city and drop off—with no penalty—in another. The country's high-speed autobahns are free, too, unlike the highways in most other European countries. (Gas isn't cheap, but at least the tiny Euro-cars get terrific gas mileage.) Watch out for traffic jams, though. Even on the high-speed roads, weekends, holidays and rush-hours can bring horrific gridlock. Our tip? Try driving during lunchtime or on a Sunday. Rates in France and Austria aren't too bad, and deals can sometimes be had in the U.K. or Ireland with advance booking while still in the United States.

Expensive places to rent? Denmark, Sweden, Norway, Switzerland, and Italy aren't cheap. (We didn't dare rent in Spain, Portugal or Greece—try driving for a day alongside the daredevil locals and you'll see why.) And learn how to drive a stick shift, for gosh sakes: It can cost you up to *twice as much* per day for an automatic-transmission car.

By all means try to book your rental ahead from your home country. It's cheaper. We don't know why. It just is. Rentals will set you back $40 to $70 US a day for a small car, and that might or might not include heavy taxes and insurance tacked onto the price. As we've said, an automatic-drive car will be more expensive.

If you can, rent or lease long-term through a company such as Kemwel (877–820–0668 or www.kemwel.com), a good firm that books long-term rentals for a fraction of the daily rate if you book ahead from your home country. They do short-term rentals as well. The big-name

American companies you know back home also rent in Europe, though rates can be quite a bit higher.

Speeds and distance in Europe are usually measured in kilometers. (But in Ireland, England, Scotland, and Wales, miles still rule!) Just to remind you, 1 kilometer is a little less than 0.6 mile, and 100 miles equal roughly 160 kilometers. Here are some common speed limits and distances you might see on road signs, with their U.S. equivalents:

40 kph	**=**	**25 miles per hour**
100 kph	**=**	**62 miles per hour**
50 kilometers away	**=**	**31 miles away**

Gas is measured in liters, and there are roughly four liters to the U.S. gallon. Gas prices are listed per liter, so multiply by four and then convert into home currency to estimate the price per gallon you'd pay back home—you'll be shocked. Want a bike yet?

What else? Well, in the U.K. (that's England, Scotland, and Wales) or Ireland, you drive on the left, which takes a lot of getting used to. In continental Europe, however, you drive on the right. Local laws must be paid attention to: Swiss laws require you to stop at all crosswalks, for example. European drivers tend to be fairly aggressive, especially in open-highway situations—that supercharged car in your rear-view might have just been doing 100 miles an hour. Pull over and let him go. And no giving the finger back to the guy. You can get tossed in the pokey or fined heavily for it—yes, really.

phones

Two words: phone card.

Dealing with pay phones can be frustrating, so don't bother pumping change unless you're truly desperate. Instead, buy phone cards at tobacco shops, train station windows, or small markets and stick 'em into the slots in the phones.

Don't bother trying to call Mom and Dad back home with these cards. Instead, get a phone card from the United States or your home country before you arrive. It'll be cheaper and easier, though a few phones might block your phone card.

You dial differently depending on whether you are in the country or not; we have indicated, in each country introduction, specifically how to do it. Remember that it's cheaper to make coin calls at night, and that directory assistance can get expensive.

There are cheaper alternatives for calling home. Right now, all three giant communications corporations have seemingly monopolized the way you call home—and we hate this development. Many of the larger hostels in Europe have special phones that have been installed by big companies like AT&T, MCI, and Sprint. The calls come with a weighty per-call charge, which can add up real fast, in addition to the exorbitant rates they charge per minute. What's more, you can use these phones only if you have an existing account with the carrier. The situation is made more frustrating because these companies sometimes won't accept a credit card.

money

You'll need it, that's for sure.

First things first. Remember this simple rule about cash: Get it from an ATM whenever possible, as that's almost always the easiest and lowest-cost way to get it.

Second, pay attention to where you are. European countries used to have their own unique money, and that was something of a pain. You often had to pay big fees to change money when traveling from one country to another. And you also had to get rid of all your loose change before you left each country, since change bureaus won't change coins. Basically, it was a use-it-or-lose-it situation.

However, in 2002 many European countries—including many, but not all, of the countries covered in this book—changed over to a single unified currency called the euro. Though it's a shame to see lire, schillings, and francs disappear, it does make life easier for travelers because you won't need to change money while traveling between these countries. Just keep forking over the euros.

In this book we have listed prices in euros for those countries that now use them. The euro symbol looks like so: €. It's easy to estimate costs in euros. One euro averages a little over one U.S. dollar. In this book, €1.00 = 1.25 US as we go to press but the value can fluctuate. For all countries that still use their own currencies, such as England, we have printed prices in the local currency and have also laid out the current conversion rates to U.S. dollars. A handy Web site for performing currency conversions is www.xe.com. Click on "currency converter" and convert to your heart's content. You can perform exchange rate calculations on the Internet using live, up-to-the-minute rates.

Having trouble remembering which countries use the euro now, and which don't? Here's a handy reminder we came up with: "BAFFLING PIGS are in." The first letters remind you that **B**elgium, **A**ustria, **F**rance, **F**inland (not covered in this book), **L**uxembourg, **I**taly, (the) **N**etherlands, **G**ermany, **P**ortugal, **I**reland, **G**reece, and **S**pain are now *in* the euro game. Norway, the U.K. (including Northern Ireland), Denmark, Sweden,

Switzerland, and all the Eastern European countries—including Hungary and the Czech Republic, which are covered in this book—are still using their own money, though that could always change. Denmark and the Czech Republic have debated converting in the near future, for example—but that is hardly a certainty.

If you must still change money—let's say you're traveling from England to Switzerland (both still use their own money), won't be coming back to England, and want to get rid of all your English pounds—try to find a big bank instead of a tourist office, train station, bureau de change, or small bank. Their rates are all terrible, and they figure you won't know the difference.

safety

As exciting as hostelling your way through European cities might be, you've got to be on the alert at all times and remember that you're in a city. Avoid wandering unfamiliar streets at night, and try to stay in well-lit areas with plenty of foot traffic. Expect to be jostled by crowds, assaulted by noise, panhandled, and pickpocketed. Guys, if you carry a wallet, keep it in a front pants pocket instead of a back pocket. Gals, if you carry a purse, carry it across your body rather than over your shoulder. (Even backpacks aren't fail-safe: thieves will sometimes use razors to slash off the straps and grab 'em.) Above all, get a good map and study it before you go out—the worst feeling in the world is that of being utterly lost, late at night, in a dicey area without a cop or friendly face in sight.

OK, now that we've got you completely paranoid, don't forget to have a good time.

travel insurance

Travel insurance might seem like a useless expenditure, but it might come in handy, too. This insurance typically covers everything from baggage loss and injuries in an air travel accident (nah, that won't happen, don't even think about it) to medical expenses incurred while you're traveling. It's also helpful if someone puts a dent in that rental car and you have waived the necessary coverage to save bucks.

We'd recommend buying some sort of travel insurance. The best we've found so far for European travel is AIG Travel Guard (800–826–4919 or www.travelguard.com) in Wisconsin.

speaking european

English will get you by in touristed areas and cities of Europe, which probably covers most of the places you're going. However, occasionally you'll want to get way off the beaten track, where you might have a little more trouble. Just think: This might be your only chance to forge a meaningful bond while getting the right bus tickets, too.

So learn a little language before you go, and don't despair. You'll be OK with a bit of brushing up and a little sign or body language where necessary. Hereforth, a short primer on the Big Four: French, Italian, German, and Spanish.

BON **COURAGE!** BUONA **FORTUNA!**
VIEL **GLÜECK!** ¡Y BUENA **SUERTE!**

français (french)

What they say	How they say it (approximately)	What they mean
oui	we	yep
non	no!	nope
peut-être	put ed	maybe
un	uh	one
deux	do	two
trois	twa	three
quatre	cat	four
billet/billets	B.A.	ticket/tickets
première classe	premier class	first class
deuxième classe	do-zyem class	second class
autobus	aw toe booze	bus
non fumer	naw foo may	nonsmoking
passe d'Eurail	pass door rail	Eurail pass
train	tren	train
quai/voie	kay/vwa	platform/track
voiture	vwa-choor	car number of a train
voiture-lit	vwa-choor leet	sleeping car of a train
place	plass	seat
pardon	par don	excuse me/I'm sorry
de Nice	de niece	from Nice
à Paris	ah, pear "E"	to Paris
je voudrais	zhuh food ray	I'd like . . .
j'ai besoin de	J.B. swan, duh	I need . . .
merci	mare "C"	thank you
merci bien	mare CBN	thanks a lot!
bonjour	bon sure	good morning, good afternoon
bon soir	bon swar	good evening, good night
au revoir	oh, vwar	good-bye
à bientôt	ah, be in tote	see ya soon
de rien	darien	you're welcome
monsieur	miss yew	sir
madame	ma damn	ma'am
mademoiselle	madam was hell	miss
mesdames	may damn	ladies
messieurs	may sure	sirs
ceci	sir see	this one
cela	sir la	that one

italiano (italian)

What they say	How they say it (approximately)	What they mean
si	see/she	yes
no	no	no means no
una/uno	ooh nah/noh	one
due	do "A"?	two
tre	tray	three
quattro	kwa-tro	four
biglietta/biglietti	Billy eta/Billy A.T.	ticket/tickets
prima classe	preema class "A"	first class
seconda classe	sick on da class "A"	second class
non fumatori	naw foo ma tory	nonsmoking
passa di treno	passa the traino!	train pass
treno	traino	train
binario	beanario	platform/track number
scusami	skoozame	excuse me
mi dispiace	me "D" spee-ah-chee	I'm sorry
grazie	gratsy	thank you
grazie mille	gratsy mealy	thanks a lot!
bongiorno	bon journo	good morning
buona sera	wanna Sara	good afternoon, good evening
ciao	chow	hi; bye
ciao-ciao	chow-chow	bye-bye
arrivaderci	a-riva-dare-chay	good-bye
prego	prego	you're welcome
pronto	pronto!	yes?
da Roma	d'aroma	from Rome
per Firenze	pear friends, ah	to Florence
Vorrei	Vhooray	I'd like . . .
Ho bisogno di	obi sanyo "D"	I need . . .
Questa	kwest-ah	this one
Quella	kwell-ah	that one

deutsch (german)

What they say	How they say it (approximately)	What they mean
Guten tag	Goo ten tag	hello, good day
bitte	beetah	please; excuse me; may I help you?
danke	Don K	thanks
danke schöne	Don KeShane	thank you very much
ein	ine	one
zwei	dzvye	two
drei	dry	three
zug	zoog	train
U-Bahn	oo baan	subway
S-Bahn	S baan	commuter/suburban train
Bahnof	baa-noff	train station
Hauptbahnof	how baa-noff	main train station
Bus	boose	bus
Ich möchte	Eek mookta	I'd like . . .
ein Fahrkart	eine far carta	a ticket
Jugendherberge	you get her burger	hostel
Doppelzimmer	dopple zimmer	double room
platz	plats	square
sprechen	spricken	speak
Sie Englisch	zee English	English

español (spanish)

What they say	How they say it (approximately)	What they mean
sí	see!	yes
no	no	no
buenos dias	Wayne-O's "D."S.	good day; hello
señor	say NYOUR	sir; mister; dude
señora	say NYOUR-a	ma'am; Mrs.
señorita	seen yer EATer	miss; dudette; cutie
¿Como está?	comb "A" star?	how's it hanging?
Esta bueno	"A" star WAYNE-O	goin' great
¿Como se llama?	COME oh, say YA-ma?	what's your name?
soy Pablo	soy PAH-blow	I'm Paul
se habla	say HAH-blah	do you speak…
Inglés	een-GLAY-say	English
iglesias	"E" CLAY-see-us	I can be your hero (oops—it means church)
donde está	Don-day "A" stah	where's
la estación de tren	la stash he OWN, day TRAIN	train station
uno	ooh, no	one
dos	dose	two
tres	trace	three
boleto	bow LAY toe	ticket
boletos	bow LAY toast	tickets
tren	train	train
pista	PEE-stah	train track
numero	NEW-mare-oh	number
a Madrid	ah ma DREED	to Madrid
de Barcelona	day BARTH a LOANer	from Barcelona
hoy	oy	today
mañana	moneyANA	tomorrow
por favor	pour fah-VOUR	please
gracias	GRASS-see-us	thanks
muchas gracias	MOOCH-us GRASS-see-us	thank you so so much
obrigado	oh Brie, GOD, oh	thank you (Portuguese)
de nada	day NAH dah	you're welcome
plaza	plAza	public square
buenas noches	Wayne-O's Nachos	good night
hasta la vista	Ah stah la VEE stah (baby)	bye
hasta luego	Ah stah lou EGGo	so long!

the
hostels

austria

Only a shred of its former size and glory, Austria is still one of Europe's best unknown travel getaways—cheap, safe, friendly, unbelievably scenic, and even a little exotic, with reminders of various empires, good and bad, that passed this way. Travelers can pick from Vienna's urban mishmash, Salzburg's *Sound of Music* cuteness and classical music, Innsbruck's position at the foot of towering mountains, Bregenz's lakeside quiet . . . and those are just the places you've heard about. There are many more. Contact ANTO, the Austrian National Tourist Office (www.austria.info), for lots more information on this wonderful, mountainous country; they have tons of info on skiing, snowboarding, food, rustic hotels, golf—just about everything.

And remember: Austria remains a good value for your travel dollar; the conversion to euros hasn't changed that one bit. A typical dorm room here costs about €12 (about $15 US).

practical details

Austrian trains are good quality, not great. Too many cars have six-seated compartments, where you're staring down five people you don't know for the next six hours or so. And distances are long; bring a book. It's also likely that at some point you will need to supplement your train travel with some form of gondola, lift, bus, cog railway, steam train . . . something. That can add to the fun. The Austrians also have an interesting system of getting you to the sticks called a postbus. Long, sleek, and comfortable, postbuses will take you up mountain passes and into tiny hamlets where no train would dare venture. They're cheap, too.

On a few occasions you might be cruising lakes or rivers; a Eurail pass covers some (though not all) of these journeys. Donaudampfschiffahrtsgesellschaft (DDSG), the tongue-twisting transport organization, for instance, runs one ferry a day on summer Sundays from Vienna up the Danube to Krems and Dürnstein and then back. It leaves Vienna (on the river, obviously, just on the bridge next to the U-Bahn stop) at 8:30 in the morning, starts back in midafternoon, and finally arrives at around 9:00 P.M. Other ferry companies run boats along the more pastoral stretch of the river between Krems and Melk. Additional ferries run around Lake Konstanz (Constance, Bodensee) between Switzerland, Austria, and Germany; there's a popular steamer service on Lake Luzern, too.

Austria's country code is 43. To call most Austrian hostels from North America, dial 011–43 and DROP THE ZERO from the numbers printed in this book. To call most Austrian hostels from within Austria, dial the number and SUBSTITUTE 00 as the international long-distance code. Vienna has special rules—see below. To call home from Austria, dial 001 and then the number you are calling.

Note: You cannot make toll-free calls from public pay phones in Austria. Instead you have to go to the post office, where there are phone booths for making international or long-distance calls, and you must use a long-distance service like AT&T or Sprint.

vienna (wien)

For most travelers Eastern Austria can be defined in just one word.
Vienna.

Actually it's pronounced "Veen," or something like that, but no matter. This city is one of the world's distinctive places—as instantly recognizable as Venice and yet not a place stuck in the past. Thousands of persons live and breathe here, enjoying life with a fullness rarely seen elsewhere. Beer, wine, chocolate, lingerie, ice cream, clubs, discos, cafes . . . it goes on and on, in neighborhood after neighborhood of university students, well-heeled locals, and others.

The place has amazing history, too. The Hapsburg emperors once ruled this part of Europe with an iron hand from the Hofburg Palace and assorted villas around town. There are even some Roman ruins here, in two places downtown.

Basically, independent travelers and backpackers flocking to Vienna can be divided into two camps: those seeking the old, historical city centered on palaces and cathedrals and those in the know who realize that this town is shaking off that dusty image with an explosion of trendy restaurants and cafes, clubs, and a provocatively dressed local population.

Those in the latter camp will be found snuffling through the district west of the city center, near the largest concentration of hostels. The area is dominated by Neubaugasse and Neustiftgasse Streets and is one of the most interesting and entertaining neighborhoods in Europe. You can do your grocery shopping, check out a cafe or bar, browse through a bookstore, or even convert to a different faith. Of course the hostels here are nearly always full at all times of the year, so it's best to call well ahead of your scheduled arrival. We recommend at least six months to a year ahead if you're coming during the high season of June, July, and August.

vienna
(wien)

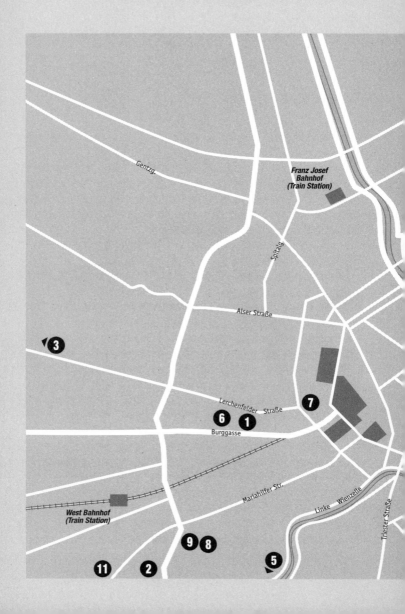

The other camp comes to see what made Vienna a rival to Paris and London during the eighteenth and nineteenth centuries; that is, the stupendous architectural achievements brought to you by the Hapsburgs. Tourists can save themselves a lot of hassle by taking the #1 and #2 trams that circle Ringstrasse in opposite directions, giving a quick overview of the big sights. Or, if you take the U-Bahn to St. Stephan's Cathedral, just walk up the stairs to the exit and you will be within easy walking distance of the cathedral—which manifests itself immediately upon exit—as well as the pedestrian Kartnerstrasse, where you can watch humanity in all its glory or lameness.

Be prepared for milling crowds watching in awe as some guy manipulates a faux piano-playing puppet to the strains of Beethoven's *Fifth Symphony* or Kurdish political groups demonstrating against the capture of their leader. Either way, with milling crowds come the ubiquitous pickpockets, who are always on the lookout for clueless Americans stepping away from a handy ATM machine, stuffing their wad of newly acquired bills into their already bursting wallets.

Other places to hit in Vienna include the Prater amusement park and beaches on the Danube. Because Vienna gets way more sun than western Austria and is blessed with consistently good, warm weather, sightseeing isn't normally marred by rain.

Finally, if you've really got some serious problems, there's always the Sigmund Freud Museum in the ninth district, at Berggasse 19. Check out the famous couch and reflect upon the meaning of cigars.

getting around

Getting around Vienna is ridiculously easy. A comprehensive network of streetcar ("tram"), subway, electric railway, and bus lines crisscrosses the city, ensuring that you'll never have to walk too far for anything. At night, after the normal transit stops running, a series of "night buses" ferry partygoers from the action back out to their homes or hostels in the burbs. Good system. Cars are here, too, of course, but they aren't as thick on the ground as in some other cities.

To get the most out of the transit network, buy a twenty-four-hour ticket from a tobacco and cigarette shop ("Tabak"); it costs about $5 US. You push the ticket into an orange machine to stamp the time and date on it just before your first ride (not sooner), and then for the next twenty-four hours you can ride anywhere on the city transit system without a bother. Unlike in most other European cities, you don't have to keep buying tickets or even showing your ticket to the conductor—it works on the honor system. (If you get caught without a proper ticket by a surprise inspection, though, you could be fined the equivalent of up to $200 US. Ouch!)

Public transportation is very advanced in Vienna. Dig this, for instance: Cars have to stop for pedestrians in crosswalks (but if the walk signal's red, don't cross), and they have to stop for any child or elderly person crossing, even if it's not at a crosswalk. The city's network of trams, U-Bahns, and buses (bearing the Austrian flag) means that you'll never have to walk far.

Stephansplatz is the city's central node for subway lines going into and out of the historic center, and the West Bahnhof train station is handy for many other destinations. All the instructions are usually in German, so make sure you get the correct information. Ask someone trustworthy to confirm train, track, or subway information.

vienna hostels
at a glance

	RATING	PRICE	IN A WORD	PAGE
Wombat's	◣◣	€17–€50	crazy	p. 52
HI-Ruthensteiner	◣◣	€13–€30	central	p. 41
HI-Wilhelminenberg Castle	◣◣	€18–€50	scenic	p. 42
Believe It or Not	◣	€12–€14	tiny	p. 40
Strawberry Hostel	◣	€21–€40	pricey	p. 50
HI-Myrthengasse	◣	€16–€20	good	p. 46
Strawberry Hostel Bürgerspitalgasse	◣	€21–€40	new	p. 49
HI-Wien-Brigittenau	◣	€16–€20	huge	p. 43
HI-Hütteldorf-Hacking	◣◗	€13–€50	remote	p. 45
Panda Hostel	◣◗	€13.50–€15.00	rubble	p. 48
Don Bosco	◔	€10	horrible	p. 51

believe it or not

Myrthengasse 10, Apartment #14, A-1070 Vienna
Phone: 01–526–4658

E-mail: believe_it_or_not_vienna@hotmail.com
Rates: €12–€14 (about $15–$19 US) per person
Credit cards: No
Beds: 15
Private/family rooms: No
Kitchen available: Yes
Season: Open year-round
Office hours: Vary; call ahead
Lockout: 10:00 A.M.–12:30 P.M.
Affiliation: None
Extras: Kitchen, Internet access, lockers, TV

If you're into communal living situations (everything's a little tight and coed), this is a better-than-okay place to bunk down for the night in a neat area of Vienna.

This small place with the unusual name is located just across the street from two massive and group-filled "official" hostels. The crowd here, though, is vastly different. Most guests are youthful adults traveling singly or in pairs; it's more like an apartment run by the owner, who has gotten better at answering the door and the phone during the day. It's important that you call during the evening and ahead of arrival; a week before you plan to come to town isn't too early to secure a bed.

It's basically an apartment packed with two rooms of laid-back hostellers. Most people love this place for such a cozy and real-life-like atmosphere (some say a little too cozy—those triple bunks are quite a climb if you've been assigned one on the top level). It's usually kept surprisingly clean. There's a self-catering kitchen, with all you'll need for a spaghetti or ramen noodle feed. And perks like Internet and TV have also been added recently. You may have to present proof of age since

Best bet for a bite:
Naschmarkt

Insiders' tip:
Knock on the correct door

What hostellers say:
"Like sleeping with ten friends!"

Gestalt:
Believable

Safety:

Hospitality:

Cleanliness:

Party index:

word on the street is that guests under age thirty sometimes aren't allowed, but our spies tell us the rule is rarely (ever?) enforced. People tend to drift in and out all night—hope they're hostellers—and traffic noise is a bit annoying when windows are left open, but the (female) owner's so friendly and personable you might not care.

how to get there:

By bus: Take #5 streetcar or #13 bus to hostel.
By car: Call hostel for directions.
By subway: Take U-Bahn U2 or U3 line to Volkstheater stop, or U6 line to Burggasse stop.
By train: From West Bahnhof Station, take U-Bahn U6 line to Burggasse stop and change to #48A bus to Neubaugasse. From Südbahnhof Station, take #13A bus toward Haltestelle to Kellermanngasse stop.

---

hostel ruthensteiner

Robert Hamerlinggasse 24, A-1150 Vienna
Phone: 01–893–4202 or 01–893–2796

Fax: 01–893–2796
E-mail: info@hostelruthensteiner.com
Rates: €13–€30 (about $16–$38 US) per HI member; doubles €48–€54 (about $60–$68 US)
Credit cards: Yes
Beds: 74
Private/family rooms: Yes
Kitchen available: Yes
Season: Open year-round
Office hours: Twenty-four hours
Affiliation: None
Extras: Courtyard, Internet access, breakfast ($), kitchen, laundry, bar, lockers

---

This hostel's odd. It's practically right next to Vienna's main train station and thus has a decent location on a sidestreet. The private rooms are nice, the attitude is laid-back, and you might hear lots of foreign languages here.

There's one enormous dorm room (thirty beds? gotta be kidding!) where hostellers are simply crammed in. We can tell that the very friendly staff cares, but that's more sweaty socks than we usually care to commune with. You have to pay a bit extra for breakfast, too.

A smallish kitchen (enhanced by an outdoor patio with grill), Internet terminal, and popular courtyard have to be counted as

Best bet for a bite:
Pizzeria Mafiosi

Insiders' tip:
Local ice cream

What hostellers say:
"Pretty groovy."

Gestalt:
Ruthless

Safety:

Hospitality:

Cleanliness:

Party index:

pluses, and this is certainly a very convenient place to sleep when you've gotten to town very late. The bar gets raves; quaff a local brew. The all-night reception is happy to let you in—it's just great to find the place open and convenient. There are no curfews, either, and it's both sparkly clean and full of good vibes.

Since it's so small, though, book well ahead of your arrival.

how to get there:

By bus: Call hostel for transit route.
By car: Call hostel for directions.
By train: From West Bahnhof Station, walk out the extreme right side, cross busy street, and continue to Robert Hamerlinggasse on right. Turn right and walk down street to hostel on left.

jugendgästehaus schlöss herberge am wilhelminenberg (wilhelminenberg castle guest house hostel)
Savoyenstrasse 2, A–1160 Vienna
Phone: 01–481-0300

Fax: 01–485–850–3702
E-mail: shb@hostel.at
Rates: €18–€50 (about $23–$63 US) per HI member; doubles €54–€78 (about $68–$98 US)
Credit cards: Yes
Beds: 164
Private/family rooms: Yes
Kitchen available: No
Season: Open year-round
Office hours: 7:00 A.M.–midnight
Lockout: 9:00 A.M.–2:00 P.M.
Affiliation: HI-ÖJHV
Extras: Minigolf, table tennis, TV, laundry, breakfast, meals ($), Internet access

This nice though very way-out-of-the-way hostel, owned by Vienna's tourist board, gets big points for stunning surroundings and beautiful rooms. But being in the burbs, it sure does attract busloads of school groups. So consider yourself forewarned, and be aware that your journey will entail at least three changes of transportation and a long ride unless you've got a car. Also keep in mind that you'll turn into a pumpkin if you stay out past 11:45 P.M., as that's the last bus out to this remote location. Thankfully, a key-card system means there are no curfews.

Most rooms here are quads with their own bathrooms (yea!), and you can wash your duds in the hostel laundry. They've got a television lounge, meal service, incredible free breakfast included with the expensive price, and even a minigolf course and woods and views adjacent. This is Vienna's best hostel for visiting families.

Best bet for a bite:
Heurigen (wine cellars)

Insiders' tip:
24- or 72-hour transportation pass

What hostellers say:
"Thought I'd never get here!"

Gestalt:
Savoy special

Safety:

Hospitality:

Cleanliness:

Party index:

All in all, it's super-friendly, clean, and quiet. However, if you have an early train to catch, you may want to consider one of the more central Viennese hostels.

how to get there:

By bus or train: From West Bahnhof, take the U3 to Ottakring, then the #46B or #146B bus to Schloss Wilhelminenberg. Look for hostel on the left of big hotel.

From Südbahnhof, take D tram to Volkstheater and follow bus directions as above.

By car: Call hostel for directions.

jugendgästehaus wien-brigittenau (vienna brigittenau guest house hostel)

Friedrich Engelsplatz 24, A–1200 Vienna
Phone: 01–332–8294

Fax: 01–330–8379

E-mail: jgh.1200wien@chello.at
Rates: €16–€20 (about $20–$25 US) per HI member
Credit cards: Yes
Beds: 410
Private/family rooms: Yes
Kitchen available: No
Season: January 1–31; February 14–December 31
Office hours: Twenty-four hours
Lockout: 9:00 A.M.–1:00 P.M.
Affiliation: HI-ÖJHV
Extras: TV, foosball, pool table, vending machines, in-room lockers, Internet access

This hostel usually has tons of decent beds—a plus—but it's also overrun with school groups and is located in a really depressing and bland suburban neighborhood alongside a major traffic artery. It's a huge edifice with zero character but a lot of frills, including vegetarian meals, many rooms with private bathrooms, and, for the most part, friendly and helpful staff—some of whom are native English speakers, which can be a relief for some. You make the call.

The hostel is actually two buildings, one of which is fairly new and is designated for families and couples. The main building is where the groups stay. Noise tends to travel through the walls here, and double rooms consist of a bunk bed instead of the two twins one would expect. At least some of the rooms are fairly spacious.

key to icons

Attractive natural setting	Comfortable beds	Visual arts at hostel or nearby
Ecologically aware hostel	A particularly good value	Music at hostel or nearby
Superior kitchen facilities or cafe	Wheelchair-accessible	Great hostel for skiers
Offbeat or eccentric place	Good for business travelers	Bar or pub at hostel or nearby
Superior bath-room facilities	Especially well suited for families	Editors' Choice: Among our very favorite hostels
Romantic private rooms	Good for active travelers	

Given the out-of-the-way and bland location, you're not going to be hanging out in the neighborhood, so hop the U-Bahn or the S-Bahn (you get endless rides on both if you buy a twenty-four-hour pass) to other points. The Donauinsel, a riverside beach and park, isn't far, for instance, nor is the Prater amusement park—fun for an afternoon— just a couple stops away by suburban train, which is covered by the city's twenty-four-hour tickets. Also of note: A huge office tower with large-screen theater, bowling, bars, mall, and food court is just a few blocks away. Still hungry for nightlife? Catch one of the night buses that stop right in Friedrich Engels Platz.

Best bet for a bite:
Zielpunkt supermarket

Insiders' tip:
Buy that twenty-four-hour transport pass

What hostellers say:
"Too far from town."

Gestalt:
Outer Space

Safety: ◩

Hospitality: ◩

Cleanliness: ◩◩

Party index: 🎉🎉🎉

how to get there:

By bus: Take the #11A or #5A bus to Friedrich Engels Platz and, following hostel logo sign, walk 50 yards to hostel.
By ferry: Take boat to Reichsbrucke dock, then walk 1½ miles to hostel.
By subway: Take U-Bahn subway U6 line to Handelskai stop and walk ⅓ mile to hostel, or take the #5A bus at the Handelskai stop for three stops, exit, and walk under overpass to hostel.
By tram: Take N, #31, or #32 streetcar to Friedrich Engels Platz and walk 50 yards to hostel.

jugendgästehaus wien ◩◩
hütteldorf-hacking
(vienna/hütteldorf–hacking guest
house hostel)
Schlossberggasse 8, A–1130 Vienna
Phone: 01–877–1501

Fax: 01–877–02632
E-mail: jgh@hostel.at
Rates: €13–€50 (about $16–$63 US) per HI member; doubles €40–€60 (about $50–$75 US)
Credit cards: Yes

Beds: 307
Private/family rooms: Yes
Kitchen available: No
Season: Open year-round
Office hours: Twenty-four hours
Lockout: 9:30 A.M.–3:00 P.M.
Curfew: 11:45 P.M.
Affiliation: HI-ÖJHV
Extras: Laundry, TV, VCR, foosball, table tennis, meals ($), Internet access, lockers, information desk, garden, playground

---

A huge six-story bunker on leafy grounds near Hütteldorf Station, this place is ruthlessly efficient, if distant and sometimes unfriendly. It's not the greatest place in town—only so-so.

A key-card system lets you in, where you'll find four singles, eleven doubles, three triples, eleven quads, twenty-four sixes, and six eight-bedded dorms—none with private bathrooms. They serve breakfast, maintain a television lounge, and really cater to families. Witness the playground area, game room, and meal service; kids will also love the Internet access.

Best bet for a bite:
Duran sandwich joints in town

Insiders' tip:
Satellite train station here

What hostellers say:
"Good place, so-so location."

Gestalt:
Huttel house

Safety: ◼

Hospitality: ◼◼

Cleanliness: ◼◼

Party index: 🔺🔺

how to get there:

By bus: Take #53B bus and walk 20 yards to hostel.
By car: Call hostel for directions.
By subway or train: Take U-Bahn U4 line to Hütteldorf stop and walk ⅓ mile to hostel.

---

jugendherberge wien ◼ myrthengasse (vienna myrthengasse hostel)
Myrthengasse 7/Neustiftgasse 85, A–1070 Vienna
Phone: 01–523–6316

Fax: 01–523–5849

E-mail: hostel@chello.at
Rates: €16–€20 (about $20–$25 US) per HI member
Credit cards: Yes
Beds: 260
Private/family rooms: Yes
Kitchen available: Yes
Season: Open year-round
Office hours: Twenty-four hours
Lockout: 11:00 A.M.–2:00 P.M.
Affiliation: HI-ÖJHV
Extras: TV, lockers, store, information desk, meeting room, disco, patio, breakfast, meals ($), laundry, Internet access, kitchen

If you're like most other hostellers, you'd probably think that a hostel with so many beds would be easy to waltz into and grab a bunk at the last minute.

Well, you couldn't be more wrong. You'll have to book it at least six months in advance if you have any hope of gracing its bunks during the summer. But it's not individual travelers who are booking the place out. It's groups from all over Europe, sometimes in numbers totaling fifty or more. Multiply that by six, and there is no chance you'll get a bed. In fact, management prefers groups because they bring in more money, what with the meals and all. So you'll just have to be really forward-thinking, because this is among the best-located hostels

> **Best bet for a bite:**
> Amerling beer joint or pizza
> on Neustiftgasse
>
> **Insiders' tip:**
> Book six months ahead
>
> **What hostellers say:**
> "No beds in July?
> But it's February!"
>
> **Gestalt:**
> Group mentality
>
> **Safety:**
>
> **Hospitality:**
>
> **Cleanliness:**
>
> **Party index:**

in town: It's right smack in the middle of the hippest district in Vienna, otherwise known as Neustiftgasse.

Staff is surprisingly laid-back and lacks that authoritative look we've come to expect from a place dealing with gangly rugrats. Rooms are pretty clean and accommodating, though the place has been remodeled to eliminate doubles. All the four- to six-bedded dorms come with their own shower and toilet. Staff is variably friendly, but certainly not terrible at all.

The hostel has organized a really useful information board, including many nearby cash machine locations and transportation information. Common areas include a very tranquil patio with picnic tables, ivy-covered walls, and one of those antique-looking water fountains so common in Europe. There is a television lounge with cable TV. The dinners (weekdays only) are basic—stuff like spaghetti, soup, and local Viennese specialties—but they have added vegetarian and organic options now.

Overall, management runs a good hostel despite its preference for groups. Maybe they can apply this efficiency and open a real hostel for travelers and backpackers, which a great city like Vienna so richly deserves.

how to get there:

By bus: Call hostel for transit route. At night, take the N46 bus to Skodagasse.

By car: Call hostel for directions.

By subway: Take U-Bahn U2 or U3 line to Volkstheater stop, or take U6 line to Burggasse stop.

By train: From West Bahnhof Station, take U-Bahn U6 line to Burggasse stop and change to #48A bus to Neubaugasse. From Südbahnhof Station, take #13A bus toward Haltestelle to Kellermanngasse stop.

---

panda hostel

Number 7, Third Floor
Kaiserstrasse 77, A–1070 Vienna
Phone: 01–522–5353

E-mail: panda_vienna@hotmail.com
Rates: €13.50–€15.00 (about $17–$19 US) per person; doubles €50–€60 (about $62–$75 US)
Credit cards: No
Beds: Number varies
Private/family rooms: Yes
Kitchen available: Yes
Season: Open year-round
Office hours: 8:00 A.M.–midnight
Lockout: 10:00 A.M.–2:00 P.M.
Affiliation: None
Extras: TV, lockers

This hostel is kind of the same deal as the Believe It or Not Hostel—this one's also in an apartment building and doesn't hold too many folks.

When the place is open (which is not always), our hostel snoops say the expensive doubles here are quite good (they're in separate apartments). Dorms consist of thirty bunks squashed in three-high, however, a big negative. There are lockers to stash your stuff, although you'll have to supply your own lock. If you stay in the off-season, which runs from November to Easter, you'll be charged a reduced rate. The kitchen is too minimal and desk staff got a few complaints for being evasive about bunk prices.

The street the hostel is located on is full of restaurants and other diversions. It's somewhat of an extension of the Neubaugasse/Burggasse area, only slightly closer to the West Bahnhof Station.

Best bet for a bite:
Supermarkets in neighborhood

Gestalt:
Panda bear

Safety:

Hospitality:

Cleanliness:

Party index:

how to get there:

By bus or train: From West Bahnhof Station, take #5 tram to Burggasse. From Südbahnhof, take #18 tram to West Bahnhof then change to #5 to Burggasse.
By car: Call hostel for directions.

strawberry hostel
bürgerspitalgasse
Bürgerspitalgasse 19, A-1060, Vienna
Phone: 01–597–9347

E-mail: strawberryhostels@hotmail.com
Rates: €21–€40 (about $26–$50 US per person); doubles €50 (about $63 US)
Credit cards: Yes
Beds: 15
Private/family rooms: Yes
Kitchen available: Yes
Season: July 1–August 31
Office hours: Twenty-four hours
Affiliation: None
Extras: Kitchen, breakfast, laundry, storage, TV

The newer of Strawberry's two Vienna hostels is a winner so far: single rooms and double rooms (that's right, no huge jail-like dorms), each with en-suite bathrooms and mini-fridges. (No, the fridges aren't *in* the bathrooms, wise guy.) The rooms themselves are clean and fresh—as we said, it's new—but pretty spare.

A communal kitchen, hosteller laundry, breakfast, bike storage area, and TV room add to the experience. Just don't come expecting rockin' times and beer blasts; it's not that kind of place. But the central location, decent facilities, and low-key vibe all play in its favor. Give it a look.

Best bet for a bite:
Wiener schnitzel

What hostellers say:
"I like it!"

Gestalt:
Strawberry alarm clock

Safety:

Hospitality:

Cleanliness:

Party index:

how to get there:

By car: Contact hostel for directions.

By bus: Contact hostel for transit route.

By train: Take U3 line to Westbahnof; from station, cross Mariahilfer Gürtel and turn right onto Bürgerspitalgasse. Continue to hostel.

---

strawberry hostel vienna
Mittelgasse 18, A–1060 Vienna
Phone: 01–5997–9660

E-mail: strawberrywien@hotmail.com
Rates: €21–€40 (about $26–$50 US per person); doubles €54 (about $69 US)
Credit cards: No
Beds: 80
Private/family rooms: Yes
Kitchen available: Yes
Season: July 1 to August 31
Office hours: Twenty-four hours
Affiliation: None
Extras: Laundry, storage, TV, Internet access

This Strawberry's not a perfect peach yet, but it's definitely not a lemon.

A summer-only hostel from the same folks who run the Strawberry in Prague, this basic and functional place does deliver decent-enough-quality bunks. Sure, it's expensive—one of the two most expensive hostels in the city, in fact—but worth it, especially if you're stuck for a safe bunk and the better places in town are fully booked already.

They tout the showers in each room, the lack of curfews/lockouts, the twenty-four-hours reception, the luggage storage, and a laundry, and these are all laudable things. Have to say the cleanliness was variable, though—sometimes good and sometimes hurting. Other than that, we wouldn't find anything else bad to point a finger at. The position close to Westbahnhof is good, as well.

Best bet for a bite:
Reinthalers

What hostellers say:
"Fun place."

Gestalt:
Strawberry bunks forever

Safety:

Hospitality:

Cleanliness:

Party index:

how to get there:

By car: Contact hostel for directions.

By bus: Contact hostel for transit route.

By train: From Westbahnhof, exit and walk along Bürgerspitalgasse 2 blocks to Mittelgasse. From Südbahnhof, take #18 streetcar nine stops to Mariahilfergürtel, then walk five minutes to Mittelgasse.

turmherberge don bosco
Lechnerstrasse 12, A–1030 Vienna
Phone: 01–713–1494

Rates: €10 (about $13 US) per HI member
Credit cards: No
Beds: 53
Private/family rooms: No
Kitchen available: Yes
Season: March 1–November 30
Office hours: 7:30 A.M.–noon; 5:00–11:45 P.M.
Lockout: Noon to 5:00 P.M.
Curfew: 11:30 P.M.
Affiliation: HI-ÖJHW
Extras: Bugs, breakfast ($)

Reports about this former church tower vary—from "run-down but cheap" to downright "grim." Owned by a church group, this may be one of the worst hostels in Europe, and we've got proof.

The building itself does have an interesting layout, occupying several stories of the tower, but it lacks caring management. The kitchen's dirty and underequipped; dorms are cramped and contain old wooden beds and flimsy mattresses. Bugs appear to run rampant—our hostel reviewer showed us his marked-up limbs as proof. The poor guy also had all his money stolen from him as he slept. The clientele are sleazy characters who appear to have taken up permanent residence in search of a job.

Overlook this place despite the fact that it's really cheap. (They charge for sheets, so that's an extra hidden cost.) Do yourself a favor and seek out other accommodations.

Best bet for a bite:
Fleas

Insiders' tip:
Don't do it

What hostellers say:
"Ouch, ooch, ouch!"

Gestalt:
Flea circus

Safety: 🔪

Hospitality: 🔪

Cleanliness: 🔪

Party index: 🎉🎉🎉

how to get there:

By bus: Call hostel for transit route.
By car: Call hostel for directions.
By train: From West Bahnhof and Südbahnhof, take the U3 line to Kardinal-Nagl Platz stop and walk toward Erdbergstrasse; take a right and continue until you reach Lechnerstrasse.

wombat's backpackers
Grangasse 6, A–1150 Vienna
Phone: 01–897–2336

Fax: 01–897–2577
E-mail: office@wombats-vienna.at
Web site: www.wombats.at
Rates: €17–€50 (about $21–$63 US) per person; doubles €50 (about $63 US)
Credit cards: No
Beds: 296
Private/family rooms: Yes
Kitchen available: Yes
Season: Open year-round
Office hours: Twenty-four hours
Affiliation: None

Extras: Breakfast ($), Internet access, laundry, bike rentals, roller skate rentals, in-line skate rentals, bar, bicycle tours, lockers, games, darts, movies, terrace, kitchen

You get a free drink when you walk into this place, and that should tell you something—though not everything—about it. There's more to this cool independent entry than just booze, and it's conveniently located almost right behind the city's main international train station. Hey, you've got to love a place that rents roller skates, right?

The hostel opened three new floors. Room arrangements now consist of nineteen doubles, four triples, thirty-four quads, and eighteen six-bedded dorms—with a shower and bathroom inside every room. People frequently write in the guestbook that the rooms are clean and the beds comfy, so it must be true, right? The kitchen's a big help, and the staff and management seem amazingly receptive to hosteller comments, complaints, and suggestions.

Best bet for a bite:
Schwejk (Bohemian cuisine)

What hostellers say:
"Let's rock it."

Gestalt:
Wombatmobile

Safety:

Hospitality:

Cleanliness:

Party index:

key to icons

Attractive natural setting	Comfortable beds	Visual arts at hostel or nearby
Ecologically aware hostel	A particularly good value	Music at hostel or nearby
Superior kitchen facilities or cafe	Wheelchair-accessible	Great hostel for skiers
Offbeat or eccentric place	Good for business travelers	Bar or pub at hostel or nearby
Superior bathroom facilities	Especially well suited for families	Editors' Choice: Among our very favorite hostels
Romantic private rooms	Good for active travelers	

The pub with the sun terrace is the most popular place, of course, even though it's only open from 8:00 P.M. to 2:00 A.M. It's one great party spot, that's for sure. But they do other stuff, too. You get your own locker and key for storage safety. Breakfast costs a bit; they've got four Internet terminals and a Laundromat. Even better, they rent bikes and skates for exploring the city. Reception also helps arrange local walking tours from May through October for around $12 US each, as well as longer tours extending to the Wachau region and even Budapest. The hostel also continues to be a stop on the Busabout circular backpacker bus route around Europe, a bonus if you're using this service.

The train-station neighborhood may not be the most posh (or safest) in town, but it certainly does provide a selection of ethnic eateries to pick from. And the hostel's close to Vienna's great city transit. Its buzz is really spreading, though, so try to arrive before noon—or, better yet, call ahead to reserve your bunk because this *is* now Vienna's top hostel.

how to get there:

By bus: Contact hostel for transit details.
By car: Contact hostel for directions.
By train: From West Bahnhof, exit station and turn right onto Mariahilfer Strasse. Follow to #152 (at the corner of Rosinagasse); bear right at Rosinagasse and continue to Grangasse, then make a left and continue to hostel on right.

belgium

If you've never been to Belgium, you're going to be in for a bit of a surprise: It's a heckuva fun place to visit, in spite of the mostly flat terrain and frequently drab weather. Kick back and enjoy the friendly people, low cost of traveling, and good food and drink.

The famous squabbling between the Dutch-speaking half of Belgium (the north) and the French-speaking part in the south has even spilled over to hostelling: There are actually two separate organizations for the country, and—to make matters worse—if you're Belgian you have to declare allegiance to one or the other. Pretty silly. But as a hosteller you can pretty much ignore it.

Given a short period of time in Belgium, we'd probably head first for Brugge—a beautiful little city with tons of sights to offer and a likable, small-town feel within the compact city center. Then we'd go for Brussels—a noisy, sprawling place that makes up in culture what it lacks in physical beauty. Finally, we'd skip down to the Ardennes for a few days of back-roading.

Oh, and if you happen to find yourself in the country on July 21—good for you! It's Belgium's National Day, sorta like our Fourth of July. And they celebrate it the same way, too, with fireworks and general merriment.

practical details

Lots of airlines fly into Brussels. Virgin Express has the most cheap flights here, because that's its hub. Sabena has the most flights overall here—from everywhere—because the airline is based in Belgium.

To get to Belgium from London, you can also take the train to Dover on the southeastern tip of England, then a ferry across the English Channel. Ferries and trains are timed to meet each other, but once in a while they don't. If the boat runs late because of weather, for instance, the train won't wait. Be prepared.

Once you're here, Belgian trains are comprehensive, comfortable, and inexpensive, though not particularly fast. You can get from anywhere to anywhere else, just about, in this small country—but count on usually making lots of stops along the way.

Brussels is the main rail hub for the country and also for much of Europe. The city's Midi/Zuid Station (it has two confusing names) connects quickly to London, Paris, Nice, and other distant points; too

brussels

bad it's in an odd, unattractive neighborhood far from the city center and the hostels. It lacks an ATM, too, but does have a grocery store and a pharmacy. If you're heading right into town, get off at Centraal Station if possible. Nord (North) Station is another good option, handy for many of the Brussels hostels though not a particularly attractive area—especially at night.

The Benelux TourRail Pass is no longer an option; now you have to buy a much more expensive "Germany 'n' Benelux Pass." At press time it cost about $295 US for a five-day (within one month) second-class pass and $395 US for a pointless first-class pass good for the same length of time. "Partners" traveling with you, or travelers under the age of twenty-six, get a 33 to 40 percent discount on some country and regional passes. A regional pass is ideal if you're also going to be traveling in Luxembourg and the Netherlands, but there is also a slightly cheaper Benelux-and-France pass now available, too.

Buses run around Belgium—and internationally—from North Station in Brussels. Because of Belgium's density, buses can take even longer than trains: one hour to get from Brussels to Ghent, for example, which is twice as long as the train takes. But they do cost less. And Euro-lines buses go from Brussels to Paris, London, Germany—heck, even Copenhagen.

The unit of currency in Belgium is now the euro. A large bag of fries purchased late at night might cost you €1.80 plus another €0.25 for curried ketchup on top. (You gotta try it, trust us.) Your €11 dorm room is also extremely cheap.

Belgium's phone code is 32. To call Brussels hostels from the United States, dial 011–32 and then DROP THE ZERO from the numbers listed in this book. To call Brussels hostels from within Belgium, dial the numbers exactly AS PRINTED in this book.

brussels

As a city, you're not going to do much better than this—if you can overlook the place's fairly bland (even ugly) physical appearance. You'll find food that's as good as Paris's, beer that's as good as Munich's, people as friendly as in your hometown, and costs surprisingly low.

Belgium's capital city, Brussels (also known as Bruxelles), is fairly centrally located in the country and is actually a good mix of the two cultures plus lots more people who come here to work for the EU's home offices. Though the city can be gray and bland—it seems that these people never met a green park they liked as much as a new store or parking garage—it's also quite hip and happening these days if you go to the right places, and it's full of good food and drink. The hostel situation here is amazingly good, too: For once, four of five hostels here are pretty centrally located—no more than a ten-minute walk from the main downtown square known as the Grand-Place.

transportation

Hostels near North Station (Jacques Brel, Sleep Well, and CHAB) are all fine but located in blah, slightly dodgy areas. There used to be a botanical garden here, but it's been mostly paved over. Auberge Generation is beautiful but pretty far to the north and in a bad part of town; the Bruegel Hostel is the most-central, best-located of the whole five-pack.

To help you get around, Brussels has loads of mass transit, but it takes a little figuring out to master. There are Metro subway lines, augmented by a system of streetcars that dip and dive above and beneath ground. There's also a pretty good bus system. Transit isn't cheap, but a *carte du jour* (day pass) can reduce your costs; for a few dollars, the pass gets you all-day access to the web of buses, trams, and subways around Brussels. Maps in the stations aren't much help, though; it's best to ask a ticket vendor, hostel staffer, or conductor before climbing aboard. Make special note of where your train ends—that's critical. The train or tram or bus will have its final destination posted, and that's the only clue you'll have about where it is going.

At least all these options are quick and efficient. It's easy to buy a ticket, too; you can get one from ticket sellers in the Metro stations or from automatic machines scattered around town and concentrated inside the stations. The tickets are good on any kind of transit, plus a transfer in the same direction within one hour; one ride in town costs about €1.50–€2.00 (about $2.00–$2.50 US), but buy a five-ride card and the price drops. Buy a ten-ride card or a daily pass (€4, about $5 US) that you use a lot, and it drops quite a bit more.

attractions and nightlife

Most tourists come here for the obvious sights: the EU's home offices, the offices of NATO, stuff like that. But to our eye, by far the hippest places to get a bite now are in the Ixelles neighborhood, which isn't right downtown but is very reachable—it's got a melange of veggie, ethnic, and Belgian food—and in the burgeoning Sainte-Catherine neighborhood close to downtown.

Hip Ixelles is the area where Brussels's nouveau rich kids (if this were London, we'd be calling them "trustafarians") boogie the nights away in bistros and discos. Otherwise it's a rather dull area, with the European Union's massive edifices and a couple museums and administrative buildings for company. Most eateries around here cater to diplomats' tastes and so probably aren't gonna be in your price range. Hike down to the Grand-Place and its surrounding maze of streets for ethnic options of all kinds instead. Sainte-Catherine is livelier and more interesting, we think, livened up by a number of strip joints, student-y bars, and the like.

Though a lot more touristed, there are also plenty of good bars and restaurants in the streets around the *Mannekin Pis* (an inexplicably popular statue of a peeing boy). The Port-Namur area is Brussels's Fifth Avenue, good for those looking to lighten their wallets before heading on to the next destination.

No matter where you're going, though, this is an easy city to get lost in—no central arteries or grids of streets to orient yourself—kinda like Paris, except about ten times worse. So get a good map, head for the Grand-Place or some other obvious landmark, and begin fanning out from there. Note that all the streets and stations in Brussels are schizophrenically named, both in French and Flemish, and the names often bear no resemblance to each other. This can be hell if you're not sure where you're going.

brussels hostels
at a glance

	RATING	PRICE	IN A WORD	PAGE
CHAB Hostel	◣	€18–€33	fun	p. 66
Bruegel Hostel	◣	€18–€31	modern	p. 61
Jacques Brel Hostel	◣	€16–€31	good	p. 62
Sleep Well Hostel	◣	€17.50–€29	central	p. 68
Auberge Generation Europe	◣◥	€16–€31	distant	p. 65

auberge de jeunesse bruegel

2 Heilig Geeststraat/rue Saint-Esprit 2, Brussels 1000
Phone: 02–511–0436

Fax: 02–512–0711
E-mail: brussel@vjh.be
Rates: €18–€31 (about $23–$39 US) per HI member
Credit cards: Yes
Beds: 135
Private/family rooms: Yes
Kitchen available: No
Season: Open year-round
Office hours: 7:00 A.M.–1:00 A.M.
Lockout: 1:00–2:00 P.M.
Curfew: 1:00 A.M.
Affiliation: HI-VJ
Extras: Currency exchange, TV, breakfast, meals ($), conference rooms, disco, lockers, patio, bar

By far the best located of Brussels's good five-pack of hostels, the Bruegel is certainly a good bunk—and, unlike almost all the rest of the city's budget lodging, is actually in a halfway interesting area: central, even if the actual street is small and hard to find if you're not a local. Which you're not.

It sits on top of a little hill that leads to Brussels's so-called "upper town": the part, of course, where the richest folks live, where the European Union officials have met to hash out details of integrating the euro and bad pop music, and so on and so forth.

However, an interesting thing happens around the corner from the hostel. Before you get to the hoity-toity, beautiful-homes-of-diplomats district, you hit a little working-class area at the base of beautiful Notre Dame de la Chapelle church. This is a place where you can still get a beer for less than two bucks instead of the ripoff prices they'll charge you in the richer area. After all, this is beer country! Inquire about happy hour specials.

Inside, the hostel's the usual situation. They serve good meals here daily, often featuring chicken or pasta but sometimes slipping

Best bet for a bite:
Snack La Chapelle or
Chez Léon

What hostellers say:
"I can see for miles . . ."

Gestalt:
Back to Bruegel-oo

Safety:

Hospitality:

Cleanliness:

Party index:

a regional Flemish specialty into the mix just to see if you're paying attention. (When you start going, "What the heck is that on my plate??" it's probably a local specialty.)

After dinner there are three main areas to congregate in. Outside, there's a beautiful little nook of a terrace, enclosed in ivy-covered brick walls and laid out with tables for hanging out. That would be our first choice. There's also a good television lounge, although who cares? Downstairs (ignore the sewery smell on the way) there's a bar/disco area that features a combination of Euro-pop, strobe lights, and the usual Belgian bar with a couple great (local) and awful (American) beers on tap. The bartender will sometimes even play CDs you bring him! Can't beat that for service.

The beds are pretty good; some hostellers raved they were hotel-quality, though we don't know if we'd go quite *that* far. How many hotels ask you to shower with strangers?

Oh, yeah, the room layouts. There are five singles, twenty-one doubles (all of them twin bunk beds, of course, not real double beds), two triples, nine quads, one five-bedded room, one six-bedded room, and three still larger ones. They're all nicer than you'd expect for the price, and some rooms even come with TVs, sinks, and/or showers. They've got lockers for your valuables, too.

There is a drawback to all this; it isn't perfection. Staff could be a lot friendlier and more helpful than they are. They match the impersonal quality of the place. So it's good, adequate—but not great.

The interesting pocket neighborhood is okay, and if you continue walking uphill you'll be in Armani (and also Notre Dame) territory. You're also—perhaps the best reason of all to stay here—maybe five minutes' walk from the city's central train station and a little bit farther from the Grand-Place at the center of the city and all its associated eateries.

how to get there:

By bus: Take #20 bus to La Chapelle and walk 50 yards to hostel.
By car: Call hostel for directions.
By train: From Centraal Station, walk 300 yards down Boulevard de l'Empereur to hostel. From Midi Station, take #20 bus to La Chapelle and walk 50 yards to hostel.

auberge de jeunesse jacques brel

30 rue de la Sablonnière, Brussels 1000
Phone: 02–218–0187

Fax: 02–217–2005

E-mail: brussels.brel@laj.be
Rates: €16–€31 (about $20–$39 US) per person; doubles €45 (about $56 US)
Credit cards: Yes
Beds: 171
Private/family rooms: Yes
Kitchen available: Yes
Season: January 2–December 16
Office hours: 7:30 A.M.–1:00 A.M.
Lockout: Noon–3:00 P.M.
Affiliation: HI-LAJ
Extras: Courtyard, laundry, conference rooms, bar, restaurant ($), lockers, Internet access, library, tourist information, table tennis, currency exchange, TV

This hard-to-find hostel sits not too far from Brussels's North Station on a quiet side street just off the bustle near the city's former botanical gardens. (Today it's more of an arts and entertainment complex; you'll see more guitars and concrete than flowers.) The Jacques Brel's wing is the real star—and it shows that this Hostelling International chapter has paid close attention to the services and design quirks that have made independent backpacker-style hostels so competitive over the past decade.

Outside, the unassuming three-story building looks as prim and proper as a schoolhouse. Inside, though, you enter a very mod-looking reception area decorated with movie posters, sleek furniture, and other cool stuff. This part of the hostel doubles as a travel store, honor-system lending library, and game room with *Risk* and other multilingual favorites—not to mention a major hangout area. A jovial staff calls out requests on an intercom and generally keeps this very busy hostel moving; the guests often are groups—American, French, or German—plus the usual motley crew of good-hearted backpackers. Slackers don't tend to stay here, we noticed.

They have four meeting rooms with TVs, VCRs, and flipcharts, in case you've brought the entire soccer team along with you and want to diagram plays in secret. Forget that and head instead for the sitting

Best bet for a bite:
Downtown

What hostellers say:
"C'est magnifique!
Mais où est la centre-ville?"

Gestalt:
Brel done

Safety:

Hospitality:

Cleanliness:

Party index:

areas, with plenty of neato furniture like glass tables, hipper than hip Eurochairs, skylights, and the like. The exposed rooftop terrace gets lots of action during the summer, when Polish girls work on their tans to the appreciative oohs and aahs of working-class Belgian guys walking by on the street. There is no curfew of any kind here—a big plus and frankly quite surprising given that this is a Hostelling International–affiliated joint.

One big drawback, however: There is neither a kitchen for hostellers to cook in nor meals (unless you've come along with a big group). The only food is served in the beautiful little bar, all freshly painted and clean and serving brews on tap. They've got toast and snacks like that, so you could probably make a meal of it if you added a couple great Belgian beers to the mix. Beer, after all, is just liquid bread when you think about it.

But we digress. The bar—painted in a pleasing stars, angels, and moons motif—comes complete with a piano and other instruments like a tambourine, congas, shakers, and more.

Rooms, as you would expect, come in a variety of configurations: There's one single room, about twenty doubles, five triples, eleven quad rooms, six six-bedded dorms, and three larger dorms of thirteen and fourteen beds in the older wing. (You don't want to get stuck there.) You get into rooms with key-cards, which is nice, and most have lockers and cupboards for arranging your stuff; many come with showers, as well. Cleanliness is just so-so, not pristine.

As for the neighborhood, that's one minus in an otherwise good hostel. It's not a bad area, and it's not a great area, safety-wise. There's just little of interest. At least there are a couple bars and cafes and a bit of shopping as well on the ring highway that encircles Brussels. To get there just take the Metro a couple of stops, or during the day hike a half mile or so.

Note that some hostellers complained of security issues—not sure if hostellers or outsiders are to blame for that, but keep an eye on your stuff.

Hey, things could be worse.

how to get there:

By bus: Take #61 bus to Botanique and walk to hostel; or take #92, #93, or #94 streetcar to Botanique and walk 200 yards to hostel.
By car: Call hostel for directions.
By train: From Gare du Nord, walk 1 mile north up rue Royale to hostel. From Centraal Station, take Metro Line M2 to Botanique or Madou stop and walk to hostel; or take #91, #92, #93, or #94 streetcar and walk to hostel.

auberge generation europe

4 rue de l'Eléphant, Brussels 1080
Phone: 02–410–3858

Fax: 02–410–3905
E-mail: brussels.europe@laj.be
Rates: €16–€31 (about $20–$39 US) per HI member; doubles €45 (about $56 US)
Credit cards: Yes
Beds: 164
Private/family rooms: Yes
Kitchen available: No
Season: Open year-round
Office hours: 7:45 A.M.–12:30 A.M.
Affiliation: HI-LAJ
Extras: Breakfast, meals ($), garden, laundry, conference rooms, library, Internet access, lockers, disco, table tennis, TV

This place was once a foundry; now it's a hostel. It's not elaborate, and it's the least central of the city's five—but it's packed with welcome extras like a garden, laundry, and Internet access. Too bad the neighborhood is unsafe and that this element filters into the hostel itself.

The three-story conversion features modern, airy architecture—think lots of arching windows open to the gray sky—and newish, mostly quad rooms. The dining area's roomy enough to hold a small dance in (if you cleared away the homey tables, that is), and they've got five meeting rooms here, too, in case you need 'em.

There are an unusual number of private rooms here—ten doubles and twenty-four quad rooms—plus two six-bedded dorms and four bigger ones. The facilities here are incredibly modern: Try Web cruising, a disco (well, that's actually retro, but in Europe it's modern), meeting rooms, and lockers, for starters. You get the picture. It's well done.

Unfortunately, the place isn't near any train stations; it'll require a Metro ride plus a good-sized walk to get here. And the neighborhood is just plain terrible.

Best bet for a bite:
Downtown

What hostellers say:
"Hello? Police?"

Gestalt:
Generation Ex

Safety:

Hospitality:

Cleanliness:

Party index:

Sorry, but we gotta tell it like it is. Take a car here at night, or walk at your own risk. Groups are in the best position, because they've got a bus to ferry them to and from the city's central attractions. Lone hostellers really need to be careful here, and we heard reports of dodgy people staying here, too. Needless to say, there's also nothing of interest to do in the area. It's just a bed in a beautiful building that's been plunked down in Skid Row City.

Otherwise this hostel is just as good as the rest of the city's places—maybe better.

how to get there:

By bus: From Midi Station, take #18 streetcar to Porte de Flandre stop and walk ⅓ mile to hostel.
By car: Call hostel for directions.
By train: From train station, take Metro to Comte-de-Flandre stop and walk to hostel.

---

chab vincent van gogh hostel
8 rue Traversière, Brussels 1210
Phone: 02–217–0158

Fax: 02–219–7995
E-mail: info@chab.be
Web site: www.chab.be
Rates: €18–€33 (about $23–$41 US) per person; doubles €52 (about $65 US); second night cheaper
Credit cards: Yes
Beds: 228
Private/family rooms: Yes
Kitchen available: Yes
Season: Open year-round
Office hours: 7:30 A.M.–2:00 A.M.
Lockout: 10:00 A.M.–2:00 P.M.
Affiliation: None
Extras: Laundry, pool table, courtyard, breakfast, Internet access, solarium, garden, lockers, bar

---

Note: **Must be age eighteen to thirty-five to stay.**
This is one of the nicest of the Brussels Fun Bunch—okay, we'll give it the narrow nod as *the* best; better than it has to be. But not perfect.

A pretty central hostel, it's not too far from town, either. It's close to the city's northern train station and no more than a leisurely half-hour stroll from the central square—though it isn't a terribly exciting walk and we'd probably end up taking the expensive city subway instead of being bored out of our minds.

The main reception area opens onto a bar area (here's a tip: cheap bar) with a small but fun pool table and a lounge with a nicely designed solarium. The kitchen is aces. Then there's a kiosk for Internet access and a locker room for your stuff (the room itself is locked, giving double security). Out through the back is the best part of all—a pretty enclosed courtyard, surrounded by ivy, with a rose garden that blooms in spring.

That's where most of the kiddies are groovin' and mingling.

The crowd doing that mingling is a real melange of cig-smoking French girls, youth groups, young Americans, rasta guys . . . just think young. We didn't see anybody over the age of twenty when we stopped in, so it's not really the sort of place where lots of families with kids show up.

Rooms are standard and nothing to write home about—usually six to a room but sometimes four or eight to a room. Amazingly, some doubles

Best bet for a bite:
L'Isole Buissoniere

Insiders' tip:
Ultieme Hallucinatie (bar)

Gestalt:
van Go!

Safety:

Hospitality:

Cleanliness:

Party index:

key to icons

	Attractive natural setting		Comfortable beds		Visual arts at hostel or nearby
	Ecologically aware hostel		A particularly good value		Music at hostel or nearby
	Superior kitchen facilities or cafe		Wheelchair-accessible		Great hostel for skiers
	Offbeat or eccentric place		Good for business travelers		Bar or pub at hostel or nearby
	Superior bathroom facilities		Especially well suited for families		Editors' Choice: Among our very favorite hostels
	Romantic private rooms		Good for active travelers		

come with private bathrooms. But the cheapest dorms are packed and the bathrooms are shrimpy overall. These are downtown city hotel rooms at hostel prices, folks; snap 'em up quick if you can.

how to get there:

By bus: Take #91, #92, #93, or #94 streetcar to hostel.
By car: Call hostel for directions.
By train: From Nord (North) Station, walk or take Metro to Botanique stop and then walk down rue Royale to rue Traversière; take a right and walk to hostel. Or take #61 bus to Botanique Metro stop and walk down rue Royale to rue Traversière; take a right and walk to hostel. From Centraal Station, take Metro Line 1 to Arts-Loi stop and change to Line 2, then continue to Botanique stop. Walk down rue Royale to rue Traversière; take a right and walk to hostel.

sleep well hostel
23 rue du Damier, Brussels 1000
Phone: 02–218–5050

Fax: 02–218–1313
E-mail: info@sleepwell.be
Web site: www.sleepwell.be
Rates: First night €17.50–€29.00 (about $22–$36 US) per person; doubles €52 (about $65 US); subsequent nights cheaper
Credit cards: Yes
Beds: 236
Private/family rooms: Yes
Kitchen available: No
Season: Open year-round
Office hours: 7:00 A.M.–midnight
Lockout: 11:00 A.M.–3:00 P.M.
Affiliation: None
Extras: TV, tours, currency exchange, bar, garden, Internet access, restaurant ($), breakfast

Another nice place?! We couldn't believe it—Brussels knows hostels. This is the newest joint in town, and it's super.

However, the surrounding area looked like a bomb shelter when we rolled in to check it out. In any event, this is perhaps the closest hostel of all to the central Grand-Place square. And, as a major bonus, there are two English-speaking businesses just down the street: a small bookstore and a Marks & Spencer, the English combination department-grocery store Londoners so fondly miss when they're away.

Lots of work has been done to spruce up this hostel. Beds come in singles (eight), doubles (fourteen, plus an annex), triples (ten), quads (thirteen more), six-bedded dorms (eight), and just one eight-bedded dorm. The hostel also has a hotel-like thirty-two-room annex of all double rooms called the Star. All have private bathrooms, TVs, and *no lockout!* This site also has a bar, club, and other upgrades. In other words, you're probably going to have a cozy small room, and that's a nice feeling. There are a surprising number of other amenities here for the traveler as well: Try an

Best bet for a bite:
Grand Place

Insiders' tip:
Lop Lop (bar) near
Grand Place

What hostellers say:
"It's O.K."

Gestalt:
Sleeping beauty

Safety:

Hospitality:

Cleanliness:

Party index:

Internet bar/cafe and fax service, in the main hostel, for starters. They do breakfast and meals, too, and store luggage for you during the day. There's even an outdoor terrace. It's all doled out by mostly friendly staffers who don't lean on rules to keep you out.

We found only one drawback to this place, in fact: a long 11:00 A.M. to 3:00 P.M. lockout, a bit discouraging in tiring Brussels. Sure, the city is fun and has some attractions—but not that much fun. We needed a rest after hours of pounding the pavement. (While we're complaining, can we say a word about the push-button-style showers, too? Argh!)

There's one other problem when you've got such a successful hostel: popularity! This place requires some serious advance booking, especially during European school holidays (May, July, August, September), when the place is swamped with not only German and French schoolkids but the occasional American bunch as well. Don't show up here on short notice, even a day ahead, expecting to find a bed, 'cause it won't happen.

how to get there:

By bus: Take #91, #92, #93, or #94 streetcar to hostel.
By car: Call hostel for directions.
By train: From Gare du Nord, walk down rue du Progrés to rue de Malines, then make a right onto rue du Damier. Or take Metro to Rogier stop and walk to hostel.

czech republic

Part of the former Czechoslovakia, the Czech Republic remains one of the most popular visitor destinations in the former Soviet bloc—in large part thanks to the lovely city of Prague.

Hostels aren't nearly as prevalent here as they are in some other European countries, but the low cost of lodging means you might not need one—except when you get to Prague, where a continuing increase in hotel prices is suddenly making hostels a very good business to get into.

practical matters

The unit of currency in the Czech Republic is the koruna (crown), abbreviated as Kč. There are between 25 and 30 Kč per U.S. dollar, so a 300 Kč dorm room costs about $11.50 and a 60 Kč beer costs $2.30.

The country code, if you're dialing ahead from the United States or elsewhere in Europe, is +420. When dialing the numbers listed here from abroad, do NOT drop the initial zero as you normally do when calling Europe. (You don't need a double zero, though, just one.)

The Czech Republic is served by its own decently efficient train company, but this is NOT a Eurail country. You'll need either a special pass or to buy tickets right from conductors and at train stations. There's a Czech pass, Austria 'n Czech pass, and a pass including Hungary. (If you're in Germany and want to go to Prague on a whim, you can also get one in Munich at the terrific EurAide office.)

prague (praha)

Think two words when you think Prague: beautiful and changing.

Prague today is a city on the move. Prices are going up, phone numbers change constantly, political figures come and go, and capitalism is on a serious upswing.

The sights here range from the grand (Hradčany Castle) to the sobering (the wonderful Jewish neighborhood known as Josefov) to the Old World (the mazes of streets, bars dispensing pilsner, and the faces of merchants and children). It's best to just dive in—with a good map—or else hire a reputable city tour guide, available through many of the hostels listed below.

There's one downtown hostel run by the Hostelling International affiliate CKM, but at least a dozen others run by independent owners and outfits. Most notable among them is the Travellers chain, which currently includes about a half dozen hostels, most open only during the summer months—and each year it's unclear which ones will reopen. We haven't included those in this guide, but you can get all the details from the main Travellers hostel, which is open year-round (see page 91).

Note that Prague's hostels are particularly finicky, and any hostel listed in these pages could well be closed by the time you get there. CALL OR E-MAIL AHEAD just before you visit.

orientation and getting around

Hlavní Nádraží, less than a mile east of the river that splits the city, is the main train station and your likely arrival point. It's also a good orientation point. From here, going directly west and a little north, you would soon pass through Old Town; go west and a little south, and you would pass through New Town. Most of the hostels are in these two neighborhoods. Just north of Old Town lies Josefov, another neighborhood you'll surely want to see.

Once here, the best way to get around the city is to use public transit. Prague's subway system consists of three lines—labeled A (green line), B (yellow line), and C (red line)—that run about every two minutes (yes, every two minutes) from approximately 5:00 A.M. until midnight. Fast streetcars (also known as trams) and buses supplement the subway, running about every ten minutes, though less frequently at night or on weekends. Big maps at the stations show you where the lines run; it's important to know which end point your subway car is heading toward before you get on, because the train will be labeled according to end-point.

During the night you must use night buses or night trams (streetcars), most of which pick up every forty minutes or so from downtown. Many of these lines pass through the Metro Station Lazarská, one of the hubs for the entire transit system. For more-out-of-the-way places, a few bus lines run out to the city's outlying districts, usually with numbers in the 300s; these are more expensive rides, but you can buy these tickets (and these alone) right on the bus.

You can buy tickets at ticket offices, at Information Centers of the Prague Public Transit Company, at selected stores, and from ticket machines. For almost all practical purposes, you will always be within "the zone," the central fare area. (There is also another zone in

prague
(praha)

Prague, the "finishing zone," and four suburban zones; prices below apply only to the two central zones.) There are several kinds of tickets: a more expensive ticket (about 80 cents US) allows sixty minutes of riding and free transfers among Metro, bus, and tram (streetcar) lines. The normal single ticket (about 50 cents US) gives you fifteen minutes of riding or up to four subway stops; get them at machines in the stations. (If you need to travel farther than four stops, you have to buy the more expensive ticket.)

If you'll be around for a while, offices also sell passes valid for twenty-four hours or three, seven, and fifteen days. They cost from about 80 Kč (about $3 US) for one day to about 280 Kč (about $10 US) for a week; that's a deal only if you'll be riding around a lot. Also remember that if your luggage is bigger than about 10" x 18" x 28"—and many backpacks are—you'll also need a cheap extra (about 25 cents US) ticket for it. Don't try to ride without a ticket, either: Cops are much more common here than on other European transit systems, and fines can be steep.

To find out more, visit the transit system's Web site: www.dp-praha.cz.

safety and crime

You'll need to be careful in Prague to avoid getting separated from your cash: Bad hostels, pickpockets, dishonest taxi drivers, and bogus currency exchangers are just a few of the potential pitfalls.

First, the hostels. You'll be surrounded by "touts" or "runners"—guys who get paid to rope in hostellers for a hostel—at the train station or even on the train going to Prague. Ignore them; you've got this book as a guide, and we're unbiased. NEVER get in a car with a hostel representative at the station. If you're truly interested, ask to see on a map where the hostel is located, then take public transit or a cab. More often than not, these places are located wayyyyy out of town, and they're very poor quality. Exceptions are rare.

There are lots of pickpockets, especially active in crowded buses and subway cars. If you feel a hard shove, grab your wallet and backpack pronto—it's probably a thief. Better yet, take off your backpack and hold it tightly in front of you, even if there isn't much space on the subway; thieves can use knives to cut them off your back. Crowded public squares like Charles Bridge, Old Town Square, or at the Hlavní Nádraží (main train station) also require caution.

Taxis are another problem; rip-offs are unfortunately all too common, and I'd recommend avoiding them altogether while in Prague. They're just not worth the potential hassle of arguing with some guy late at night in a dodgy neighborhood.

You'll also find gambling cons and prostitutes in Prague. Try to avoid all that—and keep your eyes open in the Third District and Wenceslas Square—and focus on why you came: the city.

communications

To dial Prague hostels from within Prague, dial the numbers as printed.

To dial Prague hostels from elsewhere within the Czech Republic, dial 02 plus the number printed.

To dial Prague hostels from outside the Czech Republic but within Europe, dial +00–42–02 plus the number printed—KEEP THE ZERO, unlike in most other European countries.

To dial Prague hostels from the United States, dial +011–42–02 plus the number printed. Again, KEEP THE ZERO.

prague hostels at a glance

	RATING	PRICE	IN A WORD	PAGE
Boathouse		350–420 Kč	communal	p. 77
Miss Sophie's		330–2,190 Kč	chic	p. 86
U Melounu		390–950 Kč	plush	p. 93
Sir Toby's		250–1,000 Kč	comfy	p. 89
Czech Inn		290–1,200 Kč	hip	p. 81
Sokolska Hostel		€7–€20	okay	p. 90
Faculty Guest House		750–1,200 Kč	collegiate	p. 84
Atlas		300–1,800 Kč	conservative	p. 76
Pension Týn		400 Kč	central	p. 87
Travellers' Dlouhá		380–1,300 Kč	rockin'	p. 91
Elf		260–1,200 Kč	groovy	p. 82
Hostel Advantage		400–800 Kč	average	p. 85
Clown and Bard		300–380 Kč	fun	p. 79

atlas hostel

Ve Smečkách 13, Praha 1
Phone: 222–10500

Fax: 222–10500
E-mail: hostel@atlas.cz
Web site: www.hostelatlas.cz
Rates: 300–1,800 Kč (about $12–$72 US) per person; doubles 800–1,200 Kč (about $32–$48 US)
Credit cards: No
Beds: 50
Private/family rooms: Yes
Kitchen available: No
Season: Open year-round
Office hours: 8:00 A.M.–8:00 P.M.
Affiliation: None
Extras: TV lounge, Internet access
Neighborhood: Staré Město (Old Town)

Václavské náměstí (Wenceslas Square) is the dominant influence in this part of Prague, yet it's quite surprising how quiet the street with this hostel is. Though the square itself used to be the city's main red-light district, it has gradually transformed itself into one of Prague's most exclusive shopping and business places.

Best bet for a bite:
Cafe around corner

What hostellers say:
"Like a rehab center for dudes."

Gestalt:
Atlas rugged

Safety:

Hospitality:

Cleanliness:

Party index:

The positive thing about the location is that you're directly in the heart of downtown. This might be among the best located of the city's hostels. The place is full of life, with many exclusive shops, theaters, and pubs—more a place for window-shopping and party-hopping all night long, though you will want to be careful and keep an eye out.

The hostel itself? It's a surprise again, a quiet—almost conservative—place with owners who are dedicated to what they provide for their guests. It's all clean and well maintained, within walking distance of the main train station and not at all party-central. It has been renovated recently. On the downside, there's no kitchen in the common areas, only in the private apartment section. That's five floors *up*. . . and no elevators. Other complaints? Showers are balky, and the dorms are a bit cramped.

It's easy to feel at home here, though. The lounge TV gets prominent news channels, and if you pay more you can stay in an attached apartment with a small kitchen. Then you'll *really* feel at home. There's no curfew, no lockout, and the owners are amazingly friendly, so that's something. And they recently added slowish Internet access.

Note: Don't confuse this hostel with the nightclub called Atlas at #31 on the same street.

how to get there:

By bus: Contact hostel for transit route.
By car: Contact hostel for directions.
By train: From Hlavní Nádraží, walk or take Metro subway one stop to Muzeum.

boathouse hostel
1 Lodnická, Praha 4
Phone: 417–700512

Fax: 417–76988
E-mail: boathouse@volny.cz
Web site: www.aa.cz/boathouse
Rates: 350–420 Kč per person (about $14–$17 US)
Credit cards: No
Beds: 58
Private/family rooms: None
Kitchen available: No
Season: Open year-round
Office hours: Twenty-four hours
Affiliation: None
Extras: Breakfast, shop, lockers, luggage storage, games, laundry
Neighborhood: Braní

The "Boathouse Gang" run this very unconventional hostel, located right next to the Vltava River in a green area with stupendous views. (It was hit so hard during Prague's 2003 floods that it was practically an island in the river.) It takes work to get here, but do get here: This might be one of Europe's top hostels. Vera and her crew ensure a happy stay with their incredible customer service. You have to walk through the woods and climb stairs to a dark wood building to get here. As soon as you open the door, you'll like the look of things: The interior is amazing, from the colors to the photos on the walls showing previous guests to the big lounge. By the time you've wandered into the reception area—a living room, really—you've got the full flavor of the place. It's as laid-back as can be, and staff prefer personal contact with guests.

Best bet for a bite:
Right here, right now

What hostellers say:
"We are family . . ."

Gestalt:
Love Boathouse

Safety:

Hospitality:

Cleanliness:

Party index:

This is a true hostel, so the beds are simple. You won't find any double rooms at all—just two big nine-bedded dorms and a collection of three-, four-, and five-bedded rooms. There are lockers in these rooms, every guest has a key, and you can't get in without it. Luggage storage at the reception is free. The free included breakfast is hot and almost too good to be true. The hostel shop is basically a convenience store, with everything from beer to smokes, film, tissues, chewing gum, transit tickets, and so forth.

Really, though, the focus here is on creating an ad hoc family of travelers. A glance at the photos on the wall makes that point: One features loads of guests sitting together on Christmas Eve for dinner. In other shots people are playing music or singing together. The whole place seems like a giant summer camp where hostellers stay in rather than go out at night, sitting in the lounge or on the terrace playing cards or chess, talking, or writing some of the free postcards you get as a welcome present. In summer they sit singing around a fire, work the grill, or play guitar—all with a pilsner in hand, of course.

As we've said, this place is all about fun; no worries that it might get rowdy, as the helpful staff keep everything running smoothly. They know what they expect—and they will tell you. For example, dinner is at 7:30 P.M. *sharp* and you've gotta order it by afternoon—so do it! It's cheap, good, hearty Czech food, with some good additions they got from guests, and nobody tries to miss it. (Much of the cuisine uses poultry, if that's any help. The house tomcat undoubtedly forages carnivorous leftovers.)

Curfew? Lockout? Please! This place is way too cool for all that stuff, and the streetcar ride from downtown—the only mild drawback to this place—might mean people getting locked out. They'd never let that happen.

All in all, a great pick—the best. Just be careful walking to the boat late at night.

how to get there:

By bus: Contact hostel for transit route.

By car: Contact hostel for directions.

By streetcar: Take #54 streetcar from the Charles Bridge, or #17 streetcar from Holešovice Station to Černý Kůň; follow yellow signs to river and hostel.

By train: From Hlavní Nádraží Station, cross through the park and walk straight through to Jeruzalemská Street. Catch #3 streetcar Line 3 at Jindřišská to Černý Kůň stop, then walk toward river several hundred yards, following signs. From Nádraží Holešovice Station, take #17 streetcar to Černý Kůň stop.

clown and bard hostel

Bořivojova 102, Praha 3
Phone: 222–716453

Fax: 222–719026
E-mail: clownandbard@clownandbard.com
Web site: www.clownandbard.com
Rates: 300–380 Kč (about $12–$15 US) per person; doubles 1,000 Kč (about $40 US)
Credit cards: No
Beds: 142
Private/family rooms: Yes
Kitchen available: Yes
Season: Open year-round
Office hours: Twenty-four hours
Affiliation: None
Extras: Currency exchange, city tours, bar, laundry service, ski information, luggage room, Internet access
Neighborhood: Žižkov

The hoppin' Clown and Bard may be the most famous hostel in Prague. It got most of its reputation for the kavárna (basically, a bar) that is run on the same premises—and also for the offbeat people working the reception or staying as guests. It certainly deserves its reputation as an offbeat place.

Staff are friendly and cool, though, and the hostel has hugely expanded (eighty new beds) in recent years. But upkeep has slid downhill a lot, and there's a strangeness to the place as well. The rooms themselves are on several floors of a typical Prague house;

you'll find everything from small twin rooms to a big dorm in the attic holding more than thirty beds. All of these rooms have enough daylight and make a clean and comfortable (if bare) impression, what with the whitewashed walls and such. There's a lot of wood here—in fact, the whole place looks half-timbered.

The attic-dorm is a little odd, though. There are bunk beds and even overhead beds—three layers of snoring people in one hosteller sandwich—plus a lot of screeching sounds from the wooden bunks. You don't even get lockers here, so deposit your valuables in the safe at the reception or try to avoid that dorm if you can. Other rooms may not look as cool, but they are actually much quieter and safer, and bathrooms are modern, even futuristic.

Best bet for a bite:
Pizzeria Mestre

Insiders' tip:
Internet cafe Pl@neta
nearby if hostel is full

What hostellers say:
"Fun, fun, fun."

Gestalt:
Class Clown

Safety:

Hospitality:

Cleanliness:

Party index:

While the linen and the rooms are nice, the state of the showers of the large dorm is bad—not nearly clean enough, bordering on scuzzy at times. Who's been cleaning this place?? Nobody, apparently. Also on the downside, there are a lot of long-term guests here (the hostel offers discounts for long stays), and they tend to be possessive of public areas and such. Not a good thing for a hostel. The breakfast is overpriced and terrible, too.

On the upside, the attached kavárna is mighty popular in the evenings, and justly so. Hostellers enjoy the draft beer and atmosphere, and the place is so good that even locals blend in regularly—come to Czech out the Czechs. Watch for live music nights with bands, too; there are even some open-mike nights if you're feeling inspired.

There's a kitchen with *very* minimal equipment, so you'll probably need to go out to eat. Fortunately the location here in Žižkov is one of the few pluses. Starting from the Flora Metro station there are some interesting cemeteries, including a small Jewish one, as well as a park in Vozová next to the hostel with a green area for hanging out. You'll find a large choice of shops and restaurants here, as well. Lost in the back streets? Just look for the big TV tower, one of the most prominent buildings in the hostel neighborhood.

how to get there:

By bus: Contact hostel for transit route.

By car: Contact hostel for directions.

By streetcar: Take #55 or #58 night tram.

By train: From Hlavní Nádraží Station, catch any streetcar (#5, #9, or #26) one stop to Husinecká. Take the first right on Krásova Street, up the hill, then take second right down Bořivojova Street. (Entrance is through a metal door; descend stairs into the Kavárna to find reception.) From Nádraží Holešovice Station, take Metro red line (Line C) to Muzeum Station, then change to the green line (Line A) and continue toward Skalka to Jiřího z Poděbrad Station. Get off the escalators and take the right-hand exit to Slavíkova Street; walk 300 yards and turn right at the bottom of Ježkova. Continue to Bořivojova.

By plane: Take #119 bus to last stop (Dejvicka). Walk downstairs to green Metro line (line A) and follow directions above.

---

czech inn

76 Francouzski, Prague 2
Phone: 672-67600

Fax: 672-67601
E-mail: info@czech-inn.com
Web site: www.czech-inn.com
Rates: 290–1200 Kč (about $12–$48 US) per person; doubles 1,200-1,600 Kč (about $48–$64 US); apartments more
Credit cards: Yes
Beds: Number varies
Private/family rooms: Yes
Kitchen available: Yes
Affiliation: None

The *Washington Post* once said that this place is "almost too hip to be a hostel," or something to that effect. Well, guys, deal with it.

It is, in design at least. Dorm rooms are clean, efficiently designed, and slightly modern-artish, even if the bunks themselves are just your basic everyday bunks. (There are some one-, two-, and even three-room apartments both on and off the premises costing substantially more, and these are obviously nicer.)

The big hit here so far is the cafe, which serves meals and Czech beers from early morning (well, don't drink then) until late at night. Security is good.

Best bet for a bite:
Right here

What hostellers say:
"Cool . . . for a hostel"

Gestalt:
Czech mates

Safety:

Hospitality:

Cleanliness:

Party index:

---

how to get there:

By bus: From Flŏrenc bus station, take Metro C line (red line) toward Haje to I.P. Pavlova (three stops) station. Walk upstairs to street level and walk 15 minutes along Francouska Street to hostel. Or take #4, #22, or #23 streetcar to Krymska (three stops) and walk 50 yards uphill to hostel on left.

By car: Contact hostel for directions.

By train: From Hlavní Nádraží station, take Metro C line (red line) toward Haje to I.P. Pavlova station (two stops); walk upstairs to street level and walk 15 minutes along Francouska Street to hostel, or take #4, #22, or #23 streetcar to Krymska (three stops) and walk 50 yards uphill to hostel on left. From Holešovice station, take Metro C line (red line) toward Haje to I.P. Pavlova station (five stops) and follow the same directions.

elf hostel

Husitská 11, Praha 3
Phone: 225–40963

Fax: 225–40927
E-mail: info@hostelelf.com
Web site: www.hostelelf.com
Rates: 260–1,200 Kč (about $10–$48 US) per person; doubles 760–1,440 Kč (about $30–$58 US)
Credit cards: No
Beds: 110
Private/family rooms: Yes
Kitchen available: Yes
Season: Open year-round
Office hours: Twenty-four hours
Affiliation: None
Extras: Free tea, laundry ($), city tours, garden, patio, store, grill, garden
Neighborhood: Žižkov

This whole place has been painted by art students, friends of the owners—three women who wanted to try something new and started this hostel in the summer of 2000. All of them seem to have been connected to the musical *Hair:* The whole place is very hippie-like.

No wonder long-termers like the Elf; they like the eccentric hostel as well as the area. And the prices are something to be considered, too—it's simply cheaper than most. There are a lot of guitars at this hostel, people grilling in the small garden terrace, trains coming by with waving engineers, and the like. The hostel shop sells everything from condoms to soda.

Best bet for a bite:
Einstein for pizza

What hostellers say:
"Peace."

Gestalt:
Age of Aquarius

Safety:

Hospitality:

Cleanliness:

Party index:

Attention has been paid to details: There's a nice historical pattern from the early 1900s painted underneath the ceiling at the reception. A small kitchen allows basic meals to be cooked. There's free tea all day and a laundry service. The heating in winter is among the best in town, too.

Unfortunately there are no lockers or a safe. Showers aren't very good, and the place ranges from so-so clean to downright dirty. Security would seem to be lax. But there's always somebody at the reception— one night shift even brought a very alert (though otherwise quiet) watchdog! All in all, the Elf is hippy-dippy, but also iffy-iffy.

Don't miss the atmospheric local bar, the U Vystřelenýho Voka, around the corner. The whole area, while a little rough around the edges, is just full of places like this: characteristic Czech rock clubs, discos, coffee and tea houses, skate shops, a sex shop . . . quite crazy, all in all. Come now, though, for the times they are a-changing—it might be scrubbed and polished up in a few years.

how to get there:

By bus: From Flörenc bus station, walk ¼ mile to hostel or take #133 or #207 bus one stop.

By car: Contact hostel for directions.

By train: From Hlavní Nádraží Station, take Metro Line C or walk ½ mile to Flörenc station, then continue ¼ mile to hostel or take #133 or #207 bus one stop.

From Nádraží Holešovice Station, take Metro Line C to Flörenc station, then follow directions above.

faculty guest house

Protestant Theological Faculty, Univerzita Karlova
Cerná 9, Praha 1
Phone: 219–88214

Fax: 219–88215
E-mail: majordomus@etf.cuni.cz
Web site: www.etf.cuni.cz/ubyt
Rates: 750–1,200 Kč (about $30–$48 US) per person; doubles 1,800 Kč (about $99 US)
Credit cards: No
Beds: 25 (winter), 35 (summer)
Private/family rooms: Yes
Kitchen available: Yes
Season: Open year-round
Office hours: Twenty-four hours
Affiliation: None
Extras: Breakfast ($), in-room phones, computer room, Bibles
Neighborhood: Suburbs

The interesting thing about this Charles University student dorm is that it offers beds all year long—even during the academic year—to travelers, making it a great pick for families, older travelers, and those who want more amenities. You still share kitchens, bathrooms, and showers, but at least there's a sink in each room and the place was specially designed to be wheelchair-accessible.

Best bet for a bite:
Tesco

What hostellers say:
"Will there be a pop quiz on this?"

Gestalt:
Prague-matic

Safety:

Hospitality:

Cleanliness:

Party index:

The location of the place is very central. Close by is the National Theater; opposite this is the cafe Slavia. In the early 1900s, this was very popular among the local cafe society, including artists, politicians, and other celebrities; it recently reopened.

Sure, it's a bit institutional (and pretty expensive for Prague), but this place definitely fills the bill in every other way except being a place to socialize. Oh, and ignore the church ties—they don't proselytize, as far as we could tell.

how to get there:

By bus: Contact hostel for transit route.
By car: Contact hostel for directions.
By streetcar: At night take #51, #52, #53, #55, #56, #57, or #58 night tram.
By train: From either Hlavní Nádraží or Nádraží Holešovice Station, take Metro Line C (red line) to Flörenc Station, then change to Line B (yellow line). Get off at Národní třída and walk along Ostrovní, keeping left and continuing to Cerná.

hostel advantage
Sokolská 11–13, Praha 2
Phone: 249–14062

Fax: 249–14067
E-mail: reservations@jsc.cz
Web site: www.jsc.cz/advantage
Rates: 400–800 Kč (about $16–$32 US) per person; doubles 1,100–1,650 Kč (about $44–$66 US)
Credit cards: Yes
Beds: 118
Private/family rooms: Yes
Kitchen available: No
Season: Open year-round
Office hours: Twenty-four hours
Affiliation: HI-CKM
Extras: Luggage storage, shop, TV room, fax ($), breakfast, Internet access
Neighborhood: Nové Město (New Town)

Of the city hostels affiliated with IYHF, this one is not as good as the Dlouhá 33 Travellers (see page 91) but close to town and small enough to be friendly. It's very cheap and central. What's also remarkable is that the sheets are perfectly clean.

The hostel's located on a major street, which brings both access to the city and noise. Some of the dorm rooms inside have new furniture, and some of them are quite spartan. Still, rooms are pretty spacious—one quirk of the place is that all rooms can be locked, but sometimes you must walk through another dorm room in order to reach your own. Some hostellers also complained to us of street noise and grubby and shabby bathrooms—they don't even have doors!

Despite only middling facilities, though, staff are friendly even for Prague—give 'em credit for that, at least—and they'll never hassle you

Best bet for a bite:
Radost FX

What hostellers say:
"So-so."

Gestalt:
Dissed advantage

Safety:

Hospitality:

Cleanliness:

Party index:

about lockouts or curfews. The little on-site store is quite well maintained. And the small television lounge right next to the reception is hopping, contributing very much to the atmosphere of the place. Yet one more welcome addition: an Internet station offering hostellers free access.

how to get there:

By bus: Contact hostel for transit route.

By car: Contact hostel for directions.

By streetcar: At night take #57 tram from the National Theater.

By subway: From Hlavní Nádraží or Nádraží Holešovice Station, take Metro Line C (red line) to I.P. Pavlova Station and take the stairs to the left side. Walk to Ječná Street and turn left into Sokolská. Hostel is on right.

By plane: Take #119 bus to Dejvicka Station, then Metro Line A to I.P. Pavlova Station and follow directions above.

miss sophie's hostel
Melounova 3, Prague 2
Phone: 296–303532

E-mail: reservation@miss-sophies.com
Rates: 330–2,190 Kč (about $13–$88 US) per person; doubles 1,450–2,390 Kč (about $58–$96 US) per person
Credit cards: Yes
Beds: Number varies
Kitchen available: Yes
Private/family rooms: Yes
Affiliation: None
Extras: Terrace, Internet access

They tout "the real Prague" at this place . . . and hostellers agree. It does deliver that, and more. This looks more like a boutique hotel (reception staff are dressed up!) than a centrally located, clean and safe hostel.

Leather couches, modern art, glass coffee tables, a sleek kitchen, hotel-quality apartment beds . . . not to mention a brick lounge in the basement, that cool kitchen for hostellers' use, and all no-smoking policy (is this Europe??)—it all adds up to family-friendly fun. They have dorms with three, four, and five beds, single and private/ family rooms with up to three beds, and some nicer (if somewhat pricier) apartments with private bathrooms and full kitchens. One drawback is the lack of a true restaurant, cafe, or bar in house. But that's a small quibble for such an amazingly nice place.

Best bet for a bite:
In-house

What hostellers say:
"Arty and luxe."

Gestalt:
Art Attack

Safety:

Hospitality:

Cleanliness:

Party index:

how to get there:

By bus: From Flörenc bus station, take Metro C line (red line) toward Haje three stops to I.P. Pavlova station; exit to left and upstairs. Cross over to Katerinska Street, passing Pricewaterhousecoopers and Novotel, then take first right onto Melounova Street and continue to hostel on left.

By car: Contact hostel for directions.

By train: From Hlavní Nádraží station, take Metro C line (red line) toward Haje two stops to I.P. Pavlova station; exit to left and upstairs. Cross over to Katerinska Street, passing Pricewaterhousecoopers and Novotel, then take first right onto Melounova Street and continue to hostel on left. From Holešovice station, take Metro C line (red line) in direction of Haje five stops to I.P. Pavlova station and follow same directions.

pension týn
Týnská 19, Praha 1
Phone: 248–08333

Fax: 248–08333
E-mail: backpacker@razdva.cz
Web site: www.hostel-tyn.web2001.cz
Rates: 400 Kč (about $16 US) per person; doubles 1,100–1,200 Kč (about $44–$48 US)
Credit cards: No
Beds: 50
Private/family rooms: Yes
Kitchen available: No
Season: Open year-round

Office hours: Twenty-four hours
Affiliation: None
Extras: Luggage storage, Internet access, breakfast ($)
Neighborhood: Staré Město (Old Town)

This place has perhaps the best location in town, yet it's amazingly quiet—and is among the cleanest hostels in town. That should count for something. Though it's also quite minimal in some ways (there are few extra amenities, for instance), it's definitely worth a look *if* you can get through to the staff, who mostly speak minimal to no English.

Best bet for a bite:
U Rudolfa

Insiders' tip:
Hermes Internet cafe
on Nekázanka

What hostellers say:
"Pretty simple."

Gestalt:
Central perk

Safety:

Hospitality:

Cleanliness:

Party index:

The hostel's situated between the Old Town and the Jewish quarter. Being so close to the river, it's even within walking distance of the Karlův most (Charles Bridge) and the Prague castle (Hradčany), two of the most important sights in Prague.

Rooms contain up to six beds each, so you're almost guaranteed a nice small room without too many other snoozers, and bathrooms are shared but clean. Reception does a very efficient job of running things for your usual international crowd. The hostel security system is simple but very effective, there's a safe at the reception, and the luggage room is free. There aren't lockers in the rooms, however. Need to do some laundry? Just as you do to eat, you'll need to go outside the building once again, but reception should help.

There are tons of galleries on Old Town Square next to the hostel, a brewery around the corner, and you won't go hungry either. Ask at the tourist information office on the square to find out which galleries are really worth visiting.

how to get there:

By bus: Contact hostel for transit route.
By car: Contact hostel for directions.
By train: From Hlavní Nádraží or Nádraží Holešovice Station, take Metro Line C (red line) to Muzeum Station, then change lines and continue one stop to Staroměstská Station. Hostel is located behind

Týn church. Walk around Cathedral, keeping to the left, to find hostel behind.

sir toby's hostel
Delnická 24, Praha 7
Phone: 838–70635

Fax: 838–70636
E-mail: reservation@sirtobys.com
Web site: www.sirtobys.com
Rates: 250–1,000 Kč (about $10–$40 US) per person; doubles 1,200–1,450 Kč (about $48–$58 US)
Credit cards: No
Beds: 90
Private/family rooms: Yes
Kitchen available: Yes
Season: Open year-round
Office hours: 8:00 A.M.–6:00 P.M.
Affiliation: None
Extras: Free coffee, grill, laundry, Internet access, backyard, library, bar
Neighborhood: Holešovice

There are a few hostels you might actually plan to return to one day. Sir Toby's definitely is one of them—everybody loves the place.

The hostel is inside a historical building in the Holešovice area of Prague, very close to the city's secondary train station (and many incoming trains stop here first, so check with a conductor). This neighborhood is shifting from a mixed business and residential center to a predominantly residential area, and there are several big parks nearby, as well as the Pražská Trznice (Prague Market)—a huge place to buy in quantity at low prices. As befits this interesting area, the people who come to stay here seem both offbeat and sophisticated.

Best bet for a bite:
Rustika

What hostellers say:
"Small is beautiful!"

Gestalt:
Yes, Sir!

Safety:

Hospitality:

Cleanliness:

Party index:

It's a fairly quiet place, though the kitchen "can be pretty crazy." If you have been staying at a party place and need some days to relax, you might do well to sleep here for a night or two. The dorms are relatively small, each room with its own design—one has its own piano, and even though it's out of tune a lot it's kinda fun. Everybody hangs out in the first-floor kitchen anyway, with a tape player and tapes—many of the guests bring their own recordings—plus dining table, chairs, and lots of sofas. Always you'll find tea and coffee for free.

Despite the so-so 'hood, security is tops. Bedroom and bathroom facilities here are very good; there's even a tub and very nice, hot water, plus comfortable beds. And the area seems safe. If you want to make sure your bed has a locker underneath it, just ask when reserving; usually there are enough. (They do require padlocks, however.)

The subterranean bar is where the action is, and conviviality reigns supreme. Highly recommended. Sir Toby's also has a phone, a small library, a meditation and prayer room, a small backyard where barbecues are held at least once a week during the summer, laundry service, one Internet terminal, and a small supply of event tickets. Don't be surprised when the same person who checked you in during the afternoon suddenly appears on stage that night. Families pay 25 percent less—a nice incentive to stay here—and everyone gets a handout at check-in with house picks of the local sights and hot spots.

The Art Nouveau building has recently gotten a facelift, uncovering some of its former beauty. Management also added sixty more beds in the renovation.

Staff couldn't be better, either. They like their jobs, and they are big fans of Prague. After a stay here, you will be, too.

how to get there:

By bus: Contact hostel for transit route.
By car: Contact hostel for directions.
By train: From Hlavní Nádraží, take Metro Line C (red line) two stops to Vltavska. From outside station, take any streetcar departing to the left. Get off at the Delnická tram stop (second stop), walk to the corner of Delnická Street and turn left. From Nádraží Holešovice train station, take Metro to Vltavska and follow directions above.

sokolska hostel

52 Sokolska, Prague 2
Phone: 242–67200

Fax: 242–67200

E-mail: hostel52@gmail.com
Rates: €7–€20 (about $9–$25 US) per person
Credit cards: Yes
Beds: 50
Private/family rooms: No
Kitchen available: No
Season: Open year-round
Office hours: Vary
Affiliation: None
Extras: Free Internet access, laundry, airport pickups, travel information desk
Neighborhood: Staré Město (Old Town)

No curfew. No lockout. No hidden charges. No smoking.

It may look like a no, but so far the newish (2005) Sokolska seems to be a yes. Cleanliness is okay (not perfect; it varies), bunks could be airier, but this is not a bad place. You choose from twelve-bedded, five-bedded- and four-bedded coed (not single-sex dorms); be aware of that if you're on the shy side. The bunks are a bit flimsy but seem clean enough.

What hostellers say:
"No personality, great location."

Gestalt:
Central perks

Safety:

Hospitality:

Cleanliness:

Party index:

Best of all is the location: The famous Staré Město (Old Town) section of Prague is quite close, and so is Vaclavske Square, with its shopping, eats, and National Museum (the city's oldest).

how to get there:

By car: Contact hostel for directions.
By plane: From Ruzyne Airport, take bus N 119 to the Dejvicka subway station; this takes twenty minutes. Take Metro Line A (green line) from Dejvicka to Muzeum station, then change to Line C (red line) and continue one stop to I.P. Pavlova station. Exit here, cross the road to Sokolska Street, and walk to #52.

travellers' dlouhá hostel

Dlouhá Pension and Hostel
Dlouhá 33, Praha 1
Phone: 248–26662 or 248–26663

Fax: 248–26665

E-mail: hostel@travellers.cz
Web site: www.travelers.cz
Rates: 380–1,300 Kč (about $15–$52 US) per person; doubles 1,300–1,500 Kč (about $52–$60 US)
Credit cards: No
Beds: 164
Private/family rooms: Yes
Kitchen: No
Season: Open year-round
Office hours: Twenty-four hours
Affiliation: HI-CKM
Extras: Bars, disco, TV, store, bicycle rental, in-line skate rental, Internet access, laundry service, city tour, breakfast, jukebox
Neighborhood: Staré Město (Old Town)

You will feel the pulse at this place—literally. The pulse of techno, that is: The Roxy dance club is located directly underneath it.

Headquarters for the growing Prague hostel chain called Travellers, this year-round place attracts a young crowd that's here to party—and they won't stop until 5:00 A.M. Maybe. Only then do the four bars in the Roxy close down, and the international crowd (including plenty of Brits) crawls home.

The location of the hostel—between the Old Town and the Josefov (Jewish neighborhood)—is as central as can be. The style of the rooms is a mixture of Empire and Bavarian, with carpeting everywhere except in the bar, where it would soon be destroyed. The bar is really attractive. All in all the place is loads of fun, though not so quiet. If you want to have a good time and stay centrally, this might be your top pick in town.

Best bet for a bite:
Apetit (buffet)

What hostellers say:
"Do a little dance . . .
get down tonight."

Gestalt:
HQ to the rescue

Safety:

Hospitality:

Cleanliness:

Party index:

Showers aren't exactly numerous, however, and cleanliness is sliding downhill fast. Couple that with indifferent, even rude staff and you've got trouble.

The free included breakfast, served from 8:00 to 10:30 A.M., is one of the best in town, more buffet than continental. The third-floor bar also serves as breakfast room in the morning; then, about

7:00 at night, it changes personality and dons shades. The bar serves draft beer and hot snacks, has a cable TV, and the view over the Old Town is great from up there. Reception also sells beer, soda, sandwiches, and more. You can rent bicycles and in-line skates at the desk, they've got two fast Internet terminals in the lounge, and laundry service is available. There's also the Universal Nod art gallery above the dance club. Stash your stuff in the free luggage room and get the daily punch-code that lets you in for free.

Worried about safety at night? Don't be. There's a police station around the corner, and the centrality means plenty of foot traffic even at night. Your biggest threat is from fellow travelers: We heard a number of reports of intra-hostel theft.

how to get there:

By bus: Contact hostel for transit route.
By car: Contact hostel for directions.
By train: From either train station, take #5 streetcar to Dlouhá trída stop.

u melounu hostel
Ke Karlovu 7/457, Praha 2
Phone: 249–19330

Fax: 249–18322
E-mail: info@hostelumelounu.cz
Web site: www.hostelumelounu.cz
Rates: 390–950 Kč (about $16–$48 US) per person
Credit cards: Yes
Beds: 54
Private/family rooms: Yes
Kitchen available: Yes
Season: Open year-round
Office hours: Twenty-four hours
Affiliation: None
Extras: Breakfast, food shop, phone cards, parking, Internet access, grill, garden
Neighborhood: Nove Město (New Town)

The self-proclaimed Rolls Royce among Prague's hostels (its name means "watermelon"; go figure) this place is next to a maternity hospital and about as quiet. Don't come for a party or centrality to the action, but do come if you're with a family or treasure space and relaxation.

It's in the midst of a green area in New Town. The building has only one floor, and right in the middle is a beautiful garden. Dorms are six-bedded, which is nice, and the double rooms all have private baths—even nicer, especially for couples. There's a small kitchen with a stove and a fridge on the first floor, plus a common room in which the included breakfast is served; you can even specify a vegetarian breakfast if you order a day in advance. (Prices are a little high, thus the free sheets, towels, and breakfast.)

Best bet for a bite:
Radio Bar

What hostellers say:
"It's a palace!"

Gestalt:
Green acres

Safety:

Hospitality:

Cleanliness:

Party index:

The good hostel shop sells sandwiches, cookies, and soda as well as phone cards, beer, and more. They'll even do wake-up and taxi calls for you and arrange group barbecues if enough people ask for it. Still, staff here want the place to be quiet, so be ready to go into town and hit a pub if you really want to get rowdy.

This hostel is particularly interesting for people with dogs—they're accepted for free, and they'll love the surroundings—as well as those with cars: There's a garage on premises.

how to get there:

By bus: Take #504 night bus. From Flörenc bus station, take red line (Metro Line C) to I.P. Pavlova Station, then follow directions below.
By car: Contact hostel for directions.
By train: From Hlavní Nádraží Station, take Metro Line C two stops to I.P. Pavlova Station. Use main escalator and take exit on left; cross the street and turn left into Sokolská, then make an immediate right onto Na Bojišti and continue to end. Turn left and walk down Ke Karlovu to hostel on right.

From Nádraží Holešovice Station, take Metro five stops to I.P. Pavlova Station. Take main escalator and exit on left; cross street and turn left into Sokolská, make an immediate right onto Na Bojišti and continue to end. Turn left and walk down Ke Karlovu to hostel on right.

denmark

Of all the countries in Europe, we're casting our early vote for Denmark as having the best system of hostels. Oh, Ireland is right there with a great network, too, and so is Switzerland. But Denmark's hostels, most of them affiliated with Hostelling International, are absolutely wonderful: clean, friendly, efficient, and—in a country where everything is expensive (an American soda can cost the equivalent of four bucks, a sandwich almost ten)—a godsend at less than half the price of even a budget hotel.

The rural hostels are awesome, among Europe's best. This book deals only with urban hostels, however, and in Denmark you'll *really* save money at these places—despite the fact that they're not as quiet or green as the ones out in the sticks.

practical details

Denmark's national rail service, known as DSB, is extremely efficient—and also very popular among the Danes. As a result, during the high summer season it can be difficult or impossible to reserve a spot on certain international or city-to-city trains, which you're often required to do. This is a country where you need to plan in advance, rather than try to wing it.

If you'll be traveling a great deal in Denmark, Sweden, and Norway (or even two of those three countries), get a ScanRail pass. Expensive but still one of the all-time great rail pass deals, it gets you free riding on almost all Danish trains, plus half-price discounts on most ferries.

The unit of currency in Denmark is the Danish krone or crown (DKK). There are about 5 Danish kroner to one U.S. dollar at this writing—so that 90 DKK dorm room costs about $18 US and that 65 DKK sandwich cost you . . . thirteen bucks?! Yikes! Things are expensive here, so plan accordingly; you'll spend more than you ever believed possible, believe it.

Denmark's country code is 45. When calling from within Denmark, dial the numbers AS PRINTED. When calling from outside of Denmark, dial 45 and DROP THE FIRST ZERO from the numbers printed in this book. Remember: A phone card is very useful here, and directory assistance is expensive.

århus

You might not think of Århus (pronounced *oar'-hoos*) as a real destination, but we're here to tell you that it belongs there. This is a university town—comparable to, say, Madison or Chapel Hill—with the resulting concentration of cool bars, clubs, and restaurants. Plus there's a set of beaches right in the city and historical attractions, including a folk museum. Interestingly, the two hostels here in town have very different feels and are located in vastly different neighborhoods, but both are excellent and either one makes for a good overnight stay. It just depends on what you want: sun, fun and relaxation, or the buzz of the city.

The city's train station is small enough to figure out with a minimum of trouble. Public transit here consists of a set of fairly efficient bus routes (although one of the hostels is quite far out of town, so you'll ride for a while). If you're staying in town, you're lucky: You can simply stroll through some of the city's oldest streets and get a feel for the place en route to the hostel.

århus hostels
at a glance

	RATING	PRICE	IN A WORD	PAGE
Århus Pavillonen Hostel	◪◪	140–496 DKK	beachy	p. 96
Sleep-In Hostel	◪	120–125 DKK	central	p. 98

århus pavillonen hostel
Marienlundsvej 10, Århus
Phone: 086–212–120

Fax: 086–105–560
E-mail: info@aarhus-danhostel.dk
Web site: www.aarhus-danhostel.dk

Rates: 140–496 DKK (about $28–$99 US) per HI member; doubles 448–496 DKK (about $90–$99 US)
Credit cards: No
Beds: 146
Private/family rooms: Yes
Kitchen available: Yes
Season: January 12–December 28
Office hours: 7:00–11:00 A.M.; 4:00–10:00 P.M.
Affiliation: HI-Danhostel
Extras: Laundry, breakfast ($), store, parking, playground, kitchen, beach access, TV lounge

This former motel has been converted into a very good hostel. The only disadvantage is its remote position about 2½ miles out of the center, but that's actually a plus if you need a break from cities.

Dorms can get tight in summer, but about a dozen double rooms are simply old motel units and thus better than the usual dorm room. Trouble is, Danish families have booked most of these up well in advance of you.

Even so, there are grills outdoors and a very simple kitchen for cooking—you need to bring your own utensils and plates—which will keep you in the social mix. You'll find lots of families and cyclists here beside you, not partiers, and that can be a

Best bet for a bite:
Juice Pause, downtown

Insiders' tip:
Beach is a five-minute walk

What hostellers say:
"Nice and quiet out here."

Gestalt:
Beach ball

Safety:

Hospitality:

Cleanliness:

Party index:

welcome switch. Staff are incredibly friendly here, too (the manager is a cycling nut). They'll help you out with directions, pack your breakfast in a sack to eat as a picnic lunch at the beach, and point out bike routes.

how to get there:

By bus: Take #1, #6, or #9 bus from downtown to Marienlund stop and walk 300 yards to hostel.
By car: Contact hostel for directions.
By train: From train station, catch #1, #6, or #9 bus to Marienlund stop and walk 300 yards to hostel.

sleep-in hostel

Havnegade 20, Århus
Phone: 086–192–055

Fax: 086–191–811
E-mail: sleep-in@citysleep-in.dk
Web site: www.citysleep-in.dk
Rates: 120–125 DKK (about $24–$25 US) per person; doubles 380–460 DKK (about $76–$92 US)
Credit cards: Yes
Beds: 127
Private/family rooms: Yes
Kitchen available: Yes
Season: Closed December 19–January 10
Office hours: Twenty-four hours
Affiliation: None
Extras: Bike rentals, cafe, game room, laundry, Internet access ($), TV lounge, grill, breakfast ($)

Most of Europe's so-called Sleep-Ins are nothing more than a bunch of mattresses on the floor of a gym—about what you'd expect in a Salvation Army or a disaster relief center—but this one, thankfully, is quite different. It's a better choice than the official hostel if you want to spend most of your time pub-hopping and clubbing. This place is steps away from nightspots, unlike the other place, which requires some transit waits and rides to get in and out of the central city.

key to icons

Attractive natural setting	Comfortable beds	Visual arts at hostel or nearby
Ecologically aware hostel	A particularly good value	Music at hostel or nearby
Superior kitchen facilities or cafe	Wheelchair-accessible	Great hostel for skiers
Offbeat or eccentric place	Good for business travelers	Bar or pub at hostel or nearby
Superior bathroom facilities	Especially well suited for families	Editors' Choice: Among our very favorite hostels
Romantic private rooms	Good for active travelers	

Dorms are decent, better than expected, in fact, and staff keep the activities rolling. There's a cafe with a good notice board, they rent bikes, and the double rooms are dirt-cheap and very acceptable given the high, high price of sleeping in a hotel bed in this town. Just don't expect the peace and quiet of the other hostel—you are smack dab in the center, and there may be occasional traffic noises or drunks passing by or what-have-you. Also note that this hostel tends to ding you for extra charges, everything from sheets to towels to food. And bathrooms aren't spic-and-span, either.

Best bet for a bite:
Swing Cafe

Insiders' tip:
Some trains stop at
Europaplads

What hostellers say:
"Great place."

Gestalt:
Sleep tight

Safety:

Hospitality:

Cleanliness:

Party index:

For fun, there's plenty of walking to do—including an authentic folk museum and several old, old churches and squares—but we'd hit the Åboulevarden, a twin strip of lanes that bookend the city canal. These streets are incredibly hip, packed with restaurants, pubs, jazz bars, and clubs—some of which rock until late at night. Just make sure you're looking sharp: These Danes sure know how to dress.

how to get there:

By bus: From train station, take #3, #7, or #14 bus two stops to Europaplads. Cross street to hostel.
By car: Contact hostel for directions.
By train: From train station, walk north ¾ mile to Europaplads platform; cross street to hostel.

copenhagen

Copenhagen is, to put it quite bluntly, one of the coolest cities in Europe. More than a decade ago it wasn't even on the radar; but now, new buildings, restaurants, and clubs are going up faster than you can say "boo," as the Danes enjoy a long-overdue renaissance. The hostel situation here is pretty good, too—more than a half dozen to pick from, none of them bad at all.

You'll arrive at Copenhagen's Central Station, a massive all-inclusive complex that can be a bit confusing with all the fast-food joints and shops competing for your attention. Plus, there are two separate ticket

copenhagen

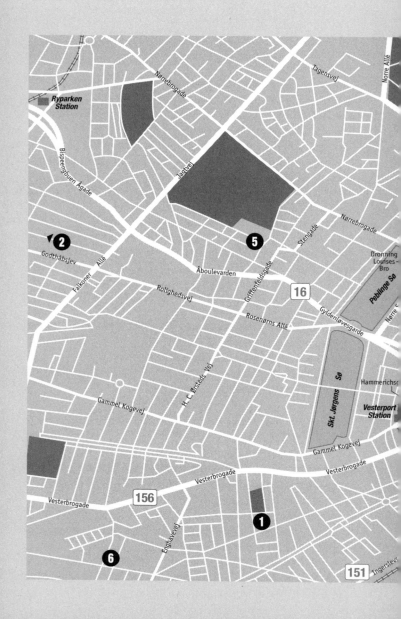

offices and a travel agency that *also* sells tickets. Our tip? Hit the grocery store near the ticket offices for sustenance, then go for the machines. You need to take a number and get in long lines for the ticket windows; it can take nearly an hour.

copenhagen hostels
at a glance

	RATING	PRICE	IN A WORD	PAGE
Amager Hostel		120 DKK	big	p. 103
Bellahøj Hostel		120 DKK	efficient	p. 104
Copenhagen City Hostel		130–165 DKK	enormous	p. 107
Sleep-In Green Hostel		120 DKK	crunchy	p. 108
City Public Hostel Vesterbrø		110–140 DKK	crowded	p. 105
Sleep-In Heaven Hostel		€17.50	poor	p. 109

If you're hard up for info on what to do in town, exit the station and walk a block up the street to the city's main tourist office, called Wonderful Copenhagen (or WoCo for short).

There's so much to see that you'll need a strategy. Want to focus on people-watching? Head for Nyhavn (pronounced *New'-howen,* or something like that), a harborside area with bobbing boats and glamorous Danes drinking beer, eating great food, or just generally hanging out with one another. Or get up to Nørrebrø, on both sides of the river, a very hip district with enough hostels, eateries, clubs, and bars to keep you going.

Whatever you do, though, don't miss Tivoli, a sprawling amusement park very near the train station. Come at night, when it's lit up and especially pretty. The local Copenhagen Card can help ease the pain of the high admission price, too. Buy the card and you get free local transit and museum entry, plus free Tivoli.

amager hostel

Vejlands Allé 200, 2300 Copenhagen S
Phone: 032–522–908

Fax: 032–522–708
E-mail: copenhagen@danhostel.dk
Web site: www.copenhagenyouthhostel.dk
Rates: 120 DKK (about $24 US) per HI member; doubles 360–450 DKK (about $72–$90 US)
Credit cards: Yes
Beds: 512
Private/family rooms: Yes
Kitchen available: Yes
Season: January 2–December 16
Office hours: Twenty-four hours
Affiliation: HI-Danhostel
Extras: Laundry, meeting rooms, parking, TV, currency exchange, Internet access

This monster hostel named for its neighborhood (say *ah-mar'*), south of the city center but beside a large sports complex, is pretty good and there are transit connections to the areas where the action is. As one of the two "official" Danhostel properties in town, standards of cleanliness and order are a bit higher than elsewhere in town, too.

Just don't expect a party at the hostel itself: This is among the biggest hostels (some say *the* biggest) in all Europe, and size naturally subtracts from the intimacy of the place. Still, staff are professional and upbeat and keep the hostel running very smoothly indeed.

A big glass atrium and the obligatory Danish flag welcome you to the property. All the dorms are two-, four-, or five-bedded rooms, and they're more than acceptable, not to mention far less expensive than comparable hotel rooms in Copenhagen. Other good things here include a laundry, kitchen, television lounge, and a lack of back-breaking rules such as lockouts and curfews. However, the hostel does receive a lot of school groups

Best bet for a bite:
Pølse wagons

What hostellers say:
"Clean and modern."

Gestalt:
Amagervelous

Safety:

Hospitality:

Cleanliness:

Party index:

debarking from school buses here, so we can't guarantee peace and quiet in the hallways.

The surrounding neighborhood isn't very interesting, so you'll want to get into town to see Tivoli, the clubs, and all the rest. It takes a little fiddling with the public transit schedules to do that, but you're rewarded with a very comfortable sleep once you get back at night—especially for the price.

how to get there:

By bus or train: From main train station, take either the #46 bus or S-train Line C to the Sjælør stop, then change to a #37 bus and continue to the Holmens Bro stop.
By car: Contact hostel for directions.

bellahøj hostel
Herbergvejen 8, 2700 Brønshøj (Copenhagen)
Phone: 038–289–715

Fax: 038–890–210
E-mail: bellahoej@danhostel.dk
Rates: 120 DKK (about $24 US) per HI member; doubles 350 DKK (about $70 US)
Credit cards: No
Beds: 248
Private/family rooms: Yes
Kitchen available: Yes
Season: February 1–December 2
Office hours: Twenty-four hours
Affiliation: HI-Danhostel
Extras: Parking, TV lounge, Internet access, luggage storage, laundry, grill, snacks

A ways out in the northern suburbs, about 3 miles from downtown, this hostel scores points from families for clean and quiet facilities. If only it were closer to town.

The reception floor is the most popular area, with a good little TV lounge, plenty of chairs, and very popular Internet access. Staff will sort you out, get you your sheets, sell you an ice-cream bar, then send you off into the building, which holds more beds than at first appears. There are seven quad rooms, thirty-one six-bedded rooms, and then three larger dorms of more than six beds all told. A few double rooms are especially nice but quite limited in supply, so don't plan on snagging one of them. The regular dorms, frankly, are too cramped.

The basement's also the place to find the kitchen, which gets heavy use—since the hostel is nowhere near any restaurants—and is very well organized, if not always cleaned-up. The laundry's also down here.

Breakfast is served in a big main-floor dining room that opens onto a surprisingly green backyard, which borders a little bog and field area. And are those goats next door?

The place is always busy with Europeans of all stripes coming and going, so this is a very good place to meet fellow travelers. Find one with a car and you're set for wheels.

Best bet for a bite:
Better eat here

What hostellers say:
"Fun place."

Gestalt:
Great Dane

Safety:

Hospitality:

Cleanliness:

Party index:

how to get there:

By bus: Catch #2 bus from train station or #11 bus to from Rådhus to Bellahøj or Brønshøj stop, then walk 200 yards to hostel. At night catch #82N bus.
By car: Contact hostel for directions.
By train: Catch #2 bus from train station to Bellahøj or Brønshøj stop and walk 200 yards to hostel. At night catch #82N bus.

city public hostel vesterbrø
Absalonsgade 8, 1658 Copenhagen V
Phone: 033–312–070

Fax: 033–550–085
Rates: 110–140 DKK (about $22–$28 US) per person
Credit cards: No
Beds: 205
Private/family rooms: None
Kitchen available: Yes
Season: May 5–August 19
Office hours: Twenty-four hours
Affiliation: None
Extras: Lockers, breakfast ($)

You're not far from most of Copenhagen's top sights and Central Station in this open-longer-than-usual summer-only hostel run by the

Best bet for a bite:
Farmers' market on
Israelsplads

Insiders' tip:
Free Internet at Use It

What hostellers say:
"Hej, hej, hej."

Gestalt:
Close to the Vesterbro

Safety:

Hospitality:

Cleanliness:

Party index:

Vesterbro Youth Center. For the surprisingly expensive price of a bed, though, you trade in privacy: The biggest dorm on the bottom floor tops out at seventy (!!!) beds and is quite irritatingly loud, but you might get lucky and score a "smaller" (i.e., hotter and smellier) room of just twenty beds, or even—pray that you do—a more bite-sized room of four as you go up the stairs. Beds are flimsy, squeaky, pillow-less, and unclean. Just plain uncomfortable. Get my drift?

The good news is that a kitchen is available for guest use: Stock up on fresh veggies from the farmers' market at Israelsplads, or try one of the small grocery store chains like Irma, Netto, or Brugsen. And staff couldn't be nicer. Too bad security is nonexistent. Still staying here for its cheap price and centrality? Fine. Hang out in the groovy hostel lounge or lawn in front and be thankful there's no curfew or lockout; you're not gonna want to spend much time here, or in the seedy surrounding area.

key to icons

Attractive natural setting

Ecologically aware hostel

Superior kitchen facilities or cafe

Offbeat or eccentric place

Superior bath-room facilities

Romantic private rooms

Comfortable beds

A particularly good value

Wheelchair-accessible

Good for busi-ness travelers

Especially well suited for families

Good for active travelers

Visual arts at hostel or nearby

Music at hostel or nearby

Great hostel for skiers

Bar or pub at hostel or nearby

Editors' Choice: Among our very favorite hostels

Bottom line? They should be ashamed of charging you this much money. Heck, they should be paying *us*.

how to get there:

By bus: Take #6 or #16 bus to Vesterbro Station.
By car: Contact hostel for directions.
By train: From Central Station, take S-train to Vesterbro Station.

---

copenhagen city hostel
H.C. Andersens Boulevard 50, 1553 Copenhagen V
Phone: 033–118585 or 033–188332

Fax: 033–118588
Rates: 130–165 DKK (about $26–$33 US) per HI member; doubles 520–660 DKK (about $104–$152 US)
Credit cards: Yes
Beds: 1,020
Private/family rooms: Yes
Kitchen available: Yes
Season: January 2–December 20
Office hours: Twenty-four hours
Affiliation: HI-Danhostel
Extras: Laundry, kitchen, television, Internet access, cafe

This hostel is the best-positioned in the city, *if* you're interested in two key tourist attractions: Tivoli (a cool combination amusement park/dining area) and Christiansborg, the hippie enclave to end all hippie enclaves. Unbelievably, it's steps away from both, and also only 3 blocks from the back side of the city's busy central train station.

It's also the biggest. . . . Not in Copenhagen. Not in Denmark. In freakin' Europe! Now that renovations are complete, the hostel is filled with more than a thousand bunks, all of them brand-new. You've just gotta love the modern design

What hostellers say:
"Like a hotel."

Gestalt:
Right on the (Den)mark

Safety:

Hospitality:

Cleanliness:

Party index:

scheme, which is so Copenhagen to a "T": stylish little beds slung low on scando-blonde wood floors you could eat off (so far); scarlet pillow covers; and oh-so-Danish little night lamps. The dining room looks like an IKEA cafeteria outtake, for heavens' sake. By Copenhagen standards this is a tall building, so upper floors come with great views of the city, Opera House, and islands.

But with all this luxury and location comes a price. This is among the most expensive bunks in C-town, and there's a steep, steep 60 DKK ($10 US!) surcharge for linens. Breakfast isn't free, and the kitchen's pretty minuscule.

Still, we can't complain too much, other than commenting on the impersonal, swept-clean element to it all. This almost isn't hostelling. It's hotelling.

how to get there:

By car: Contact hostel for directions.
By train: Contact hostel for transit details.
By bus: Contact hostel for transit details.
By plane: Contact hostel for transit details.

sleep-in green hostel
Ravnsborggade 18, Copenhagen
Phone: 035–377–777

Rates: 120 DKK (about $24 US) per person
Credit cards: No
Beds: 68
Private/family rooms: None
Kitchen available: No
Season: June 12–October 31
Office hours: 10:00 A.M. to 10:00 P.M.
Lockout: Noon–4:00 P.M.
Affiliation: None
Extras: Breakfast ($), storage

Denmark has always been a leader in world environmental issues, and it stands to reason that Copenhagen would proudly sport its own earth-friendly hostel. This is it. Sleep-In Green hostel is open the longest of Copenhagen's seasonal hostels and is situated—in our opinion—in the hippest neighborhood of them all: Nørrebro, a five-to-ten-minute bus ride from Central Station.

You'll find low-flow showers and toilets, nontoxic paint, recycling facilities, healthy, untouched-by-chemicals food, and so on. Dorms are nicely painted, though rather large and noisy; there aren't any private rooms here. The biggest dorm sports some forty beds; the rest of the bunks are split between two other dorms. Expect to get to know your neighbors, who'll quite possibly be European students with leftish political stands. And don't expect perfectly clean rooms and bath-rooms—the earthy ethos seems to extend to the accumulation of dirt and muck in the wrong places. Note that the formerly low bed price has been jacked up and is somewhat offset by the a la carte charges for lots of little extras like breakfast and sheets; what seemed like a good deal at $11 a night suddenly becomes $20. Bottom line? Bring your own sheets and food to save money.

Best bet for a bite:
Nørrebrø area

Insiders' tip:
Free bikes in the city

What hostellers say:
"It's not easy bein' green."

Gestalt:
Green achers

Safety:

Hospitality:

Cleanliness:

Party index:

Still, staff are cool, there's a nice view of the backyard (no, you can't use it), we applaud the green-friendly message, and this is the best-located hostel in town along with Sleep-In Heaven (see next entry). If you don't mind big crowds of non-deodorant-wearing young hippies, this should be your pick.

how to get there:

By bus or train: Take Nørrebrø bus #5 or #16 or night bus #81N or #84N. Or contact hostel for transit route.
By car: Contact hostel for directions.

---

sleep-in heaven hostel
Struenseegade 7 (Seventh floor), Copenhagen
Phone: 035–354–648

E-mail: morefun@sleepinheaven.com
Web site: www.sleepinheaven.com
Rates: €17.50 (about $21 US) per person
Credit cards: No
Beds: 100
Private/family rooms: Yes

Kitchen available: No
Season: Open year-round
Office hours: Twenty-four hours
Affiliation: None
Extras: Lockers, free Internet access, breakfast ($), bar, pool table, earplugs

"It's more fun" is the motto here. Well . . . we wouldn't go that far. This place is more popular with backpackers than with family types, and it's run by a couple of cool Danish guys who provide loads of bunks at a fair price. You're in hip and trendy Nørrebrø, where there are scads of great restaurants, bars, and nightclubs, as well as being in the thick of the university area so the vibe is very young. However, the place itself frankly sucks. It's way too noisy; security is lax; guests tend to be obnoxious; and cleanliness is an issue.

Best bet for a bite:
Community House nearby

Insiders' tip:
Playtime magazine for listings

What hostellers say:
"Great place!"

Gestalt:
Heaven 17

Safety:

Hospitality:

Cleanliness:

Party index:

The dorms are large rooms divided into compartments, but you'll still feel like a sardine. There are also two coveted private rooms. You'll have to pay for sheets and breakfast, which might dent your budget slightly, but outside the hostel there's a private garden in which you can chill out and strike up conversations with other hostellers. One positive: the joint is open year-round, a blessing for those searching for accommodations in the dead of the Danish winter, when nearly all hostels are closed down. Staff are friendly, and they dispense good beer. So—it's not all bad; just mostly bad.

how to get there:

By bus or train: Contact hostel for transit details.
By car: Contact hostel for directions.

france

It's easy to get to France from the United States directly, often cheaper than flying to London first and taking the train. From elsewhere in Europe, Eurolines France (28, avenue du Général-de-Gaulle, Paris; telephone 08–9289–9091) runs buses to Paris and other points.

practical details

Once you're here, France's train system is among the world's best—especially the TGV superfast bullet trains that blast you from Paris out into the countryside at upwards of 100 miles an hour. TGV trains always cost a little extra, however, and you must reserve a ticket at least ten minutes before your departure; it costs about $3 US per ticket for the reservation.

For short hops in France, you buy one-way ("sample") or return ("ray-tour") tickets at the train stations. Always remember to punch your train ticket before you get on the train. There will be an orange machine in every station that stamps the current date and time on the ticket's magnetic strip, giving you twenty-four hours to use it or lose it. France also has its own individual country pass. The France Railpass is simple as pie: It gives you three (formerly four) days of travel in a month for $227 to $267 US. You can add extra days for about $35 a pop, and students and seniors get cheaper rates.

Remember that trains don't run as frequently on weekends; Saturday is usually the worst day to travel within France. International trains and sleeper cars usually run seven days a week, and Friday and Sunday are feast or famine; check schedules and think like a local. If you want to go to the south of France, for example, lots of trains will be running from the cities to the country on Friday afternoon. Sunday, everyone's either going to the beach or going home.

To take the bus in France, you buy short-hop bus tickets from the drivers and long-distance tickets at bus stations. Again, always remember to punch your ticket on the bus; there will be a machine on every bus that stamps the current date and time on the ticket's magnetic strip. Most are good for one hour.

Dealing with French pay phones can be frustrating, so don't bother pumping change unless you're truly desperate. Instead, buy France Telecom phone cards at tobacco shops or other small markets and stick 'em into the slots in the phones. (Push the card in lightly, with the little computer chip facing up.) Local calls won't eat up much of these cards, but long-distance calls within a country will; figure about ten to fifteen minutes per card at most.

France's phone code is 33. To call French hostels from North America, dial 011–33 and DROP THE FIRST ZERO from all numbers in this book. To call French hostels from within France, dial them AS WRITTEN. And to dial a hostel from within its home city, DROP THE CITY CODE (the part beginning with zero).

France's unit of currency is now the euro.

lyon

Lyon doesn't get much press over here, but the French—and foodies anywhere—love it. Restaurants are excellent, the architecture isn't bad, and it's more manageable than Paris in a day, if a lot less beautiful. Use this city as a hub for Provence and the south of France; you can get anywhere from the train station. To get around town use the one-line subway (Hey! these trains don't have drivers!). The only problem is finding the stations, sometimes hidden behind a store or a surprisingly ornate (and small) Metro sign.

lyon hostels
at a glance

	RATING	PRICE	IN A WORD	PAGE
Lyon-Vénissieux	◗	€11.80	distant	p. 114
Vieux Lyon	◗	€16.20	fun	p. 112

auberge de jeunesse ◗
du vieux lyon
41–45 Montée du Chemin Neuf, Lyon, Rhone 69005
Phone: 04–78–15–05–50

Fax: 04–78–15–05–51
E-mail: lyon@fuaj.org

Rates: €16–€20 (about $20 US) per HI member
Credit cards: Yes
Beds: 180
Private/family rooms: Yes
Kitchen available: Yes
Season: Open year-round
Office hours: 7:00 A.M.–noon; 2:00 P.M.–1:00 A.M.
Affiliation: HI-FUAJ
Extras: Garden, patio, bar, e-mail, tourist information, bike storage, laundry, breakfast

Lyon's central Hostelling International hostel is every bit as good as the other, farther out one! (See next listing.) Amazing, especially since this city really isn't a big destination; visitors are usually rushing through on their way to somewhere else.

Breakfast is included, and you can send or receive e-mail. There's a laundry, kitchen, patio, extremely popular bar, and garden. Views of downtown Lyon from the upper floors are absolutely awesome, and the building has been completely renovated in recent years, so it's in pretty good shape.

The beds consist of doubles, quads, and about twenty bigger bunkrooms with an average

Insiders' tip:
Metro is great

What hostellers say:
"This place rocks and rolls."

Gestalt:
Lyon sleeps tonight

Safety:

Hospitality:

Cleanliness:

Party index:

nine beds each—definitely a little too big, the only drawback here. There are also four wheelchair-accessible rooms and a wing of family rooms that can be delightfully cool or dreadfully chilly, depending on time of year.

Social life is the real draw here, though. The happy-go-lucky staff keep the fun (and booze) flowing and serve a free and popular breakfast of juice, cereal, bread, and coffee. Lyon as a town is also surprisingly fun—packed with eateries and clubs and other fun stuff, plus a gorgeous church right beneath your window. Come on, check it out—it's only two hours by fast train from Paris, after all.

how to get there:

By bus or train: From Part Dieu Station, take #28 bus to St-Jean–St-Just stop; from Perrache Station, take #31 bus.

By car: From Paris, take A6 to Lyon; from Marseille, take A7 to Lyon; call hostel for directions.

By subway: From downtown, take D subway line to St-Jean stop.

lyon-vénissieux auberge de jeunesse internationale

51, rue Roger Salengro, Vénissieux (Lyon), Rhone 69200
Phone: 04–78–76–39–23 or 04–78–15–05–50

Fax: 04–78–77–51–11
E-mail: lyon_sud@fuaj.org
Rates: €11.80 (about $15 US) per HI member
Credit cards: No
Beds: 71
Private/family rooms: Yes
Kitchen available: Yes
Season: January 15–December 15
Office hours: 7:00–11:00 A.M.; 5:00–11:00 P.M.
Lockout: 11:00 A.M.–5:30 P.M.
Curfew: 11:00 P.M.
Affiliation: HI-FUAJ
Extras: Laundry, meals ($), TV, patio, bar, breakfast, Internet access, snack bar, pool table

This joint is really nice—reason enough to stop in Lyon for the night even when you're bound for Paris or Nice. The location, however, stinks; it reminds us of some forlorn East Coast expressway burb back home. Oh, well.

Free breakfast is just the start of the experience. The rooms consist of doubles, quads, and bunkrooms with an average six beds apiece. They're fine. The real star here is the common facilities: There's a bar, Internet access, a cool patio and deck, meal service, and more. It all adds up to superior socializing with the other folk who've landed in Lyon for the night.

The city, by the way, has some of France's biggest outdoor produce

Best bet for a bite:
Markets galore

What hostellers say:
"Kinda far out."

Gestalt:
Lyon's share

Safety:

Hospitality:

Cleanliness:

Party index:

markets; hit the one on the banks of the Saone Tuesday through Sunday. The city also possesses a wide array of excellent (though somewhat snobbish) restaurants.

how to get there:

By bus or train: From Part Dieu Station, take #36 bus to Viviani stop and walk 300 yards to hostel. From Perrache Station, take #35 bus to hostel.

By car: Take Laurent Bonneway ring road to Lyon Etats-Unis exit, turning toward Vénissieux.

By subway: Take D subway line to Vénissieux.

marseille

Marseille is definitely one of the most exotic—and dangerous—places in France. This old, old port city has long been the meeting place for sailors from Africa and points beyond, and you'll find it a sensory assault—crazy traffic, barking market vendors, dingy streets, and the beautiful sea.

marseille hostels
at a glance

	RATING	PRICE	IN A WORD	PAGE
Auberge Bonneveine	☒	€11.80	beachy	p. 115
Chateau de Bois-Luzy	☒	€11.30	distant	p. 117

auberge bonneveine ☒
47, avenue Joseph-Vidal (Impasse du Dr. Bonfils), Marseille, Bouches-du-Rhône 13008
Phone: 04–91–17–63–30

Fax: 04–91–73–97–23

E-mail: marseille-bonneveine@fuaj.org
Rates: €11.80 (about $15 US) per HI member
Credit cards: Yes
Beds: 150
Private/family rooms: Yes
Kitchen available: No
Season: January 19–December 18
Office hours: 7:00 A.M.–1:00 A.M.
Curfew: 1:00 A.M.
Affiliation: HI-FUAJ
Extras: Meals ($), breakfast, laundry, lockers, bar, bike rentals

As it's almost on the beach, this hostel is the first pick in town of the Euro-beach bums. You know the type: wraparound shades, Jetsons-era rave clothes, cigarettes perpetually dangling from their mouths, and attitudes out to here. If you, too, want to hang with a young, partying crowd, by all means come.

What hostellers say:
"At least it's near the beach."

Gestalt:
Marseille what?

Safety:

Hospitality:

Cleanliness:

Party index:

Breakfast is included with your bed here, they serve other meals, and there's a laundry for washing your bathing suit afterward.

Be warned, though, that crime is a problem in the area—and at the hostel. Use the lockers they offer, but also take other precautions; even lockers aren't crook-proof. In fact, since you're in the heart of the Marseille waterfront, some extra caution is definitely in order. This work-about area is about as diverse as any you'll find in France—a sweltering melting pot of cultures and economic classes all scrabbling to wheel and deal themselves into a better (if not exactly straight-arrow) life.

This might be the town where the expression "thick as thieves" was invented, so be very, very careful at night. Heck, even during the daytime, try to travel with a group.

how to get there:

By bus: Take #44 bus to Place Bonnefons stop or #583 bus to Bourse Square.
By car: Call hostel for directions.
By subway: Take #2 Metro (subway) line to Prado stop.
By train: Marseille/St-Charles Station is 3 miles; from station take #2 Metro (subway) line to Rond Point du Prado stop.

chateau de bois-luzy
Allée des Primevères, Marseille, Bouches-du-Rhône 13012
Phone: 04–91–49–06–18

Fax: 04–91–49–06–18
Rates: €11.30 (about $15 US) per HI member
Credit cards: No
Beds: 90
Private/family rooms: Yes
Kitchen available: Yes
Season: January 5–December 20
Office hours: 7:30 A.M.–noon; 5:00–10:30 P.M.
Lockout: Noon–5:00 P.M.
Curfew: 10:30 P.M.
Affiliation: HI-FUAJ
Extras: Meals ($), laundry, TV, bike storage

This nineteenth-century mansion is much superior to the beachside hostel in town. Know why? It's pretty darned far out of town, that's why! Try almost 5 miles from the smoggy city center. But if you can negotiate public transit and strap on your walking shoes—or somehow have brought a car to the coast (are you nuts??)—then this is hostel heaven: simple, clean, attractive, and above all peaceful.

Rooms come in a variety of shapes, sizes, and colors. You've got your basic double rooms, your triples, and your quads.

Finally, there are a few larger dorm rooms—but none has more than eight beds, and most have about six.

The facility is surrounded by green fields, some of which are used for sports contests. Plenty of shops and restaurants are nearby, too, though they won't be anywhere as cheap or gritty as the stuff you can get right in the heart of Marseille. Ah, well, what price paradise?

What hostellers say:
"Not too close to town."

Gestalt:
Marseille hey!

Safety:

Hospitality:

Cleanliness:

Party index:

how to get there:

By bus: Take #6 or #8 bus to J. Thierry or Marius-Richard stop.
By car: Call hostel for directions.
By train: Marseille/St-Charles Station is 3 miles; call hostel for transit route.

paris

Paris, City of Lights: Practically every other European traveler begins or ends a European adventure here, so it's not really surprising that there are more hostels concentrated in the greater Paris area than in just about any other city on the Continent. Some are okay; some are dingy; some are central; some are miles out in the burbs. We've done our level best to separate the wheat from the chaff here.

Getting into town is no problemo. A ring of train stations surrounds Paris, shuttling travelers to and from all points in Europe; all the city's train stations are on the subway.

Once you're here, though, parking is atrocious. Chances are you're not hauling your car into the city, but if you are—well, just don't. Get rid of it at a parking garage or lot or rental drop-off area in the burbs, or just don't rent one until you leave town. Besides the fact that driving in Paris can needlessly consume hours of vital sightseeing time, you won't need a car anyway. Instead, rely on that Metro subway system—one of the world's best—and the buses that race all over the city. Taxis are expensive and scarce except at the train stations, but they're quite useful when you need to make a desperate dash.

Before doing anything else, take time to figure out the Metro map—which can be quite confusing at first glance—and orient yourself according to line number (*ligne* in French). You need to know what stop is at the END of the line you're traveling in order to figure out which side of the platform to get on. Got it? Let's say you wanna take Line #5 away from town to the north. That line ends at Bobigny Station. Okay! Now, in the station look for a sign with a 5 in a circle that says DIRECTION BOBIGNY. Presto, that's your line.

You can buy books of ten tickets (way cheaper than the €1.50 single tickets) at any station; ask for a carnet—say "un carnay"—and fork over €11.10. As you enter the subway, place the skinny blue ticket into the slot in the gate and take it out again when it pops up. You'll have a few seconds to get through the gate, so be speedy, and don't push your luggage ahead of you to avoid getting it caught in the doors. That's it: In seconds you'll be elsewhere in town. Hang onto the ticket 'til you get off, too, since conductors will occasionally demand to see it.

The RER (suburban railway) is a related system, even more effi-cient (there are lots fewer stops), and your Metro ticket gets you on board at no extra cost unless you need to go outside city limits to the airports or Disneyland Paris. Check the map; you can often zip from a station to the action much faster using the RER. Each station also has helpful boards posting the next incoming train and where it'll be stopping—one advantage over the Metro.

We'd avoid most of the Paris buses except as a cheap sightseeing tour. To get to the airport, use Air France buses because they have luggage compartments.

Once you're here, act like a local. Don't stand in those huge aboveground lines to get into the Louvre; go late in the day, and take the underground mall stairway instead of the aboveground cattle call. Score cheap clothes at flea markets. Buy food at farmers' markets. Watch yourself at night in dimly lit alleys like in Saint-Germain or around the train stations.

paris hostels at a glance

	RATING	PRICE	IN A WORD	PAGE
FIAP Jean-Monnet	◩	€24.50–€54.00	educational	p. 132
Woodstock	◩	€18–€22	hoppin'	p. 137
AJ Jules Ferry	◩	€19.50	strict	p. 127
CISP Maurice Ravel	◩	€18.50–€34.00	clean	p. 131
AJ le D'Artagnan	◩	€22	lively	p. 128
AJ Leo Lagrange	◩◩	€19.50– €22.00	quiet	p. 130
La Maison Hostel	◩◩	€19–€21	okay	p. 133
AJ Cité des Sciences	◩◩	€19.50– €22.00	distant	p. 124
Le Village Hostel	◩◩	€24–€30	newish	p. 134
Aloha	◩◩	€19–€23	small	p. 122
Young & Happy	◩◩	€21–€23	tiny	p. 138
AJ des Jeunes	◪	€13–€17	chaotic	p. 126
Three Ducks	◪	€19–€25	dirty	p. 136

As for the hostels: Not one of them really knocked our socks off. We'd guess that Paris is so popular you could rent out a paper bag and charge ten bucks for it, and maybe that's why. For what it's worth, the HI-affiliated hostels are cleaner and better run than almost all the independent ones—but they're much worse located.

The independents tended to be more relaxed. Too relaxed, actually. Most of them (six, to be exact) are run by the same group, called

paris

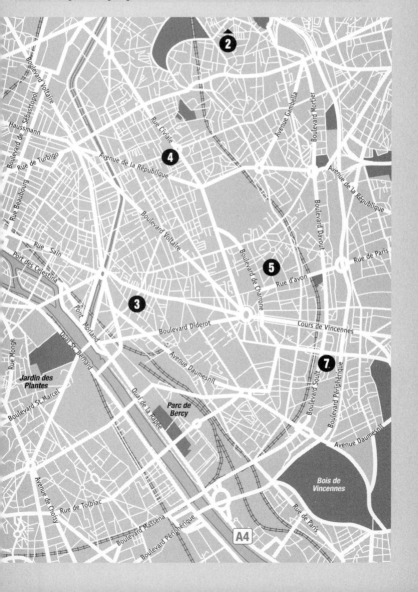

C.H.E.A.P. These hostels vary wildly in quality from pretty nice to funky/yucky; definitely check our reviews before booking into these places. All are in great locations, at least, so if you can stand the beds, you'll probably love the surroundings.

In case all the good hostels are full, there are two other sets of accommodations you might want to know about: MIJE and BVJ. (Their French names are too long to deal with just now.) We haven't included them in this book because they discriminate based on age: You can't get in unless you're under a certain age. Since that would exclude some of our readers, we're not giving up the goods on those guys. But there's a fantastic BVJ almost under the nose of the Louvre and another in the heart of Paris's Latin Quarter; contact the organization to learn more about these and other BVJs.

Also call to learn about MIJE's network, which in Paris consists of three fine hostels for young people only in the Marais neighborhood.

aloha hostel

1, rue Borromée, Paris 75015, Fifteenth Arrondisement
Phone: 01–42–73–03–03

Fax: 01–42–73–14–14
E-mail: friends@aloha.fr
Web site: www.aloha.fr
Rates: €19–€23 (about $24–$29 US) per person; private/family rooms €46–€50 (about $57–$62 US)
Credit Cards: No
Beds: 130
Private/family rooms: Yes
Kitchen available: Yes
Season: Open year-round
Office hours: Contact hostel for hours
Lockout: 11:00 A.M.–5:00 P.M.
Curfew: 2:00 A.M.
Affiliation: None
Extras: TV, breakfast, bar

We'd place this joint in the lower third of the pack among Parisian hostels: not the best, but certainly not the absolute worst. Actually, location-wise it's got many of the rest of them beat hands-down. So it's worth a look for that reason, and that reason only.

Just don't expect the lap of luxury. This place, despite the high bed number, is small and feels small. Dorms contain two to six beds each, and although they're in surprisingly good condition, they're also kinda tight. There's one huge dorm, too. The upper-floor bunk beds are atmospheric, beneath a sloping roof and giving views down onto the hopping streets. They also have a very few double rooms; by all means try to get those if you can.

But as for bathrooms, kitchen . . . well, they're teensie-weensie, not much space at all. We're talking just one little shower—it's in a closet that opens into a hall—and just a couple of toilets for the whole darned place. And it's extremely dirty, worse than in previous years. So resign yourself to waiting in line and bumping into people constantly. You might never get that shower, but at least your dorm room likely has a sink; it could be sponge-bath city. The outdoor kitchen, as mentioned, is minuscule, and common space consists of a couple tables in the lobby.

Best bet for a bite:
Rue Cler

What hostellers say:
"Tight quarters."

Gestalt:
Hawaii five-oh

Safety: 🔳🔳

Hospitality: 🔳🔳

Cleanliness: 🔳

Party index: 🔺🔺🔺🔺

Staff will sell you beer and wine from the check-in desk sometimes, which oils conversation considerably. But that's about all they'll do; they were not friendly and helpful, generally speaking. We liked the bright-red gas pumps in the bar area. (Points off for the official hostel motto, though: "Fun . . . that's the point, isn't it?" Boy, is that lame.)

The real draw here, anyway, isn't the hostel but rather the neighborhood. Everyone who stays here remembers one thing about it: The

key to icons

🌲	Attractive natural setting	🛏	Comfortable beds	🎨	Visual arts at hostel or nearby
🌍	Ecologically aware hostel	S	A particularly good value	🎵	Music at hostel or nearby
🍴	Superior kitchen facilities or cafe	♿	Wheelchair-accessible	🎿	Great hostel for skiers
🎉	Offbeat or eccentric place	💼	Good for business travelers	🍺	Bar or pub at hostel or nearby
🚿	Superior bathroom facilities	👪	Especially well suited for families	🏅	Editors' Choice: Among our very favorite hostels
❤	Romantic private rooms	🚴	Good for active travelers		

Eiffel Tower is around the corner, and when you turn that corner—
well, it's almost a religious experience. You've arrived in Paris. And
nearby are those quintessential Parisian cafes, produce markets,
student fast-food eateries, and even a laundry and a post office. Not
a bad place at all to base yourself.

    Annoyingly, though, lots of Americans and Brits stay here, possibly
detracting a bit from that purely French experience you wanted.

how to get there:

By bus or train: Call hostel for transit route.
By Metro: Take Metro to Volontaires stop, then walk west on rue de
Vaugirard; turn right at rue Borromée and continue to hostel.
By plane: Two large airports outside Paris; call hostel for transit
route.

---

auberge cité des sciences
**24, rue des Sept Arpents, Le Pré Saint-Gervais
(Paris) 93310
Just outside Nineteenth Arrondisement
Phone: 01–48–43–24–11**

Fax: 01–48–43–26–82
E-mail: paris.cite-des-sciences@fuaj.org
Rates: €19.50– €22.00 (about $24–$27 US) per HI member
Credit cards: Yes
Beds: 184
Private/family rooms: Yes
Kitchen available: Yes
Season: January 1–November 9 and December 1–31
Office hours: Midnight to 11:00 A.M. and 4:00 P.M. to midnight
Affiliation: HI-FUAJ
Extras: Breakfast, laundry, lockers, bike rentals

This place is pretty far out from central Paris—in fact, it's technically
not in the city but in the suburb called Le Pré Saint-Gervais—but you
might get stuck here because the rest of the hostels are filled. At least
it's on a Metro line and quite handy to several northern Parisian rail
stations. But that cuts both ways; train station neighborhoods tend not
to be the greatest.

    Beds here come two to six to a room, and things can get a little tight.
On the plus side, they keep the common room open all day during the

room lockout and maintain a laundry and an ironically itsy-bitsy kitchen. For the laundry, about €2.00 ($2.50 US) in coins is needed (frustratingly, reception doesn't always have enough change on hand).

Accommodations are a little sterile, and not clean enough. Rooms in the newer of the two buildings have big, big windows with absolutely no awnings or curtains. (Don't come bopping out of the shower au naturel, if you know what we mean.) The four-bed private rooms for families and other folk come with their own washing facilities—a sink that shoots cold water for about two seconds. The shower, also push-button, shoots hot water—but there's no curtain. Toilets are not included; you have to clomp down the hallway and pray the WC is free. The newer building is more crowded but also more congenial, a lot more conducive to the sort of social mixing you came here to do.

The scene here consists of people gathering in the big common room to write postcards, practice their French, and listen to live music performed by locals who tend to dress in drag. You can also make phone calls with phone cards purchased from the vending machine. Laundry facilities are located in the basement, along with the gigantic storage area.

Unfortunately, there's virtually nothing to do at or around the hostel except sit at one of the outdoor tables watching the street. Pinch us. Since the neighborhood's so blah and distant and potentially dodgy, you'll need to whip out your Metro pass and ride the rails to see anything of note. At least the crowd here at the hostel tends to be lively and friendly, and staff—those who will deign to speak English with you, anyway—are okay.

Oh, and if you're into high-tech museums, the Cité des Sciences nearby does a great job of letting you touch, feel, and even smell science and nature up close and personal. Not too Parisian, but it's a cool rainy-day trip.

Best bet for a bite:
Bakery near Metro exit

Insiders' tip:
Sidewalks too narrow
for luggage

What hostellers say:
"Your French stinks."

Gestalt:
Blinded by science

Safety:

Hospitality:

Cleanliness:

Party index:

how to get there:

By bus: Take PC or #170 bus to Port de Pantin stop, then walk 200 yards to hostel.

By Metro: Take #5 Line toward Bobigny to Hoche stop.

auberge internationale ◥ des jeunes

10, rue Trousseau, Paris 75011, Eleventh Arrondisement
Phone: 01–47–00–62–00

Fax: 01–47–00–33–16
Web site: www.aijparis.com
Rates: €13–€17 (about $16.50–$21.00 US) per person
Credit cards: Yes
Beds: 40
Private/family rooms: Yes
Kitchen available: No
Season: Open year-round
Office hours: Twenty-four hours
Lockout: 10:00 A.M.–3:00 P.M.
Curfew: 1:00 A.M.
Affiliation: None
Extras: Laundry, breakfast, Internet access

Chaos.

That's a good word to describe this hostel, Paris's cheapest—and possibly its best located—but also one of the most crowded.

Most dorms contain two to four beds, and it's a bit cramped here.

Best bet for a bite:
Monoprix

What hostellers say:
"Another night? Umm . . . no."

Gestalt:
French fried

Safety: ◥◥

Hospitality: ◥◥

Cleanliness: ◥◥

Party index: 🎉🎉🎉🎉

The bigger the room, paradoxically, the worse it gets. The bathrooms have also seen better days. At least all the quad rooms have their own, er, facilities. Sure, they give you free breakfast—but nobody liked it. The daytime lockout is annoying, too, though this is far from the only Paris hostel to indulge in that practice.

But the location's good, near La Bastille—once a famous French jail. But now the jail is gone and it's a hip, edgy neighborhood of bars, immigrants, and shops. (You can't hear the action from your bunk, which is a plus.) You can mail letters, stock up on grub at one of four supermarkets, and take care of other errands all within a block or two. A number of cool clubs are located here, too, though they tend to specialize in bad imitation soul music.

how to get there:

By bus: Call hostel for transit route.

By Metro: Take #8 Line to Ledru-Rollin stop; walk east on rue du Faubourg St-Antoine 1 block to rue Trousseau; turn left.

By train: From Gare du Lyon, walk to Ledru-Rollin; turn and walk east on rue du Faubourg St-Antoine 1 block to rue Trousseau; turn left.

---

auberge jules ferry

8, boulevard Jules Ferry, Paris 75011, Eleventh Arrondisement

Phone: 01–43–57–55–60

Fax: 01–43–14–82–09
E-mail: paris.julesferry@fuaj.org
Rates: €19.50 (about $24 US) per HI member
Credit cards: Yes
Beds: 99
Private/family rooms: None
Kitchen available: No
Season: Open year-round
Office hours: Twenty-four hours
Lockout: Noon–2:00 P.M.
Affiliation: HI-FUAJ
Extras: Laundry, breakfast, cafeteria ($), lockers, bicycle storage, travel agency

An extremely light breakfast is included at this big but not super-huge Paris hostel, which is as efficient as the rest of the Hostelling International joints in and around town—and a whole lot more hoppin' than you'd expect. The joint's placed in an excellent location near two cool neighborhoods, La Bastille and the Marais, and is definitely one of the better hostels in the city.

Expect slightly cramped rooms, a sorry excuse of a kitchen, and variable cleanliness. Yeah, this place is definitely not perfect, but it's a lot better than some of the other dives in town. Consider that.

Staff are pretty strict about curfew-busting, food-snatching, or using too much water in the showers, but you can probably deal with it because it's still one of the best deals you'll find in town, and they're not bad once you get to know them. The atmosphere, in particular, is surprisingly laid-back once you return after the lockout. Yes, people actually have fun here! The Hostelling International office right next door serves as an information depot, travel agency, and more, so take full advantage of it.

Arrive early at the trim six-story building, though, for two simple reasons: First, they don't ever take advance reservations by phone. Second, this is always one of the first places to fill up in the morning.

Best bet for a bite:
Brasseries around République

What hostellers say:
"Wheee!"

Gestalt:
Ferry tale

Safety:

Hospitality:

Cleanliness:

Party index:

how to get there:

By bus: Take #75, #46, #54, #56, #65 or #96 bus to République or Jules Ferry stop and walk 200 yards to hostel.

By Metro: Take Metro to République stop; walk east along rue du Faubourg du Temple to boulevard Jules Ferry; turn right.

By plane: From airport, take #350 bus to hostel.

By train: Call hostel for transit route.

auberge le d'artagnan
80, rue Vitruve, Paris 75020, Twentieth Arrondisement
Phone: 01–40–32–34–56

Fax: 01–40–32–34–55
E-mail: paris.le-dartagnan@fuaj.org
Rates: €22 (about $28 US) per HI member
Credit cards: Yes
Beds: 435
Private/family rooms: Yes
Kitchen available: No
Season: Open year-round
Office hours: 8:00 A.M.–1:00 A.M.
Lockout: Noon–3:00 P.M.
Affiliation: HI-FUAJ
Extras: Laundry, meals ($), breakfast, bar, disco, movies, lockers, concerts, piano, climbing wall, Internet access ($), shop

This huge edifice is in kind of a weird area for a hostel, in a drab neighborhood that's really only close to a train station and giant

Père-Lachaise Cemetery (where Jim Morrison and others now rest). So if you've come to lay flowers at the Lizard King's feet, well, this is the hostel for you. Otherwise it's just too, too far from the action.

At least there are tons of activities here. They show free movies every week, host concerts, and run a bar in the basement. Did we mention the discotheque? (Nobody dances, but that's beside the point.) All that, plus a laundry, family and private rooms, and meals.

Free breakfast is included with your bed, though it wasn't as sumptuous as the staff-only lunch spread that's off-limits to hostellers.

Drawbacks? Try the attitude sometimes displayed by a hipper-than-you'll-ever-be staff, who'd rather watch you fumble for hours with unresponsive pay phones than explain that they don't work. The in-house cafe attempts cowboy cooking with a Tex-Mex menu that just doesn't quite cut it, and plumbing is outdated and not always in good repair. Most annoying, groups of French schoolkids tend to book the place and make a lot of noise in the halls at night.

Best bet for a bite:
Bastille area

What hostellers say:
"Got a light?"

Gestalt:
Lachaise lounge

Safety: ◣◣

Hospitality: ◣◣

Cleanliness: ◣

Party index: 🎉🎉🎉🎉

Still, it's a good place, safe and reasonably clean. Dorms are generally three- to four-bed affairs (though there are also some eight-bedded dorms), kept fairly clean. They're a welcome change from the gargantuan dorms we'd feared when we laid eyes on the place. All the activity from below does occasionally filter upward; try to get a top-floor bunk if you don't want noise or the omnipresent cigarette smoke hovering about.

The real trade-off here, as we said, is location; you need to hoof it to the Metro, then ride awhile, to get to most places you want to be. Otherwise, this isn't a bad hostel at all.

how to get there:

By bus: Euroline terminal is ½ mile from hostel.
By Metro: Take #3 Metro Line to Porte de Bagnolet stop; walk ⅓ mile to hostel.
By plane: From airport, take #351 bus to hostel.
By train: Gare de Lyon is ½ mile from hostel.

auberge leo lagrange

107, rue Martre, Clichy (Paris) 92110
Just outside Seventeenth Arrondisement
Phone: 01–41–27–26–90

Fax: 01–42–70–52–63
E-mail: paris.clichy@fuaj.org
Rates: €19.50– €22.00 (about $24–$28 US) per HI member
Credit cards: No
Beds: 338
Private/family rooms: Yes
Kitchen available: Yes
Season: Open year-round
Office hours: Twenty-four hours
Affiliation: HI-FUAJ
Extras: Breakfast, lockers, bar

Breakfast is included, and so are free sheets, at this grim-looking hostel on the outskirts of Paris—in fact, it's a couple blocks outside Paris, in the suburb of Clichy if you're gonna get picky about things.

Best bet for a bite:
Try Montmartre

What hostellers say:
"Far out. Literally."

Gestalt:
Lagrange hall

Safety:

Hospitality:

Cleanliness:

Party index:

Bunkrooms are small—just two to four beds in all of 'em—and FUAJ has provided free breakfasts, a bar, and lockers for hostellers' enjoyment. Don't forget to hang out with your new buds in the balcony chairs, either. All in all, a place removed from the frenzy of most other Parisian hostels. But the rude staff, poorly maintained bathrooms, and noise should make you think twice.

This is fairly close to both Montmartre and the Champs-Elysées, although you'll need to do a little fancy footwork to get there. And, as with FUAJ's other hostels, you'll need to hop Le Metro to get to downtown's chief attractions.

how to get there:

By bus: Take #54 or C bus.
By car: Call hostel for directions.
By Metro: Take #13 Metro Line to Mairie de Clichy stop and walk 100 yards to hostel.

By plane: From airport, take Orlybus or Roissybus to hostel area.
By train: St-Lazare Station, 2½ miles; call hostel for transit route.

cisp maurice ravel
6, avenue Maurice Ravel, Paris 75012, Twelveth Arrondisement
Phone: 01–44–75–60–00 or 01–44–75–60–06

E-mail: cisp@cisp.asso.fr
Web site: www.cisp.asso.fr
Rates: €18.50–€34.00 (about $23–$42 US) per person; doubles €50 (about $62 US)
Credit cards: Yes
Beds: 600
Private/family rooms: Yes
Kitchen available: No
Season: Open year-round
Office hours: 6:30 A.M.–1:30 A.M.
Affiliation: CISP
Extras: Restaurant ($)

This place is so cheap, and so clean, that it's a wonder more hostellers haven't discovered it yet.

Well, okay, not so fast. Like a lot of Paris hostels, it *is* located a half-hour out from the center of town in a fairly dodgy suburb where you'll want to be careful at night. And, it's kinda spartan on the furnishings. Still, rooms this clean and airy ought to be commanding hotel rates. And the big breakfast is positively energizing. Note that it's pretty hard to make friends here at the hostel itself, owing to the layout—and the fact that everybody's headed into town anyway. But if you can put up with that, and the remote location, this might be one of the better picks in town.

What hostellers say:
"Great breakfast"

Gestalt:
Ravel rouser

Safety:

Hospitality:

Cleanliness:

Party index:

Note: There's a great annex, known locally as Kellerman, in the Thirteenth Arrondisement; ask about it when booking or checking in.

how to get there:

By bus: Contact hostel for transit details.
By car: Contact hostel for directions.
By train: Contact hostel for transit details.

fiap jean-monnet

30, rue Cabanis, Paris 75014, Fourteenth Arrondisement
Phone: 01–43–13–17–00 or 01–43–13–17–17

Fax: 01–45–81–63–91
E-mail: fiap@fiap.asso.fr
Rates: €24.50–€54.00 (about $30–$65 US) per person; doubles €70 (about $84 US)
Credit cards: Yes
Beds: 500
Private/family rooms: Yes
Kitchen available: No
Season: Open year-round
Office hours: Twenty-four hours
Lockout: 9:00 A.M.–2:30 P.M.
Curfew: 2:00 A.M.
Affiliation: UCRIF
Extras: Cafeteria ($), laundry, club, conference rooms, game room, classes, tourist information, breakfast, Internet access

If tour groups didn't get first dibs on the beds here, it would be darned near perfect. As it is, this great hostel might not have any space when you call—especially in summer—for individual hostellers. But we're including it because if they do have room, it's a great place to hang.

Clean and educational, that's what this place is. How educational? Try French classes taught right in the hostel! Plus concerts and shows in the hostel's lounge and a tourist info desk to point you the right way in the city of lights. On the practical

What hostellers say: "Huge but fun."

Gestalt: Monnet, Monnet

Safety:

Hospitality:

Cleanliness:

Party index:

side, there's a laundry and cafeteria plus a game room for idle pursuits.

And the rooms—well, they're every bit as clean and nice as you'd expect, in configurations of two to eight beds each; en-suite bathrooms are often present, too.

Only problem is, if it's summertime you're probably not going to get a bunk. That doesn't seem fair. And there is a brutal 9:00 a.m. checkout . . . no exceptions. But that's the way it is. So come off-season.

how to get there:

By bus or train: Call hostel for transit route.

By Metro: Take Metro to Glacière stop, then walk down boulevard St-Jacques to rue Ferrus; make a left, then immediate right onto rue Cabanis.

By plane: Two large airports outside Paris; from Charles de Gaulle, take RER Line B to Denfert Rochereau; from Orly take Orlybus to Denfert Rochereau.

la maison hostel

67 bis, rue Dutot, Paris 75012, Twelfth Arrondisement
Phone: 01–42–73–10–10

Fax: 01–42–73–08–08
Web site: www.mamaison.fr
Rates: €19–€21 (about $24–$26 US) per person; private/family rooms €45–€48 (about $56–$60 US)
Credit cards: Yes
Beds: Varies
Private/family rooms: Yes
Kitchen available: Yes
Season: Open year-round
Office hours: 8:00 A.M.–2:00 A.M.
Lockout: 11:00 A.M.–5:00 P.M.
Curfew: 2:00 A.M.
Affiliation: None
Extras: Breakfast, Internet access

Another in the string of six well-situated C.H.E.A.P. hostels around Paris, La Maison used to be better. Now it's losing some of its gloss—okay, it's falling apart a bit—but it's still a doable option practically under the nose of that big iron tower some of you are going to Paris to see.

Rooms come in usually small (two- to four-bed) configurations. The dining room's nice, and a decent amount of work has gone into making this one of the two best in the C.H.E.A.P. chain. Staff are quite friendly and the crowd is pretty cool.

You're not far from the Eiffel Tower, as we mentioned, and also pretty close to the Montparnasse train station if you're heading out for points south and west.

What hostellers say:
"Dude, check out the Tower."

Gestalt:
Maison hall

Safety:

Hospitality:

Cleanliness:

Party index:

how to get there:

By bus: From station, take Metro to Volontaires stop.
By train: From any station, take Metro to Volontaires stop.

le village hostel

20, rue d'Orsel, Paris 75108, Eighteenth Arrondisement
Phone: 01–42–64–22–02

Fax: 01–42–64–22–04
E-mail: bonjour@levillagehostel.fr
Rates: Rates: €24–€30 (about $30–$36 US) per person; doubles €60 (about $75 US)
Credit cards: No
Beds: 95
Private/family rooms: Yes
Kitchen available: Yes
Season: Open year-round
Office hours: 7:30 A.M.–2:30 A.M.
Lockout: 11:00 A.M.–4:00 P.M.
Curfew: 2:00 A.M.
Affiliation: None
Extras: Breakfast, bar, Internet access, fax, terrace, TV room

So you're walking downhill off Sacre Coeur, still blown away by the church (and hordes of Americans snapping pics of it), and you turn a corner; there it is, a big blue neon hostel sign. You've found the newest hostel in Paris, already a darling of certain cheapie guidebooks but one that still has kinks to work out.

The beds are good, so far, though the mostly Aussie and American crowds appear to be beating up the furniture fast. Bunks come in rooms with from two to four beds (in summer they add more to reduce your privacy, but the price is also less); some coveted doubles are available.

What hostellers say:
"Montmartre rocks!"

Gestalt:
Village people

Safety: 🔳🔳

Hospitality: 🔳

Cleanliness: 🔳🔳

Party index: 🔺🔺🔺

This place has the best views and terrace in Paris, so that's definitely worth something. Management and staffing are hit-or-miss, while the small bar appears to be where the socializing gets done. Cleanliness is hit-or-miss, too: Some rooms are pristine, some itchy and scratchy. Also, we *really* hate the push-button showers here. Push this.

Internet access is available, though it's a so-so service at best. Also, though they claim to have a kitchen, it's really just a hot plate-and-microwave combo. So we can't consider that the real deal.

how to get there:

By Metro: Take Metro to Anvers stop; walk up rue Steinkerque to rue d'Orsel and turn right; walk ½ block. Hostel is on left.

key to icons

🟥 Attractive natural setting

🟥 Ecologically aware hostel

🟥 Superior kitchen facilities or cafe

🟥 Offbeat or eccentric place

🟥 Superior bathroom facilities

🟥 Romantic private rooms

🟥 Comfortable beds

🟥 A particularly good value

🟥 Wheelchair-accessible

🟥 Good for business travelers

🟥 Especially well suited for families

🟥 Good for active travelers

🟥 Visual arts at hostel or nearby

🟥 Music at hostel or nearby

🟥 Great hostel for skiers

🟥 Bar or pub at hostel or nearby

🟥 Editors' Choice: Among our very favorite hostels

three ducks travelers hostel

6, place Etienne Pernet, Paris 75015, Fifteenth Arrondisement

Phone: 01–48–42–04–05

Fax: 01–48–42–99–99
Rates: €19–€25 (about $24–$30 US) per person; doubles €46–€52 (about $57–$65 US)
Credit cards: Yes
Beds: 95
Private/family rooms: None
Kitchen available: Yes
Season: Open year-round
Office hours: 8:00 A.M.–2:00 A.M.
Lockout: 10:00 A.M.–5:00 P.M.
Curfew: 2:00 A.M.
Affiliation: None
Extras: Storage, lockers, courtyard, breakfast, sheets ($)

Beaten-down and packed with beer-guzzling North Americans, this place is Party Central—and that's about it. This is Paris's worst hostel in every way except one: If you're absolutely intent on getting bombed off your pierced butt and then hitting on some other soused hosteller in the process, then you'll love it.

What hostellers say:
"Partyyyy!"

Gestalt:
Daffy ducks

Safety:

Hospitality:

Cleanliness:

Party index:

But first things first. The rooms here—which contain two to eight beds apiece—are cold, cramped, and dirty. There's no heat in winter, and some beds don't even have pillows. That's right. No pillows. It's BYOP, apparently. Bathrooms are even worse, not even approaching cleanliness or hotness of water. (That's what happens when scrungy hosteller after hos-

teller kneels before the porcelain god at the end of a long drunk.) Management somehow gets away with locking you out of the place all day long, too, though they don't appear to use that free time to do much cleaning or upkeep.

Some hostellers told us that the staff here were tough to deal with, while others claim staff are helpful; it probably depends on what you're wanting. If it's a party, then they'll help you out. Got a complaint? Tough luck. Breakfast is free but not terribly nutritious; when we stopped in, it was weak hot chocolate and a cheapo baguette. They also charge for sheets, towels—heck, everything.

The bar—the only reason people could possibly want to stay here—throbs all night long with bad music, making sleep all but impossible. The atmosphere resembles a twenty-four-hour hookah party, with hostellers traipsing in and out, smoking, drinking, and becoming ill from dusk till dawn.

Our call? This is about the equivalent of lying down and sleeping in the middle of the Champs Elyseés, we'd say—and sleeping in the street is about twenty bucks cheaper!

how to get there:

By bus or train: Call hostel for transit route.

By Metro: Take Metro to Commerce stop. Walk south on rue du Commerce toward church; hostel is on right.

By plane: Two large airports outside Paris; call hostel for transit route.

---

woodstock hostel

48, rue Rodier, Paris 75009, Ninth Arrondisement
Phone: 01–48–78–87–76

Web site: www.woodstock.fr
Rates: €18–€22 (about $22–$27 US) per person; doubles €42–€50 (about $52–$63 US)
Credit cards: No
Beds: 75
Private/family rooms: Yes
Kitchen available: Yes
Season: Open year-round
Office hours: Twenty-four hours
Lockout: 11:00 A.M.–5:00 P.M.
Curfew: 2:00 A.M.
Affiliation: None
Extras: Bar, laundry, breakfast, Internet access ($), foosball

---

By the time we got to Woodstock . . . ah, never mind. This hostel dubs itself "The American Youth Embassy in Paris," and—as the name implies—the place is partly staffed by folk from the US of A. So it feels

Best bet for a bite:
Grocery store on corner

What hostellers say:
"Which state are you from?"

Gestalt:
Back to the garden

Safety:

Hospitality:

Cleanliness:

Party index:

very American. If you're looking for the quintessential French hostel experience, you've come to the wrong place—but every so often it's comforting to bunk with those who know where you're coming from.

The bar on the ground level is the nerve center of the place, and the music blaring twenty-four hours a day creates an exciting social atmosphere (if you like rock music). Luckily, walls in the bunkrooms are thick enough to block out most of the sound waves. So the party ends when you want it to. There's a nice mix of doubles, triples, and dormitory-style rooms, all within a very fair price range for Paris. Another room is available to store your packs for the day, suitable as long as you trust your roomies.

A breakfast is included with your overnight stay, itself not very American. But the hostel baguettes, jelly, coffee, and hot chocolate should give you the French jump start necessary to get through that first museum after a late night. As a bonus, the hostel's just 2 blocks from the Metro, close to the famous Sacre Coeur church, and also just a short walk from Paris's pulsing red-light district.

Only drawback? Prices are rising here; the word must be getting out.

how to get there:

By bus or train: Call hostel for transit route.
By Metro: Take Metro to Anvers stop, then walk across street to park with gazebo; walk through park and make a right on avenue Trudaine, then turn left on Rodier. Hostel is on left.
By plane: Two large airports outside Paris; call hostel for transit route.

young & happy (y&h) hostel
80, rue de Mouffetard Paris, Fifth Arrondisement
Phone: 01–47–07–47–07

Fax: 01–47–07–22–24
Rates: €21–€23 (about $26–$29 US) per person; doubles €46–€52 (about $57–$65 US)

Credit cards: Yes
Beds: 75
Private/family rooms: Sometimes
Kitchen available: Yes
Season: Open year-round
Office hours: Call hostel for hours
Lockout: 11:00 A.M.–4:00 P.M.
Curfew: 2:00 A.M.
Affiliation: None
Extras: Breakfast, fax, Internet access, bar, kitchen

This fairly new Paris hostel tries to be good to you, but its small space and odd management practices don't quite mesh with ideal hostelling.

It's somewhat unclean (though, inexplicably, popular with Japanese visitors) and crams you in: The watchword here is *tiny.* Rooms (two to six beds apiece) are close quarters, hallways are narrow, and there's little common or eating space. A small breakfast and showers are free. Things are semi-clean, but the staff . . . oy-vay. Among the worst in Europe? It's possible.

Safety:

Hospitality:

Cleanliness:

Party index:

The real draw here is the surrounding area, which is fairly cool—if a bit distant from the central city. It's yet another Parisian neighborhood of shops, bars, and student hangouts where real Parisians live. Come to the Mouffetard market, the city's oldest, where farmers and others hawk their goods. It's not the best market in the city, not by far, but if you want a quickie introduction to the market phenomenon (and you like fresh fruit), check it out.

how to get there:

By bus or train: Call hostel for transit route.
By Metro: Take Metro to Monge stop; follow rue Ortolan to rue Mouffetard.

germany

This is it: the land that inspired Walt Disney World—a land of great rivers, wines, oompa-loompa sounds, and some of the best damn beer in the world. If only Germany's "official" hostels reflected this spirit. Unfortunately, they reflect another side of Germany—the cold, efficient one. The independent hostels of Germany, however, are quite another story: lots of variety and craziness in both Berlin and Munich, and you'll find picking through the options fun.

practical details

Deutsche Bahn (DB), the national train company, is incredibly efficient; their trains are usually fast (sometimes very fast), clean, comfortable and—obviously—quite punctual. Ticket agents all speak English and have access to DB's lightning-fast trip-planning software, which can get you where you want to go faster than you can. Trust us. While these rail systems cross an incredible variety of landscape, even the iron horse can't get everywhere. It's likely, at some point, that you might need to supplement your train travel with some form of gondola, lift, bus, cog railway, or steam train.

The German Railpass gets you four days of rail travel in one month. It costs $358 US for first-class seating ($558 for two people traveling together in first class); $277 for second-class seating ($412 for two people traveling together in second class); and $139 to $179 per child under eleven years old. You can buy additional Railpass days, too, for $32 to $48 per day per adult, less for children.

Remember that a German pass or Eurail pass saves you big on Romantic Road and Castle Road bus tours and gets you a free ride on most Rhine and Moselle River ferries.

If you're gonna be around for a *really* long time, you can buy a BahnCard in German train stations for around $100 to $180 US, depending on your age. That gets you a half-price discount on second-class tickets for a whole year, and the savings can really add up.

A few other things to keep in mind:

- The EurAide offices in the Munich and Berlin train stations are an absolute godsend for trip planning. They'll set up your train reservations, reserve sleeper-train beds, give tours, whatever you need—usually at little cost, and always in perfect English.

- Germany is a big country. Going from Berlin to anywhere else is gonna take you half a day, at least, maybe all day. The superfast InterCity Express (ICE) trains blast along at 80 or more miles an hour, and they can save you time, but they also cost a little extra— reservations are required, too. Definitely go for second-class tickets on these babies unless you're loaded.

- Big-city German train stations and their neighborhoods can get a little rough late at night. Ever heard of skinheads? Germany invented them, and they're still actively circulating the streets and stations of East Berlin, among other places. Stay away from those guys with the jackets and white-laced boots. You don't need the trouble.

German's country code is 49. To call German hostels from North America, dial 011–49 and DROP THE FIRST ZERO from the numbers printed in this book; to call from within Germany, dial the numbers AS PRINTED. To call the United States, Canada, or wherever else you might hail from, dial 001 and then the number you are calling. Remember: It's cheaper to make coin calls at night, and directory assistance (dial 11833) can get expensive.

Germany's unit of currency is now the euro.

berlin

Population 3.5 million and growing, Berlin's one crazy place these days. Flush with its position as capital of a reunified Germany (let's face it, you never realized Bonn was the old capital anyway), construction projects are sprouting like mad. There's a palpable energy as entrepreneurs, artists, clubbers, and just about everyone else tries to carve out an exciting new direction. It might be the most exciting city in the world right now—no kidding.

That's not to say it's a physically attractive place, though. Years of Iron Curtain life have turned chunks of the city into run-down quarters and fascist-architecture hotels and housing projects. You come here for the culture and the fascinating history, not pretty buildings and quaint alleyways. Fortunately, some parks provide a bit of green relief from the concrete, and some are quite close to the central sightseeing districts.

getting oriented

Zoologischer Garten Station—almost always called Zoo Station or Bahnof Zoo—is big and confusing, but it will probably be your introduction to Berlin and it's the best place to orient yourself and get ready for the party. Want a big hint? The place to get all your local tourist tips—not to mention make onward train reservations—is the American-run EurAide office at Zoo Station. Also at the train station you'll find tour companies such as Berlin Walks, a very good one (try the Third Reich tour).

For purposes of organizing your visit to this sprawling city, we've divided Berlin into a few areas. Going from west to east, the huge downtown area is composed of the western districts known as Charlottenberg, Tiergarten, and Schöneberg; two central areas near the old Berlin wall, Mitte ("middle") and Kreuzberg; and two eastern neighborhoods, Prenzlauer Berg and Friedrichshain. Each of these areas has its own individual character, and collectively they are chock-full of hostels. Any hostel that's outside these five areas is probably gonna take some time to get to.

In each write-up we've indicated in which of these areas a hostel is located. If a hostel's not in one of these areas, we've labeled it as being in the Outer Districts.

getting around

Berlin's so big that it had to gradually build a tremendous transport network to get everyone around—and it did. What's amazing is that when East and West Berlin joined hands in 1989, the two networks were seamlessly joined. Today, tons of buses, streetcars, subways, and commuter trains ensure that things keep moving.

Subways (the U-Bahn) are marked by a "U." Aboveground trains (the S-Bahn, free with Eurail passes) are marked by an "S." Bus and streetcar stops are marked with an "H" by the side of the road, and night buses (those with an "N" in the number) run all night long, though less frequently than day buses do.

Buy a transit pass each day (or every couple days), then use it—a lot—to sightsee and get around. You might pay a little bit extra, but if you're gonna be hopping around a lot, it works out as a better deal than individual tickets. And it's *really* worth the time you'll save not having to stand in line or trying to decipher ticket machines.

Transit passes come in several levels. The Tageskarte, the daily transit pass, costs about $7.50 US per day; three to five people doing all their traveling together can save by buying a Gruppentageskarte for about $18.00 US per day. There's also a one- and three-day Welcome Card and a 7-Tage-Karte-Card (about $20 to $30 US) for those staying a little longer. Do the math and you'll see why they save you money over the long run.

what to see

You could spend days and days in Berlin, alternating between Cold War sightseeing and bar-hopping among the city's hundreds of enjoyable *kneipen* (pubs).

To see the sights, we'd possibly begin with a quick walk or ride. From Zoo Station, you might take a public transit ride over to Charlottenburg

Palace. It's every bit as impressive as you'd expect; there are spacious grounds, plus museum after museum filled with regal items. A closer site to the station would be the Kaiser-Wilhelm-Gedächtniskirche memorial church, about a block away.

In the other direction, toward the Wall, you might try a get-acquainted stroll along famous Kurfurstendamm Boulevard (Berliners-in-the-know just call it Ku-damm), a long, wide, and drab—but oh-so-Berlin—collection of department stores, restaurants, and bars.

After getting that first taste of the city, we'd hop a bus for the Mitte district, where the sights come fast and furious near the former border checkpoint that divided East and West known as the Checkpoint Charlie House.

The Brandenburg Gate, built in the late 1700s, is the usual starting point on a walking tour from west to east and a point of pride for Berliners, who now consider it the heart of their city. The huge radio tower—with its 1,200 feet of steel and antenna right in the center of town—is the next obvious point on a tour. You can ascend to a platform halfway up and check out the new German capital from high in the air. From there, head east along wide Unter den Linden ("Under the Lime Trees") Boulevard for a really grand look at Berlin's pre-Nazi glories.

Or make a short hop over to Museumsinsel, a small island in the Spree River stocked with enormous and impressive museums; look for such landmarks as the huge cupola of the Berliner Dom (cathedral). Some of the offerings include the Altes Museum (Old Museum), Alte Nationalgalerie (Old National Gallery), Bode Museum, and Pergamon Museum.

Nearby you'll find a number of churches that testify to the atrocities of World War II, including the Nikolaikirche (first begun in the thirteenth century). Also close by, the Nikolaiviertel section is the city's most ancient. Begin at the Nikolai church and filter through alleys and squares, stopping for a bite or a beer when you get the urge.

Most of the same key sights, in roughly the same order, can be seen by jumping onto the city's #100 bus at Zoo Station and riding from west to east. That's the cheap way. For a more romantic look at things, find out about one of the city boat tours running along the Spree River.

the hostel scene

The hostels in Berlin, predictably enough, range from near-dumps to boring warehouse-style places to near-pristine palaces. (We did note that an amazing number of the places here, no matter what they're like, charge you extra dough just to get sheets. Boo to that!)

We've found that the backpacker-style joints here are about as groovy as any in Europe—there's a very laid-back feel to them, which is at odds with the normal hostels-in-Germany way of doing things. In

berlin

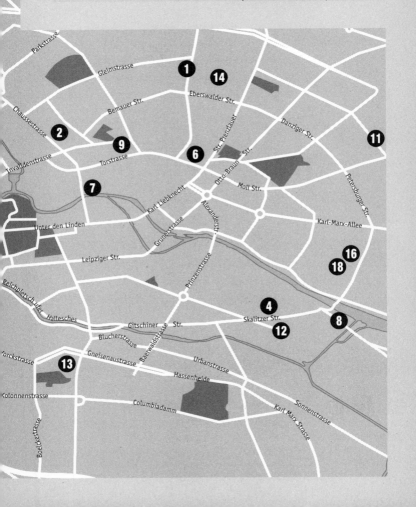

other words, the difference between an "official" hostel and an "independent" one in this city is huge in terms of atmosphere.

berlin hostels
at a glance

	RATING	PRICE	IN A WORD	PAGE
Circus Hostel	⬛⬛	€17–€46	cool	p. 155
Die Fabrik Hostel	⬛⬛	€18–€38	fun	p. 158
Eastener Hostel	⬛⬛	€12–€35	tiny	p. 160
Odyssee Globetrotter	⬛	€10–€36	rockin'	p. 171
Freiraum Guest House Hostel	⬛	€20	historic	p. 165
Hotel Transit Hostel	⬛	€21–€62	great	p. 166
Backpacker Mitte Hostel	⬛	€13–€30	arty	p. 148
Lette 'm Sleep Hostel	⬛	€17–€26	relaxed	p. 168
Backpacker's Paradise	⬛	€8–€9	campy	p. 150
Generator Berlin	⬛	€10–€30	huge	p. 163
Clubhouse Hostel	⬛	€13–€19	clubby	p. 157
Nordufer Hostel	⬛	€19.90	okay	p. 170
Ernst Reuter Hostel	⬛	€17	quiet	p. 161
Sunflower Hostel	⬛	€10–€35	fine	p. 173
Jugendherberge Berlin	⬛	€21	blah	p. 153
Alcatraz Hostel	⬛	€13–€45	remote	p. 147
Wannsee Hostel	⬛	€21	distant	p. 174
A & O Hostel am Zoo	⬛◻	€10–€30	worn	p. 176
BaxPax Hostel	⬛◻	€12–€30	new	p. 151
Student Hotel Hubertusallee	NR	€30–€48	adequate	p. 172

alcatraz backpacker hostel

Schönhauser Allee 133a, 10437 Berlin
Phone: 030–4849–6815

Fax: 030–4172–5804
E-mail: ok@alcatraz-backpacker.de
Web site: www.alcatraz-backpacker.de
Rates: €13–€45 (about $16–$56 US) per person; doubles €42–€60
(about $53–$75 US)
Credit cards: No
Beds: Number varies
Private/family rooms: Yes
Kitchen available: Yes
Season: Open year-round
Office hours: Twenty-four hours
Affiliation: None
Extras: Internet access, breakfast, bike rentals, safe, luggage storage, library,
yard, television, kitchen

Located in Prenzlauer Berg

There's nothing wrong with this hostel. On the other hand, there's
almost no reason to stay here. Puzzled? Read on. . . .

The big coed dorm here is cheapest, of course, but they also have
double, triple, and quad rooms, and
they will try to give you a single-sex
room if you ask and they're not full
up. Beds and bunks were a bit
skinny, yet everything—including
bathrooms—is funkily decorated,
and nicely clean. The modern
kitchen alcove was also well kept,
and certainly adequate for the task
of preparing nosh. The friendly staff
serves breakfast, points you to
Internet access, rents bikes, and
will store your valuables or luggage.

What hostellers say:
"Um, where's Berlin?"

Gestalt:
Escape from Alcatraz

Safety:

Hospitality:

Cleanliness:

Party index:

Other nice features included trippy murals and a nice back garden
with picnic tables covered by umbrellas.

However, the hostel felt a bit sterile—no party action at all. And
while it's technically located in the fun Prenzlauer Berg 'hood, there's
actually little to do in the surrounding area either. You're a little bit
marooned. (No wonder they call it Alcatraz! Now we get it.) That
means you've got to use public transit and get away from here to have
any fun, then get back later.

The consensus among our pals was this, then: The hostel itself is just fine. Better than fine. Management seems to be doing a good job, and they've earned our thumbs-up (for now). Unfortunately, Berlin is such a fantastic city that you need to be in the action to sample and enjoy it, and that simply isn't possible at this location. So we can't recommend you stay.

how to get there:

By bus or train: Take U-Bahn line U2 toward Pankow to Eberswalder-strasse Station. Exit station to Allee and continue to hostel on left at number 133a.
By car: Contact hostel for directions.

backpacker mitte hostel
Chausseestrasse 102, 10115 Berlin
Phone: 030–2839–0965

Fax: 030–2839–0955
E-mail: info@backpacker.de
Web site: www.backpacker.de
Rates: €13–€30 (about $16–$37 US) per person; doubles €46–€56 (about $57–$70 US)
Credit cards: Yes
Beds: 60
Private/family rooms: Yes
Kitchen available: Yes
Season: Open year-round
Office hours: 7:00 A.M.–10:00 P.M.
Affiliation: None
Extras: Bike rentals, laundry, tours, Internet access, linens ($), television

Located in Mitte
This superfriendly, arty place gets big points for being a hoppin' hangout in the heart of the Mitte neighborhood and all its pleasures. The character isn't so much Berlin, however, as a get-together of dudes and dudettes from California and Jersey and Australia, places like that. You'll hear lots of sentences beginning with grating constructions like "Like, you know, it was, like, so, like cool, when we, like, threw up on the bartender."

If that sets your heart racing with joy, by all means head for this place. If it doesn't, enjoy the rooms at night, but spare yourself the lame conversations.

Okay, okay, we'll talk about the hostel instead of the hostellers. We noted several different kinds of decor in the rooms, which are surprisingly fancy and decorated in a typical Mitte-90s design (you'll have to see it to see what we mean; for example, the color orange is prevalent, and one room has an underwater theme). Other rooms are a little more sedate, with flowery motifs, but all are a welcome change from the depressing or institutional

Best bet for a bite:
Humboldt University Mensa

What hostellers say:
"Like, you know . . ."

Gestalt:
Mitte you there

Safety: 🚩

Hospitality: 🚩

Cleanliness: 🚩🚩

Party index: 🎉🎉🎉🎉

walls of your usual hostel. This one almost feels homey. The dorms contain two to six beds each. (One big room way up on the top floor, euphemistically called "the Penthouse," has a lot more beds; avoid it if you can.) Sheets do cost extra, but there's a laundry on the premises. They offer all the usual services, too, renting bicycles and even giving advice on work and work visas and stuff like that. All in all, this is a very hosteller-friendly sort of place—and staff are fluently English-speaking and friendly, too, which really helps.

The self-serve kitchen, unusual for a Berlin hostel, is handy and extremely well equipped—especially since there's a market just around the corner for groceries in case you want to whip up a creative feast. If you abhor the thought of cooking, though, the hostel has an arrangement with a Turkish/Italian restaurant downstairs that offers significant discounts on meals to its guests. The restaurant also serves breakfast for a few bucks.

Wanna see the city with a bunch of other hostellers? No problem. The hostel has also made an arrangement with a tour company, Berlin Walks; you can meet tour guides at the reception desk for a walk around town. (Yes, it costs money.) Ask at reception for more details. Future plans include a cool backyard where you can chill and grill to your heart's content. And if you're tripping through Berlin during November through February, you'll be rewarded with an ample discount off the cost of your bed. If you're part of a foursome or more, one of you may receive a free night. Unfortunately, those discounts don't carry over into the peak season. And tack on €2.50 per person for sheets, if you don't have any.

As we've said, there is really nothing special about the atmosphere here; you'll likely spend a lot of your free time hanging around drinking beer with Australians. Fun, we suppose, but you're here to see Berlin—and this place is very near the center of Berlin's active, almost crazed nightlife. The nighttime action in Mitte is intense, as it has been since the days of playwright Bertolt Brecht and the cabaret scene of the 1920s. Think Liza Minnelli belting "Life is a ca-bah-ray old chum" in pseudo-S&M gear—except with more piercings, tattoos, and multicolored hair—and you've more or less got the picture.

how to get there:

By bus: Contact hostel for transit details.
By car: Contact hostel for directions.
By train: From Zoo Station, take U-Bahn line U6 to Zinnowitzer Strasse stop; walk to hostel.

---

backpacker's paradise
Ziekowstrasse 161, Berlin
Phone: 030–433–8640

E-mail: backpackersparadise@web.de
Rates: €8–€9 (about $10–$11 US) per person
Credit cards: No
Beds: 260
Private/family rooms: No
Kitchen available: No
Season: June 15–September 2
Office hours: Twenty-four hours
Affiliation: None
Extras: Laundry, breakfast ($), bonfires, kitchen, lockers, Internet access, bike rentals

Located in the Outer Districts
Note: Must be under age twenty-seven to stay (flexible).

This is incredibly far from the interesting parts of Berlin you've come to see—it's more than an hour by public transportation from the city center. And get one thing straight: The place consists mainly of a tent. Yeah, a tent. Germany's so nutty these days that it's not even the only tent in the country, either—there's a tent hostel in Munich, too, more famous and probably a better overall place. But we digress.

Before you show up salivating, get another thing straight. You don't come here for great beds, not at all. In fact, a "bed" here could mean anything from a pad under the tent to a cot—but it will be extremely simple, no matter what. How do you think they manage to charge so little? (This is by *far* the cheapest place in town.) They manage because you're not getting much. Take maximum advantage of the campfires.

Best bet for a bite:
Penny Markt

Insiders' tip:
Zitty for
entertainment info

What hostellers say:
"Duuuuude, got a light?"

Gestalt:
Tent pole

Safety:

Hospitality:

Cleanliness:

Party index:

If you can get past that flaw and sleep twisted like a pretzel, however, the laid-back staffers do offer two key services in the morning: They lay out a breakfast buffet that's dirt cheap, and they also run a laundry. The age limit mentioned above probably will be waived if you try to get in. Does that give you some idea of what this place is about? It's about the vibe, daddy-o, and restrictions just get in the way. So away with 'em.

If you're short on cash and show up in summer, this is easily your best bed—er, tent—in town. Just remember that, as we've warned you previously, it's quite a ways from the action; a lengthy train ride, and *then* a bus ride, is required just to get here.

how to get there:

By bus or train: From train station take S-Bahn line S25 or U-Bahn line U6 to Alt-Tegel Station, then change to #222 or N22 bus and continue to Titusweg stop; walk to hostel.
By car: Contact hostel for directions.

baxpax hostel
Skalitzer Strasse 104, 10997 Berlin-Kreuzberg
Phone: 030–695–18322

Fax: 030–695–18372
E-mail: info@baxpax.de
Web site: www.baxpax.de
Rates: €12–€30 (about $15–$37 US) per person; doubles €44–€46 (about $55–$57 US)

Credit cards: No
Beds: 65
Private/family rooms: None
Kitchen available: Yes
Season: Open year-round
Office hours: Twenty-four hours
Affiliation: None
Extras: Bike rentals, tours, Internet, pool table, movie theater, sheets ($)

Located in Friedrichshain/Kreuzberg

BaxPax is the second hostel from the folks who brought you the
Backpacker Mitte (see page 148).

The building is an old factory that once produced men's bowler
hats. Keying into the hip Oranienstrasse neighborhood, it caters to
hostellers who need little privacy; there are no private rooms here at all. Rooms contain between four and ten beds—*real* beds, not bunks. Bathroom facilities are shared and rooms are coed, although there is also one dorm just for women, and the quality of the showers leaves something to be desired.

Although it's located in a highly trafficked area, the sleeping rooms face the back of the building, providing some quiet. The hostel sets aside a place behind the desk for backpacks and other luggage—we'd rather see lockers—and there's a safety box for smaller valuables like passports and nose rings. You'll have to shell out extra dough for sheets and towels, though. The public phone here only takes change, no phone cards. Sheesh! Staff will sell you various transport tickets, including long-distance bus tickets for one of the new intra-Europe coach companies.

Best bet for a bite:
Kaiser's Markt

Insiders' tip:
See last paragraph

What hostellers say:
"Good new place."

Gestalt:
Pax a punch

Safety:

Hospitality:

Cleanliness:

Party index:

The place is quite roomy—it was a factory, after all—and has
plenty of common areas. Management claims you can drive a car
(maybe a Trabi) through the extra-wide hallways, though we're not
saying you should actually try.

For food, the Kottbusser Tor area is just a subway stop away. This neighborhood is populated by Turkish immigrants, and there are good and cheap markets supplying fresh fruits and veggies, which is great since there is a well-equipped kitchen to play chef in. German supermarkets also abound. If you're into other people's unwanted junk, flea markets here should keep you occupied. During the summer there's a pool at Görlitzer park to dunk your toes in.

how to get there:

By bus: Contact hostel for transit details.
By car: Contact hostel for directions.
By train: From Zoo Station, take U-Bahn line U2 one stop to Wittenberg Platz, then change to U1 and continue to Görlitzer Bahnhof. Hostel is 10 yards from station.

---

jugendherberge berlin
(berlin international youth hostel)
Kluckstrasse 3, 10785 Berlin
Phone: 030–26110–97

Fax: 030–26503–83
E-mail: jh-berlin@jugendherberge.de
Rates: €21 (about $26 US) per HI member
Credit cards: No
Beds: 354
Private/family rooms: Yes
Kitchen available: No
Season: Open year-round
Office hours: Twenty-four hours
Curfew: 3:00 A.M.
Affiliation: DJH-HI
Regional office: Berlin-Brandenburg
Extras: Cafeteria ($), Internet access, computer room, table tennis, VCR, TV room, parking, breakfast, information desk, meeting rooms, garden, luggage storage

---

Located in Schöneberg
Note: Must be HI member to stay.

Huge, German, and perfect in every way—except in terms of being offbeat, or humorous—this place is the DJH's showpiece, a contemporary design that warehouses you without making you feel that way. Too much.

Best bet for a bite:
Merz Schöneberger

Insiders' tip:
Market on Wednesday to Saturday mornings

What hostellers say:
"Kinda sterile."

Gestalt:
Warehouse district

Safety:

Hospitality:

Cleanliness:

Party index:

It's a big, bland building with a somewhat interesting postmodern sculpture on the front lawn. Inside, they've got more than 300 beds in a tremendous variety of shapes and sizes. Breakfast is included in the price, no matter what sort of room you get, and the auxiliary services they offer are incredible. Try Internet access, a computer workroom, a game room with table tennis, meeting rooms, and meals, for starters. Three lounges—including one with a television—provide areas for hanging out. Everything is cleaner than clean, for once.

But the draw here is that it's in the Schöneberg neighborhood, known as Berlin's quiet place to hang in a cafe without the crush of city noise and traffic. (It's also the center of gay Berlin, but that's another story.) This hostel is very central, close to both the Potsdamer Platz and the world-famous Brandenburg Gate, where Berliners celebrated—and continue to celebrate—the smashing of the Wall.

While in the area, you might head over to the Topographie des Terrors museum for a brutal history lesson of war-crimes exhibits. Appropriately (and chillingly) enough, it's on the same spot where the Gestapo and SS ran their operations for a dozen years, up to and through World War II. Find it by walking over (or taking the S-Bahn) to Anhalter Bahnhof Station.

Note: Call ahead if you will arrive at the hostel after 6:00 P.M. or you might not be able to check in.

how to get there:

By bus: Take #129 bus to Gedenkstätte.

By car: Take autobahn to Berlin, exiting at signs for Innsbrucker Platz; turn left at Hauptstrasse and continue to Potsdamer Strasse. Make a left onto Lützowstrasse, then make a right onto Kluckstrasse and continue to hostel.

By train: From Zoo Station, take U-Bahn line U2 toward Vinetastrasse to Wittenbergplatz stop, then take U-Bahn line U1 or U15 to Kurfürstenstrasse Station. Walk ¼ mile up Potsdamer Strasse; make a left onto Lützowstrasse, then make a right onto Kluckstrasse and continue to hostel.

circus hostel

Weinbergsweg 1a, 10119 Berlin
Phone: 030–2839–1433

Fax: 030–2839–1484
E-mail: info@circus-berlin.de
Web site: www.circus-berlin.de
Rates: €17–€46 (about $21–$58 US) per person; doubles €50–€62 (about $63–$78 US)
Credit cards: No
Beds: 180
Private/family rooms: Yes
Kitchen available: No
Season: Open year-round
Office hours: Twenty-four hours
Affiliation: None
Extras: Internet access, bar, travel office, breakfast, restaurants ($), TV room, laundry, museum tickets, city tours

Located in Mitte

Close to the action in the historic center of Berlin, this hostel (which was formerly a trading house) serves up terrifically clean and stylish rooms at surprisingly low prices. There's a laid-back atmosphere, happy and flexible staff, lack of rules, even Internet access. Not bad, not bad at all. The spiffy, modern facility began life as an annex to the original Circus building at the Rosenthaler Platz Station. Great for families and couples. It's also got eleven hotel-style apartment suites (which are more expensive), a bar, and a DJ. Oddly, you get to the rooms by elevator—no stairs—but no matter.

Dorms consist of single, double, triple, quad, five-bedded, and six-bedded rooms. Of the seven double rooms, four have a standard double bed and three have two single beds, which can be

Best bet for a bite:
Trattoria

Insiders' tip:
Oranienburger
Strasse for Indian

What hostellers say:
"I like it!"

Gestalt:
Big top

Safety:

Hospitality:

Cleanliness:

Party index:

pushed together to simulate a double. Duvets cover the beds. Only the few apartments—doubles and quads—have their own kitchens and bathrooms; other showers and bathrooms are located in hallways, and there are no communal kitchens besides those in the apartments. Luckily, supermarkets and cheap, good restaurants abound in the surrounding area.

The services here are fantastic, all administered by cool staff. They include three Internet terminals; a   bar; a booking service selling cut-rate train, bus, and museum tickets; and free breakfast (provided by one of the restaurants) with your bunk—it includes rolls, salami, croissants, and hot beverages. They've also got bicycles for rent and washers and dryers for the grungy hosteller. The television lounge gets international satellite TV, and they lay out newspapers for you to read as well. You can even book an onward bed at certain other European hostels.

Like we said, not bad at all. Put this one on your short list of places to stay.

how to get there:

By bus: Contact hostel for transit details.
By car: Contact hostel for directions.
By train: Take U8 Subway line to Rosenthaler Platz Station. Hostel is yellow building on corner.

key to icons

Attractive natural setting	Comfortable beds	Visual arts at hostel or nearby
Ecologically aware hostel	A particularly good value	Music at hostel or nearby
Superior kitchen facilities or cafe	Wheelchair-accessible	Great hostel for skiers
Offbeat or eccentric place	Good for business travelers	Bar or pub at hostel or nearby
Superior bathroom facilities	Especially well suited for families	Editors' Choice: Among our very favorite hostels
Romantic private rooms	Good for active travelers	

clubhouse hostel

Kalkscheunenstrasse 4–5, 10117 Berlin
Phone: 030–2809–7979

Fax: 030–2809–7977
E-mail: info@clubhouse-berlin.de
Web site: www.clubhouse-berlin.de
Rates: €13–€19 (about $16–$24 US) per person; doubles €46
(about $58 US)
Credit cards: No
Beds: 58
Private/family rooms: Yes
Kitchen available: No
Season: Open year-round
Office hours: Twenty-four hours
Affiliation: None
Extras: Breakfast, Internet access, bar

Located in Mitte

This place is fairly standard, but the superior location—close to a
hopping area with a serious nightlife factor—and friendly staff (some
of them Aussies when we stopped by) push it into the "thumbs-up"
category. Even better, school groups are not accepted here.

The dorms are colorfully painted and clean, with an IKEA feeling.
(That's a Swedish design firm heavy on blond woods and minimalist,
black and steel-gray fixtures.)
These rooms are divided into
triples, doubles, and singles
with no bunks. Sleep sacks
are not allowed, so you'll have
to fork over about two bucks
for sheets; at least this is a fee
you only have to pay once
during the course of your stay.
They have no kitchen and don't
offer the services of some of
the city's other backpacker-
style joints. But there is something like a lounge, where you
can hang around on fluffy
sofas and drink beer, coffee,
tea, or juices. Internet access

Best bet for a bite:
Brooklyn (American food)

Insiders' tip:
Cafe Silberstein bar

What hostellers say:
"Pretty rad."

Gestalt:
Club bed

Safety:

Hospitality:

Cleanliness:

Party index:

is available; and late sleepers will rejoice over the gracious noon checkout time. The all-you-can-eat (and drink) breakfast is yet another positive.

Remember that this place books up very early, however. Staff advise making a firm booking two to three *weeks* in advance between April and October if you want a double room, a week in advance during that time for dorms.

Why so popular? It's near one of the best parts of Mitte, that's why—right in the heart of Berlin's nightly party. There are so many sights, bars, and restaurants here you're going to be tripping over yourself. Staff told us that the hottest techno club in Berlin is steps away from the hostel and that Oranienburger Strasse and Tor are notorious for their shiny, happy club scene. Guests come from every corner of the globe to be part of it; during high season you'll encounter Americans, Brits, Japanese, Koreans, and, of course, Europeans. (In January and February, for some reason, the hostel is inundated with folks from South America living it up during their school breaks.) Staff are multilingual, obviously.

This hostel goes out of its way to provide local tours given by the owner, who worked in Berlin for the British Embassy when the city was still divided and can give hostellers an in-depth overview of the city's complicated political history. He illuminates even the drabbest, most insignificant-looking building (which other people would simply ignore). The tour lasts five hours, so wear those comfy walking shoes. If you'd rather see the city on your own schedule, the hostel staff sells transit passes. They can also make reservations and book round-Europe bus tickets for you.

how to get there:

By bus: Contact hostel for transit details.
By car: Contact hostel for directions.
By train: Take S-Bahn line S1 or S25 to Oranienburger Strasse stop or U-Bahn line U6 to the Oranienburger Tor stop; walk to hostel.

die fabrik

Schlesische Strasse 18, 10997 Berlin
Phone: 030–611–7116 or 030–617–5104

Fax: 030–618–2974
E-mail: info@diefabrik.com

Web site: www.diefabrik.com
Rates: €18–€38 (about $23–$47 US) per person; doubles €46–€72 (about $58–$90 US)
Credit cards: No
Beds: 120
Private/family rooms: Yes
Kitchen available: No
Season: Open year-round
Office hours: Twenty-four hours
Affiliation: None
Extras: Bike rentals, breakfast ($), meals ($)

Located in Kreuzberg

Once an industrial building, this hostel has been well renovated into a very good hostel-cum-bed-and-breakfast near the river that divides Berlin in half.

It's cheapest in the cavernous fifteen-bed bunkroom at the bottom, also known in Europe as a "sleep-in," but it's actually not too bad. You'll get more exercise and pay more for the privacy of smaller quad, triple, double, and single rooms as you ascend. All rooms are roomy and airy with plenty of windows. They rent bicycles, offer breakfast—though you've gotta pay extra for that—and serve meals in a cafe.

The location, in too-hip-to-be-true Kreuzberg, is ideal. This is the neighborhood to hit for the best Turkish food, not to mention oodles of punkers, longhairs, and other not-conforming-to-society folk.

Best bet for a bite:
Kleine Markthalle for chicken

Insiders' tip:
Exercise caution after dark

What hostellers say:
"Lotsa fun."

Gestalt:
Fabrik of society

Safety:

Hospitality:

Cleanliness:

Party index:

how to get there:

By bus: Take #265 or N65 bus to Taborstrasse stop; walk to hostel.
By car: Contact hostel for directions.
By train: From Zoo Station, take U-Bahn line U1 or U15 to Schlesisches Tor stop; walk to hostel.

eastener hostel

Novalisstrasse 14, 10115 Berlin
Phone: 0175–11–23–515

E-mail: contact@eastener-hostel.de
Web site: www.eastener-hostel.de
Rates: €12–€35 (about $16–$44) per person; doubles €36–€60 (about $45–$75 US)
Credit cards: No
Beds: 17
Private/family rooms: Yes
Kitchen available: Yes
Season: Open year-round
Office hours: 10:00 A.M.–noon and 6:00–9:00 P.M.
Affiliation: None

Located in Mitte

A tiny hostel in a stone apartment building near many of the coolest things in East Berlin, the Eastener consists of a grand total of seventeen beds tucked into five rooms; though some of these rooms are a bit narrow, all in all this place is immaculately clean and faultlessly friendly. The place isn't big enough to offer tons of amenities, so it makes up for it with the little things: newspapers, tea, good bunks, a partial kitchen, and free walking tours (in English!) that depart right from the front door each morning. All rooms have sinks, too.

Best bet for a bite:
Cafe across the way

What hostellers say:
"Perfect!"

Gestalt:
Star in the East

Safety:

Hospitality:

Cleanliness:

Party index:

The location is aces, too, a few minutes' walk from hip and hoppin' Oranienburger Strasse and about twenty to thirty minutes' walk from the Brandenburg Gate and Checkpoint Charlie.

The owner deserves kudos for his no-smoking policy (the lack of which has ruined many a cashmere sweater in, say, a hostel in Paris). All things considered, this is one of your best picks in the city—*if* you can score a bed.

how to get there:

By car: Contact hostel for directions.
By bus: Contact hostel for transit details.

By train: From Zoo Station, take any S-Bahn on track 5 to Friedrichstrasse. Change to U6 (toward Alt-Tegel) and continue one stop to Oranienburger Tor station. Exit station in same direction as the departing train, then walk 100 yards (passing Oranienburger Strasse); take second right onto Torstrasse, continue 100 yards, then make first left onto Novalisstrasse.

From Ostbahnhof, take any S-Bahn four stops to Friedrichstrasse. Change to U6 (toward Alt-Tegel) and continue one stop to Oranienburger Tor station. Follow directions above.

By plane: From airport, take #128 bus to Kurt-Schumacher-Platz U-Bahn station, then take U6 line to Oranienburger Tor. Exit station in same direction as the departing train, then walk 100 yards (passing Oranienburger Strasse); take second right onto Torstrasse, continue 100 yards, then make first left onto Novalisstrasse.

jugendherberge berlin
"ernst reuter" (ernst reuter
berlin hostel)

Hermsdorfer Damm 48–50, 13467 Berlin
Phone: 030–404–1610

Fax: 030–404–5972
E-mail: jh-ernst-reuter@jugendherberge.de
Rates: €17 (about $21 US) per HI member
Credit cards: No
Beds: 111
Private/family rooms: Yes
Kitchen available: No
Season: Closed December 6–January 6
Office hours: Twenty-four hours
Curfew: 1:00 A.M.
Affiliation: DJH-HI
Regional office: Berlin-Brandenburg
Extras: TV, table tennis, foosball, breakfast, meals ($), laundry, lockers, luggage storage, information desk

Located in Outer Districts
Note: Must be HI member to stay.

This hostel is located in the suburbs of Berlin, with excellent connections into the city center by public transport (night and day), despite the long haul out here. If everything else is full, it's not a bad choice.

The series of connected buildings here are made of stone, more than forty years old, and nicely decorated and painted. A great green lawn, lush overhanging trees, and picnic tables out front dress up the outside, sure, but it's also some 9 miles out of town.

Some rooms and sections are newer and better lit than others. The dorms inside are mostly five- or six-bedded affairs (sixteen of those); there are four family rooms as well. Bathrooms and showers are in the hallways; in some cases you have to walk downstairs a floor to use 'em. Ugh!

Best bet for a bite:
U-Bahn for grub

Insiders' tip:
Tip magazine for listings

What hostellers say:
"Okay."

Gestalt:
Mellow yellow

Safety:

Hospitality:

Cleanliness:

Party index:

Anyway, they have plenty of hosteller services to distract you, including Internet access, a guest laundry, a television lounge for couch potatoes, a game room with two table tennis tables, and an information desk dispensing crucial info about the city. They serve a big breakfast buffet throughout the day, then at night often serve a hot dinner for about four bucks. (There's no kitchen for hostellers to cook in.)

Jogging trails and woods surround the hostel, yet you can buy food just a couple hundred yards away when hunger pangs strike. You can also hit the nearby Alt-Tegel subway station's shops for other vital goods, often at lower prices than in the city. And here's one final tip: Rather than endure the complicated transit route to get into town, inquire about taking the local sightseeing boat from here into central Berlin; it leaves from the Tegel Greenwichpromenade. Neat.

Note: Call ahead if arriving after 6:00 P.M.

how to get there:

By bus: From Zoo Station, take U-Bahn line U9 to Leopoldplatz stop, then change to U-Bahn line U6 and continue to Alt-Tegel stop; change to #125 bus and continue to Jugendherberge (hostel) stop.

By car: From the north take Highway 111 to Berliner Ring, exiting at signs for Hermsdorfer Damm. From the south take Highway 115 and Highway 111 to Stadtring Nord, exiting at signs for Hermsdorfer Damm.

By train: From Zoo Station take U-Bahn line U9 to Leopoldplatz stop, then change to U-Bahn line U6 and continue to Alt-Tegel stop; change to #125 bus and continue to Jugendherberge (hostel) stop. From Ost

Station take S-Bahn train to Friedrichstrasse stop, then change to U-Bahn line U6 or S-Bahn line S25 and continue to Tegel Station.

generator berlin
Storkower Strasse 160, 10407 Berlin
Phone number: 030–417–2400

Fax: 030–417–24080
E-mail: reservations@generatorhostels.com
Web site: www.generatorhostels.com
Rates: €10–€30 (about $12–$37 US)
Credit cards: Yes
Beds: 854
Private/family rooms: Yes
Kitchen available: No
Season: Open year-round
Office hours: Twenty-four hours
Affiliation: None
Extras: Bar, TV room, breakfast, lockers, laundry, shop, meals, Internet access, courtyard, foosball, walking tours

Located in Friedrichshain

Modeled after the huge and strange Generator Hostel in London, this Generator may not generate quite the same buzz; that's partly because it's stuck way out by a suburban train station, partly because it attracts a school-group type crowd, and partly because we still don't get the overall sci-fi strangeness of the decor. Still, this place is good and improving. Too bad the location sucks.

Anyhoo, there are tons of beds—more than 850, at last count—divided into many, many rooms of fourteen, eight, seven, six, five, four, three, and two beds; there are also some single rooms. Only the singles, doubles, and triples can potentially have their own private bathrooms, though obviously you pay more for that privilege. All are clean.

Kudos for the other amenities, too, such as a bar/beer garden (that means it's outdoors), a television room with satellite TV, an included free breakfast, lockers in each dorm, a small laundry room, meals, and the all-important Internet access. A small free breakfast is fine, and you can pay a bit more for a heartier one. We liked the always-open, fun bar and the opportunity to take a walking tour of the city.

There's also a game room and a small shop dealing in books, essential supplies, and the like. (The food's not much good here, though; try to pack some in from a store near the station.)

Only problem is, it all feels a bit clinical. This remote nabe just doesn't have it happening, and despite the beer garden action—your best bet for fun here—you might as well have checked into a barracks for the size. Anyway, one good thing is this: The presence of a nearby station means you can potentially party late-night in the city and whisk back via S-Bahn anytime. However, check on schedules at the desk before you foray out. And take care late at night in East Berlin.

What hostellers say:
"Um . . . ."

Gestalt:
Generation Z

Safety: 🏚

Hospitality: 🏚

Cleanliness: 🏚

Party index: 🎉🎉

how to get there:

By bus: Contact hostel for transit route.

By car: **From west,** take A2 or A9 or A10 (Berliner Ring) going toward Frankfurt; continue to Dreieck Nuthetal, join A115, continue toward Berlin Zentrum to Dreieck Funkturm. Merge onto A100 going toward Hamburg. Take first turnoff (Kaiserdamm) and then B2/5 going toward Zentrum and Unter den Linden. Continue 4 miles to Alexanderplatz; cross under train overpass and take second left onto Mollstrasse, which becomes Landsberger Allee, for 2 miles. Hostel is on left. **From northwest,** take A24 to A10 (Berliner Ring) going toward Frankfurt, then merge onto A114 at Dreieck Pankow, which becomes B109; continue 1 mile, turn left onto B96a, then make a left again onto Landsberger Allee. Continue to hostel on left. **From northeast,** take A11 to A10 (Berliner Ring) going toward Hamburg, then merge onto A114 at Dreieck Pankow, which becomes B109; continue 1 mile, turn left onto B96a, then make a left again onto Landsberger Allee. Continue to hostel on left. **From east or southeast,** take A113 or follow A14 to A113; continue to end of A113, then continue along B96a into Friedrichshain. Turn left into Warschauer Strasse and continue along Petersburger Strasse; turn left into Landsberger Allee, and continue to hostel on left.

By train: From Zoo Station or Ostbahnhof, take S-Bahn eastbound to Ostkreuz; change to Ring S-Bahn train northbound and continue to Landsberger Allee. Hostel is big blue-and-white structure beside station; walk up steps toward Syringenstrasse, turn right after wire fence, and enter hostel at right.

freiraum gästehaus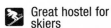
(guest house hostel)

Wiener Strasse 14, 10999 Berlin
Phone: 030–618–2008

Fax: 030–618–2006
E-mail: info@freiraum-berlin.com
Web site: www.freiraum-berlin.com
Rates: €20 (about $25 US) per person; doubles €30–€47
(about $36–$59 US)
Credit cards: Yes
Beds: 35
Private/family rooms: Yes
Kitchen available: No
Season: Open year-round
Office hours: Twenty-four hours
Affiliation: None
Extras: Apartments, pool access nearby

Located in Kreuzberg

This small, clean guest house attracts travelers of all stripes, but its lack of a common room/hangout area deters backpacker types from flocking here to meet like-minded others. It's a fairly quiet hostel that draws an older crowd who like to blend with locals, soak up the sights on their own terms—and save money in the process.

key to icons

 Attractive natural setting

 Comfortable beds

 Visual arts at hostel or nearby

 Ecologically aware hostel

 A particularly good value

 Music at hostel or nearby

 Superior kitchen facilities or cafe

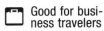 Wheelchair-accessible

 Great hostel for skiers

 Offbeat or eccentric place

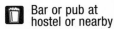 Good for business travelers

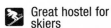 Bar or pub at hostel or nearby

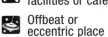 Superior bath-room facilities

 Especially well suited for families

 Editors' Choice: Among our very favorite hostels

 Romantic private rooms

 Good for active travelers

The brick-walled, ivy-covered joint started out as a mere bed-without-the-breakfast agency matching people in need of accommodations with beds. After operating the agency for seven years, the manager/owner decided that he'd rather establish an actual hostel. (He still sets folks up with beds through his agency if the guest house is full.)

Best bet for a bite:
Cafe Jolesch

Insiders' tip:
Viktoriapark for peace and quiet

What hostellers say:
"Hip 'n happening."

Gestalt:
Best guest house

Safety:

Hospitality:

Cleanliness:

Party index:

Rooms come in combinations of singles, doubles, triples, and one six-bedded dorm room. Note that you've got to rent the entire bunkroom; bring a couple pals and your rate plunges to as little as €13 (about $16 US) a night. There are also three apartments that each have a small kitchen and their own bathroom. All other hostellers must share bathrooms with their fellow guests.

You're close to green and leafy Görlitzer Park, which has an indoor pool for splashing in, as well as Spreewald Platz—always good for a cheap nosh. Oranienstrasse is a stone's throw away, too, and that's where you want to go to check out the techno clubs. Night buses (those with an "N" in the number) whisk you to and from the hostel all night long, as there's no curfew to worry about.

Ivos, the friendly manager, also runs a helpful Web page (www.net4 berlin.com) with English links to help you figure out the complicated and trendy Berlin*szene*. He's from East Berlin and can educate you on how the city has changed, then direct you to cafes and bars. One of his faves is the Anker Klause, just a few minutes' walk from the hostel.

how to get there:

By bus: Contact hostel for transit details.
By car: Contact hostel for directions.
By train: From Zoo Station, take U-Bahn line U1, U12, or U15 to Görlitzer Bahnof stop; walk to hostel.

hotel transit hostel

Hagelberger Strasse 53–54, 10965 Berlin
Phone: 030–789–0470

Fax: 030–789–04777

E-mail: welcome@hotel-transit.de
Web site: www.hotel-transit.de
Rates: €21–€62 (about $26–$75 US) per person; doubles €72 (about $90 US)
Credit cards: Yes
Beds: 290
Private/family rooms: Yes
Kitchen available: No
Season: Open year-round
Office hours: Twenty-four hours
Affiliation: None
Extras: TV room, bar, breakfast, courtyard

Located in Kreuzberg

This hotel doubles as a hostel, and it offers considerable goodies—a nice courtyard, roomy dorms, a good location, and friendly, English-speaking staff. You might forgive the slightly clinical feel and lack of common socializing, because it's a clean and safe place to rest.

The cool, cool furnishings in the loft-style dorms and doubles give you a happy feeling right away. Attempt to watch television in the room shared with the hoppin' bar, or hang in the courtyard; we don't care. Sleep in if you want, 'cause there's no lockout and a free breakfast buffet included with your bunk. Be warned, though, that this place attracts plenty of school groups. When we checked the place out on a Monday night (a night not known for being raucous), the bar was teeming with garrulous kids, making it apparent that the hostel succeeds at bringing folk together. Staff assure us that was a fluke . . . but you'll have to go yourself to find out for sure.

Best bet for a bite:
Chandra Kumari (Sri Lankan)

Insiders' tip:
Bike rentals nearby

What hostellers say:
"More fun that I thought possible."

Gestalt:
Transition abroad

Safety:

Hospitality:

Cleanliness:

Party index:

The rooms have no more than six beds each, assuring a (relative) modicum of privacy—much appreciated when you've done time in the notorious *mehrbettzimmer* (dormitories, literally "many-bedded room") in lots of other hostels. If you and your traveling companion require even more privacy, there are doubles at a slight extra cost, still well within price reach for the budget hosteller.

Breakfast is offered at no extra cost—a buffet that includes cheese, sausage, bread, cereal, and choice of coffee, tea, or hot chocolate. You can eat as much as you want, so you might make it through till dinner if you're lucky. As an additional service, the hostel works with two local tour companies to help you understand the intricate political and cultural history of this sprawling metropolis. Note that these tours do cost extra.

This a great neighborhood, as we've said before, and—as befits it—there's a great travel store called Outdoor on Bergmannstrasse. Head there to stock up on guidebooks and maps, some of them actually in English. For some nice green space in which to toss around a Frisbee, head to nearby Viktoria Park.

An equally (or perhaps even increasingly) cool annex called the Transit Loft opened in 2001 in a renovated factory in the hip Prenzlauer Berg neighborhood. Sporting forty-seven rooms of one to five beds each, it's slightly more expensive than the Kreuzberg location if you get a private room; dorms cost the same in both locations.

how to get there:

By bus: Contact hostel for transit details.
By car: Contact hostel for directions.
By train: From train station take U-Bahn line U6 or U7 to Mehringdamm stop; walk to hostel.

lette 'm sleep hostel
Lettestrasse 7, 10437 Berlin
Phone: 030–4473–3623

Fax: 030–4473–3625
E-mail: info@backpackers.de
Web site: www.backpackers.de
Rates: €17–€26 (about $21–$31 US) per person; doubles €49–€68 (about $61–$85 US)
Credit cards: Yes
Beds: 45
Private/family rooms: Yes
Kitchen available: Yes
Season: Open year-round
Office hours: Twenty-four hours
Affiliation: None

Extras: Free Internet access, TV, information desk, garden, snacks

---

Located in Prenzlauer Berg

This place is pretty good for the money. The clean-enough dorms are three- to seven-bedded. Each room has only a sink, not a bathroom, but there are plenty of other extras—a television lounge, Internet access for checking that e-mail, a hosteller kitchen, and a beer-gardeny backyard. Some of the double rooms have kitchens, a great bonus, but there's also a main kitchen for everybody to use. Staff are very helpful and friendly, speak multiple languages, and will point you toward the best sights, bars, and discount transit deals. We've heard increasing complaints about local residents and long-term hostellers contaminating the place's happy atmosphere, though, so be alert.

There are tons of rockin' clubs, pubs, and cafes nearby, so you can't possibly get bored here. Ignore the post-industrial look of the area and the half-finished buildings, and head out for a beer or a coffee. There's also a convenient Spar market close at hand. Note that although it's usually a quiet, safe neighborhood, a staffer confided a theft of the hostel TV. That incident appears to have been just an isolated blip on an otherwise calm radar screen, but keep an eye on your stuff anyway. By the way, if you want to be hip and with it, refer to the 'hood as "Prenzle Berg," just like the locals do.

Best bet for a bite:
Offenbach Stuben

Insiders' tip:
Nosthalgia bar for good
vodka

What hostellers say:
"But I don't *wanna* sleep."

Gestalt:
Prenz charming

Safety:

Hospitality:

Cleanliness:

Party index:

This hostel is extremely popular in July and August, so much so that reservations are not accepted. Staff advise that you either call and be placed on a rather lengthy waiting list or just stay the night elsewhere and show up at the hostel around midday after most folk have checked out.

how to get there:

By bus: Contact hostel for transit details.

By car: Contact hostel for directions.

By train: Take U-Bahn line U2 to Eberswalder Strasse stop, then walk down Danziger Strasse 1 block to Lychener Strasse. Turn left and continue to Lettestrasse, then turn right and walk to hostel.

jugendgästehaus nordufer
(nordufer guest house hostel)
Nordufer Strasse 28, 13351 Berlin
Phone: 030–4519–9112

Fax: 030–452–4100
E-mail: Nordufer@t-online.de
Web site: www.jugendgaestehaus-nordufer.de
Rates: €19.90 (about $24 US) per person
Credit cards: No
Beds: 130
Private/family rooms: Yes
Kitchen available: No
Season: Open year-round
Office hours: 7:00 A.M.–5:00 P.M. (sometimes later)
Affiliation: None
Extras: Pool access ($), breakfast, meals ($)

Located in Outer Districts

Note: Must be under age twenty-seven to stay *unless* traveling as a family.

This place is definitely off the beaten track, outside the city central sightseeing zone—though actually very well equipped if you don't mind the commute.

Best bet for a bite:
Schleusenkrug Müller
(by the canal)

Insiders' tip:
#100 bus for cheap
sightseeing

What hostellers say:
"I feel so relaxed!"

Gestalt:
Pool party

Safety:

Hospitality:

Cleanliness:

Party index:

They've got everything from singles to doubles to larger dormitories. It's all quiet enough and well managed, and staff are relaxed enough to lay back on what rules there are here. Breakfast is included with your bed, by the way, and it's very good and plentiful. You can also pay a bit extra for access to a swimming pool next door, or head for the lake instead.

Of all the "Outer District" hostels in town, this one is the closest; it's just across the canal from Tiergarten. You won't find tons and tons of nightlife around here, but strap on your walking shoes and you'll find parks aplenty.

how to get there:

By bus: From Zoo Station, take U-Bahn line U9 to Leopoldplatz stop; change to line U6 and continue to Seestrasse stop, then take #126 bus to hostel.

By car: Contact hostel for directions.

By train: From Zoo Station take U-Bahn line U9 to Westhafen stop, then cross bridge and continue to Nordufer Strasse. Or take U-Bahn line U9 to Leopoldplatz stop; change to U6 line and continue to Seestrasse stop, then take #126 bus to hostel.

odyssee globetrotter hostel
Grünberger Strasse 23, 10243 Berlin
Phone: 030–2900–0081

Fax: 030–2900–3311
E-mail: odyssee@globetrotterhostel.de
Web site: www.globetrotterhostel.de
Rates: €10–€36 (about $13–$45 US); doubles €30–€54 (about $50–$73 US)
Credit cards: No
Beds: 82
Private/family rooms: Yes
Kitchen available: No
Season: Open year-round
Office hours: Twenty-four hours
Affiliation: None
Extras: Bar, lockers, breakfast ($), pool table, Internet access, foosball, meals ($)

Located in Friedrichshain

This is it: Berlin's most party-hearty hostel (and that's saying something in a town where almost every hostel must have a bar to survive). Even when you're not partying, you'll be socializing. It's fun, fun, fun, if not completely clean, clean, clean.

The rooms? They've got doubles, quads, six-bedded dorms, and eight-bedded ones, too; per usual, the cost of your bunk drops with each incremental drop in privacy. They've got lockers, a pool table, e-mail access, and the bar's open till *dawn.* (No, silly, there's no curfew here.) In fact, someone at the hostel told us that it never closes!

Overall, there's a young and funky vibe, great for twenty-one-year-olds and not too ideal for traveling families or older folks.

You can shoot some stick in the pool room and store stuff in lockers. Even the absence of a laundry is somewhat mitigated by the fact that there's one right around the corner—ask the staff for details.

Best bet for a bite:
Dachkamer

Insiders' tip:
Pentascop's a freaky bar

What hostellers say:
"Wilde."

Gestalt:
Space Odyssee

Safety:

Hospitality:

Cleanliness:

Party index:

The place is located in Friedrichshain, Berlin's drab-looking yet quickly developing nightspot-of-the-moment. It is actually starting to get a little expensive to live around here, which must seem incredible to the old-timers in the neighborhood.

how to get there:

By bus: From Ost Station take #147 or #250 bus to hostel.
By car: Contact hostel for directions.
By train: From Zoo Station take any S-Bahn train east to Warschauer Strasse stop, then walk north up Warschauer Strasse; turn left at Grünberger Strasse. Hostel is on right.

---

student hotel hubertusallee NR
Delbrückstrasse 24, Berlin
Phone: 030–891–9718

Fax: 030–892–8698
Rates: €30–€48 (about $36–$60 US) per person; doubles €44–€66 (about $55–$82 US)
Credit cards: No
Beds: Number varies
Private/family rooms: Yes
Kitchen available: No
Season: Year-round, but students only October to February
Office hours: Twenty-four hours
Affiliation: None
Extras: Breakfast

Located in Outer Districts

Situated a couple miles southwest of the city center, near a small lake, this one's hardly worth mentioning—it's neither easy to get to nor superattractive. You can only rent singles or entire doubles, triples, or quads—bring friends. And they charge you for sheets, besides.

On the other hand, let's give them credit for this: Every room in the joint has a bathroom and shower in it, and that's saying something. Consider it a good desperation pick if you happen to have a car (yeah, right). Otherwise it's probably best to cross it off your list.

Best bet for a bite:
U-Bahn stop

Insiders' tip:
Buy a transit pass

What hostellers say:
"Nice bathrooms."

Gestalt:
Shower power

Safety:

Hospitality:

Cleanliness:

Party index:

how to get there:

By bus: Take #119 or #129 bus to hostel, or contact hostel for transit details.
By car: Contact hostel for directions.
By train: Contact hostel for transit details.

sunflower hostel

Helsingforser Strasse 17, 10243 Berlin
Phone: 030–440–44250

Fax: 030–577–96550
E-mail: hostel@sunflower-hostel.de
Web site: www.sunflower-hostel.de
Rates: €10–€35 (about $12–$43 US) per person; doubles €38–€45 (about $47–$56 US)
Credit cards: Yes
Beds: 100
Private/family rooms: Yes
Kitchen available: No
Season: Open year-round
Office hours: Twenty-four hours
Affiliation: None
Extras: Breakfast ($), bar, Internet access, foosball

Located in Friedrichshain

This newish place out in the far reaches of East Berlin is getting excellent early buzz from happy hostellers.

They operate a coin-op laundry, serve cheap beer, and maintain a (pricey) Internet access terminal. Our guys say it's clean and well-run, though hardly the most rocking place in the world—the distant location could account for this. Bedding consists of one big dorm, plus a supply of double, triple, and quad rooms at slightly higher prices per person. Some rooms have balconies, and the kitchen is airy. But bathrooms could be better and you're stranded in Nowheresville.

Gestalt: Sunflower children

Safety: ▨

Hospitality: ▨

Cleanliness: ▨

Party index: ▨▨▨

how to get there:

By bus: Contact hostel for transit route.
By car: Contact hostel for directions.
By train: Take S-Bahn train to Warschauer Strasse Station and walk to hostel.

jugendgästehaus berlin ▨
"am wannsee" (berlin-wannsee guest house hostel)

Badeweg 1, 14129 Berlin
Phone: 030–803–2034

Fax: 030–803–5908
E-mail: jh-wannsee@jugendherberge.de
Rates: €21 (about $26 US) per HI member
Credit cards: No
Beds: 288
Private/family rooms: Yes
Kitchen available: No
Season: Open year-round
Office hours: Twenty-four hours
Curfew: 1:00 A.M.
Affiliation: DJH-HI

Regional office: Berlin-Brandenburg
Extras: Lake, disco, garden, table tennis, parking, laundry, TV room, luggage storage, volleyball, chess, pool table

Located in Outer Districts

Note: Must be HI member to stay.

To get here you make a very long trip out to what turns out to be a peaceful, sleepy neighborhood that comes with its own lake. That's correct: It's set right on Berlin's biggest lake.

It's a depressing building once you arrive, however, with an exceptionally plain post-industrial design even for a German hostel. Think a concrete structure with multicolored flags. On second thought, think "bomb shelter." A few bright splotches of paint here and there do help a bit. All seventy-two rooms here are four-bedded rooms, and they've decked the place out with everything modern you'd need. There's a disco of sorts, a game room containing a table tennis table, a television lounge, a luggage room, and a guest laundry. It's all adequate if a bit boring. Caution, however, before booking your bunk:

Best bet for a bite:
Better eat here

Insiders' tip:
Peacocks on Pfaueninsel

What hostellers say:
"Nice lake!"

Gestalt:
See side

Safety:

Hospitality:

Cleanliness:

Party index:

Schoolkids often book this big place absolutely full, meaning this peaceful quiet neighborhood is occasionally overrun with the pitter-patter of restless German youths. But the big, good breakfast and camp fires by the lake might still entice you.

To escape you might head for the lake and walk, swim, or boat. There's also the depressing Wannsee Museum, commemorating (if that's the word) the place where the Nazis met in 1938 and decided to proceed with the mass extermination of Jews.

Note: Call ahead if you want to check in after 6:00 P.M.

how to get there:

By bus: Take #118 bus to Badewag stop and walk 30 yards to hostel.

By car: From Berliner Ring take Highway A 115, following signs toward Mitte to exit for Spanische Allee; make a left onto Kronprinzessinnenweg and another left onto Badeweg.

By train: From Zoo Station take S-Bahn line S1 or S7 to Nikolassee Station. Exit station at Strandbad sign and make a left onto Fußgängerbrücke; cross bridge and make a left onto Kronprinzessinnenweg. Hostel is on right.

---

a & o hostel am zoo
(zoo guest house hostel)
Hardenbergstrasse 9a, 10623 Berlin
Phone: 030–312–9410

Fax: 030–312–550–330
Rates: €10–€30 (about $12–$37 US) per person; doubles €34 (about $42 US)
Credit cards: No
Beds: 350
Private/family rooms: Yes
Kitchen available: No
Season: Open year-round
Office hours: 9:00 A.M.–midnight
Lockout: 10:00 A.M.–2:00 P.M.
Affiliation: None
Extras: Breakfast (groups only), bar, television, Internet access, bike rentals

---

Located in Charlottenburg
As you can tell from the name of this hostel, it's the closest one to the city zoo—and, by extension, huge Zoo Station.

However, the hostel frankly leaves some things to be desired. In fact, speaking of negative first impressions, the first time we dropped by the place, nobody opened the door as we rang and pounded on it—despite the long hours that reception claims the place is open. Imagine if it had been the freezing cold and dark of winter, we had just stumbled off a late-arriving train, and the door refused to open!

Anyway, *somebody* must be opening that door, because the place has been very popular in recent years due to its location near the station—maybe too popular for its own good. The bunks are beat up; breakfast is served to groups only, not individual saps like yourself. At least it's close to a few bars and clubs.

The Erotic Museum, right near the main train station, isn't the best in Europe, but it's fine as a quick stop if you've really got sex on the brain. One of our favorite discoveries in the neighborhood, though, is Savignyplatz, a square just a block or two away from the train station (going west). Its jazz bars, clubs, and pubs are among the city's classiest and most atmospheric, and they're not too expensive, either. The area *right* around the hostel, mind you, is harmless.

That city zoo is actually pretty decent as such things go. And don't forget to take a minute and drop by the giant KaDeWe department store, Europe's most humongous department store and a famous relic of the former GDR. Our hot tip is that you can check your e-mail cheaply on the fly inside the store. Head for the electronics section and flag down a clerk.

Best bet for a bite:
Mövenpick Marché on Ku'dammom

Insiders' tip:
Ewige Lampe for jazz

What hostellers say:
"Couldn't be any closer to the station."

Gestalt:
Zoo Station

Safety: 🏴🏴

Hospitality: 🏴🏴

Cleanliness: 🏴🏴

Party index: 🎉🎉🎉

how to get there:

By bus: Take #145 bus to Steinplatz stop; walk to hostel.
By car: Contact hostel for directions.
By train: From Zoo Station exit back of train station; walk down Hardenbergstrasse to hostel. From Ost Station take U-Bahn line U2 or U9 or S-Bahn to Zoologischer Garten (Zoo Station). Exit back of Zoo Station; walk down Hardenbergstrasse to hostel.

key to icons

🍁 Attractive natural setting

🌎 Ecologically aware hostel

✕ Superior kitchen facilities or cafe

💥 Offbeat or eccentric place

🚿 Superior bathroom facilities

♡ Romantic private rooms

🛏 Comfortable beds

💲 A particularly good value

♿ Wheelchair-accessible

💼 Good for business travelers

👫 Especially well suited for families

🚲 Good for active travelers

🎨 Visual arts at hostel or nearby

🎵 Music at hostel or nearby

🎿 Great hostel for skiers

🍺 Bar or pub at hostel or nearby

🏅 Editors' Choice: Among our very favorite hostels

munich (münchen)

Ah, Munich, city of monks. That's what the name means. Honest. Of course you'd never know it—it's the least German of German cities. In other words, it's easygoing, fun-loving, and (relatively) sunny compared to the rest of 'em. This ain't fast-paced Berlin; it's the kind of place where people sit around for three hours in the midday sun drinking beer. And those are people with jobs.

Still, it's a little hard at times to reconcile all this merrymaking with a recent past as the nerve center of Nazi activity during the dark years of World War II.

orientation and getting around

You'll most likely start your visit at the big and confusing Munich Hauptbahnhof, one of the busiest train stations in Europe. Getting off the train, you're confronted with a jumble of tracks, each bunch earmarked for a specific type of travel: Slow local trains, slick intercity trains, speedy international trains, and ultramodern overnight trains all have their own areas.

Before you even leave, make your first stop the EurAide office, on the quiet side of the station beside track #11. The staff at this American-run office (funded by the Germans) speak perfect English and help you find your way through train schedules, make train reservations for a small charge (it's worth it, trust us), or book a tour. The station itself contains any services you need under one roof—a travel agency, twenty-four-hour lockers and luggage storage, restaurants, a currency exchange, a cool Internet cafe (upstairs near the exit), a newsstand, a tourist office, and bike rentals. There are public phones everywhere that accept German phone cards (buy 'em at the post office or newsstand).

Surprisingly, the immediate area surrounding the train station is not as shabby as it could be. But there's not much to see here if your hostel is elsewhere; you'll probably be making a beeline for the U-Bahn or S-Bahn station to check into your hostel. Wanna get an immediate taste of the city? Head straight out of the station and follow the crowds to Marienplatz through a no-car walking zone. This is where most of the tourist action can be found (see What to See, later in this section).

Of the in-town neighborhoods, Schwabing is by far the coolest. It's the heart and soul of Munich, located between the enormous and lively English Garden and even bigger Olympic Park. The "Jugendstil" of art was born here, and many beautiful buildings survived World War ll bombings. Though Schwabing has gotten a little too hip for its own good—there are suits and cell phones all over the place now—the area still has Munich's best cafes, pubs, good-value restaurants, and cinemas. Bottom line? This is as laid-back as Germany ever gets. Come here.

getting around

Getting around should be no trouble, as the city maintains a topflight transit network of buses, commuter trains (S-Bahn), and subway cars (U-Bahn). The system is efficient, fairly clean, and always busy. Look for an "S" on a green circle for commuter rail stations and a "U" on a blue square for subway stations. Bus stops are marked by street signs with an "H" on them.

You can purchase single tickets for this system starting at €2.00 (about $2.50 US) or—to save time and money while hopping around—a transit pass such as the following:

- The one-day pass (Single-Tageskarte) starts at €5.00 (about $6.25 US) or at €9.00 (about $11.00 US) for two adults (called a Partner-Tageskarte).
- The three-day pass (3-Day Pass) goes for €12.30 (about $15.00 US) for one adult, €21.00 (about $26.00 US) for two.

It's probably better to buy one of these passes rather than going for the complicated Streifenkarte ("strip ticket") book of ten tickets, which can work out cheaper but is also a pain to use if you're not a local. Also note that two people traveling together can buy "partner" tickets for about a 15% discount, and that the rates above apply to inner-city trips. Rides to outlying hostels cost more than those listed above; you pay extra for longer trips on the Munich system.

Remember to "validate" (punch) your ticket at the blue box as soon as you board your streetcar, bus, or subway car. Don't forget to do this. Secret transit police may be riding alongside you, dressed like normal Munichers, and they'll fine you big if you "forgot" to stamp your ticket.

There are two things to keep in mind when using the subways and commuter trains:

Number one: This is one of those rare cities where the S-Bahn's aboveground trains are actually handier for getting to most of the sights and hostels than the subway, so when in doubt go for the S-Bahn signs instead of the U-Bahn signs.

Number two: If you've got a Eurail pass, you can use the S-Bahns for free—yes, free!—as long as you have penciled the current date in the

munich
(münchen)

box. This is *not* a good idea normally because it wastes a day. However, if you have already used the pass to get into town, pencil in that date.

Feeling flush? In a hurry? Taxis troll for passengers at the exit near track #11. They are beige, clean, and fairly inexpensive.

what to see, drink, and eat

The main tourism information office is located just outside the train station (follow the signs). It's open Monday through Saturday, 8:00 A.M. to 8:00 P.M., and 9:00 A.M. to 6:00 P.M. Sunday. They are among the friendliest and most helpful tourist officers we've ever met.

After picking up maps and getting their advice, begin in the Altstadt ("old town"), where the Marienplatz is the focal point for the worthwhile sights and beer. Even without much time, you can taste the mood of the city within a few minutes in this sunshine-filled pedestrian zone containing the majestically twin-towered Frauenkirche, St. Michael's Kirche, the Rathaus, and the royal Residenz.

A little southeast and you'll be walking through the Isartor—a gate built in the early fourteenth century, the last remaining piece of the ring that formerly closed Munich—toward the Viktualienmarkt. You've gotta see this place: an open market teeming with foodies in search of plump olives, freshly squeezed carrot juice, shaded beer gardens, and tons of small restaurants. Eat here now!

Culture vultures might head in the other direction, to art museums such as the Alte and Neue Pinakotheks and the modern Haus der Kunst. You'd also do well to entertain yourself at the huge and fun Deutsches Museum (on the other side of the Isar River) or the informative BMW and Siemens museums.

If the weather's good, skip the museums and head instead for the Englischer Garten (English Garden), Europe's oldest public park, with several great beer gardens, fields, and sunbathers—basically one of the best places to discover Munich in a nutshell.

Note that almost all the Munich museums and sights are closed on Monday, so do something else.

The beer, of course, flows in a never-ending river through this town. This is arguably the best beer in the world—if you like dark beers, it *is* the best in the world—so suck it up and suck some down. You can get a draft or bottle or keg of the stuff anytime anywhere, but it's especially obvious during beery festivals in March (March Beer Festival), May (Maibock), and September (Oktoberfest). Beer garden listings are included in some of the hostel write-ups that follow.

Finally, know that Munich's restaurants are pricey—even more so in crowded areas such as around the station, as there are loads of tourists to rip off there. A better choice might be the many pizza and falafel

munich hostels
at a glance

	RATING	COST	IN A WORD	PAGE
Pullach Hostel	◩	€21	regal	p. 196
Wombat's	◩	€12–€68	fun	p. 199
Easy Palace	◩	€14–€65	promising	p. 186
Euro Youth Hotel	◩	€12.50–€32.50	beery	p. 187
Kapuziner (The Tent) Hostel	◩	€7.50–€10.50	groovy	p. 192
CVJM Jugendgästehaus Hostel	◩	€26.50–€41.00	Catholic	p. 184
Neuhausen Hostel	◩	€20.50–€23.50	institutional	p. 194
Haus International Hostel	◩◩	€25–€48	big	p. 191
4 You München	◩◩	€17.50–€44.00	green	p. 189
Thalkirchen Hostel	◩◩	€20.50–€23.50	strict	p. 197

take-out joints, the Wienerwald fast-food chain, or the Mickey D's outlets in the station, if you can stand them.

the hostels

Munich's hostels are, for the most part, clean and safe. Some even manage to be fun and interesting. Despite the huge annual beer fest, they don't have the same fluctuations in standards that similar party-oriented cities like Amsterdam do.

There's a big difference between DJH hostels and the rest here. Travelers older than twenty-six will be turned away at the "official" DJH-affiliated hostels but not at most of the more laid-back independent ones. The DJH joints here also tend to have inconvenient locations, harsher rules, and loads of noisy (sometimes bratty) schoolchildren. On the other hand, the independent places tend to slide a bit in terms of quietness and cleanliness. You make the choice.

Be aware, too, that during Oktoberfest—which actually takes place the last two weeks of September, strangely enough—all hostel prices listed here probably jump at least 10 percent and as much as 100 percent, depending on the greed of the hostel managers. (We're kidding. Some places don't raise the rate at all, and others double it! The point is, they could charge the moon and you'd still *pay* it, wouldn't you?)

Note that a number of these hostels are located very close to the main train station. There's lots of red-light business to be found here, as well as the usual suspects hanging out in the station, so be a bit more cautious at night—though Munich is, generally speaking, a very safe place.

cvjm jugendgästehaus hostel
(ymca guest house hostel)
Landwehrstrasse 13, 80336 Munich
Phone: 089–552–1410

Fax: 089–550–4282
E-mail: muenchen@cvjm.org or hotel@cvjm-muenchen.org
Web site: www.cvjm-muenchen.org/en/hotel
Rates: €26.50–€41.00 (about $33–$51 US) per person; doubles €57–€64 (about $68–$77 US)
Credit cards: Yes
Beds: 85
Private/family rooms: Yes
Kitchen available: No
Season: Closed December 25–January 6
Office hours: 7:00 A.M.–midnight
Curfew: 12:30 A.M.
Affiliation: None
Extras: Restaurant ($), breakfast

Note: There is a 10 percent surcharge for guests over twenty-six and discounts in winter.

Bring those rosary beads if you wanna stay at this hostel, 'cause it's run by the local Catholics. As a result, it's humdrum but serviceable.

After a complete renovation, the place looks more like a posh bank than a hostel. Staff is surprisingly friendly and keeps everything looking as though no hosteller had ever used it before. There are only single rooms, doubles, and triples available; none of them are very large, but all sport relatively new furniture. They actually resemble nice hotel rooms, not barnyard floors (which a couple other places in town resemble). Ask for an off-the-street room, some of which face a court-yard and are pleasantly quieter. However, note that there are only two showers on each floor (there are sinks in the room). The hostel also has its own restaurant, bar, and common room.

While even some HI-affiliated hostels have recently trashed their ridiculously outdated rules, these folks are Catholic enough to hold the line. You'll have to deal with rules rules rules—among them: strict curfews, no unmarried couples sharing a room, no smoking, single male travelers are discouraged, no booze, and you have to be in by 12:30 at night. There are also no scandalous, licentious extras like Internet access or a laundry. That's just the beginning. The whole attitude here really is almost like being back in Catholic school (for those who remember such a thing); you half expect nuns to bring out the rulers and begin whacking your knuckles.

Best bet for a bite:
La Vecchia Masseria for pizza

Insiders' tip:
Head for the Augustinerkeller beer garden

What hostellers say:
"Jeez—I mean, gosh—too many rules."

Gestalt:
Church chat

Safety:

Hospitality: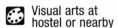

Cleanliness: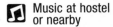

Party index:

key to icons

 Attractive natural setting

Ecologically aware hostel

Superior kitchen facilities or cafe

Offbeat or eccentric place

Superior bath-room facilities

Romantic private rooms

Comfortable beds

A particularly good value

Wheelchair-accessible

Good for busi-ness travelers

Especially well suited for families

Good for active travelers

Visual arts at hostel or nearby

Music at hostel or nearby

Great hostel for skiers

Bar or pub at hostel or nearby

Editors' Choice: Among our very favorite hostels

But, OK, the staff are friendly. Sheets and breakfast are included for free. And everything's kept spic-and-span, just as you'd expect. There's an extra charge here if you're over twenty-six years old.

At least it's mighty central, just steps from that huge train station where you're undoubtedly going to be arriving.

Party? You'll have to pray for one.

how to get there:

By bus: Contact hostel for transit details.
By car: Contact hostel for directions.
By train: From the main train station, turn right and walk down Schillerstrasse; take the second street on the left.

easy palace

Mozartstrasse 4, 80336 Munich
Phone: 089–558–7970

Fax: 089–558–79797
E-mail: info@easypalace.com
Web site: www.easypalace.com
Rates: €14–€65 (about $19–$78 US); doubles €79–€89 (about $99–$111 US)
Credit cards: No
Beds: 300
Private/family rooms: Yes
Season: Open year-round
Kitchen available: Yes
Office hours: Twenty-four hours
Affiliation: None
Extras: Meals ($), laundry, kitchen, lockers, Internet access

One of the Euro Youth Hotel's managers opened this Munich hostel in the summer of 2003. The building itself was built in the '50s as a low-end hotel, then made into a doss house. When the old lads weren't exploring the bottom of their glasses, they obviously did all they could to wear down their "palace."

So, before the place was converted into a hostel, each of the rooms was equipped with a toilet, shower, and small kitchen. Most of these were in such bad condition that management decided to remove some of those facilities and use the extra space for bunks. A few rooms here still have two beds and a bathroom (some of them even have kitchens), but most have four to six beds and share bathroom facilities. The big eight-bedded dorms are probably Munich's best deal.

Unfortunately, if you intend to mingle with fellow backpackers, this hostel is about as hot as your fridge. There would be enough space for common rooms or even a bar downstairs, but no dice so far, the renovation of dorm rooms is still the top priority, apparently. The staffers do all they can to compensate with a friendliness and efficiency we appreciated just as well. The additions of a kitchen and hostel laundry, as well as Internet, have also been most welcome. A very good breakfast is served in the restaurant next door, and hostellers get great discounts on their meals; no wonder many end up hanging out there in the evening over a few glasses of Hofbräu beer. There's not really a kitchen here, you should know.

Adding it all up, this place still has its flaws, but there's enough enthusiasm to make it better (we'll keep an eye on it for you), the price is nice, and even the location—a bit off the shady station area where several other hostels are located—is decent. Our verdict so far? The envelope please . . . thumb up!

Best bet for a bite:
Place next door

Insiders' tip:
Oktoberfest just 2 blocks away

What hostellers say:
"Ain't no palace."

Gestalt:
Million Dollar Hotel

Safety:

Cleanliness:

Hospitality:

Party index:

how to get there:

By bus: Contact hostel for transit route.

By car: Contact hostel for directions.

By train: From Hauptbahnhof, take U-Bahn U1 or U2 line one stop to Sendlinger Tor Station, then change to U3 or U6 line and continue one stop to Goetheplatz station. From Goetheplatz, walk to Mozartstrasse; hostel is on right. Or, from Hauptbahnhof, simply walk 1 mile along Goethestrasse and turn right onto Mozartstrasse at Goetheplatz.

euro youth hotel
Senefelderstrasse 5, 80336 Munich
Phone: 089–599–0880

Fax: 089–5990–8877

E-mail: info@euro-youth-hotel.de
Web site: www.euro-youth-hotel.de
Rates: €12.50–€32.50 (about $15–$40 US) per person; doubles €45–€60 (about $56–$75 US)
Credit cards: No
Beds: Number varies
Private/family rooms: Yes
Kitchen available: No
Season: Open year-round
Office hours: Twenty-four hours
Affiliation: None
Extras: Bar, breakfast ($), laundry, information

We heard very good reports of this place, but when we finally got there we were greeted by an extremely rude receptionist who refused to give us any info at all (too busy playing video games). That's unfortunate, because it's got to be one of the best choices in town—if you don't mind a little noise and beer.

Best bet for a bite:
Mövenpick at Karlsplatz

Insiders' tip:
Beer gardens in
Viktualienmarkt

What hostellers say:
"Pour me another!"

Gestalt:
Beer guardian

Safety:

Hospitality:

Cleanliness:

Party index:

Housed inside a once-posh hotel just next to Munich's train station, the place opened in 1999. They've got everything from a cheap, monsterlike thirty-bed dormitory to more expensive quad and double room digs (with shared bathrooms, of course; this ain't the Ritz). Upstairs rooms are small and quite decent, despite a short supply of showers. The ground-floor big dorms aren't worth your money, though—right behind the bar, they're smoke-filled and noisy. There's zero security here. And you have to trek to the basement to use showers and bathrooms.

The best thing of all here, though, isn't the bed or the company—it's the beer. It is owned lock, stock, and barrel by one of Munich's (and Germany's) finest breweries, Augustiner. Needless to say, there's a constant flow of the suds, and the price isn't bad: Less than €2 for a half-liter draft is less than you'll pay just about anywhere else in town.

Friendly? Central? Absolutely yes on both counts. The laundry is a huge bonus after traveling on the train, and you can pay extra for breakfast. It's a little expensive by Munich standards, however, so bring a few extra bucks and you'll be all right.

how to get there:

By bus or train: Contact hostel for transit details. Or from main train station, exit right-hand side and turn down Bayerstrasse; continue to Senefelderstrasse.

By car: Contact hostel for directions.

4 you münchen hostel

Hirtenstrasse 18, 80335 Munich
Phone: 089–552–1660

Fax: 089–552–16666
E-mail: info@the4you.de
Web site: www.the4you.de
Rates: €17.50–€44.00 (about $22–$55 US) per person; doubles €50–€64 (about $63–$80 US)
Credit cards: Yes
Beds: 212
Private/family rooms: Yes
Kitchen available: No
Season: Open year-round
Office hours: Twenty-four hours
Affiliation: None
Extras: Cafeteria ($), breakfast ($), tours, luggage storage, kindergarten, lockers

Note: There is a 10 percent surcharge for guests over twenty-six.

A group of enthusiasts once took over a run-down five-story 1950s-era hotel with a mission: Start up Munich's first independent hostel. But they focused so much on ecology, on making it a "green hostel"—they even added wooden light switches—that they forgot to use a little business sense. And "green" didn't always equal "clean."

The project flopped. The place changed hands, passing to newer, more savvy (if less idealistic) management. Bottom line? Things look to be straightening out.

The place *needs* improvement: Right now, it's only so-so. The building, located on a quiet little street just inches from the train station's craziness, has seen better days, and the somewhat beat-up dorm rooms (which have large lockers, by the way) are just too used-looking. The bunk beds are decent but not superior and are too tightly packed in. The showers are abysmal and frustrating. At least everything is kept clean (except for the showers), a very recent improvement after the cleanliness and upkeep standards had really begun to slide. Check out the walls, floors, beds, and everything else while you're here; they've probably been recycled, depesticided, and left unpainted. You get the drift.

Best bet for a bite:
Buxs (near Viktualienmarkt) for veggie

Insiders' tip:
Sussman's has newspapers in English

What hostellers say:
"Duuuuude."

Gestalt:
2 cool 2 be 4gotten

Safety:

Hospitality:

Cleanliness:

Party index:

Prices are cheaper for younger folks; more expensive as you age or your room improves. Breakfast and other meals—you have to pay for them—are tasty, organic, and healthful, possibly as an antidote to all the beer and city fumes you'll be swilling the rest of the time. A few basic extras like Internet access and a laundry are also planned; but the lack of either a bar or kitchen has to be considered a negative.

The place is still very politically and ecologically correct. Smoking is allowed only in a "smoker room," and the hostel kindergarten takes care of kiddies during the daytime. Nevertheless, we've gotta admit one thing: This is already one of Munich's best hostels in which to meet fellow travelers, though school groups occasionally take over the place and render the hallways noisy and smoky.

Note that the hostel also includes a pricier "hotel" section upstairs, part of the same complex but with better-equipped single and double rooms (they're more expensive, of course); these rooms all come with private bathrooms, and breakfast is included.

All things considered, this is one to consider since it's very close to the city's central train station.

how to get there:

By bus or train: Contact hostel for transit route. Or from main train station, exit left-hand side to Arnulfstrasse; take an immediate right onto Pfeffenstrasse, then another quick right onto Hirtenstrasse.
By car: Contact hostel for directions.

haus international hostel

Elisabethstrasse 87, 80797 Munich
Phone: 089–120–060

Fax: 089–1200–6251
E-mail: info@haus-international.de
Web site: www.haus-international.de
Rates: €25–€48 (about $31–$60 US) per person; doubles €56–€76 (about $70–$95 US)
Credit cards: Yes
Beds: 545
Private/family rooms: Yes
Kitchen available: No
Season: Open year-round
Office hours: Twenty-four hours
Affiliation: None
Extras: Restaurant ($), swimming pool, TV room, disco, bar, garden, patio, table tennis, breakfast ($)

In one word, this hostel is huge and ugly—and inconveniently located, too. Wait, that's more than one word.

You can't believe how huge this '70s-style building is—it's one of two hostels in town that have 500-odd beds—yet, remarkably, it's often quite full due to the unending parade of school kiddies who provide the hostel with its bread-and-butter clientele.

The common area on the ground floor looks practically Soviet, and the rooms and floors have taken lots of abuse. Double rooms here are in acceptable condition, though the bigger ones are overpriced for what you get: cigarette burns through the carpets, loose closet doors, and graffiti. For "fun" there's a large, mostly empty disco in the basement, where you can also improve your skills in '80s video games (think Pac-Man, Ms. Pac-Man, Frogger, Super Mario). Teenyboppers congregate there, so you head downtown instead.

Best bet for a bite:
Pizzeria da Tanino

Insiders' tip:
BMW museum near Olympic park

What hostellers say:
"Big but bland."

Gestalt:
Haus of horrors

Safety:

Hospitality:

Cleanliness:

Party index:

Despite the incredibly bland and beat-up fixtures and rooms, though, it's surprisingly expensive—thirty bucks a night?!—and the U-Bahn doesn't come anywhere near here, so you've gotta hoof it quite a ways or take a bus (#33 bus from Rotkreuzplatz) that doesn't run at night. You might have to split a taxi, kiddies, so factor that into your budget.

The only good things are the swimming pool, beer garden area, meals in a cafeteria, and a television lounge. Not good enough. Perhaps most important, though, the hostel's in approximately—and we stress approximately, not exactly—the same part of town as the Schwabing neighborhood, which some have compared with New York's Greenwich Village, it's so cool (though it's a lot cleaner and safer). Okay, Schwabing actually stretches from the city center to Munich's northern border, and the Haus International is even quite a bit north of this hoppin' district, but you could conceivably see Schwabing on the same journey you're making out to the hostel.

The hostel is exceptionally close to the city's Olympic Stadium, however, with its awe-inspiring tinted-glass suspended roof. You can take a dip in the swimming pool, too, which is open to the public; in winter rent skates and take to the ice. Other highlights of the park include tours of the grounds and a speedy lift to the top of the Olympic Tower.

how to get there:

By bus or train: Take U-Bahn line U2 toward Feldmoching to Hohenzollernplatz stop, then walk to hostel; or change to #12 tram or #33 bus and continue to Barbara Strasse stop. Hostel is next to gas station.

By car: From any highway into the city, take Mittlerer Ring to Schwabing exit and continue to hostel.

---

kapuziner (the tent)
In den Kirschen 30, Munich
Phone: 089–141–4300

Fax: 089–175–090
E-mail: see-you@the-tent.com
Web site: www.the-tent.com
Rates: €7.50–€10.50 (about $9–$13 US) per person
Credit cards: No
Beds: Nobody's sure how many

Private/family rooms: No
Kitchen available: Yes
Season: Open June 15–October 15
Office hours: Twenty-four hours
Affiliation: None
Extras: Bike rentals, lockers, breakfast, meals ($), campfires, movies, campground, transit pass discounts, Internet access, city tours, laundry, volleyball

Note: Must be under age twenty-seven to stay.

Spartans have found a new joint in town to celebrate: "The Tent." This place, quite simply put, is a regular three-ring circus (minus the animals)—very appropriate, given that it is located beneath, yes, a giant tent.

That's right: A bed here isn't really a bed; it's a mattress on the floor of the tent—talk about urban camping—with a skimpy blanket. On warm nights you might not mind, though you're obviously sacrificing tons of privacy and amenities and security. Oh, they've got some plain bunk beds, too, marginally more like home but not much. Still, it's all in good fun and the skank-factor isn't too too high. Plumbing facilities consist of camp-style showers and toilets.

Best bet for a bite:
HL Markt for picnic supplies

Insiders' tip:
Bring earplugs

What hostellers say:
"Roll another one!"

Gestalt:
Big Top

Safety:

Hospitality:

Cleanliness:

Party index:

They show movies, sell cheap city transit passes (that city ownership really comes in handy), offer free breakfast, rent bikes, have an Internet terminal, and maintain lockers for your stuff. The real draw, though, is the ambience, which is as groovy as they come. They light bonfires at night, grill stuff, bring out the guitars and the red wine . . . what a great feeling developing under the stars.

It's in a bit of an inconvenient location, but there's always space, and the enthusiastic staff are great. They are soooo laid-back here, it's scary. Age limit? Chances are 50–50 that these folk won't even care. There's a three-night maximum stay rule, too, but we imagine that's flexible; depending on the mood of the receptionist, who knows?

Note that this hostel is sponsored by the city of Munich and kept on a tight budgetary leash, so its future is not secure. It could be gone by the time you crack this book, or it could be around forever. Also, the hostel is summer-only and thus closes before Oktoberfest.

how to get there:

By bus or train: From main train station take #17 tram to Botanischer Garden stop, then walk up Franz-Schrank-Strasse to In den Kirschen; hostel is on right. Or take U-Bahn line U1 to Rotkreuzplatz stop, then change to the #12 tram to Botanischer Garden stop; walk up Franz-Schrank-Strasse to In den Kirschen.

By car: Contact hostel for directions.

---

jugendherberge
münchen-neuhausen (munich
neuhausen hostel)

Wendl-Dietrich-Strasse 20, 80634 Munich
Phone: 089–131–156 or 089–164–545

Fax: 089–167–8745
E-mail: jhmuenchen@djh-bayern.de
Rates: €20.50–€23.50 (about $25–$29 US) per HI member
Credit cards: Yes
Beds: 351
Private/family rooms: Yes
Kitchen available: Yes
Season: Closed December 1–31
Office hours: Twenty-four hours
Affiliation: HI-DJH
Regional office: Bavaria
Extras: TV room, bike rentals, bistro ($), meeting rooms, foosball, patio, garden, breakfast, luggage storage, laundry, lockers, information desk, bar, games, bike tours ($)

Note: Must be under age twenty-seven to stay.

As more and more competitors continue to enter the Munich hostelling market, things have recently improved even at the city's Hostelling International–affiliated hostels—especially at this one. Built and opened way back in 1927, between the wars, this was Hostelling International's very first city hostel and Europe's biggest until 1991. Now, minus the curfew and lockout that once made it a bad choice, it is finally starting to meet backpackers' needs. Though the furniture doesn't seem to have changed too much since, um,

1927, things are being kept in one piece and acceptably clean. It's so-so and boring, but we'll give it a nod.

It's located 2 miles west of the central train station but reachable by public transit. Once there, you'll find the hostel compound is actually made up of several linked stone buildings with a nice garden and bar between them. Three big stone arches frame the front doors; behind, you'll find a few double rooms and mostly six-bedded dorms.

However, take heed: There's one giant thirty-bed dormitory they call the "stable," with stinking socks and snorers all round; if you end up here you'll want to lock your stuff up fast. (Thankfully, lockers in the rooms are big enough for backpacks.) This huge room must be a real treat around Oktoberfest, what with the various scents of beer, sweat, urine, and other fluids wafting through the air.

There are also seventeen doubles, twenty-four quads, and thirty-six six-bedded rooms in addition to the monster dorm, if that gives you some sense of the size of this place. Bathrooms and showers are in the hallways, not in the rooms.

There are good and bad things about the place. On the downside of the ledger, rooms on the street can

Best bet for a bite:
Santa Fe

Insiders' tip:
Sheets are free here

What hostellers say:
"Getting better."

Gestalt:
Institutionalized

Safety:

Hospitality:

Cleanliness:

Party index:

be noisy, and the showers are closed down at 10:00 P.M. The neighborhood is not great at all. They have a kitchen, sure, but it comes without pots, plates, or other helpful items—you've gotta bring your own. None of the private rooms come with private bathrooms, which is too bad. Finally, it's likely to be packed with annoying school groups April through October.

On the other hand, staff are quite friendly, and they certainly offer plenty of services: You can arrange bike tours for a fee at the front desk, for example. There's a television lounge and tourist information desk. And check out the rather unusual on-premises restaurant, too—it's set in a streetcar. Yep. You heard us. Kinda cool, plus there's a patio for chilling as well. You have the option of paying for a half-board or full-board plan that includes meals, and vegetarian food can be ordered as long as you tell 'em in advance. As for party potential, this is a good place to meet people, if not exactly to rock hard.

The hostel's located in Neuhausen, the neighborhood most commonly associated with the Schloss Nymphenburg palace, and some say it's got a snooty attitude to match. It shouldn't be too proud, though, since most of the buildings here were completely destroyed during World War II, and the ones that still stand reflect a monotonous architectural conformity. There are a few cheap restaurants around—ask the receptionist—plus an Internet cafe nearby on Nymphenburger Strasse; access is free, but you have to eat or drink to use it. Our tip? You might do best to contemplate life in the Hirschgarten, one of the nicer beer gardens in the city.

Just remember that this place is always popular; you'll want to book ahead or arrive before noon to stay the night.

how to get there:

By bus: Take #12 or #17 streetcar and walk ¼ mile. Or, from main train station, take U-Bahn line U1 to Rotkreuzplatz Station; walk along Wendl-Dietrich-Strasse ½ mile to hostel.
By car: Entering city, follow signs for Olympiapark, then make a right onto Nymphenburger Strasse. (If coming from Lindau, make a left.)
By train: From main train station take U-Bahn line U1 to Rotkreuzplatz Station; walk along Wendl-Dietrich-Strasse ¼ mile to hostel.

---

jugendherberge burg schwaneck (pullach hostel)

Burgweg 4–6, 82049 Pullach (Munich)
Phone: 089–7448–6670

Fax: 089–7448–6680
E-mail: info@jugendherberge-burgschwaneck.de
Rates: €21 (about $26 US) per HI member
Credit cards: Yes
Beds: 132
Private/family rooms: Yes
Kitchen available: No
Season: Closed December 21–January 15
Office hours: 7:30 A.M.–5:30 P.M.
Curfew: 11:30 P.M.
Affiliation: HI-DJH
Regional office: Bavaria
Extras: Meeting room, grill, pool table, meals ($), terrace, breakfast, bowling, sports facilities, patio

Note: Must be under age twenty-seven to stay.

If you're staying here, you're in for some amazing castle (yeah, castle) hostelling . . . but you're so distant from the action that once you check in you might never get into Munich at all—at the very least you'll have to work to get in and out of town via the S-Bahn (commuter train) in time for the brutal curfew. If you're wanting a country break between cities, though, this is just ideal.

Situated in a park, in a real-life castle with some history to match (ask the staff about the parties that were thrown here back in the nineteenth century), it's full of four- to eight-bedded dorms. Good breakfasts are included with your bunk, which is gonna probably be more comfortable than you expected. The views are stupendous from the patio, and they've decked the place out with some nice touches: bowling, some sports facilities, a game room, stuff like that.

They don't take reservations in advance, however, so you need to call from the Munich train station on the same day.

Best bet for a bite:
Meals on-site

Insiders' tip:
Prinz for entertainment listings

What hostellers say:
"Fit for a king!"

Gestalt:
Royal flush

Safety:

Hospitality:

Cleanliness:

Party index:

how to get there:

By bus: Contact hostel for transit details.
By car: Head south from Munich on Highway B11 to Pullach.
By train: From Munich take S-Bahn line S7 to Pullach Station, then walk along Margarethenstrasse to Heilmannstrasse; turn right on Charlottenweg and continue to hostel, about ½ mile total.

jugendgästehaus thalkirchen (thalkirchen munich guest house hostel)

Miesingstrasse 4, 81379 Munich
Phone: 089–723–6550 or 089–723–6560

Fax: 089–724–2567
E-mail: jghmuenchenthalkirchen@djh-bayern.de
Rates: €20.50– €23.50 (about $26–$30 US) per HI member
Credit cards: No
Beds: 352
Private/family rooms: Yes

Kitchen available: No
Season: Open year-round
Office hours: Twenty-four hours
Lockout: 9:30 A.M.–2:00 P.M.
Curfew: 1:00 A.M.
Affiliation: HI-DJH
Regional office: Bavaria
Extras: TV room, playground nearby, foosball, pool table, parking, luggage storage, table tennis, garden, cafeteria ($), laundry, lockers, breakfast, bike rentals, meeting rooms

---

Note: Must be under age twenty-seven to stay.

Far out of town and not exactly full of warm fuzzies, this may not be your first choice in Munich, despite its modern look—all elevated walkways and glassy rooms admitting much more light and sunshine (when there is sunshine) than most other German hostels.

Best bet for a bite:
Cafeteria here

Insiders' tip:
Stay in town!

What hostellers say:
"Getting better."

Gestalt:
Tough as nails

Safety:

Hospitality:

Cleanliness:

Party index:

Dorms contain from two to fifteen beds. They've got fifty-six twin rooms—that means two single beds, not one double bed—plus fifty-five rooms with three to six beds each and then six much larger dormitories. The dorms are all segregated by sex, as is usual in an HI-affiliated joint, and to share a family room you have to be over eighteen and married. All bathrooms and showers are in the hallways, but at least breakfast is included with your bunk.

The pluses include a television lounge, game room with table tennis and a pool table, meeting room, bikes for rent, and a cafeteria serving meals and selling bag lunches. There's a locker in your dormitory room, which costs a few euros to use (and you get the money back later), then another bigger luggage room in the basement of the hostel for your big stuff; it's free. Get a key at the front desk. Generally speaking, this place is charmless, but it does seem to have improved a bit recently.

Beware, however: Staff are Germanly trained, and some managers have actually been known to ask for wedding certificates when couples want to share a room. (Hopefully that practice has been discontinued by now.) And, as we mentioned, it's a pain in the keister to get here. The hostel's situated in Thalkirchen, southwest of the city and some distance. Although close to the zoo, the Isar River, and woods and parks, you'll need wheels or some major public-transit time to even think about it as an option.

Given the staff's nitpicking nature, we'd think about skipping it.

how to get there:

By bus: Take #3 streetcar to Thalkirchen stop and walk ¼ mile to hostel. Or take U-Bahn line U1 to Sendlinger Tor Station, change to U-Bahn line U3, and continue to Thalkirchen Station and walk ¼ mile to hostel. Or take line U3 to Thalkirchen and walk ¼ mile to hostel.

By car: Follow signs to Mittlerer Ring, then to Zoo; from Thalkirchen follow signs to hostel.

By train: From main train station take U-Bahn line U1 to Sendlinger Tor Station, then change to U-Bahn line U3 and continue to Thalkirchen Station. Or take line U3 directly from Marienplatz toward Furstenried West to Thalkirchen; from Thalkirchen walk ¼ mile to hostel.

wombat's backpackers munich
Senefelderstrasse 1, D-80336 Munich
Phone: 089–5998–9180

Fax: 089–5998–91810
E-mail: office@wombats-munich.de
Rates: €12–€68 (about $15–$85 US) per person; doubles €58–€68 (about $72–$85 US)
Credit cards: No
Beds: 300
Private/family rooms: Yes
Kitchen available: No
Season: Open year-round
Office hours: Twenty-four hours
Affiliation: None
Extras: Internet access, laundry, pool table, bar, patio, breakfast ($)

Unless hostellers abuse the heck out of this place and reduce it to rubble (or chaos), this Munich entry looks like a real winner. Brought to you by the same folks who started up the great Wombat's hostel in

Vienna, this place has an equally chill vibe: a party, yes, but not one that's raging out of control.

It's an amazingly modern-looking place from the outside. Inside, in a big yellow lobby with a parquet floor fronting a glassed-in atrium with potted trees, you get a free welcome drink, free sheets for your bed, and city maps. Bunkrooms are clean and airy enough, fresh-painted if functional. At least you're not crammed in like a sardine. All rooms have en-suite bathrooms. And, dig this: Most doubles here have balconies! That is not a misprint. The rooftop patio bar is the star of the show, though, a place for convivial hanging out and getting to know your fellow hostellers.

Safety: 🗲

Hospitality: 🗲

Cleanliness: 🗲

Party index: 🎉🎉🎉🎉

how to get there:

By car: Contact hostel for directions.

By train: From the platforms, take the right-most exit out of the building onto Bayerstrasse. Cross the road, turn left, then turn down the first street on the right (Senefelderstrasse); the hostel is on the left.

By plane: Take S-Bahn lines S1 or S8 to the main railway station "Hauptbahnhof" (approximately forty-five minutes). At the station, you will find yourself in a maze of underground passages. Look for the exit to Bayerstrasse Ost. After you come up the escalator, make a U-turn, walk up Bayerstrasse, and take the first street to the left (Senefelderstrasse). Wombat's is the second house on the left.

greece

Greece is well known for sun-washed islands in blue seas. But it's also becoming increasingly known for the hedonism that descends upon it, summer or winter, in the form of British, Swedish, and American tourists (among others) seeking sun, sand, ruins, clubs, olives, ouzo, and feta cheese. That all adds up to one of the most interesting countries in Europe—a little disorganized, a little bit chauvinist, a lot hot in summer, but nevertheless one of those places that draws travelers back time and again.

practical details

As might be expected, Athens shifted into overdrive for the 2004 Olympics; among the city's improvements were a greatly expanded Metro (subway) and a new airport. The Metro's three modern lines are slowly being expanded to the suburbs, but the city center is now already decently serviced. Check at the train station or your hostel for a map. A single ride on the subway costs about €0.80 (about $1.00 US), while a one-day city transit pass—which includes access to all buses and streetcars—costs €3.00 (about $3.75 US). If you're really pinched for cash, note that buses do cost only half as much as the subway, but are far less efficient—and often require some serious local knowledge to figure out routes, schedules, and stops.

The new, modern airport is located about 20 miles southeast of the city center, and is served by all the usual international carriers; log onto www.aia.gr for more info. A direct train link to downtown Athens opened in 2004. Express buses also connect the city with the airport 24/7/365; the E95 runs farthest into the center of town, stopping at Syntagma Square and its Metro stop (serving lines 2 and 3), while the E94 runs to another, less central Metro stop served only by line 3. The express buses cost about €3.00 (about $3.75 US) one-way. There's also a new six-lane highway if you're brave enough to rent a car and attempt driving in Athens.

Eurail passes cover certain ferry lines from Bari and Brindisi, Italy, to Patras, a ferry port three and a half to five hours' train ride from Athens. Find out which lines are accepting the pass—the lineup sometimes changes—and don't be swayed by whatever the ticket-sellers in Italy tell you; there are plenty of crooked outfits trying to cash in on your ignorance. READ YOUR EURAIL GUIDE CAREFULLY FIRST. Also note that the pass covers only your ticket; you'll have to pay a little extra for an actual seat, quite a bit extra for a sleeping cabin.

The unit of currency in Greece is now the euro. Prices for food and drink are generally low in Greece, but higher in Athens.

Greece's country code is 30 and Athens's city code is 210. To call Athens hostels from the United States, dial 011–30 PLUS THE NUMBERS PRINTED in each listing. To call Athens hostels from Greece, dial NUMBERS EXACTLY AS PRINTED.

athens

Smoggy, crowded, and historic, Athens is a sensory blitz and not to be lingered in. It's best to catch it on your way into Greece, soak up the amazing concentration of sights and humanity, then get the heck out of town before it drives you nuts—and get to one of those sunny islands you've heard so much about. There's a rudimentary subway system, but many travelers end up having to cope with the crowded city buses. Athens isn't really walkable, and in summer it's too hot to think about walking anyway.

athens hostels
at a glance

	RATING	PRICE	IN A WORD	PAGE
Pella Inn Hostel		€15–€50	adequate	p. 207
Student & Traveller's Inn		€15–€20	good	p. 209
Hostel Aphrodite		€9–€30	fun	p. 206
Athens International		€9.20–€10.90	busy	p. 203

athens international hostel

Victor Hugo 16, Athens 10438
Phone: 210–523–4170

Fax: 210–523–4015
E-mail: info@aiyh-victorhugo.com
Rates: €9.20–€10.90 (about $12–$15 US) per person
Credit cards: No
Beds: 142
Private/family rooms: Yes
Kitchen available: Yes
Season: Open year-round
Office hours: Twenty-four hours
Affiliation: HI
Extras: Laundry, breakfast, luggage storage, Internet access, information desk, lunch ($), kitchen

The only "official" hostel in Greece, the Athens hostel is pretty far from the hub of the city's activity (the Plaka), but it does offer a ton of amenities and demonstrates a desire to modernize by offering computer stations for Net cruising. (It also closed for a time but reopened under new management.) The place is very busy and popular, and it's relatively cheap. Therefore you'll need to reserve wayyyy ahead of time. (It's part of the International Booking Network, so if you're, say, in Edinburgh and want to be in Athens in forty-eight hours or so, you can secure and prepay for your bed from a participating IBN hostel.)

Best bet for a bite:
Bretania Cafe

Insiders' tip:
PNYX (near Acropolis) for peace and quiet

What hostellers say:
"No, I *don't* want a good time."

Gestalt:
Greece is the word

Safety:

Hospitality:

Cleanliness:

Party index:

This, despite the so-so nature of the place. Some dorms are downright skuzzy (but some private rooms are nicer).

Rooms here are small and rather (okay, very) basic. There are about eleven doubles and twenty-nine quads, eliminating that crowded feeling so common in hostels that feature huge dormitories. However, there's a drawback: Once you leave the confines of the hostel and venture into chaotic Omonia Square, you'll get nothin' but noise—from cars, buses, and people. Little coffee shops line the square, but they mostly seem patronized by (again, loud) elderly folk. There's

athens

Leoforos Alexandras

Lofus Strefi

H. Trikoupi

Iprokratous

Likavitos

Koniari

Solonus

Akzdhimias

Vasilissis   Sofias

Vasileos Alexandrou

Filelimon

Irodou

Alikou

Ethnikos Kipos

Vasileos Konstandinou

4

Leoforas Amalias

Dikearhou

Eftihidou

stadio

Dhrakou

Ardhittou

Imitou

not much peace or quiet in these parts, sorry to say. And be wary at night; prostitutes overtake the area, drawing a seedy element to the neighborhood. Not the best place to stick a hostel, even if the staff are extremely friendly and helpful.

how to get there:

By bus: Take A7 or B7 bus to Kanigos Square, then walk 400 yards to hostel.

By car: Contact hostel for directions.

By subway: Take Metro line #2 to Metaxourhio Station, then walk 150 yards to hostel.

By train: From train station, walk ⅓ mile; or take #1 or #12 streetcar to Agiou Konstantinou and walk 300 yards to hostel.

hostel aphrodite

Einardou Str. 12, Athens 10440
Phone: 210–8839–249 or 210–8810–589

Fax: 210–8816–574
E-mail: info@hostelaphrodite.com
Web site: www.hostelaphrodite.com
Rates: €9–€30 (about $12–$36 US) per person
Beds: 80
Credit cards: Yes
Private/family rooms: Yes
Kitchen available: No
Season: March 1–November 1
Office hours: Twenty-four hours
Affiliation: HI
Extras: Currency exchange, laundry, meals ($), luggage storage, safe, sunroof, breakfast, bar, travel information desk

This whitewashed tenement block, on a neighborhood corner close to Athens's main train stations, may not be the most exciting hostel in the world. But it is darned close to some prime attractions, and as such it's worth a look. The staff has even improved in recent years. It's not superb, but still good enough to recommend.

They've got a supply of singles, doubles, triples, and quads—nothing spectacular, but some do have private bathrooms. Among the local attractions are the Acropolis (just half a mile away!), the National Arch Museum, and tons of little eateries and locals-only haunts. Buses to the beach pick up just a couple blocks away. They run a bar, which is obviously the most popular room in the house, and you can hang out on a sunroof overlooking the city. The luggage room is iffy, the laundry and meals more welcome.

how to get there:

By bus: Contact hostel for transit details.

By car: Contact hostel for directions.

By plane: From airport, take #090 or #091 bus to Syndagma Square stop, then change to #1 trolley bus and continue to Proussis stop. Walk north along Mikhail Voda to hostel on left.

By subway: Take Metro to Victoria Station and walk to hostel.

By train: From Larissis Station, cross street and walk straight out along Philadeleias Loulianou to Mikhail Voda and turn left. Continue down Mikhail Voda to hostel on left.

From Pelopennes Station, cross footbridge to Larissis Station. Cross street and walk straight out along Philadeleias Loulianou to Mikhail Voda and turn left. Continue down Mikhail Voda to hostel on left.

Best bet for a bite:
Market next door

What hostellers say:
"Somebody's been taking happy pills."

Gestalt:
Aphrodisiac

Safety:

Hospitality:

Cleanliness:

Party index:

---

pella inn hostel

Ermou Str. 104, Athens 10554
Phone: 210–325–0598 or 210–321–2229

Fax: 210–321–2229 or 210–325–0598
E-mail: info@pellainn.gr
Web site: www.pellainn.gr
Rates: €15–€50 (about $18–$63 US) per person; doubles €40–€50 (about $50–$63 US)
Credit cards: No
Beds: Number varies
Private/family rooms: Yes
Kitchen available: No
Season: Open year-round
Office hours: Twenty-four hours
Affiliation: None
Extras: Fax service, sundeck, garden, meals ($), laundry service, phones, air-conditioning, luggage storage, currency exchange, Internet access, car rentals, book exchange, breakfast

This place is really more a hotel than a hostel, which usually means that staff are probably more interested in making a buck than in fostering international peace and understanding—or in distributing warm fuzzies or keeping rates low, for that matter. That said, however, they do offer a lot of amenities here.

Best bet for a bite:
Souvlaki stands around Syndagma

Insiders' tip:
Drop off extra guidebooks at book exchange

What hostellers say:
"Not bad."

Gestalt:
GoodPellas

Safety: ◩

Hospitality: ◩◪

Cleanliness: ◩

Party index: ▲▲

Rooms are either singles, doubles, triples, or quads—many with private bathrooms, which cost more, of course. Like most other hostels in Athens, you aren't forced to share your sleeping space with more than four souls at a time.

You won't believe the great view of the Acropolis from the rooftop garden, though it's tainted by smog, of course. If you want to get away from that smog and head to the more desirable islands, staff will rent you a car for cheap. They'll also change your currency, hook you up with Internet access, do your laundry, and cook you a meal (all for a fee). Other amenities include a fax service, breakfast, a luggage storage area, and a free book exchange.

key to icons

▨ Attractive natural setting	▨ Comfortable beds	▨ Visual arts at hostel or nearby
▨ Ecologically aware hostel	**S** A particularly good value	▨ Music at hostel or nearby
✖ Superior kitchen facilities or cafe	▨ Wheelchair-accessible	▨ Great hostel for skiers
▨ Offbeat or eccentric place	▨ Good for business travelers	▨ Bar or pub at hostel or nearby
▨ Superior bathroom facilities	▨ Especially well suited for families	▨ Editors' Choice: Among our very favorite hostels
♡ Romantic private rooms	▨ Good for active travelers	

how to get there:

By bus: From city bus terminals A and B, take city bus to Omonia Square, then change to Metro and continue one stop to Monastiraki Station. Walk 50 yards along Ermou Str. to hostel at #104.

By car: Contact hostel for directions.

By plane: From airport, take Express Bus #091 to Syntagma Square, then walk along Ermou Str. to hostel at #104.

By subway: From port area, take subway seven stops to Monastiraki and walk 50 yards along Ermou Str. to hostel at #104.

By train: From train station, take #1 trolley bus to Syntagma Square, then walk along Ermou Str. to hostel at #104.

student & traveller's inn
Kydathineon 16, Athens 10558
Phone: 210–324–4808 or 210–324–8802

Fax: 210–321–0065
Web site: www.studenttravellersinn.com
Rates: €15–€20 (about $18–$24 US) per person; doubles €45–€50 (about $50–$62 US)
Credit cards: Yes
Beds: Number varies
Private/family rooms: Yes
Kitchen available: No
Season: Open year-round
Office hours: Twenty-four hours
Affiliation: HI
Extras: Laundry, safe, currency exchange, meals ($), travel agency, courtyard, bar

Students, travelers, and everyone else would be all too happy to find decent accommodations near the Plaka—and the Student and Traveller's Inn, sister hostel to the Aphrodite (see page 206), offers a better location with many of the same amenities. This is *the* best hostel in Athens, and with an amazing location to boot.

Rooms are bright and spacious with smooth wooden floors, real beds (instead of bunks), and nice

Best bet for a bite:
Authentic *tavernas* near (but not in) Plaka

Insiders' tip:
Greek folk museum is nearby

windows that open to all the sensory experiences that are Athens. A nice patio festooned with grapevines and tables makes a good place

What hostellers say:
"G'day mate."

Gestalt:
Inn-Sync

Safety:

Hospitality:

Cleanliness:

Party index:

to schmooze with your newfound friends, partaking of meals offered as well as the occasional ouzo. Staff are most likely Aussies or Brits, so English is not normally a problem; they can help you negotiate your way around this big and confusing city. You're also positioned near the Acropolis, which helps when making your sightseeing plans for the day.

how to get there:

By bus or train: Contact hostel for transit details.
By car: Contact hostel for directions.

hungary

Hungry for a little Hungary? The former Eastern Bloc-er is experiencing new life as a tourist destination, and Budapest is by far the prime attraction. It's even inexpensive to reach and travel in, if a little remote. That's because, unlike the Czech Republic's system, Hungary's train network is covered by Eurail passes. That means you won't need to buy extra tickets from your departure station, usually Vienna (three to four hours away), Prague (six hours), or Paris or Berlin (overnight trains)—though reservations are required on many of these long-distance trains, and those do cost a few bucks.

practical details

Hungary's unit of currency is the Forint (abbreviated Ft.). At this writing, 1,000 Ft. equaled about $5.50 US.

The bills come in the following denominations:

200 Ft.	=	approximately $1.10 US
500 Ft.	=	approximately $2.80 US
1,000 Ft.	=	approximately $5.60 US
2,000 Ft.	=	approximately $11.00 US
5,000 Ft.	=	approximately $28.00 US
10,000 Ft.	=	approximately $56.00 US

The coins come in pieces worth:

1 Ft.	=	approximately ½ cent US
2 Ft.	=	approximately 1 cent US
5 Ft.	=	approximately 2 cents US
10 Ft.	=	approximately 5 cents US
50 Ft.	=	approximately 28 cents US
100 Ft.	=	approximately 55 cents US

Hungary's country code is 36, and the Budapest city code is 1. To dial Budapest hostels from the United States, dial 011–36, then the numbers listed below. To dial Budapest hostels from within Hungary but outside the city, dial 06, pause, and then the numbers listed below EXACTLY AS PRINTED. To dial Budapest hostels from within Budapest, just dial the number's seven digits.

budapest

Thermal baths, bridges across the Danube, a castle on a hill . . . Budapest remains a wonderful city simply to wander through, tasting goulash or checking out the relics of the Communist era. (It's two cities, really—Buda and Pest—divided by the river.)

There are dozens of places in Budapest calling themselves a "hostel"—and you'll be accosted at Keleti Station by mobs of hustlers—but many are low-end hotels, and others are open only a very short summer season. To make matters worse when sorting through it all, the lineup changes each year as new fly-by-night places open and others close for good.

First things first: Don't be pressured into a bad decision. Observe two rules if you're thinking about an independent hostel. First, make them show you the location on a city map, and be sure the hostel is within the central city before agreeing to go for a ride—you might decide not to stay, and you don't want to be lost or stranded. Second, hand over no cash until *after* you've seen a room. If they won't agree to these two conditions, they're probably dishonest.

There are a couple "official" hostels in the city, plus loads of independent ones. The Hotel Marco Polo Hostel (see page 220) is the flagship of the Universum chain. Mellow Mood (yes, really), operates a string of summer joints. This chain runs "tourist information" booths in Keleti Station. The information really consists of getting you to stay in their hostel, but this chain does offer free rides. It has some good places and some not-so-good places, but the locations change so quickly that we weren't confident enough to rate them or give you the addresses. (We don't want you ending up in the boonies.)

For the purposes of this chapter, we have rated the one hostel (the Hotel Marco Polo) that stays open year-round. We haven't summarized the Strawberry hostels because none of them are open year-round and there's no true headquarters hostel. You can always get up-to-the-minute details about the current offerings of all three chains from the phone numbers we have included in those listings.

Note: Almost all these hostels have kitchens and Internet access, and all provide sheets, but almost none take credit cards. Also note that many smaller hostels here link their rates to the U.S. dollar, meaning that if the dollar is strong, they'll raise prices. That means the prices listed in this book aren't written in stone. City tours and car rentals are often available, though the hostels get a commission for these. Finally, smaller hostels tend to be run by just one or two staffers, so don't plan on checking in at 3:00 in the morning or checking out very early without letting them know ahead of time.

budapest hostels
at a glance

	RATING	PRICE	IN A WORD	PAGE
Red Bus Hostel	▚	3,600–9,500 Ft.	great	p. 223
Backpack	▚	3,000–3,500 Ft.	tops	p. 217
Hotel Marco Polo Hostel	▚	12,600–17,600 Ft.	plush	p. 220
Caterina Hostel	▚	2,000–6,800 Ft.	clean	p. 218
Museum Youth Guest House	▚	€20–€31	fun	p. 221
Station Guesthouse	▚▚	2,300–3,600 Ft.	boppin'	p. 224
Aquarium Hostel	▚▚	3,000 Ft.	tiny	p. 216
Yellow Submarine	▚	2,500–9,000 Ft.	cramped	p. 226

budapest

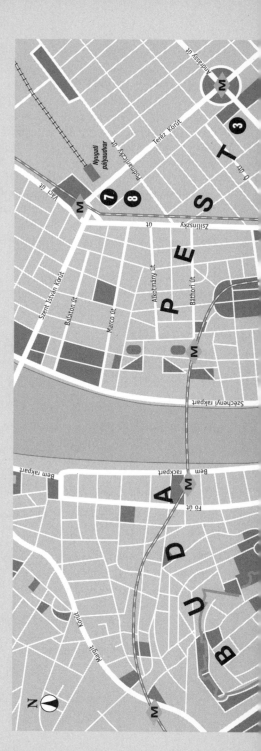

BUDA

PEST

aquarium hostel

Alsoerdosor út. 12, Second Floor, Budapest
Phone: 1–322–0502

Rates: 3,000 Ft. (about $17 US) per person; doubles 10,000 Ft. (about $56 US)
Credit cards: No
Beds: 15
Private/family rooms: Yes
Kitchen available: Yes
Season: Open year-round
Office hours: Contact hostel for current hours
Affiliation: None
Extras: TV room, free Internet access, laundry, lockers

S

For really lazy hostellers and their comrades, this is the only hostel within walking distance of Budapest's international train station.

Best bet for a bite:
At the station

What hostellers say:
"Never seen one this small."

Gestalt:
Train in vain

Safety:

Hospitality:

Cleanliness:

Party index:

There are only a handful of beds here, though, including the one double room, so you had better run there now or else reserve way ahead of time—it's unbelievably small and cramped, and very poorly lit besides.

You get a bunk, the same weird rabbit-cage lockers as at another hostel in town (must be a Budapest thang?), and all the basic extras you need like a kitchen, free Internet access, a laundry (cost: about four bucks per load), and the inside of a central downtown apartment. Unfortunately, the staff here just don't seem to care about much of anything, except keeping their cigarettes lit.

One good thing, though: You can enjoy a real bathtub in the bathroom for a change. Just don't push it, or you'll make ten enemies in a hurry—this is the only bathroom in the place.

how to get there:

By bus: Contact hostel for transit details.
By car: Contact hostel for directions.

By train: From Keleti pu. Station, cross Baross tér to Rakoczi út. and turn left onto the second street after the bridge. If you aren't there after 200 yards, you're probably lost. Backtrack and try again.

backpack guesthouse
Takacs Menyhért út. 33, Budapest
Phone: 1–385–8946

Fax: 1–385–8946
E-mail: backpackguest@hotmail.com
Web site: www.backpackbudapest.hu
Rates: 3,000 Ft.–3,500 Ft. (about $17–$19 US) per person; doubles 9,000 Ft. (about $50 US)
Credit cards: No
Beds: 50
Private/family rooms: Yes
Kitchen available: Yes
Season: Open year-round
Office hours: Twenty-four hours
Affiliation: None
Extras: Kitchen, TV room, bar, city tours, laundry, free Internet access, outdoor excursions, lockers, camping

Put this house closer to the city center and we would recommend this small, personable, and very cheap hostel above all the others in Budapest. Unfortunately, it's a loooooong way to Tipperary. But once you've done the bumpy bus ride out here—they claim it's only twelve minutes, believe it or not—you know this is where you belong. Forget downtown Budapest for a night and simply have a good time.

Truckloads of paint went into and onto Attila (yes, really) and Tori's house, making it look like nothing else on earth.

No two rooms are alike; there are two cozy doubles (neither with private bathroom, however), and a few dorm rooms with six or eight beds—and fans—each. There's a mellow kitchen scene, a comfy combination bar-and-TV room (which, we noticed, is stocked with 300 class-A videos in English), and the reception produces both good mood and groovy tunes all day and night long. There's a laundry (four bucks per load), Internet access (less than $4 per hour), a small garden in front of the house, and another, bigger one behind it. It's summer? Sleep in the treehouse! (Yes, Virginia, they have hammocks.)

Oh, and in case you're still interested in far-off Budapest, there's an information-packed board next to the reception. You can also book a tour with one of the helpful staffers, well worth a few extra bucks to have a local guide. Food? If it's not Sunday night—when they dole out free *gulash* (stew)—order a pizza. Daily orders go out around 6:00 P.M., just before the big group "where to go out today" conference, so you don't have to find the way back alone at night.

Best bet for a bite:
Free *gulash* on Sundays

Insiders' tip:
Bring your crampons

What hostellers say:
"This is heaven!"

Gestalt:
Leader of the (back)pack

Safety:

Hospitality:

Cleanliness:

Party index:

All this good feeling, spirit, and general cleanliness make for a good hostel. However, the buzz about this place is spreading rapidly, so advance reservations are essential. Even harder than getting a spot here is leaving. Some still haven't made it out: That's the reception crew.

how to get there:

By bus or train: From Keleti pu. Station, walk across street to Pizza Hut and catch #7 or #7A bus to Tetenyi út. (fifth stop after crossing river). Walk back underneath railway overpass, turn left, and continue to third right.

By car: Contact hostel for directions.

caterina hostel

Teréz krt 30, Budapest
Phone: 1269–5990

E-mail: info@caterinahostel.hu
Web site: www.caterinahostel.hu
Rates: 2,000–6,800 Ft. (about $11–$38 US) per person; doubles 6,000–6,800 Ft. (about $34–$38 US)
Credit cards: No
Beds: 38
Private/family rooms: Yes
Kitchen available: Yes
Season: Open year-round
Office hours: 8:00 A.M.–10:00 P.M.

Affiliation: None
Extras: TVs, Internet access, laundry, city tours

Basically a ramshackle, third-floor apartment that is really difficult to find, this is the kind of hostel you really only find in Central Europe. It's operated by cool owner Joe and a mother-daughter tag-team, each named, yes, Caterina, and it's conveniently located just off central Oktogon Square (with Metro, trolley, and bus stops all almost right in front of the hostel entrance). "Caterina always cleaning, yes, much cleaning!" they told us. Needless to say, the place is *extremely* clean.

Best bet for a bite:
Cactus Juice for steaks

What hostellers say:
"Sure is clean."

Gestalt:
Mama mia

Safety: [icon]

Hospitality: [icon]

Cleanliness: [icon]

Party index: [icon]

Or places, to be precise. There are two apartments on both sides of the Oktogon, one with eighteen beds, the other one with twenty more. And then there are another two apartments to rent for small groups (up to four people on a per-person basis). The bright and spacious dorm rooms come with four, six, or eight beds apiece. There are no lockers, but considering the hostel's small size, safety shouldn't be an issue. Three of the rooms have their own televisions.

There are two cozy double rooms as well—along with the apartments, these are an incredible bargain, but they're weirdly constructed. The floors are a little tall, maybe 10½ feet high, so they've gone and wedged in an extra step-up "floor" above the bunks—a double with a curtain instead of a door. You have to climb up steps to get there, kind of like climbing to a treehouse, and once there you can hardly stand upright or scramble back down during middle-of-the-night emergencies. Not the most comfortable setup, more like a tiny train compartment. Anyhow, Internet access costs about $2 per half hour, while the laundry runs you about three bucks per load.

This place is a good choice if you value cleanliness, hospitality, and quiet—which we do.

how to get there:

By bus: From main bus station, walk to Deák tér Station. Take Metro M1 line in direction of Mexicói út three stops to Oktogon stop.
By car: Contact hostel for directions.

By train: From Keleti pu. Station, take Metro Line #2 (red line) three stops toward Déli pu. to Deák tér Station, then change to orange line (#1) and continue to Oktogon Station. The hostel is right on the corner of Andrassy út. and Oktogon Square.

From Nyugati Station, take Metro M3 line toward city center (in the direction of Köbánya-Kispest) two stops to Deák tér Station. Change to M1 line and continue in direction of Mexicói út. three more stops to Oktogon stop.

hotel marco polo hostel

Nyar út. 6, Budapest 1072
Phone: 1–323–2999

Fax: 1–323–2998
E-mail: info@hostelmarcopolo.com
Web site: www.hostelmarcopolo.com
Rates: 4,000–12,000 Ft. (about $22–$67 US) per person; doubles 10,000–17,000 Ft. (about $56–$95 US)
Credit cards: No
Beds: 140
Private/family rooms: Yes
Kitchen available: Yes
Season: Open year-round
Office hours: Twenty-four hours
Affiliation: HI
Extras: Restaurant ($), free breakfast, baby beds, bicycle storage, currency exchange desk, newspapers, city maps, postcards, wake-up calls, Internet access, laundry, TV room, pool table, foosball table, city tours, TV rentals, car rentals, hair dryers, pickups

They call it the "pearl of a new generation of hostels," a suspiciously B.S.-sounding slogan, but this place—located in a six-floor, turn-of-the-twentieth-century downtown building—really is something else. By Hungarian standards, the Marco Polo charges incredibly high prices, but you get what you pay for—a comfy (if bland) place with superior (if expensive) rooms.

Let's start with free pickups from the central train station, a real bonus in a city where you don't know enough about the layout or the language to figure out public transit. Once you're here, you'll find that the rooms are immaculate, everyone has his or her own shower (towel and soap included), and what's this? A telephone! Certainly we've never seen *that* before in a hostel. When you've got calls to make, this is definitely the place for you.

If that still isn't enough for you, spoiled dude/dudette, head back to the reception and get yourself a TV set—they rent 'em. Or a car—they rent those, too, if you care. Then an interesting twist on the usual dorms: These dorms have twelve beds, but they're divided into little compartments, each containing a bunk and two lockers. Breakfast is included, and other meals are served in the large and spotless restaurant in the basement, where you also find a corner with a pool

Best bet for a bite:
Here and now

What hostellers say:
"Damn, no butlers?!"

Gestalt:
Polo club

Safety:

Hospitality:

Cleanliness:

Party index:

table and a dart machine (you'll have to visit to see what we mean). Other touches include Internet access (a deal at about $2 per half hour), an in-house Laundromat ($3 per load), and special beds they'll lend you if you're traveling with kids. Basically, this is everything you could want in a hostel—and more. But forget a party—you won't find one here.

Everything is clean here, if not antiseptic, and the reception staff run the extra mile for you (except if you try to snag a second slice of cheese at breakfast). This is the top bunk in town, no question about it.

how to get there:

By bus: Call hostel for free pickup or transit details.
By car: Contact hostel for directions.
By train: From Keleti pu. Station, call hostel for free pickup. Or take Metro Line #1 (red line) one stop to Blaha L. tér, or walk to Blaha L. tér Station. Walk straight along Rakoczi út. to third street on right and turn right onto Nyar út.

museum youth guest house
Mikszath Kalman tér 4, First Floor, Budapest
Phone: 1–318–9508

E-mail: museum@budapesthostel.com
Rates: Rates: €20–€31 (about $25–$39 US) per person; doubles €63.50–€76.50 (about $80–$95 US)

Credit cards: No
Beds: 22
Private/family rooms: No
Kitchen available: Yes
Season: Open year-round
Office hours: Contact hostel for current hours
Affiliation: None
Extras: Free Internet access, free postcards, laundry, TV room, book swap

Note: This hostel charges by the euro.

Budapest's coziest (i.e., tiniest) hostel is on the first floor of a castle-like old apartment building in the middle of the student ghetto, conveniently located just south of the city center.

Best bet for a bite:
Throw a rock; you'll hit something

What hostellers say:
"Excellent."

Gestalt:
Museum piece

Safety:

Hospitality:

Cleanliness:

Party index:

There are two "doubles" (they're above each other; remember that 8½ floor in *Being John Malkovich?* No? Oh, never mind . . .). The other rooms are of a more normal height and are well furnished with four or six beds, plenty of armchairs, and carpets about everywhere except the ceiling. Try to work out a computer agreement with the staffers: You let them play games until 7:00 P.M., and after that it's your turn to use the Net . . . for free! (They're supposed to charge you, but, hey, be nice and they might not.) Are you getting the point? This is a fun place, in a fun area of the city. However, hostellers have noted problems with upkeep and cleanliness. And you have zero privacy due to the layout. In spite of that, most everybody seems to like the place.

There's also a book swap you can take advantage of, a kitchen attached to the TV room, and a Laundromat where laundry costs about $4 US per load. The neighborhood, being a student area, has loads of pubs and pizzerias; you can't possibly go hungry or thirsty.

how to get there:

By bus: Contact hostel for transit route.
By car: Contact hostel for directions.
By train: From Keleti pu. Station, take Metro Line #1 (red line) to Astoria Station; exit at Muzeum Korut exit and walk past National Museum. Turn left at Pepsi sign onto Baross út., then bear left at

fork onto Reviczky út. Continue to Mikszath Kalman square; hostel is on square.

red bus hostel
Semmelweis utca 14, Budapest
Phone: 1–266–0136

Fax: 1–266–0136
E-mail: redbusbudapest@hotmail.com
Web site: www.redbusbudapest.hu
Rates: 3,600–9,500 Ft. (about $20–$53 US) per person; doubles 9,500 Ft. (about $53 US)
Credit cards: Yes
Beds: 50
Private/family rooms: Yes
Kitchen available: Yes
Season: Open year-round
Office hours: Twenty-four hours
Affiliation: None
Extras: Free breakfast, Internet access, tours, kitchen

The Red Bus Hostel actually consists of two places in the city center of Budapest—neither one is in a bus, however (huh?), so don't start trolling the streets looking for one. They are set in typical old Hungarian buildings; booking and check-in are handled at the office listed above.

Although both facilities are a little hard to find, once you get there you'll be thrilled. The rooms are attractive and clean, with beautiful high ceilings; the dorms hold six to eight beds each, and there's a supply of doubles and triples as well. Because of its downtown location, this is an ideal base from which to do all of your Budapest sightseeing and partying. As we said, there's also Internet access to keep in touch with fellow road-mates, the hostel's open twenty-four hours for night owls, the kitchen is huge, and management maintains (and actually tries to enforce) a friendly no-smoking policy—good if you're sensitive to the smoke that often

Best bet for a bite:
Eklektika

Insiders' tip:
Bookstore next door

What hostellers say:
"Slept like a baby."

Gestalt:
This Old Hostel

Safety:

Hospitality:

Cleanliness:

Party index:

pervades independent European hostels. All in all, it's a great addition to the lineup.

Note: Many hostellers have complained that this hostel loses reservations routinely. Double-confirm before arriving, and have a backup plan just in case.

how to get there:

By bus or train: Take Metro to Astoria Station. Exit station and follow exit sign for Kossuth Lajos út. Walk along Kossuth Lajos út. just 15 yards and take first right onto Semmelweis utca. Hostel is at end of street, on the left.

By car: Contact hostel for directions.

station guesthouse hostel

Mexikói út. 36/B, Budapest
Phone: 1–221–8864

Fax: 1–383–4034
E-mail: station@mail.matav.hu
Rates: 2,300–3,600 Ft. (about $13–$20 US) per person; doubles 7,200 Ft. (about $40 US)
Credit cards: No
Beds: 68
Private/family rooms: Yes
Kitchen available: Yes
Season: Open year-round
Office hours: Twenty-four hours
Affiliation: None
Extras: Internet access, laundry, breakfast ($), pool table, TV room, city tours, lockers, bar, music

Note: At press time, this hostel was closed for renovations.

Don't let the name confuse you: This hostel isn't exactly close to the city's central station; it's more like a half mile or more east of it, where things already start to look suburban. The hostel appears a rather dull yellow house from outside, but it's completely different once you're inside: You are supposed to leave graffiti on the walls—and the hostel provides you with *free paint* to do it.

Only in Europe.

The beds do have to be paid for, though. If you don't like sleeping with fifteen or so other people in the same room, reserve ahead and ask not to be put on the third floor. Up there, they lay mattresses out on that floor till every square inch is used up, and we wouldn't want you to go through that—especially since there's no air-conditioning, either, of course. There's another room with a double bed (no private bathroom here), while others have four to eight beds each. All the beds themselves are sort of unremarkable steel-pipe bunks, though everyone does get a locker.

Best bet for a bite:
Chinese restaurant at bus stop

What hostellers say:
"Good enough for me."

Gestalt:
Graffiti bridge

Safety: ◨

Hospitality: ◨

Cleanliness: ◪

Party index: 🎉🎉🎉🎉🎉

The vibe is hippie and party-hearty all the way; if you're a wallflower or a neat freak or a light sleeper, stay elsewhere. There's both a smallish kitchen for cooking and a television room on the second floor, but the main draw here is the common room—with a bar and occasional live music—downstairs, much hipper than you would expect from a Hostelling International–affiliated joint. This is where the slackers hang out until dawn, and rooms on the ground floor can be pretty noisy for that reason. Also, there have been serious cleanliness issues; in summer of 2003, health inspectors actually closed the place for ten days. Let's hope they've learned their lesson.

Other amenities include an Internet access terminal (about four bucks

key to icons

🍁 Attractive natural setting

🌍 Ecologically aware hostel

✕ Superior kitchen facilities or cafe

🍳 Offbeat or eccentric place

🚿 Superior bathroom facilities

♥ Romantic private rooms

🛏 Comfortable beds

Ⓢ A particularly good value

♿ Wheelchair-accessible

💼 Good for business travelers

👪 Especially well suited for families

🚴 Good for active travelers

🎨 Visual arts at hostel or nearby

🎵 Music at hostel or nearby

🎿 Great hostel for skiers

🍺 Bar or pub at hostel or nearby

🏅 Editors' Choice: Among our very favorite hostels

per hour, charged by the minute), a laundry (about $2.50 US per load), and breakfast for the equivalent of little more than a buck. Also, if you stick around long enough, you get discounts here for every night after your third.

how to get there:

By bus or train: From Keleti pu. Station, take #7 (red) bus one stop to Hungaria krt. After bridge, turn right. After 11:00 P.M., take #78E bus and ride four stops to near hostel.
By car: Contact hostel for directions.

yellow submarine hostel
Terez krt 56, Third Floor, Budapest 1063
Phone: 1–331–9896

Fax: 1–269–4354
E-mail: yellowsubmarine@mail.interware.hu
Web site: www.yellowsubmarinehostel.com
Rates: Rates: 2,500–9,000 Ft. (about $14–$51 US) per person; doubles 9,600 Ft. (about $54 US)
Credit cards: Yes
Beds: 38
Private/family rooms: No
Kitchen available: Yes
Season: Open year-round
Office hours: Contact hostel for hours
Affiliation: None
Extras: TV room, laundry, Internet access, locker

"We all live in a Yellow Submarine . . ." Yeah, but you never knew how many "we" meant—or how small a submarine could be!

Despite the small size and close quarters, it's still a popular hostel where you really get in "touch" with your fellow travelers. There are thirty-eight beds packed into this apartment, eight to ten to each room, plus a terminal with Internet access. Each bed comes with a locker (it looks like a rabbit cage), though you've gotta bring your own padlock if you want to use it.

Showers are run-down here, and there's just one each for boys and girls. Bad enough, and the warm water supply is somewhat limited, too. The rest of the place is equally filthy. If you're heading for a party, you might not care. If you intend to sleep, though, try to avoid the room behind the kitchen—it stays noisy late into the night.

All things considered, this *is* a good party place if you're into that aspect of traveling, and it has friendly staff. On the flipside, the whole place is way too small, the showers are limited, and the toilets are smelly; checkout is also rather early. You make the call.

One big advantage to this hostel, though, is the location on a downtown avenue (again, that means there's lots of noise). You aren't far from anything, including a twenty-four-hour grocery store just around the corner, a really weirdo restaurant called Sir Lancelot, and a dance club known as Bahnhof right across the street. Check it out. It'll give you reason to stay away from the grungy beds.

Best bet for a bite:
Supermarket across from Nyugati Station

What hostellers say:
"Yikes. Refund?"

Gestalt:
Sub-par

Safety:

Hospitality:

Cleanliness:

Party index:

how to get there:

By bus or train: From Keleti pu. Station, cross square and catch #73 trolley bus in front of McDonald's. Ride eight stops to Terez Korút. Hostel is on right, at #56.

By car: Contact hostel for directions.

ireland

It's green, rainy, and musical, and there's lots of Guinness, right? Well, yes, but there's more to Ireland than just all that. Hostels, for one thing, amazingly thick on the ground around the country—and most of them are darned good. Call the independent IHH-affiliated joints first; though laid-back, they offer the best mixture of socializing and comfy beds.

To see the best of Ireland, begin in Dublin and make a counter-clockwise trip to the Southeast, the gorgeous Southwest, the West, the Northwest, and Northern Ireland—which of course is a different country, part of the United Kingdom—and finally circle back to Dublin again. There are tons of budget flights to the east and west from London and elsewhere in England. Or try taking a ferry from Wales, France (covered by Eurail), or England.

practical details

Students can get a good deal on Irish transportation by buying a Travelsave Stamp from the USIT student travel network or at Ireland's larger transit stations. You've got to be a student or under a certain age, but if you are, this stamp saves you on each long-distance bus or train ride you take while holding it.

Ireland's national rail company, Irish Rail, is part of the CIE government transport network that helps get you around the country. Contact Irish Rail (www.irishrail.ie) for schedule and fare information. You can generally get anywhere the train serves—which isn't everywhere, unfortunately—for less than €35 (about $42 US) one-way. In the Dublin area, the DART (Dublin Area Rapid Transit) suburban train calls at twenty-five stations within a good-sized radius of the city.

Consider getting an Ireland-only rail pass such as the Irish Explorer—which gives you five days of riding on the rail network for about €138 (about $171 US) within a fifteen-day window—or the Irish Rover, good for five days in Ireland and Northern Ireland for about €170 (about $213 US). Traveling a lot? Go whole hog on the more expensive Emerald Card to get longer periods of bus and rail access, plus access to Northern Ireland's Ulsterbus and Northern Irish Railways systems. That card costs around €235 to €406 ($295 to $487 US) for eight or fifteen days of riding. Remember to buy any rail pass before you get to Ireland. Not traveling so much? Buy short-distance tickets one by one at train stations instead.

Buses are cheaper than trains in Ireland, and they go many more places; as a result, you're probably going to spend some time riding them. (For a bus trip of, say, Dublin to Cork and back, you'd pay about half the train fare.) The buses are reasonably on time and scenic, with lots of locals riding alongside you happy to give advice, opinions, or soccer scores. You might have to wait around for one, but eventually there'll be a bus going wherever you're going; just remember that on Sunday and certain Mondays, some lines run less frequently.

Irish Bus is the country's national bus carrier (also known by its Gaelic name, Bus Eireann). For rates, schedules, bus station information, and other stuff peruse their comprehensive Web site—www.buseireann.ie. Local buses fill the rest of the gaps, and these can range from incredibly efficient lines to laughable ones.

Bicycling is one of the very best ways of all to see Ireland; though challenging at times, the terrain rewards cyclists with view after splendiferous view. Rental agencies are everywhere—and many hostels within this book rent two-wheelers out, as well—or you could try one of the many tour outfitters that run country-road tours of various regions. The national clearinghouse for cycling information and tours is in Dublin: Walking Cycling Ireland, with a Web site at www.irelandwalkingcycling.com.

The unit of currency in Ireland is now the euro.

All phone and fax numbers in this book are listed as you dial them from Ireland or Northern Ireland. To call Irish hostels from within Ireland, dial them EXACTLY AS PRINTED. To call Irish hostels from the United States, dial 011–353 and then DROP THE ZERO from the number printed.

dublin

This is probably why you've come to Ireland: to experience Dublin in all its hectic glory—the bookshops, rain, pubs, pictures of U2 and James Joyce plastered around town . . . and much, much more. After weeks running around the Irish countryside, coming here can be a bit overwhelming—but it's sure to inject a bit of cosmopolitan culture in any trip that has started to degenerate into a string of rainy days or dull meals. And once you've landed in Dublin, it's not far to the surrounding counties—some, in fact, can even be reached with the DART bus and train system that serves the greater Dublin area. Many of these smallish villages are popular with local tourists, and with good

dublin

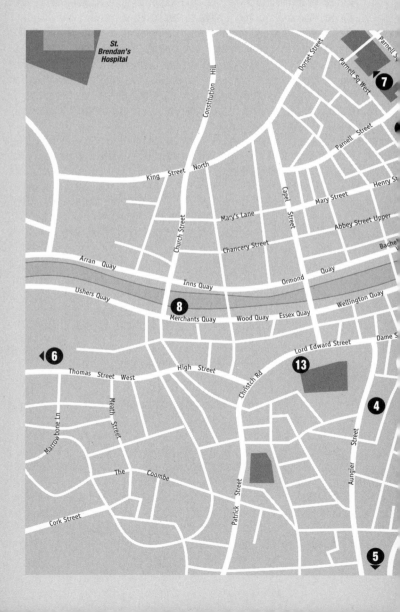

reason: They often come with their own castles, some of which have been transformed into arts centers, recording studios, or other strange (yet strangely appropriate) uses.

Getting around Dublin isn't too hard at all. The central city is very compact, based along both sides of the River Liffey, so much of it's walkable. Buses run seemingly everywhere else you want to go, too. Dublin Bus (01–873–4222, or www.dublinbus.ie on the Web) offers everything from one-day to one-month passes on its extensive network of services in both the urban and suburban areas. You can buy tickets from drivers, at more than 200 offices in the greater Dublin region, at the central O'Connell Street Station, or at still another office at Dublin Airport. (Bear in mind that not all bus drivers are able to give change.)

If you'll be using only buses while in town, get the Dublin Rambler pass. You can travel for three hassle-free days around town on the Dublin Bus (Bus Eireann) system and also use the Airlink service to and from the airport.

You can reach some hostels just outside the city using the DART suburban trains that chug north and south from the city center to such quaint-sounding places as Howth and Dun Laoghaire. The city's bus and municipal transit systems sell various passes for frequent train or train and bus users; an all-inclusive one, known as the Short Hop, will run about €9 (about $11 US) per day or €13.50 (about $18.00 US) for a family of two adults and up to four children. It's valid on almost everything except the city's special night buses and airport transit. A weekly Short Hop pass for all Dublin area buses and trains costs €30 (about $38 US).

Around town, besides the obvious Big Three draws—St. Stephen's Green, Trinity College, and the hip Temple Bar neighborhood—there are an amazing number of other old castles, buildings, and parks scattered within the city limits. Dublin Castle is the most central, but there's also Rathfarnham Castle (built in 1583 and pretty impressive), the National Botanic Gardens (more than 20,000 species of things growing here), the Pearse Museum, and the spooky Kilmainham Gaol. All have small admission charges and daytime open hours, and they can be reached by public buses.

At night? Well, what else? We love to hit the pubs, of course; you can't walk 10 feet without stumbling into another one. O'Shea's Merchant on Bridge Street is typical: The walls are plastered with photos and old knickknacks that give a real sense of continuity and history to the place. Locals file in to play the real Irish music, not the stuff you get on package tours. There's a tinge of sadness—always the sadness—but a sense, too, that people come here to acknowledge life.

That's the best of Dublin: Life pressing forward in defiant, even jubilant, celebration.

dublin hostels
at a glance

	RATING	PRICE	IN A WORD	PAGE
Globetrotters	★★★	€21–€25	fancy	p. 243
Marlborough	★★★	€17.00–€22.50	clean	p. 250
Kinlay House	★★★	€18–€31	central	p. 248
Gogarty's Hostel	★★	€18–€30	happy	p. 252
Litton Lane	★★	€17–€30	historic	p. 249
Belgrave Hall	★★	€12–€15	handsome	p. 238
Brewery Hostel	★★	€18–€22	cheery	p. 240
Abbey Court	★★	€19–€30	friendly	p. 234
Goin' My Way Hostel	★★	€15	tall	p. 245
Jacobs Inn	★★	€16–€31	iffy	p. 247
Avalon House	★★	€13–€37	tight	p. 237
Dublin International	★★	€19–€35	institutional	p. 241
Ashfield House	★★	€13–€40	okay	p. 236
Abraham House	★★	€18–€50	worn	p. 235
Four Courts	★★	€15–€29	iffy	p. 242
Isaacs Hostel Dublin	★★	€10–€16	noisy	p. 246
Mount Eccles Court Hostel	★	€14.00–€29.50	no	p. 251

abbey court hostel

29 Bachelor's Walk, O'Connell Bridge, Dublin
Phone: 01–878–0700

Fax: 01–878–0719
E-mail: info@abbey-court.com
Rates: €19–€30 (about $24–$36 US) per person; doubles €78–€88 (about $98–$106 US)
Credit cards: Yes
Beds: 228
Private/family rooms: Yes
Kitchen available: No
Season: Open year-round
Office hours: Twenty-four hours
Affiliation: IHH
Extras: Meals, Internet access ($), laundry

You can't get any closer to the famous O'Connell Bridge than this hostel; it's practically right on top of the thing.

Gestalt: Abbey Road
Safety:
Hospitality:
Cleanliness:
Party index:

They've got quite nice dorms, family rooms with twin beds and en-suite bathrooms, Internet access for a fee, and laundry, and they serve meals, too. This is a clean, secure bunk with a very good breakfast included—but try to avoid the biggest (read: tightest) dorms. You're just across the river from the hip Temple Bar area, where everybody wants to be, and Trinity College.

key to icons

- Attractive natural setting
- Ecologically aware hostel
- Superior kitchen facilities or cafe
- Offbeat or eccentric place
- Superior bathroom facilities
- Romantic private rooms
- Comfortable beds
- A particularly good value
- Wheelchair-accessible
- Good for business travelers
- Especially well suited for families
- Good for active travelers
- Visual arts at hostel or nearby
- Music at hostel or nearby
- Great hostel for skiers
- Bar or pub at hostel or nearby
- Editors' Choice: Among our very favorite hostels

how to get there:

By bus: From Busarus station, walk ¼ mile along Abbey Street or along river to O'Connell Bridge; hostel is just past bridge, on right.
By car: Contact hostel for directions.
By train: From Connolly Station, walk 300 yards to river, turn right, and continue about ⅓ mile to O'Connell Bridge. Hostel is just past bridge, on right.

---

abraham house hostel
82–83 Lower Gardiner Street, Dublin 1
Phone: 01–855–0600

Fax: 01–855–0598
E-mail: stay@abraham-house.ie
Rates: €14–€40 (about $18–$50 US) per person; doubles €76–€92 (about $95–$115 US)
Credit cards: Yes
Beds: 191
Private/family rooms: Yes
Kitchen available: Yes
Season: Open year-round
Office hours: Twenty-four hours
Affiliation: IHH
Extras: Bureau de change, breakfast, laundry, TV, pool table, restaurant ($), Internet, towels

---

Not exactly central, this place might be a good bet if you're getting in late or getting out early—it's on the way to Dublin's out-of-town airport.

Dorms come in rooms of four to ten beds, and they also do private rooms. They change currency, serve a breakfast, and maintain the usual TV room and pool table combo. Overall, the place is just so-so—possibly from heavy use, as it's always been a very popular place for some reason. (Take note and book ahead if you're really set on staying here.)

What hostellers say:
"So-so."

Gestalt:
Abraham sandwich

Safety:

Hospitality:

Cleanliness:

Party index:

Staff and management do a pretty good job here of making you feel at home. It's just that the facilities aren't Dublin's tops; complaints include worn plumbing and beds, a skimpy breakfast, erratic cleaning, and other quibbles. That's the price of popularity. Getting one of the twenty private rooms could improve the experience, though.

Let's just say that it's in the middle of the Dublin pack: unspectacular and showing wear and tear, but certainly not the pits. That distant location, though, makes it an unlikely pick.

how to get there:

By bus: Bus station in Dublin; call hostel for transit route.
By car: Call hostel for directions.
By train: Train station in Dublin; call hostel for transit route.

ashfield house
19–20 D'Olier Street, Dublin 2
Phone: 01–679–7734

Fax: 01–679–0852
E-mail: ashfield@indigo.ie
Web site: www.ashfieldhouse.ie
Rates: €13–€41 (about $17–$51 US) per person; doubles €76–€94 (about $95–$118 US)
Credit cards: Yes
Beds: 104
Private/family rooms: Yes
Kitchen available: Yes
Season: Open year-round
Office hours: Twenty-four hours
Affiliation: IHH
Extras: Breakfast, meals ($), laundry, bike rentals, currency exchange, laundry, cafe

This Dublin hostel has a really excellent position near that awesome Temple Bar area we keep telling you so much about. (Watch for U2 sightings, just in case our favorite stood-the-test-of-time band decides to show up at a pub near the hostel steps for a beer.)

Oh, the hostel. Right. It's certainly not terrible. Yet things are definitely showing wear and tear here, so the positive vibe is occasionally dampened.

The dorms at Ashfield contain the usual number of beds—in this case, usually four to twelve apiece—and they are more pleasant than we have any right to expect them to be. They even throw in a kitchen for fixing meals, bureau de change, free breakfast, laundry service (that costs money), and a cafe if you're feeling lazy.

The staff will rent you a bike, too, although we'd recommend seeing this hustle-bustle town on foot.

What hostellers say:
"What a neighborhood!"

Gestalt:
Ashfield of dreams

Safety:

Hospitality:

Cleanliness:

Party index:

how to get there:

By bus or train: Call hostel for transit route.
By car: Call hostel for directions.

avalon house
55 Aungier Street, Dublin 2
Phone: 01–475–0001

Fax: 01–475–0303
E-mail: info@avalon-house.ie
Web site: www.avalon-house.ie
Rates: €14–€36 (about $19–$45 US) per person; doubles €60–€78 (about $75–$98 US)
Credit cards: Yes
Beds: 281
Private/family rooms: Yes
Kitchen available: No
Season: Open year-round
Office hours: Twenty-four hours
Affiliation: IHH
Extras: Cafe ($), bureau de change, breakfast, laundry, TV, fireplace, lockers, Internet

We'd like to give our highest marks to Avalon House, universally checked off by our hostellers as one of Dublin's better hostels. We'd like to, but we can't; it wants to be home away from home, but it too often turns out to be more like a warehouse.

A brick building that once housed a medical school, it's quite close to wonderful Trinity College, St. Stephen's Green, and the hub of Dublin. (Would that make it Hublin?) Everything's run smoothly and interestingly by likable staff.

What hostellers say:
"It's okay, I guess."

Gestalt:
Halfalon

Safety:

Hospitality:

Cleanliness:

Party index:

The entire first floor at Avalon is a cafe with cheap, delicious food. This restaurant and coffee shop are two good bets in the city's sometimes bleak eating scene. Dorms here, in a separate area, generally contain four to ten beds, and they're okay—but can get quite crowded and loud, as they're just too small to handle the load. Some have en-suite bathrooms, which is good, but they're not as sweet and clean as they could be.

At least you can book one of the private rooms, change money, hang with fellow hostellers in the common area, and get accustomed to the coed hall bathrooms.

Oh, and one more big bonus if you're starting your Irish sojourn here: Stay a night and you can book all your future IHH nights from here to save the hassle of doing it later.

how to get there:

By bus: Call hostel for transit route.
By car: Call hostel for directions.
By ferry: Take 46A bus to downtown.
By train: From DART, take train to Pearse Station.

belgrave hall hostel
34 Belgrave Square, Monkstown (Dublin)
Phone: 01–284–2106

Fax: 01–280–5838
E-mail: info@dublinhostel.com
Web site: www.dublinhostel.com
Rates: €12–€15 (about $15–$19 US) per person
Credit cards: Yes
Beds: 50
Private/family rooms: Yes
Kitchen available: Yes

Season: Open year-round
Office hours: Vary; call for hours
Affiliation: IHH, IHO
Extras: Breakfast, bike rentals, laundry, car rentals, meals ($), Internet access, fireplace

---

Note: At press time, this hostel was closed for renovations.

Situated not in Dublin but a bit south, Belgrave Hall is pretty nicely outfitted and quite close to the Stena ferry dock in Dun Laoghaire if that town's hostel is already full up. It's better than most, thanks to a good facility with equally good management.

The early-Victorian building was constructed in 1840 and once served as the summer home of the Bishop of Meath (that's a county). Today the high-ceilinged dorm rooms contain from two to six comfortable beds each, and every room comes with a small ensuite bathroom tucked into it. The owner has added or refurbished some nice touches—wood floors, carpets, marble mantelpieces, friezes, atmospheric old chairs, dressers, detail on the ceilings, and such—that almost make the place a history lesson in itself.

What hostellers say:
"Nice views."

Gestalt:
Bay watch

Safety:

Hospitality:

Cleanliness:

Party index:

But that's not all. They've also added modern services, including Internet and e-mail access, open turf fires, and bike and car rentals. The common room here is especially nice, featuring a computer with said access as well as a comfy couch in front of a roaring fire, a writing table, and a chess board.

Ah, we didn't even mention the hostel's position right on Dublin Bay. Great views abound. As one more tremendous bonus, the Irish Cultural Institute is literally next door; you need walk no more than a few steps from the hostel door to catch all that traditional folk music you came here to hear.

how to get there:

By bus: From Dublin bus station, walk to Tara Street DART station; take DART train south to Seapoint Station. Walk down Seapoint Avenue to Belgrave Road, turn right, then turn left onto Belgrave Square. Go clockwise around square to number 34.

By car: From Dublin, take M50 ring road to N81 exit; exit and follow Stena Ferry signs to Blackrock, then take Seapoint Avenue to Belgrave Road. Turn left on Belgrave, then left onto Belgrave Square.

By train: From Dublin, take DART train south to Seapoint Station. Walk down Seapoint Avenue to Belgrave Road, turn right, then turn left onto Belgrave Square. Go clockwise around square to number 34.

brewery hostel
22–23 Thomas Street, Dublin 8
Phone: 01–453–8600

Fax: 01–453–8616
E-mail: brewery@indigo.ie
Web site: www.irish-hostel.com
Rates: €18–€22 (about $23–$28 US) per person; doubles €75 (about $94 US)
Credit cards: Yes
Beds: 52
Private/family rooms: Yes
Kitchen available: Yes
Season: Open year-round
Office hours: Twenty-four hours
Affiliation: IHH
Extras: Breakfast, pickups, TV, VCR, grill, terrace, laundry, fax, lockers, piano

Once you get here you'll see why it's called the Brewery Hostel. Grand old Guinness is only steps away, and chances are good that you'll spend half a day in there checking out the brewing of the black beverage that's almost a religion in Ireland.

Gestalt:
Beer with us

Safety:

Hospitality:

Cleanliness:

Party index:

This place, like most IHH joints, is as relaxed as you'd want it to be. Maybe too much so—dorms tend to be mixed-sex, which some hostellers loved and others despised. But the rooms are spacious, airy, and cheery, with somewhat newish bunks. They contain four, eight, or ten beds each, all with en-suite bathrooms; they maintain some double rooms for couples, too.

Breakfast is free, there's a good kitchen, and they've added lots of social amenities like a TV room and common area with comfy couches, plus—in the warm season—an outdoor patio with a grill. Some love it, some merely like it, but most agree it's friendly and good.

how to get there:

By bus: From O'Connell or Dame Street, take #123 bus to hostel.
By car: Call hostel for directions.
By train: From Heuston Station, walk up Steevens Lane and turn immediately left onto Thomas Street. Hostel is across street, just past Guinness brewery.

dublin international hostel

61 Mountjoy Street, Dublin 7
Phone: 01–830–1766

Fax: 01–830–1600
Rates: €19–€35 (about $24–$44 US) per HI member; doubles €48–€52 (about $60–$65 US)
Credit cards: Yes
Beds: 297
Private/family rooms: Yes
Kitchen available: Yes
Season: Open year-round
Office hours: Twenty-four hours
Affiliation: HI-AO
Extras: Breakfast, meals ($), laundry, conference room, bureau de change, tours, Internet access, bike rentals, parking, TV, shuttle service, luggage storage ($), sheets ($)

A former convent packed with almost 300 beds (depends on whom you ask, on which day, at which time of year), this place is huge and uninspiring. At first glance it's got all the charm of a nun's whack on the knuckles with a ruler. It's not in the greatest neighborhood, either—a bit of a sketchy area up on the workabout north side of the city. So don't go walking around outside alone at night if you can help it; the security precautions aren't supertight.

So why'd we stay? We had to. Naw, just kiddin'. Actually, it's halfway decent, although that institutional taste never quite goes away.

Gestalt:
Nun of the above

Safety: ◪

Hospitality: ◪◪

Cleanliness: ◪

Party index: 🍾🍾

Dorms are pretty bleak—packed, big, with basic beds that are sometimes comfy and sometimes uncomfy—but the cafe and kitchen partially redeem the place. Also, some rooms have their own bathrooms, so you don't always have to fumble your way to distant loos at 3:00 A.M. and the double room prices *are* a bargain in Dublin . . . There are fewer rules here than in many An Oige–affiliated joints, too, and it's kept obsessively clean.

They also kick in plenty of services like decent food, free big breakfasts, and a currency exchange. So it's not completely terrible or anything, just kinda sterile.

Our advice: If you're still coming, come early and pay extra for a two-to-six-bedded dorm. And watch out for the ghost of Sister Mary, wielding a ruler she'll take to uncouth hostellers. Just kiddin'—again.

how to get there:

By bus: From downtown, take #10 bus 1 mile to hostel.
By ferry: Ferry from Holyhead, Wales, to Dublin dock (2½ miles away), then catch Stena bus to Central Station, 1 mile from hostel. From Dun Laoghaire (7½ miles), catch Stena bus to Central Station.
By foot: From O'Connell Street bridge, walk north to Parnell Street; make a left, then right on Parnell Square. Go 4 blocks to Mountjoy.
By plane: From airport, take #41A bus to near hostel.
By train: Connolly Station is 1 mile; Heuston Station is 2 miles.

four courts hostel ◪◪

15–17 Merchants Quay, Dublin 8
Phone: 01–672–5839

Fax: 01–672–5862
E-mail: info@fourcourtshostel.com
Web site: www.fourcourtshostel.com
Rates: €15–€29 (about $18–$36 US) per person; doubles €62–€74 (about $70–$79 US)

Credit cards: Yes
Beds: 230
Private/family rooms: Yes
Kitchen available: Yes
Season: Open year-round
Office hours: Twenty-four hours
Affiliation: None
Extras: Internet access, laundry, bureau de change, lounge, game room, pool tables, tour desk, breakfast

---

This huge, independent hostel has a riverside location (right on the Liffey), a little bit of a hike to Trinity, Grafton Street, and everything else you wanna see. It's a very convenient base hostel for exploring the city if you don't mind wearing out a little shoe leather.

It's made up of three connected Georgian mansions, fitted out with dorms containing anywhere from four to ten beds apiece. There is also a selection of double rooms for couples and families. Laundry? Parking? Front-desk security? Big-screen TVs? Kitchen? Free continental breakfast? Natch. There's even an elevator, for crying out loud.

But there are a lot of problems here, too—it's cramped and often dirty. The feeling is one of disappointment at wasted potential. Could've been so much better, guys.

Gestalt:
Courts and spark

Safety: [rating]

Hospitality: [rating]

Cleanliness: [rating]

Party index: [rating]

how to get there:

By bus: From Busarus station, take #90 bus to hostel.
By car: Contact hostel for directions.
By ferry: Take #53 or #53A bus to hostel.
By train: From Heuston or Connolly Station, take #90 bus to hostel.
By plane: From Dublin airport, take #748 bus to hostel.

globetrotters tourist hostel
46–48 Lower Gardiner Street, Dublin 1
Phone: 01–873–5893

Fax: 01–878–8787
E-mail: gtrotter@indigo.ie

Web site: www.iol.ie/globetrotters
Rates: €24–€70 (about $25–$30 US) per person; doubles €90–€120 (about $113–$150 US)
Credit cards: Yes
Beds: 250
Private/family rooms: No
Kitchen available: Yes
Season: Open year-round
Office hours: Twenty-four hours
Affiliation: IHH
Extras: Breakfast, meals, laundry, sheets, luggage storage, TV, Internet

You're not always going to get it this good.

We were amazed at the Globetrotters, which (we've gotta admit) is a word we've seen hostels around the world slap onto their front doors—often with dire consequences. Memo to managers: Just calling yerself a globetrotter doesn't mean you've accomplished it. Too often, it's the bedbugs doing the trotting.

Gestalt:
World party

Safety:

Hospitality:

Cleanliness:

Party index:

Anyhow, this dapper place scored big right off the bat with a delicious and filling breakfast buffet that's included with your bed price—and get this: It's AYCE. That's right, All You Can Eat. Some hostellers wedged themselves out the front door hours later.

key to icons

🚿 Attractive natural setting

🌍 Ecologically aware hostel

🍴 Superior kitchen facilities or cafe

Offbeat or eccentric place

🛁 Superior bathroom facilities

♡ Romantic private rooms

🛏 Comfortable beds

S A particularly good value

♿ Wheelchair-accessible

💼 Good for business travelers

👪 Especially well suited for families

🚲 Good for active travelers

🎨 Visual arts at hostel or nearby

🎵 Music at hostel or nearby

⛷ Great hostel for skiers

🍺 Bar or pub at hostel or nearby

🏅 Editors' Choice: Among our very favorite hostels

Then we discovered the nifty courtyard garden, another nicety.

Granted, some of the dorms here are ten-bed affairs, and the doubles cost a little extra. But if you've snagged one of the thirty-eight private B&B–style rooms, you know this is pretty cool anyway: B&B, plus hostelling companions, all in one shot. Even the dorms (with six, eight, ten, or twelve beds each) are relatively comfy.

What else can we say? Oh, how about this: This palatial hostel is just a block from Dublin's main bus station, maybe 2 blocks from its train station, and the neighborhood actually doesn't suffer too badly. Just in case, though, security here is tight.

how to get there:

By bus: From bus station, walk 1 block to hostel.
By car: Call hostel for directions.
By train: From train station, walk 2 blocks to hostel.

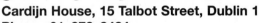

goin' my way hostel
Cardijn House, 15 Talbot Street, Dublin 1
Phone: 01–878–8484

Fax: 01–878–8091
E-Mail: goinmyway@esatclear.ie
Rates: €15 (about $18 US) per person; doubles €44 (about $55 US)
Credit cards: No
Beds: 40
Private/family rooms: Yes
Kitchen available: Yes
Season: Janurary 4–December 22
Office hours: 9:00 A.M.–midnight
Lockout: 10:00 A.M.–5:00 P.M.
Curfew: Midnight
Affiliation: IHH
Extras: Breakfast, coffee shop, meals ($)

S

Hard to find and not so wonderful that you'll want to stay for years, this hostel even changes its name periodically. And it's the only hostel in Dublin that charges you for showers, locks you out, and has a nighttime curfew. But it's dirt-cheap and better than several other places in town.

In general, it's an average joint—made less likable by the knee-straining hike to the sixth floor you might have to make if you've

---

Gestalt:
Goin' away

Safety:

Hospitality:

Cleanliness:

Party index:

---

drawn one of those rooms. Things are simple and too tightly packed (there are usually six to eight beds per tiny room), so it's definitely not a first-choice pick when in Dublin.

Only benefit? A semi-interesting Dublinesque location on a regular street above those all-knowing cogs of Irish life, the news agents.

how to get there:

By bus or train: Call hostel for transit route.
By car: Call hostel for directions.

---

isaacs hostel dublin

2–5 Frenchmans Lane, Dublin 1
Phone: 01–855–6215

Fax: 01–855–6574
E-mail: hostel@isaacs.ie
Web site: www.isaacs.ie
Rates: €10–€16 (about $13–$20 US) per person; doubles €52–€66 (about $65–$83 US)
Credit cards: Yes
Beds: 235
Private/family rooms: Yes
Kitchen available: Yes
Season: Open year-round
Office hours: Twenty-four hours
Lockout: 11:00 A.M.–5:00 P.M.
Affiliation: IHH
Extras: Cafe ($), bike rentals, lockers, bureau de change, music, meals ($), sauna

---

This eighteenth-century building was once a warehouse for a wine merchant. Now it's a rockin' hostel, almost legendary among the droves of hostellers who descend on Dublin each summer.

The place consists of singles, big but fun dorms, lots of private rooms, decent food, some bathrooms right in the rooms, and regular live-music nights to initiate you into the Irish way as soon as you've arrived.

However—and it's a big however—this place definitely isn't for light sleepers, and things have declined considerably. You couldn't sleep any closer to the train tracks if you wanted to (not that you do): They literally run right over the place. (Actually, it reminded us of the scene in *The Blues Brothers* where Jake and Elwood Blues nap in Elwood's apartment, right underneath Chicago's elevated train.)

Also, there's an annoying six-hour lockout during the heart of the day. Given that the place isn't the

Gestalt:
Train a comin'

Safety:

Hospitality:

Cleanliness:

Party index:

supercleanest, and the staff's attitude plain sucks, it's quite missable. (*Note:* This hostel added a sauna to its facilities. Okay . . . .)

how to get there:

By bus: From Busarus bus station, walk around corner to hostel.
By car: Call hostel for directions.
By train: Take DART to Connolly Station, then walk along Talbot Street to Frenchmans Lane and turn left to hostel.

jacobs inn
21–28 Talbot Place, Dublin 1
Phone: 01–855–5660

Fax: 01–855–5664
E-mail: jacobs@isaacs.ie
Web site: www.isaacs.ie
Rates: €16–€31 (about $20–$39 US) per person; doubles €62–€76 (about $78–$95 US)
Credit cards: Yes
Beds: 295
Private/family rooms: Yes
Kitchen available: Yes
Season: Open year-round
Office hours: Twenty-four hours
Lockout: 11:00 A.M.–3:00 P.M.
Affiliation: IHH
Extras: Meals ($), TV, pool table, bureau de change, laundry, lockers

Incredibly close to Dublin's main bus station, this biggish hostel manages at times to be friendly and at times to resembles a city shelter.

Gestalt:
Jacob's ladder

Safety:

Hospitality:

Cleanliness:

Party index:

It sports good-sized dorm rooms—with usually around six beds apiece—but also a good supply of doubles, triples, and quads for couples and families. Security could be better; the location is ace.

Plus there are other amenities, like a little restaurant that stays open all day long, good en-suite bathrooms in the dorms (news flash: showers seem to work), a currency exchange, a television room, and more.

how to get there:

By bus: 2 blocks behind Busarus bus station; ask at station for directions.

By car: Call hostel for directions.

By train: Take DART to Connolly Station, then walk along Talbot Street to Talbot Place; turn left to hostel.

kinlay house hostel

2–12 Lord Edward Street, Dublin 2
Phone: 01–679–6644

Fax: 01–679–7437
E-mail: info@kinlaydublin.ie
Rates: €18–€31 (about $23–$39 US) per person; doubles €60–€78 (about $75–$98 US)
Credit cards: Yes
Beds: 149
Private/family rooms: Yes
Kitchen available: Yes
Season: Open year-round
Office hours: Twenty-four hours
Affiliation: IHH
Extras: Breakfast, cafe ($), laundry, bike rentals, bureau de change, lockers, TV

This is it: the southern Dublin Temple Bar neighborhood you've heard so much about—and Irish rock stars.

And Kinlay House's brick Victorian supplies some of the best-positioned, if not the most comfortable, bunks in town. Beds come packed four to six to a room, usually, unless you grab one of a dozen or so private rooms (some with en-suite bathrooms, thank goodness). There are also three "XC" dorms with sixteen to twenty-four bunks each—lots of camaraderie, sure, but avoid this if you like privacy.

Gestalt: Kin-do

Safety:

Hospitality:

Cleanliness:

Party index:

Overall, it's a nice building, with great views of town. You'll like the laid-back atmosphere, the laundry, and the continental breakfast they throw in with your bed price. You might love or hate the mostly coed nature of the dorms, though.

how to get there:

By bus: Call hostel for transit route.
By car: Call hostel for directions.
By train: Train station in Dublin; call hostel for transit route.

litton lane hostel

2–4 Litton Lane, Dublin
Phone: 01–872–8389

Fax: 01–872–0039
Web site: www.irish-hostel.com
Rates: €17–€30 (about $21–$38 US) per person; doubles €75–€100 (about $94–$125 US)
Credit cards: Yes
Beds: 96
Private/family rooms: Yes
Kitchen available: Yes
Season: Open year-round
Office hours: Twenty-four hours
Affiliation: IHH
Extras: TV lounge, laundry, Internet access ($), breakfast

Talk about location—and history.

This hostel sits right on the River Liffey, in the thick of things, a short walk from most any part of downtown Dublin you're interested in. And it used to be a recording studio where frickin' U2 laid down tracks back before they all went techno, not to mention Vanbc—oops, Van Morrison.

Gestalt:
You, too

Safety:

Hospitality:

Cleanliness:

Party index:

They've got the standard bunkrooms, of course (breakfast is included with your rate), but also some pretty nifty apartments and private rooms. The apartments cost in the $100 range, but they're all worth it; all come with access to special family-friendly amenities like a laundry and kitchen.

how to get there:

By bus: From Busaras station, walk ¼ mile along Abbey Street or along river to O'Connell Bridge; hostel is just past bridge, on right, down Litton Lane.

By car: Contact hostel for directions.

By train: From Connolly Station, walk 300 yards to river, turn right, and continue about ⅓ mile to O'Connell Bridge. Hostel is just past bridge, on right, down Litton Lane.

marlborough hostel

81–82 Marlborough Street, Dublin 1
Phone: 01–874–7629

Fax: 01–874–5172
E-mail: mail@marlboroughhostel.com
Web site: www.marlboroughhostel.com
Rates: €17.00–€22.50 (about $21–$27 US) per person
Credit cards: Yes
Beds: 76
Private/family rooms: Yes
Kitchen available: Yes
Season: Open year-round
Office hours: Twenty-four hours
Affiliation: IHH
Extras: Breakfast, laundry, grill, bike rentals, sheets ($), storage

A nicely scrubbed and painted brick facility carved out of two restored Georgian buildings, this hostel's a fine option when in Dublin. It's quite close to the central attractions of the city, staff and crowd are cool, and the two-, four-, six-, and eight-bedded bunkrooms don't feel too bad. However, communal showers segregated by sex aren't for the shy.

Three private rooms are up for grabs, and all get a small breakfast plus use of the common room and kitchen combo.

Gestalt:
Marlborough men

Safety:

Hospitality:

Cleanliness:

Party index:

how to get there:

By bus: Bus station in Dublin; call hostel for transit route.
By car: From O'Connell Street, go north to North Earl, then turn right onto Marlborough; hostel is on left.
By train: Train station in Dublin; call hostel for transit route.

mount eccles court hostel
45 North Great Georges Street, Dublin 1
Phone: 01–873–0826

Fax: 01–874–6272
E-mail: meccles@iol.ie
Web site: www.eccleshostel.com
Rates: €14.00–€29.50 (about $18–$37 US) per person; doubles €63–€78 (about $79–$98 US)
Credit cards: Yes
Beds: 115
Private/family rooms: Yes
Kitchen available: Yes
Season: January 3–December 24
Office hours: Twenty-four hours
Affiliation: IHH
Extras: Breakfast, free parking

This eighteenth-century Georgian convent is semicentral, and they tried to outfit it with the right stuff—a mixture of various sizes of dorms and private and double rooms. Unfortunately, things don't live up to the promise. Dorms are too big—go for a double or quad—and the place isn't well-cleaned or maintained.

At least the James Joyce Center is practically next door. Otherwise,

Gestalt: Nun too soon	
Safety:	
Hospitality:	
Cleanliness:	
Party index:	

you're gonna hafta hoof it a little bit to get to the other sites, pubs, and so forth in town.

how to get there:

By bus or train: Contact hostel for transit route.

By car: Contact hostel for directions.

oliver st. john gogarty's temple bar hostel
58/59 Fleet Street, Dublin 2
Phone: 01–671–1822

Fax: 01–671–7637
E-mail: info@olivergogartys.com
Web site: www.olivergogartys.com
Rates: €18–€30 (about $23–$38 US) per person; doubles €60–€90 (about $75–$113 US)
Credit cards: Yes
Beds: Number varies
Private/family rooms: Yes
Kitchen available: Yes
Season: Open year-round
Office hours: Twenty-four hours
Affiliation: IHH
Extras: Restaurant, bar, TV

The single reason for staying at this hostel is the super location, a double whammy of good luck: One, it's in Temple Bar. Two, it's next to a pub with the same name as the hostel. So you can drown your sorrows if you don't like the bunks.

And, frankly, you might not. They come packed six or eight or more to a room and are only so-so at best. At least dorms have their own bathrooms. The

Gestalt: Beer and now	
Safety:	
Hospitality:	
Cleanliness:	
Party index:	

private apartments here aren't really part of the hostel and cost a lot more—upward of €100 (about $125 US) for a quad—but they do offer more amenities. All in all, this is a partying place, but it's better-kept than most of the hostels in town, and for that we can recommend it.

how to get there:

By bus or train: Call hostel for transit route.
By car: Call hostel for directions.

italy

Quite simply put, there's no other place like Italy in the world. Here culture, landscape, food, fashion, and *amore* (that's love) blend together in an intoxicating mixture. You might be a little apprehensive about going off to Italy, what with tales of *mafiosi* and thieves and long lines and such, but after you've been there a week I guarantee you'll probably never want to leave. Italy is the reason it's always a good idea to ask your airline about the penalties for changing your return date to a later one . . . a *much* later one.

Most hostellers will want to hit the big cities first, and we've described them below. But by all means save some time for the Italian countryside: places like Tuscany, Umbria, and Liguria possess some of the most amazing scenery (and some good hostels, too) in the world. It'll bring out the artist in you.

practical details

Alitalia is Italy's largest airline, but its fares are often higher than those of competitors. Shop around carefully, or take a train from London, Paris, Brussels, or elsewhere; you can catch an overnight train to Italy from just about everywhere in continental Europe. If you want to save money, Eurolines is a good company running comfortable long-distance buses around Europe for very competitive rates—including England to Italy and points between. In Italy, contact Eurolines Italia in Florence (via G.S. Mercadante 2b, Firenze 50144; 055–357–110) or check their Web site at www.eurolines.it.

Once you're here, trains are the best way to get around Italy—just don't count on superefficiency. Sure, it's dirt-cheap to ride by rail, even long-distance (you pay according to distance, with an extra charge on the fastest trains even if you have a Eurail Pass). But as for schedules, stations, arrival times . . . all are subject to potential change, so plan ahead to avoid missing connections—and always have a backup plan in case things go wrong. Sometimes they do.

Tickets are so cheap here that passes are useful only if you'll be traveling a lot, staying only one or two nights in each place. Italy's

Railpass is available in many different permutations, similar to the Eurailpass. Or get a flexible pass.

Remember that trains don't run as frequently on weekends; Saturday is usually the worst day to travel within Italy. International trains and sleeper cars usually run seven days a week, and Friday and Sunday are feast or famine; check schedules and think like a local. If you want to go to the Italian beaches, for example, lots of trains will be running from the cities to the country on Friday afternoon. Sunday, everyone's either going to the beach or going home.

Buses can be a cheaper (though slower) ride, and they're extremely useful in parts of Italy where trains simply don't go—reasonably on time, scenic, with lots of locals riding alongside you happy to give advice or opinions or soccer scores. Buy tickets for long-distance buses at the local bus station, and buy tickets for city buses at tobacco shops (called *tabbachi*), not from the drivers. Always remember to punch your ticket on the bus; there will be a machine on every bus that stamps the current date and time on the ticket's magnetic strip. Most are good for one hour.

Italy's country code is 39. To call Italian hostels from North America, dial 011–139 and then the numbers AS PRINTED IN THIS BOOK. To call Italian hostels from within Italy, simply dial the numbers AS PRINTED. Don't use loose change or your calling card; instead, buy the artsy Telecom Italia phone cards at tobacco shops and other small markets and stick 'em into the slots in the phones. (Push the card all the way in—*hard*—with the magnetic strip facing up.) Local calls won't eat up much of these cards, but long-distance calls within a country definitely will; figure about ten or fifteen minutes per card at most.

Italy's unit of currency is now the euro. Note that you might have trouble with some Italian ATMs if your card is on the Plus system. Just keep hunting. Banco Toscana is one that will work with Plus; BNL is another—but if you're outside Tuscany, it could take a while to find one. It's better to get a card that works on the Cirrus system, which is much more heavily used in Italy.

florence (firenze)

Firenze's wonders can't be overstated, and although you're going to have to wait in line to experience them, the place is really something.

florence
(firenze)

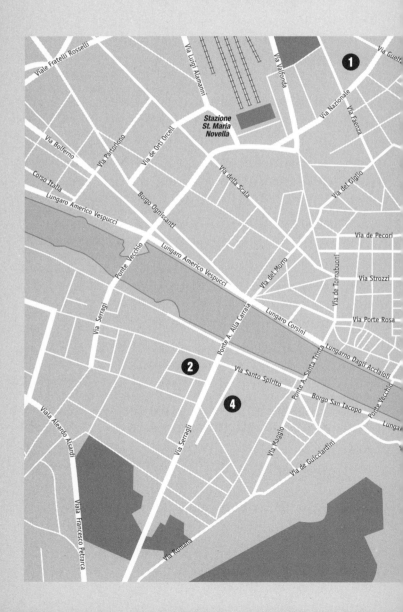

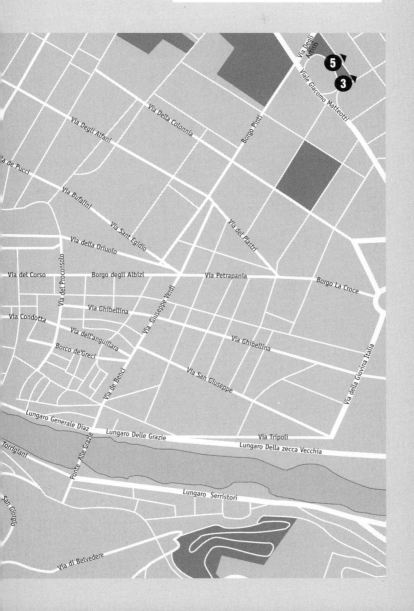

The art hanging indoors and the architecture standing outdoors rival anything else in the world. A few words here can't possibly do it all justice, so just go see it. Parts of the city are gorgeous; parts are somewhat dirty and noisy, but you probably won't care. Simply dive in and try to ignore the press of the crowds.

Getting to Florence is easy; walking downtown is, too. Streets radiate outward from the extremely convenient train and bus stations—which, for once, are actually located near the action, across from a great church and just ten minutes' walk from some of the most amazing buildings and paintings in Italy. Get a really good map and use it; the streets can be a bit maddening here. Also watch yourself late at night in dim alleys, and take advantage of lots of American-geared services around town: stores, Internet places, cafes, and the like.

The hostel situation is amazingly good here, too. This city has five decent hostels, not a really bad one in the bunch, and we can honestly say that this came as a real surprise. Most aren't central, but a fifteen-minute walk will usually get you right into town.

In short, Firenze's one of a kind. A bit of a madhouse, but we love it.

florence hostels
at a glance

	RATING	PRICE	IN A WORD	PAGE
Archi Rossi	◤	€21–€35	sociable	p. 259
Pensionato Pio X	◤	€17–€19	religious	p. 263
Ostello Villa Camerata	◤	€18–€23	rural	p. 262
Ostello Santa Monaca	◤	€15–€19	tight	p. 260
7 Santi Ostello	◤◥	€15–€31	okay	p. 265

ostello di archi rossi
Via Faenza 94r, Firenze
Phone: 055–290–804

Fax: 055–230–2601
E-Mail: info@hostelarchirossi.com
Rates: €21–€35 (about $26–$44 US) per person; doubles €80 (about $100 US)
Credit cards: No
Beds: 87
Private/family rooms: Yes
Kitchen available: No
Season: Open year-round
Office hours: 7:30–9:30 A.M.; 3:30–11:30 P.M.
Lockout: 11:00 A.M.–2:30 P.M.
Curfew: 1:00 A.M.
Affiliation: None
Extras: Movies, patio, snack shop ($), breakfast, lockers, laundry, Internet access

This newish hostel—where guests attempt to draw their own *Last Supper* on its walls with the hostel crayons—has made quite an impression on legions of enthusiasts. It isn't as grungy as many other backpacker-type places in Europe, and it isn't a twenty-four-hour party. All in all, it's not a bad option.

The entranceway could easily pass for that of a museum or nice hotel. Inside, it's just as nice: Bunks often come with en-suite bathroom, though they say you should get here by 9:00 A.M. if you want any hope of getting a bed. We'd take it one step further and advise you to get your butt over there as early as possible. Don't count on calling; they don't take reservations. The ten private rooms with en-suite bathrooms are especially in demand. Singles, triples, quads, and five-, six-, and nine-bedded dorms are also available.

Best bet for a bite:
Giardino di Barbano for pizza

What hostellers say:
"Really nice."

Gestalt:
Archi's bunks

Safety:

Hospitality:

Cleanliness:

Party index:

The hostel provides free breakfast, Internet access, hot showers, sheets, and blankets; a towel rental will cost you all of half a euro.

Guests have access to a teeny microwave and refrigerator. No stovetop here, though. Showering and other stuff you do in the bathrooms will be enhanced by the superclean facilities. And people love the nice outdoor terrace as a gathering place.

The staff are very nice and do speak some English. The best thing about this hostel is its location: It's only five minutes from the train station and ten or fifteen minutes by foot to such sites as San Lorenzo, Il Duomo, and some nice shopping areas. There's easy access to both the local orange buses that zip (okay, crawl) around Florence and the blue SITA buses, which go off to day trips in the surrounding countryside.

Just bring earplugs to block out the delightful street sounds at night—this is just 2 blocks from Florence's main train station, so it ain't superquiet even if it is superconvenient for arrivals and departures. All in all, a good retreat from the hectic hustle and bustle of Florence.

how to get there:

By bus: From bus station, walk left around corner to train station and cross through station onto via Nazionale. Walk to via Faenza; turn left. Hostel sign is neon blue. Or take via Val Fonda, turn corner at via Cennini, and follow it to via Faenza; cross street. Hostel is on right, marked by blue sign.

By car: Call hostel for directions.

By train: From Firenze Station, exit left onto via Nazionale and walk to via Faenza; turn left. Hostel sign is neon blue. Or take via Val Fonda, turn corner at via Cennini and follow it to via Faenza; cross street. Hostel is on right, marked by blue sign.

By plane: Airport is outside Florence. From airport, take bus to train station stop and walk up via Val Fonda to via Cennini; turn corner and follow via Cennini to via Faenza, then cross street. Hostel is on right, marked by blue sign.

ostello santa monaca
(santa monaca hostel)
Via Santa Monaca 6, 50124 Firenze
Phone: 055–268–338 or 055–239–6704

Fax: 055–280–185
E-mail: info@ostello.it
Rates: €15– €19 (about $18–$24 US) per person
Credit cards: Yes

Beds: 140
Private/family rooms: None
Kitchen available: Yes
Season: Open year-round
Office hours: 6:00 A.M.–1:00 P.M.; 2:00 P.M.–2:00 A.M.
Lockout: 10:00 A.M.–2:00 P.M.
Curfew: 1:00 A.M.
Affiliation: None
Extras: Lockers, laundry, TV room, fax service, Internet access ($)

This hostel, located away from the madding crowds on the other side of the Arno (but it's a short walk to the Uffizi across a pretty bridge), provides quiet seclusion and clean bathrooms, to boot.

Though not affiliated with HI, it still follows some of the stricter rules, like a brutal, 10:00 A.M.-starting lockout and a more tolerable 2:00 A.M. curfew. You can't make a reservation here, but you can put yourself on a waiting list during the morning office hours.

Dorms border on the claustrophobic, with a minimum of eight bunks and a maximum of twenty bunks. Ouch! No lockers, either, so if you're sleeping by a door you'd be smart to chain your stuff to something. However, there's a safe deposit box for small valuables like passports and traveler's checks. It's tight as a tick here, but at least it's clean.

You're bound to run into people you've seen scrambling all over Europe in other hostels. You'll look at your traveling partner and say, "Hey, wasn't that the guy who put his foot in my face as he climbed to the top bunk at the Young & Happy in Paris?" or "Wasn't she the loud American who wouldn't shut up?" Yep, they be the ones, but you might be happy when it turns out to be someone you yukked it up with or thought was cute. Anyhoo, this place attracts Americans like the Super Bowl does football fans.

Some detractors have objected to noisy rooms and small dorms with too many bunks. And although the stays-open-late kitchen is

Best bet for a bite:
Sugar Blues

Insiders' tip:
Internet cafe just
down street

What hostellers say:
"Pretty social."

Gestalt:
Santa's little helper

Safety:

Hospitality:

Cleanliness:

Party index:

free for use, alas, there are no utensils. It's B.Y.O.U. all the way. Still, most agree that it's a pretty decent place to rest your head in this culture-permeated town. Good thing the hostel has struck up a deal with a nearby eatery for meals.

how to get there:

By bus or train: Call hostel for transit route.
By car: Call hostel for directions.
By plane: Airport outside Florence; call hostel for transit route.

ostello villa camerata
(friendship village hostel)
Viale Augusto Righi 2/4, 50137 Firenze
Phone: 055–601–451

Fax: 055–610–300
Rates: €18–€23 (about $23–$29 US) per HI member; doubles €50–€60 (about $63–$75 US)
Credit cards: No
Beds: 322
Private/family rooms: Yes (not in summer)
Kitchen available: No
Season: Open year-round
Office hours: 7:00 A.M.–midnight
Lockout: 10:30 A.M.–2:00 P.M.
Curfew: Midnight
Affiliation: HI-AIG
Extras: Meals ($), bar, library, movies, laundry ($), Internet access, TV, campground, parking, breakfast

This exceptionally popular hostel asks that you reserve months in advance with a letter and credit card deposit, or several weeks ahead if you fax. Bottom line: Don't just show up expecting a bed.

Lots of folk like this huge hostel for its cleanliness, fabulous gardens, and belly-busting pasta-and-salad meals. Dorm rooms are fairly standard, although the family-room wing does contain quads with their own bathrooms—rooms that are not available during the high summer season, we should hasten to add. The dining room is a very sociable and popular place for exchanging addresses and stories, as are the handsome marble front porch, the Internet room, and about

anywhere else here. One of the best places in Italy to hook up with
others for ride-sharing, we'd say.
And breakfast is included with a
bunk.

The big minus here is the usual
Hostelling International-in-Europe
story: This is quite a jaunt from
town, although greenery is on
all sides and you're in a handsome villa. You have to take the
bus for almost half an hour from
the Duomo to get out here, and
then—if it's late at night—walk a
poorly lit half-mile-long driveway
with woods on both sides. A
little creepy feeling, although in
summer things should be hopping enough to make you feel safe. No
kitchen, either, so pack in your food—get it at the city's central market,
near the train station. There's a busy campground here, as well.

Oh, and keep in mind that you might occasionally be sharing bunkrooms with schoolchildren who could seriously cramp your style—as
will the great distance from town, the hot-and-cold staff, and the awful
10:30 A.M. lockout that boots you out to the bus stop for the day.

Best bet for a bite:
Il Latini (back in town)

What hostellers say:
"Love it."

Gestalt:
Candid camerata

Safety:

Hospitality:

Cleanliness:

Party index:

how to get there:

By bus or train: From Firenze Station, exit track 5 and take #17A or
#17B bus to hostel, walk through gates and follow signs.
By car: Call hostel for directions.
By plane: Call hostel for transit route.

pensionato pio x
(pope pius x hostel)
Via dei Serragli 106, Firenze
Phone: 055–225–044

Fax: 055–225–044
Web site: www.hostelpiox.it
Rates: €17–€19 (about $21–$29 US) per person
Credit cards: No
Beds: 64
Private/family rooms: No
Kitchen available: No

Season: Open year-round
Office hours: Vary; call for hours
Curfew: Midnight
Affiliation: None

Note: Two-day minimum stay required.

Open since the '50s, this is another great and friendly hostel for the Firenze-bound hosteller, across the river in the staid but tried-and-true Oltrarno's residential neighborhood. However, it is as quiet as a mouse. Quieter. This is *not* your best choice if you wanna party, or even meet another person on your travels. (It is good for Bible study, though. After all, it used to be a convent)

Once again, plan ahead and you'll probably snag a Spartan bunk in a room that's big but limited to just four hostellers. Pay extra for a bath in your room, but showers are included with the rate. The staff are pretty friendly, although you can only stay for up to five nights. There isn't a kitchen for cooking.

What hostellers say:
"It's *what* time in the morning?"

Gestalt:
X marks the spot

Safety: 🏔

Hospitality: 🏔

Cleanliness: 🏔

Party index: 🍷

Watch out, though, late sleepers—you might have to check out by 9:00 in the morning. Yikes!

how to get there:

By bus: Take #36 or #37 bus to first stop after crossing river.

key to icons

🍃	Attractive natural setting
🌍	Ecologically aware hostel
✗	Superior kitchen facilities or cafe
🍲	Offbeat or eccentric place
🚿	Superior bathroom facilities
❤	Romantic private rooms
🛏	Comfortable beds
S	A particularly good value
♿	Wheelchair-accessible
💼	Good for business travelers
👫	Especially well suited for families
🚴	Good for active travelers
🎨	Visual arts at hostel or nearby
🎵	Music at hostel or nearby
⛷	Great hostel for skiers
🍺	Bar or pub at hostel or nearby
🏅	Editors' Choice: Among our very favorite hostels

By car: Call hostel for directions.

By train: From Firenze Station, exit by track #16, turn right and walk to P. della Stazione. Go straight down via degli Avelli, with church Santa Maria Novella on immediate right. Cross P. Staz. Maria Novella and continue straight down via dei Fossi, over the Ponte alla Carraia Bridge, and down via dei Serragli. Or take #36 or #37 bus to first stop after crossing river.

---

7 santi ostello (7 saints hostel)
Viale dei Mille 11, Firenze
Phone: 055–504–8452

Fax: 055–505–7085
E-mail: info@7santi.com
Rates: €15–€31 (about $18–$39 US) per person; doubles €42–€52 (about $53–$65 US)
Credit cards: No
Beds: 65
Private/family rooms: Yes
Kitchen available: No
Season: Open year-round
Office hours: Vary; call for hours
Affiliation: None
Extras: Bar, TV, laundry, fax

Part of a convent beside the Church of the Sette Santi (Seven Saints), this relatively new hostel touts its central location near Campo di Marte and amenities as reasons to pay extra cash for a night's stay. To be sure, it's a big and attractive place, but not perfect. Curiously, annual infestations of mosquitoes are one of the negatives to look out for.

Singles, doubles, and bunks in quad to six-bedded dorm rooms are priced according to a fairly complicated structure based on size and bathroom availability.

What hostellers say:
"Not very close to town."

Gestalt:
Santi clause

Safety:

Hospitality:

Cleanliness:

Party index:

Positives include telephones on each floor (you may have to search for one that works), a sports field, a laundry, and fax service.

So take your pick: Save a buck and stay somewhere else, or open up your wallet and ratchet up the experience.

how to get there:

By bus: Take #11 or #17 bus to Sette Santi stop; walk one block to hostel.

By train: From Santa Maria Novella Station, take #11 or #17 bus to Sette Santi stop; walk one block to hostel.

milan (milano)

Milano, way up in the center of the flat north, is Italy's style and power capital—a city defined by Gucci fashion shows, execs power-lunching with cell phones glued to their ears, and everyone looking just a little too perfect. It's also a place experiencing a surprising recent upswing in violent crime, so look sharp at night. There really isn't as much to see in Milan as you might think—the stock exchange is more symbolic of its current role in Italian society—but the *duomo* (cathedral) here is one of the country's finest and well worth finding, even if it is quite a hike from the main train station. Take the city subway to get there.

ostello piero rotta
(piero rotta hostel)
Salmoiraghi 1, 20148 Milano
Phone: 02–392–670–95

Fax: 02–330–001–91
E-mail: milano@ostellionline.org
Rates: €19–€22 (about $24–$28 US) per HI member
Credit cards: No
Beds: 376
Private/family rooms: None
Kitchen available: No
Season: January 13–December 22
Office hours: Twenty-four hours
Lockout: 9:30 A.M.–3:30 P.M.
Curfew: 1:00 A.M.
Affiliation: HI-AIG
Extras: Internet access, gardens, TV, lockers, fax, bar

This place obviously has little of the easygoing attitude pervasive at other northern Italian hostels; the no-exceptions lockout and strict lights-out policy could sour your experience. Definitely don't come here expecting lots of warm and fuzzy vibes.

We'll concede that the hostel's location can be serene, on the outskirts of town, but this could seriously cramp your partying style, since you have to return by the 1:00 A.M. curfew. But we've also heard that, on some nights, crowds of teens gather on the front lawn, talking and smoking. There's a three-day-max stay, too. Your only consolation? Milano isn't really a destination. It's more of a business center, where fashion, design, and movie powerhouses operate and tourists find little to do. It's a mighty convenient transit hub, however, with lots of high-speed trains going all over Europe and lots of flights heading off to North America.

What hostellers say:
"Are we anywhere *near* the city?"

Gestalt:
Milan-dollar hotel

Safety:

Hospitality:

Cleanliness:

Party index:

You are almost always guaranteed a room here, at least, so don't worry too much about being shut out. (You can always call ahead to be sure.) Beds are poor-quality, though, and bathrooms are just short of a horror show. Bring your own T.P. We can't emphasize this enough.

Remember that Milano empties out in August—completely—so that's the worst time to come here. Nothing is open. Nothing. DO NOT COME IN AUGUST. There. We warned you.

Still, this is the cheapest possible lodging option in one of Italy's most expensive cities. And it's certainly clean and well run (if you like Gestapo tactics), if a tad hospital-like. No, make that dentist-like—a dentist with almost 400 chairs.

how to get there:

By bus: Take bus #68, #90, or #91 to ostello (hostel) stop, then walk 200 yards to hostel.

By plane: Two airports. Milano Linate is 15 kilometers (about 10 miles) from hostel; Milano Malpensa is 40 kilometers (about 25 miles) from hostel. Call hostel for transit routes.

By subway: Contact hostel for transit route.

By train: Centrale Station, 5 miles from hostel; contact hostel for transit route.

rome (roma)

Chances are, if you've come to Italy, you're going to end up in Rome sooner or later. We've just got two words to say before we leave you off here.

Good luck.

Seriously, though, if you're flying into Rome, don't even try to deal with the chaos while jet-lagged. Instead, we'd recommend that you grab a train straight from the airport (which is south of the city) and head away to Naples, one of its associated islands, or the beautiful Amalfi coast—somewhere south of Rome on the blue ocean where you could catch up on sleep and prepare mentally for the cauldron that is Rome.

Once there, you'd have to be nuts to rent or drive a car—and we're pretty crazy when it comes to driving. But this is one place where we threw our hands up and cried uncle. Use the bus system, which may be hard to understand at first but does the job. Taxi drivers appear to be insane but are savvy. The two Metropolitan (subway) lines are also very useful.

rome hostels
at a glance

	RATING	PRICE	IN A WORD	PAGE
The Beehive	◪◪	€20–€25	homey	p. 272
Fawlty Towers	◪	€20–€50	good	p. 274
Pensione Ottaviano	◪◪	€20–€27	tiny	p. 277
Foro Italico	◪◪	€18	plain	p. 276
Alessandro Palace Hostel	◪◪	€18–€35	okay	p. 269
Pensione Sandy	◪◪	€25–€30	small	p. 278
M & J Hostel	◪	€18–€35	mediocre	p. 275

Coming by train? Be extra careful around the Stazione Termini, the train station where most Roman hostellers first arrive. This area—as well as several of the busiest tourist areas in the city, like the Spanish Steps—is notorious for thieves and pickpockets.

So don't wear that expensive camera around your neck, don't flash too much cash, don't wear shorts that advertise your greenhorn status, don't walk alone down teenie alleys at night, and don't pay attention to the hordes of kids who'll do anything—even toss a baby in your face—to occupy you for just the moment it takes to snatch your wallet. Our advice: Wear a money belt.

Any other advice? Well, just this: When in Rome . . .

alessandro palace hostel
Via Vicenza 42, Roma
Phone: 064–461–958

Fax: 064–938–0534
E-mail: palace@hostelsalessandro.com
Web site: www.hostelsalessandro.com
Rates: €18–€35 (about $23–$42 US) per person; doubles €66–€110 (about $83–$138 US)
Credit cards: Yes
Beds: 53
Private/family rooms: Yes
Kitchen available: Yes
Season: Open year-round
Office hours: Twenty-four hours
Affiliation: None
Extras: TV, coffee, bar

A young staff, pub, and laid-back atmosphere make up—partly—for the tight fit in the dorm rooms here, the stuffy dorms, the chaotic streetside location, and lack of cleaning. You can avail yourself of cooking facilities as well as the free-flowing coffee and free pizza parties once a week.

However, lack of a curfew could mean people traipsing in at all hours of the night and making your attempts at sleep futile. *Caveat emptor.*

Legend has it that management encourages travelers to get to know one another over glasses of vino. Things seem to be getting

rome
(roma)

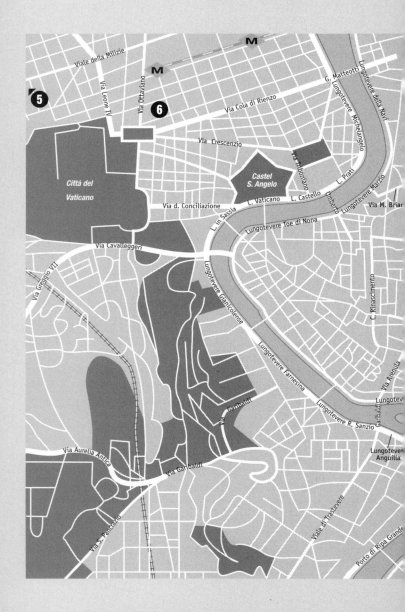

What hostellers say:
"This place isn't too
great."

Gestalt:
Chaosissimo

Safety:

Hospitality:

Cleanliness:

Party index:

better here bit by bit; give it a chance if you want a central bunk in Roma.

Note that two annexes of this hostel are now open, with the same prices as the original Palace.

how to get there:

By bus: Call hostel for transit route.

By car: Call hostel for directions.

By train: From Termini Station walk along via Marsala approximately 65 feet and turn left onto via Vicenza. Walk about 4 blocks to hostel.

the beehive hostel

Via Marghera 8, Roma 00185
Phone: 064–470–4553

E-mail: info@the-beehive.com
Web site: www.the-beehive.com
Rates: €20–€25 (about $25–$30 US) per person; doubles €70–€80 (about $88–$100 US)
Credit cards: Yes
Beds: Contact hostel for current number
Private/family rooms: Yes
Kitchen available: No
Season: Open year-round
Office hours: Twenty-four hours
Affiliation: None
Extras: Alarm clocks, hair dryer, luggage storage, walking and biking tours, earplugs, safe, garden, free Internet access, art gallery, yoga classes, cafe

Rome desperately needed a friendly and clean hostel close to the action in the hip and energetic neighborhood near one of the biggest train stations in Europe, and it got one! The owners of the Beehive, an American couple who chucked the prefab life of Los Angeles for the joy of running a small hostel in Rome, keep on keeping their guests happier than happy. The location and a slew of additions have only ramped up the cool factor here, and this is far and away Rome's best hostel.

Rooms are bright and spacious, if slightly spartan. In traditional Italian fashion, there are no rugs covering the tiled floors, but these rooms are outfitted with modern furniture, and most of them are doubles—it's almost like a secret little hotel. There's also one coed dormitory containing eight beds. Rates are reasonable for such a desirable location. Beds have reading lamps; some of the bathrooms have tubs. In all, you'll be well taken care of here, and you won't have to worry about dodgy accommodations in questionable pensiones. There is also a vegetarian cafe on the premises, which replaced the hostel kitchen and extends the green ethic.

Best bet for a bite:
Bakeries in the 'hood

What hostellers say:
"What's the buzz?"

Insiders' tip:
Great coffee bar across street from Termini

Gestalt:
Queen Bee

Safety: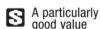

Hospitality:

Cleanliness:

Party index: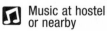

Since the Beehive moved to its present, quieter location, the owners have added a very popular garden—they refer to it as the "outdoor living room," and it is—eliminated the lockout, expanded office hours, hooked up free Internet access, and created a mini-guidebook to Rome for guests to tote around town. They've also added yoga and shiatsu classes. Future plans include a classy concierge service for snagging tickets and getting to or from the hostel, and Sunday brunch service. Rotating art exhibits showing the work of local artists have

key to icons

 Attractive natural setting

 Ecologically aware hostel

 Superior kitchen facilities or cafe

 Offbeat or eccentric place

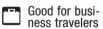 Superior bathroom facilities

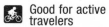 Romantic private rooms

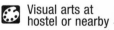 Comfortable beds

 A particularly good value

 Wheelchair-accessible

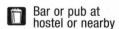 Good for business travelers

 Especially well suited for families

 Good for active travelers

Visual arts at hostel or nearby

Music at hostel or nearby

Great hostel for skiers

Bar or pub at hostel or nearby

Editors' Choice: Among our very favorite hostels

already become a reality. Could this place be any better? Honestly, we don't know.

how to get there:

By bus or train: From Termini Station, exit to right (north side of station) past Cafe Trombetta and continue straight across Via Marsala to Via Marghera; continue 2 blocks to hostel on left.
By car: Contact hostel for directions.

fawlty towers

Via Magenta 39, Roma
Phone: 064–450–374 or 064–454–802

Fax: 064–543–5942
E-mail: info@fawltytowers.org
Rates: €20–€50 (about $25–$63 US) per person; doubles €55–€85 (about $69–$106 US)
Credit cards: No
Beds: 150
Private/family rooms: Yes
Kitchen available: Yes
Season: Open year-round
Office hours: Twenty-four hours
Checkout: 9:00–10:00 A.M.
Affiliation: None
Extras: Terrace, Internet access, TV room, air-conditioning

No, there's no bumbling bellhop named Manuel here or owner Basil Fawlty finding himself constantly in compromising positions. This happenin' hostel just borrowed its name from the popular British comedy starring that ex-Monty Python guy John Cleese.

What hostellers say:
"Are you John Cleese's Italian cousin?"

Gestalt:
No Fawlty

Safety:

Hospitality:

Cleanliness:

Party index:

You're the only one who might find yourself in a compromising and unpleasant situation, though, if you don't reserve your bed well in advance. Otherwise you can look forward to camping out at the front door by 7:00 A.M. at the latest if you really want a short-notice bed. It's that popular, especially in the summer, and deservedly so.

Hostellers love the supersocial terrace that assists in bonding with fellow bunkmates. Rooms are accommodating and mostly small, some even equipped with a refrigerator and air-conditioning. (There are also dorms, which are okay, but most beds here are not bunks: a big plus. The catch? This place often books up fully because of its deserved popularity.) A wide collection of guidebooks and maps keeps travelers occupied when they're not out seeing the carnival that is Roma.

And you're right behind the train station, too.

how to get there:

By bus: Hostel is within walking distance.
By car: Call hostel for directions.
By train: Train station adjacent to hostel.

m & j hostel
Via Solferino 9, Roma
Phone: 064–462–802

Fax: 064–462–802
E-mail: info@mejplacehostel.com
Web site: www.mejplacehostel.com
Rates: €18–€35 (about $23–$42 US) per person; doubles €60–€100 (about $75–$125 US)
Credit cards: No
Beds: 50
Private/family rooms: Yes
Kitchen available: Yes
Season: Open year-round
Office hours: Twenty-four hours
Affiliation: None
Extras: Radio, TV, refrigerator, bar, ceiling fans

This hostel has it all for young backpackers in the way of varied amenities: TV, on-site bar, refrigerator, and much-needed ceiling fans. And it's certainly a convivial place, even if it gets cramped during the summer high season. However, reports of poor upkeep mar its reputation when compared with the other independent

Best bet for a bite:
Bar across from Termini

Hospitality:

Cleanliness:

Party index:

hostels in town. You can't believe how many of our snoops complain about sagging beds, grimy rooms, and creeping critters—and things aren't getting any better over time, despite the complaints. Come here if you don't mind a little grunge and smoke and are seeking travel buddies.

how to get there:

By bus: Call hostel for transit route.
By car: Call hostel for directions.
By train: Hostel is a few blocks north of Termini.

---

ostello foro italico
(italian forum hostel)
Viale delle Olimpiadi 61, 00194 Roma
Phone: 063–236–267

Fax: 063–242–613
E-mail: roma@ostellionline.org
Rates: €18 (about $23 US) per HI member
Credit cards: No
Beds: 334
Private/family rooms: Yes
Kitchen available: No
Season: Open year-round
Office hours: Twenty-four hours
Lockout: 9:00 A.M.–2:00 P.M.
Affiliation: HI-AIG
Extras: Meals ($), breakfast, bar, Internet access, fax, TV

This hostel's architecture is spookily reminiscent of the somber era of *i fascisti*—and it's no accident. It was originally built as a dormitory for Mussolini's charges. Later, it was converted to a hostel, but the gray concrete exterior, too-wide hallways, gang-style showers (slowly being converted to regular ones), and really blah location beside an expressway in the burbs remind you of its former life.

Dorms and bathrooms are mostly way too big and institutional, and staff can't always keep pace to clean them; expect groups and potentially noisy nights here, at undoubtedly the least homey of Rome's half dozen hostels. After a couple of days using transit to get all the way back to town, you'll also start wondering why the heck they picked a place so darned far away from the action. Oh, well. At least the three-night maximum stay ensures that you won't have to deal with the place for too long; for once, this rule is a blessing.

There's a vending machine in the lobby where you can purchase tickets for Rome's buses or Metropolitan subway, which makes planning a visit downtown a snap (though the trip is time-

What hostellers say:	"Um, where's the city?"
Gestalt:	Fascist architecture
Safety:	
Hospitality:	
Cleanliness:	
Party index:	

consuming). If you're driven to drink by the boring neighborhood, they also run a small cafeteria/bar downstairs with local characters dishing up light meals, snacks, drinks, coffee, and mineral water. There's a garden out back, a famous sports complex nearby, and the premier's villa next door, which should make you feel a little better.

And, actually, staff are as professional and friendly as can be, for the most part—some of them even are multilingual. Maps on the wall help guide you around what can be an intimidating city. And that basement eatery isn't bad at all; during one visit, a Lithuanian women's chorus practiced beautifully sad songs that echoed through the halls.

See? We find the good side of everything.

how to get there:

By bus: Take Metro Line A to Ottavino, exit onto via Barletta, and take #32 bus (from the middle of the street) to Cardorna. Get off before Stadio del Nuoto.
By car: Call hostel for directions.
By train: Call hostel for transit route.

pensione ottaviano
(ottaviano home hostel)
Via Ottaviano 6, Roma 00192
Phone: 063–973–8138 or 063–973–7252

Fax: 063–974–0809
E-mail: info@pensioneottaviano.com
Web site: www.pensioneottaviano.com
Rates: €20–€27 (about $25–$34 US) per person; doubles €100 (about $125 US)
Credit cards: No

Beds: Number varies
Private/family rooms: Yes
Kitchen available: No
Season: Open year-round
Office hours: 7:00 A.M.–midnight
Lockout: 10:00 A.M.–2:00 P.M.
Affiliation: None
Extras: TV, lockers, Internet access

This independent hostel sits close to St. Peter's, a mere block from the Vatican.

Yes. *That* Vatican.

What hostellers say:
"Let's go shopping."

Gestalt:
Popeless

Safety:

Hospitality:

Cleanliness:

Party index:

Run by the same folks who own Fawlty Towers and Pensione Sandy, it's close to the action. It's also clean and has both some private rooms and fairly tidy bathrooms. Staff are mostly helpful.

Some of the rooms even have their own refrigerators, so you can store all of that San Pellegrino mineral water we all love so well. Access all of Rome's wonders from the Metro stop a short stroll away; just don't expect too much in the way of scintillating conversation. The ambience is rather bland, and common space is almost a nonentity. Bathrooms are so-so at best. The crowd is almost 100 percent Aussie and American.

No matter. It's a good inexpensive bunk in a town where decent beds are normally outrageous. You're welcome to use the hostel's Internet facilities, too, to keep in touch with your envious pals back home.

how to get there:

By bus or train: Call hostel for transit route.
By car: Call hostel for directions.

pensione sandy
(sandy's home hostel)
Via Cavour 136, Roma
Phone: 064–884–585

E-mail: info@sandyhostel.com
Web site: www.sandyhostel.com

Rates: €25–€30 (about $30–$36 US) per person; doubles €70–€106 (about $88–$133 US)
Credit Cards: No
Beds: 30
Private/family rooms: No
Kitchen available: No
Season: Open year-round
Office hours: 7:00 A.M.–midnight
Affiliation: None

Bring your Tiger Balm to soothe your back after you schlep your backpack up the four flights of stairs to reach this small hostel. But once here, you'll be welcomed into a warm (not in winter—there's no heat!) and hoppin' scene. Beds are cots rather than bunks, but at least you'll be sharing your room with only two to four other folk.

Safety:
Cleanliness:
Hospitality:
Party index:

It's not as clean as Fawlty Towers—in fact, a few of our snoops claimed it's among the dirtiest in Europe—but it's really close to the Coliseum: just a couple blocks. In fact, you're central to a lot of the sights that attracted you to the "mother of civilization" in the first place, like the Santa Maria Maggiore church. However, since you're also painfully close to the Stazione Termini—Rome's main station and a noted home of lowlifes, pickpockets, and worse—you'll want to watch yourself after dark.

how to get there:

By bus or train: Take #9, #16, #27, #70, #71, or #204 bus.
By Metro: Take Line B; Cavour Colosseo.
By train: Stazione Termini near hostel.

venice (venezia)

You're gonna come here, so deal with the facts: First, the only way to get around is by boat or by foot. When you arrive at Santa Lucia train station, the first thing you want to do is grab a *vaporetto* (commuter boat) downtown. Take the #82 line to get to the center fast if you must, but we prefer the #1 boat—it's superscenic and gets you right into the sights at once.

To walk around, get a great map and watch for little bridges and side canals; when you get lost (you will), ask locals to point you back toward San Marco plaza at the center of it all, or else just find signs and troop off again.

Quite convenient are the many smaller picturesque gondolas: They appear to have been built for tourists, but actually they ferry residents across the bigger canals all day long for a pittance. Avoid the rip-off gondola tours and buy a regular commuter ticket on a cross-city boat instead; it's just as good.

venice hostels
at a glance

	RATING	PRICE	IN A WORD	PAGE
Casa Gerotto Calderan		€18–€36	decent	p. 280
Ostello Santa Fosca		€19	quiet	p. 281
Ostello Venezia		€20–€24	okay	p. 284

There's a surprising and serious lack of hostel beds here, though. The only big and legit one is the huge HI joint—and it's not even in Venice proper, but on another island. Two little places rent out dorm beds, but they only partly resemble true hostels. Lots of religious organizations in Venice maintain dorms as well, but their strict curfews and no-unmarried-couples rules kept 'em out of this book.

casa gerotto calderan
Campo S. Geremia 283A, Venezia
Phone: 041–715–562 or 041–715–361

Fax: 041–715–361
Rates: €18–€36 (about $23–$42 US) per person; doubles €45–€60 (about $56–$75 US)
Credit cards: No

Beds: 30
Private/family rooms: Yes
Kitchen available: No
Season: Open year-round
Office hours: Vary, contact hostel for current hours
Curfew: 12:30 A.M.
Affiliation: None
Extras: Internet access ($)

This little hostel, which also doubles as a nice hotel, offers both bunks and private rooms, giving hostellers the best of both worlds. And, bully for you, showers are included in the rate. They're pretty nice for hostel showers, that's for sure. And the place is both kept clean *and* staffed by friendly folks.

Gestalt:
Venetian blinds

Safety:
Hospitality:
Cleanliness:
Party index:

Although it boasts a location near the train station, where you'll almost surely arrive, it's not central to the rest of the medieval action for which Venice is justly famous. You might enjoy this location, though, in a quiet Venetian suburb if you need to get in late or get out early.

how to get there:

By boat: From Venezia Station, call hostel for transit route.

ostello santa fosca
Santa Maria dei Servi, Cannaregio, 2372 Venezia
Phone: 041–715–775

E-mail: ostello@santafosca.it
Rates: €19 (about $24 US) per person; doubles €44 (about $56 US)
Credit cards: Yes
Beds: 140 (winter: 30)
Private/family rooms: Yes
Kitchen available: Yes
Season: Open year-round
Office hours: 7:00–9:00 A.M.; 6:00–11:30 P.M.
Lockout: 9:00 A.M.–6:00 P.M.
Curfew: 1:00 A.M.
Affiliation: None
Extras: Game room

venice
(venezia)

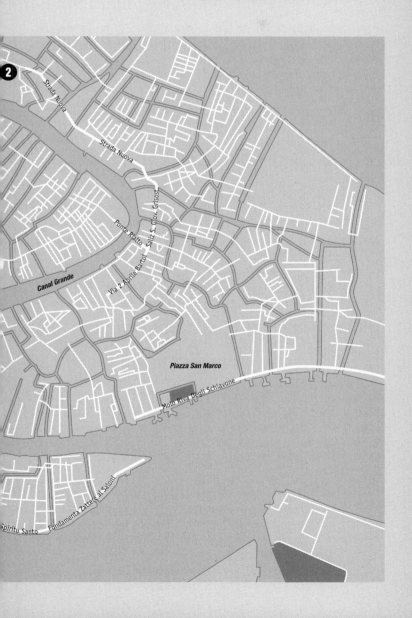

College students will certainly appreciate this really nice hostel (which is open year-round) for its relaxed 'tude and lots of diversions to keep them happy, like the omnipresent game of foosball. But you can't hang around here forever, due to ironclad rules—see below.

A former convent, the hostel has both dorm rooms and doubles; thumbs down, though, to the super-long lockout that lasts from nine in the morning till six at night. Sure, Venice is one great town, but sometimes we the jet-lagged need to kick back for a few minutes, too.

What hostellers say:
"Foosball, anyone?"

Gestalt:
Convent-ional

Safety:

Hospitality:

Cleanliness:

Party index:

how to get there:

By boat: From train station, walk left along the main street over three bridges. Turn left over bridge at the P. S. Fosca and left along canal.

ostello venezia
(venice hostel)

Fondamenta delle Zitelle, Guidecca 86, 30123 Venezia
Phone: 041–523–8211

Fax: 041–523–5689
E-mail: venezia@ostellionline.it
Rates: €20–€24 (about $25–$30 US) per HI member
Credit cards: Yes
Beds: 260
Private/family rooms: None
Kitchen available: No
Season: Closed December 12–27
Office hours: 7:00 A.M.–midnight
Affiliation: HI-AIG
Extras: Breakfast, meals ($), bar

This optimally placed former warehouse with a view of San Marco—from across the canal on the island of Guidecca, you understand—really packs 'em in and always seems booked full. Venice is probably the biggest destination for tourists in Italy, more so in summer, so reserve way in advance if you want a bunk in this somewhat strict hostel.

Still, it's fairly friendly and—best of all—efficient. Just remember that you'll have to take a little boat out to a remote island from central Venice, then haul your carcass and your backpack up steep flights of stairs. (Some hostellers compared it to Alcatraz. We can see why: You'll never escape late at night.)

Gestalt:
Blue lagoon

Safety: ▨

Hospitality: ▨▨

Cleanliness: ▨

Party index: ▨

Other complaints have been lodged about the plumbing: specifically, the showers. They have a tendency to run on the lukewarm side. Of course, being that the hostel is located next to really prime real estate, it gets supercrowded, and with crowds comes a lot of noise. Bring your earplugs to drown out the cacophony of sounds made by those who are sleeping and those who aren't. (When you see the architecture, you'll get why noise bounces around the place.)

Meals are served here, but for some reason wine and other spirits are banned. That definitely could be a bummer if you're looking to imbibe.

All in all, AIG seems to be listening to complaints and righting some of this hostel's (former) wrongs. This island-bound bunk is definitely an option. Just don't expect peace and quiet.

how to get there:

By boat: From Venezia train station, take vaporetto #82 or #2 (costs roughly €1, about half an hour). Get off at Zitelle and walk to the right to hostel.

luxembourg

This is some country to get into your itinerary: small, hilly, terribly expensive, and almost completely schizophrenic. But then, what would you expect from a place surrounded by all those other countries? And it's true that you can hear strains of German, French, and Flemish here in one place. It's worth a trip—and the countryside is nice.

There's only one big city to speak of—the capital city, with the same name as the country—and the cost of living is prohibitively high. Yet there are surprising numbers of English speakers here, possibly due to liberal banking laws that encourage foreign holding companies to place their assets here in lovely Luxy. The official tongue of this land is French, but most residents speak German and English, too, so you'll find your language pretty well understood.

Interestingly, the tiny country has always played a major role in European politics, getting a number of high officials elected to European Union and European Commission posts. The so-called "father of modern Europe," Robert Schumann, was a native, too.

The dozen or so hostels here are all generally good, geared to school groups, outdoorsy types, and families. If you're keen on seeing a number of them, you should definitely find out about the *Sentiers des Auberges de Jeunesse—or Jugendherbergs Wanderfade* in German—a series of hiking trails that connect some of the rural hostels here. They're marked with classy blue-and-white signs in the woods and proceed through stone steps and hills from hostel to hostel. *Note:* Only the "city" hostel is presented here.

practical details

Getting here isn't easy and it isn't hard. By train, you will usually connect through Strasbourg, Paris, Köln (Cologne), or Brussels. Almost all trains coming to Luxembourg go through the capital city.

By plane it's quite a bit easier; take a flight from the United States via Icelandair and you can land in Luxembourg after a quick set down in Iceland. European cities are pretty well connected to the tiny capital city, too, especially through the national carrier, Luxair (www.luxair .lu), and its direct flights from London, Paris, Nice, Rome, and other key places. British Airways also flies from London, and SAS can get you here from Copenhagen.

There are few train lines in Luxembourg, so you might need to supplement your journey with a bus ticket unless you're staying in the capital. Train passes are a waste of time here unless you'll be touring Belgium and the Netherlands extensively, so just buy point-to-point tickets. (You can find regional pass details in the Belgium and Netherlands chapters.) Hostellers *might* be wise, however, to buy a Luxembourg Card, which sets you back about €10.00 ($12.50 US) per day—you get a small discount for two- or three-day cards—and gives you free or discounted admission to lots of attractions plus free use of public transit throughout the duchy. You can get the card at many hostels, hotels, campgrounds, and tourist information offices.

Luxembourg's monetary unit is now the euro, and you'll need plenty of cash here. This is a relatively expensive country.

Luxumbourg's phone code is 352. To dial Luxembourg's hostel from the United States, dial 011–352, then the number AS PRINTED. Luxembourg is so small that there is no initial zero or city code, unlike most other European countries. From inside the country, dial the number EXACTLY AS IT'S PRINTED HERE. Mail runs efficiently, and you'll find some unusual stamps if you look for 'em; this isn't Liechtenstein, but they're still interesting enough.

luxembourg city

Luxembourg City is, quite simply, the capital of the country and its only true metropolis. It's a bit like Monaco: a city unto itself, where everyone seems to possess incredible wealth (and they do).

Getting around is a snap: The place is compact enough that you can walk anywhere—with a little huffing and puffing due to the hills—and there's also a bus system for outlying areas, though you probably won't need to worry about those at all.

To communicate on the fly, look for the Internet-style info terminals downtown on rue du Curé and inside the city's train station.

---

luxembourg city hostel

2 rue du Fort Olisy (Pfaffenthal), L–2261 Luxembourg City
Phone: 22–68–89 or 22–19–20

Fax: 22–33–60

E-mail: luxembourg@youthhostels.lu
Rates: €19.50 (about $25 US) per HI member
Credit cards: Yes
Beds: 240
Private/family rooms: Yes
Kitchen available: Yes
Season: Open year-round
Office hours: 7:00 A.M.–11:00 P.M.
Lockout: 10:00 A.M.–2:00 P.M.
Curfew: 2:00 A.M.
Affiliation: HI-AJL
Extras: Breakfast, meals ($), bar, bike rentals, laundry

This big hostel, Luxembourg's mothership hostel if you will, is a good news–bad news situation: great location, fairly central (though you'll walk uphill to reach the town's attractions), but pretty institutional— "modern" in this case meaning "characterless." Yet hostellers seem to whoop it up nonetheless in one of the five common areas, and that isn't a bad thing at all; you might actually have a little fun here. They've also got eight family rooms for couples or folk with kids.

Best bet for a bite:
(gulp) Fast food stands

What hostellers say:
"Mom, wire me more money . . ."

Gestalt:
De-Lux

Safety:

Hospitality:

Cleanliness:

Party index:

There's a surprising amount to do in this rich little capital city if you've landed at the hostel for a day or two. Take a Wenzel Walk tour down the river valley for a look at the rock upon which the castle's built plus underground tunnels, moat ruins, and more; an elevator at walk's end carries walkers back up top.

Museums also abound. The National Museum of History and Art, on Fishmarket, contains new and old art, archaeological finds, medieval weapons associated with the fort, and lots more stuff relating to the history of this city and country. The National Museum of Natural History takes on—what else—nature topics; one feature is an "ecodatabase" that is collecting records of the country's plants and animals.

Luxembourgian festivals include a peppy spring fete in early May, where townsfolk carry new tree branches in a parade through town; an April pilgrimage to the city cathedral; and Schueberfour, the huge late-summer carnival that started out as a market for shepherds but just kept growing.

Other Euro-institutions to check out while here include the Court of Justice, the Court of Auditors, the Secretariat of the European Parliament, and some offices of the European Commission, to name but a few.

how to get there:

By bus: Take #9 bus, or walk uphill 1 mile to hostel.

By car: Call hostel for directions.

By train: From station, take #9 bus or walk uphill 1 mile to hostel.

the netherlands

First things first, bub. This country is not called Holland. That's the northern part. If you're in Amsterdam (itself sometimes called A'dam by "hip" types), you're smack in North Holland— but that's just one province (kinda like a U.S. state) of the larger country. So call it the Netherlands everywhere else you go here, even though you will some-times hear A'damers referring to their fair country as Holland.

This is a *very* densely populated land. That might come as a surprise—until you hit the streets and find yourself bumping into folk. Take a train, and you'll find it's a very short distance between populated areas. But, hey, look at it this way: It's really hard to get lost with all those roads, signs, bike paths, and people in the way. Anyway, it's not New York or Tokyo crowded (except maybe on those Amsterdam trams).

Where to go? It's pretty simple. Go to Amsterdam for canals and museums; hit the Hague to see the capital buildings; the northern Netherlands have all the beaches, dunes, islands, and major cities; and the southern Netherlands has, um, some hills.

The Dutch are a hospitable people by nature, and their hostels pretty much reflect this—they're uniformly clean, safe, and, well, uniform. One trend that we didn't find great is that most of the hostels are built for school groups; except for all those independent hostels in Amsterdam, almost all the rest have remote locations, conference rooms, and lots of noisy kids. Unfortunately. We have kept our descriptions of totally-group-oriented hostels brief in these pages, because you're unlikely to find a bed here in high season—or enjoy it if you do.

practical details

There are plenty of flights into Amsterdam, the hub of the country. The budget airline EasyJet uses Amsterdam as a hub and therefore has some short hops around Europe from Schiphol airport; the airline KLM (sometimes teamed with U.S. airline Northwest) is based in Amsterdam and has tons of international flights. Schiphol airport, an increasingly major hub for both international and European traffic, is well connected to the center of Amsterdam and its train station by very frequent (seven times per hour) and quick (fifteen to twenty minutes) trains. It's a lot cheaper than a cab and possibly quicker, too; buy the train tickets at the airport.

You can also get to the Netherlands by ferry, starting from Harwich (an hour east of London by train from Liverpool Street Station) and taking a Stena fast-ferry ride of three and a half hours to Hoek van Holland, the Netherlands. The ferry runs twice daily—take the early one, unless you want to roll into your hostel bed at 2:00 A.M. From there it's about a ninety-minute train ride to Amsterdam. Total time expenditure: eight hours. Warning: Ferries and trains are planned to meet each other, but once in a while they don't. If the boat runs late because of weather, for instance, the train won't wait. Be prepared.

Eurolines is a Europe-wide company running comfortable long-distance buses around Europe for very competitive rates; it goes from Amsterdam to London, Paris, Hamburg, Munich, and beyond, for instance. In the Netherlands contact Eurolines at 020–560–8788.

Once you're here, there are two main ways to get around the Netherlands: bikes and trains. Buses and cars are secondary options, but bike or train is probably easiest in such a flat, compact, densely populated country.

To get around by train, either buy a pass at stations or buy inexpensive point-to-point tickets. A national "reduction ticket" for about €50 (about $60 US) gives you a big discount on all tickets used after 9:00 A.M. weekdays or all day on weekends. There are several kinds of trains in the country: InterCity trains are the fastest, stopping only in major cities, and sometimes charge an extra fee. Sneltreins are more regional, stopping sometimes but not everywhere. Finally, the Stoptrein is just what it says—a poky, locals-only train you will use only when you need to get to small towns and avoid otherwise. Note that the Dutch aren't very good about putting English on their signs, so you might need to ask for help, and *always* remember to punch your train ticket before you get on the train; there will be a machine in every station that stamps the current date and time on the ticket, showing the conductor that it has been "used up."

If you're traveling heavily, look into buying a Holland Pass. At press time these cost about $92–$146 US per person for a second-class pass of three to five days in a month. A wider regional pass is smarter if you're going to be limiting your trip to one or two countries, a waste otherwise. The Benelux–France Pass costs about $334 US for a four-day-in-one-month first-class pass, $290 US for a second-class pass. A second traveler gets a 50 percent discount; travelers younger than age twenty-six also get a discount.

You can rent bikes either from most of the country's railway stations—that's what the Dutch do, so don't be shy about it—or from private companies. We're talking about a country of fifteen million people here, and they own twelve million bikes! As a result, there are miles of marked paths through the Netherlands, and the local VVVs (tourist offices, pronounced *fay-fay-fay*) will sell or give you maps of them. To rent, bring a picture ID and some money or a credit card for a deposit; it shouldn't cost much. Round blue signs with white bikes point out the way to bike trails; squat white "mushroom" signs point the way to various surrounding towns and tell you the distances to them. You can also "park" your bike at train stations for a small fee (sometimes waived) or bring them on the trains themselves for about €5–€7 (about $6–$9 US).

Finally, buses can be a cheaper ride than the train or more expensive, depending on local whims. It might take you all day to make connections, but most bus drivers are helpful and knowledgeable. As a bonus, they'll sometimes let you off where you want to go even if there isn't an actual scheduled bus stop there.

The unit of currency in the Netherlands is now the euro.

The Netherlands' country code is 31. To call Amsterdam hostels from North America, dial 011–31 and DROP THE ZERO from the phone numbers listed in this book. To call Amsterdam hostels from within the Netherlands but outside Amsterdam, dial the numbers just as they are printed in the book. And to dial Amsterdam hostels from within the city, drop the initial city code (such as 020) and then dial the rest of the number as printed. Phones are pretty easy to use—you buy a phone card, available at some hostels and most newsstands or tobacco shops, to access most phones these days.

Note that if you have a U.S. calling card, you might have to buy a Dutch phone card and stick it in, then dial your toll-free access number. Unfair? You bet. But it's their country, so you might not be able to get around it.

amsterdam

Everyone, it seems, makes it to Amsterdam sooner or later—at least where young backpackers are concerned. The place has taken on a legendary status as a haven of lawlessness (prostitution and marijuana both being basically legal), and thousands of college kids come each summer to blow mommy and daddy's money on intoxicating substances and pleasures of the flesh. As a result it's become one of the single craziest places on Earth, a concentration of weirdness and vice.

These seamier aspects aside, the actual residential neighborhoods of Amsterdam—where most of the locals and some of the hostels reside—

are attractive and quiet, laced with dozens of placid (if not exactly drinkable) canals, plenty of trees, and tall, attractive town houses. The museums are terrific, most of them concentrated within a small area.

So it makes a great journey stop even if you're not into getting wasted; just remember that all this drug and sex activity has brought some crime with it. Thefts are more common here than in many larger European cities, so you've got to look sharp.

As you might expect, there's tremendous choice and variety within the hostel offerings; this is one of the very few cities we've been where every single hostel has a distinctive personality, so much so that if you say, "I'm stayin' at Bob's or the Pig," others will instantly know exactly what groove you've plugged into. Of course, the quality of the digs also varies hugely. Some of these places are out-and-out dives, especially the cheapies down by the red light district. Others around town are nicer, if sometimes a bit farther out—though nothing is really that far from the center. At the wildest ones (see write-ups), you'll smell pot and beer everywhere and find stoned hostellers sprawled on the floor while others swap bong hits.

Then again, at the two Hostelling International joints, you'll stumble across tons of school groups having good, clean fun, and facilities will be conspicuously cleaner.

There are even two "Christian hostels" here: obviously not the places to score dope or engage in an orgy, but quite nice places if you don't mind the persistent religious iconography and messages scattered throughout. The write-ups here serve as a good guide to the party places, snoozes, and dives; heed their advice. Also note that all these places get booked full up during summer, so you'd best reserve a month or more ahead (*if* the place takes reservations, and many don't). Failing that, show up in the morning before noon and put your name on a list. Once you're in, most hostels can book you into a local bike tour or other excursion if you like.

One final note: If you're staying at one of the two Hostelling International–affiliated hostels in Amsterdam, you reap an additional benefit—a staggering array of hefty discounts at museums and other attractions around the city. They range from tickets for a boat trip through the Amsterdam canals (about $3.50 US per person, 40 percent off) to Rijksmuseum tix (about $4.00–$6.00 US per person, a 10 to 55 percent savings depending on your age) or even a 10 percent break on Eurolines long-distance bus fares.

Arriving in the city's Centraal Station, you'll be confronted with complete, utter chaos—a seething mass of tourists, locals, hookers, transit employees, and others, some half-stoned and the rest completely so, moving in all directions without apparent order. Our advice? Try not

amsterdam

to come late at night, and know your bearings before you step off that train. Most of what you need is on the main level; lockers and luggage deposit are at the far left of the station (if you're inside it facing out), near track 2b. There's a change machine, too, to give you quick coins. Two ATMs sit right near the front station entrance, under a brightly lit red sign but still easy to miss amid the crowds.

Outside it gets complicated again. Unless you're staying right downtown—which is very possible in this compact city—you'll need to figure out which streetcar (tram) line goes to your hostel and buy transit tickets. The trams come and go in haphazard fashion to and from the front of the station; there are some useful diagrams showing which trams stop where just at the edge of the train-station canal. Walk straight out the front door, dodge through all the tram lines, and bear a bit right; come to the water, and check out the maps.

You can buy tram tickets at many places: tobacco shops, train stations, machines (with Dutch-only instructions), or bus stops. Even some trams sell 'em, but that's the most expensive way to get them. We normally get a transit pass in European cities, but in Amsterdam you'll walk so much—and the pass costs enough—that single tickets are probably a better deal. Those easy to buy, although a little hard to figure out; you punch out two "strips" in the machine on the tram for each in-town journey, three each time you travel to the burbs. Transfers to buses are free if you change immediately; show the tram driver your punched ticket right after you get on.

One- or two-day passes—good for all city buses, trams, the subway, and some suburban trains—cost about €5–€7 (about $6–$9 US), though you'd need to ride a lot to make 'em worth your while. Our take? The two-day pass is a much better deal than the one-day pass. Punch the tickets as soon as you get on the tram, inserting the correct end (it has an arrow usually) into the slot and waiting for the ding! sound. Sometimes the conductor will want to see it, too.

Also keep in mind:

- The circle tram line (#20) is a useful sightseeing route, where you can ride through the entire city without getting off, while the #1, #2, and #5 lines get you out beyond the center quickest.
- The city's subway is barely worth having, since there's just one short line, but it could be useful if you're visiting the outskirts. Watch yourself, though, because sleazy characters hang out downstairs in the Nieuwmarkt and other stops. It's probably best to take a tram or taxi instead.
- Boat tours of the canals are quite popular, though not always worth the charge. A ton of operators are set up around town; head for

a canal and you're sure to find one, especially down by Centraal Station. Tiny paddleboats are also popular, but we think they look silly and require a lot of pedaling for not a lot of distance gained.

- Walking is the most attractive option, of course, but remember to walk on the black tar and not the red-painted lanes—or you'll risk decapitation by one of the zillions of bicycles zooming around town without regard for traffic laws.
- If you can't beat 'em you could, of course, rent or borrow your own bike and join 'em; the city's network of bike lanes is one of the best in the world.

nightlife and attractions

Amsterdam is one of the world's great museum towns, and almost all the action is concentrated in the so-called Museumplein area—outside the central downtown but very close to three or four of the city's hostels. (Vondelpark and the Pig Palace are closest.) The big two are the Van Gogh Museum and the adjacent Rijksmuseum, which owns twenty Rembrandts as well as some of Vermeer's finest work and obviously puts on some great exhibits. The Van Gogh contains more than 700 of the painter's drawings, paintings, and letters—everything from his early Dutch Brabant work (of peasants, miners, and potato eaters) to spectacular French canvases featuring his own self-portrait, still lifes of sunflowers, and some final paintings of cornfields and crows. Other exhibits feature contemporaries and influences such as Toulouse-Lautrec, Monet, and Gaugin. And what else can we say about the famous Rijksmuseum that hasn't already been said? In addition to those twenty Rembrandts, four Vermeers, and plenty of other material documenting the history of Dutch painting, there are also collections of rare porcelain, Dutch tiles, old dollhouses, and Asian art complementing the paintings. Also note a good exhibit documenting the history of the far-reaching Dutch East India Company.

Nightlife, of course, is everywhere around town. The so-called Brown Cafes, little neighborhood bars dripping with character and great beer, are the primary draw as far as we're concerned. If you're looking for a different kind of high, there are some 200 "coffee shops" here where the Jamaican flag flies high—even though you're thousands of miles from the island. That can only mean one thing: It's not a place to get coffee; it's a place to get stoned. (There once were as many as 400 of these places, by the way, but the government has been cracking down on licenses under pressure from other countries.) The names are particularly amusing.

Now stop running down the street waving your money. You came here to sightsee, right? Didn't you? You didn't? Oh. Well, anyway, there are basically two kinds of sights here—the quaint and the decadent. If you're going for the former, hit the central city and then walk over to the Jordaan neighborhood (a mile or less due west of the train station by foot). Canals, cafes, and cute apartment buildings combine to evoke a Europe you thought existed only on postcards.

Want a different, more low-down kind of experience? The red light district here is the world's most famous, and indeed you will see legalized prostitution very much in evidence. Well-endowed women fill every available window at night, it seems—and, yes, they're for rent. A bit sad. Whatever you do, absolutely resist the temptation to snap a photograph of these gals. A bouncer will grab you before you can say "cheese."

Bar-wise, you can find an upscale concentration of places to eat and drink in Leidseplein, a nonsquare square just a block or two toward town from the museum complex; at night, it's a mishmash of fire-jugglers, tourists, and pickpockets. Note that the bars here don't stay open all night—it's kinda like England or the States, where last call probably won't be past 2:00 A.M. As elsewhere in Europe, there is also a smattering of discos and late-night clubs.

For more information on all this and more, contact the ultra-well-run VVV, the official tourism office. They've got locations all over town, including booths at Centraal Station (upstairs from track 2), the airport, and Leidseplein. They're usually open 8:00 A.M. to 8:00 P.M. weekdays and Saturdays, 9:00 A.M. to 5:00 P.M. Sundays.

Finally, this is one of the most wired cities in Europe, so there are a number of cybercafes (avoid ones that require you to buy a drink or are full of pot smoke). The national phone company has installed many "Internet phone kiosks" around town, which look just like phone booths but contain tiny screens you activate with a phone card; it's hard to type, we found, but you can certainly do some quick Web-cruising for info on the fly.

common sense

Safety-wise, remember to carry your valuables in a money belt or front pocket whenever you're out and about: Pickpockets are all over the Amsterdam trams and streets, especially in broad daylight for some reason. If ever you should feel a sudden hard shove and/or a hand groping your back or backside, immediately check for your wallet—if it's gone, turn around fast, watching for anyone exiting your tram in a hurry. That's probably your thief.

Bring an umbrella and/or raincoat, as it rains here practically every day at least for a few minutes. You think England was bad? This is worse. Even bright, sunny days tend to cloud up by noon, dump some rain on the unsuspecting, then clear up again by sunset.

amsterdam hostels
at a glance

	RATING	PRICE	IN A WORD	PAGE
Stadsdoelen Hostel		€21.40–€25.60	super	p. 327
Crown Hotel Hostel		€40–€45	great	p. 306
Vondelpark Hostel		€22.20–€31.40	big	p. 304
Bulldog Hostel		€22–€26	smokin'	p. 303
Euphemia Hostel		€25–€46	fine	p. 309
Flying Pig Palace		€13.30–€29.90	mellow	p. 314
Flying Pig Downtown		€13.90–€36.90	fun	p. 311
Shelter Jordaan		€16.00–€19.50	religious	p. 325
Shelter Downtown		€16.00–€23.50	religious-er	p. 323
Aivengo Hostel		€18–€30	basic	p. 300
Bob's Hostel		€18	wasted	p. 301
Meeting Point		€16–€30	central	p. 321
Hans Brinker		€21	raging	p. 316
White Tulip Hostel		€20–€40	middling	p. 329
International Budget		€20–€35	stoned	p. 318
Globe Centre Hostel		€18–€20	tiny	p. 315
Durty Nelly's		€22	blah	p. 309
Croydon Hostel		€35	sucky	p. 308
Kabul		€21–€50	devolving	p. 320

One final word of advice: If you're offended by porno shops or the presence of marijuana—the smell is everywhere, even on the street, and will probably get into your clothes at some point—steer clear of this town, since you won't be able to avoid them.

aivengo hostel

Spuistraat 6, Amsterdam
Phone: 020–620–1155

Rates: €18–€20 (about $23–$25 US) per person
Credit cards: No
Beds: 36
Private/family rooms: No
Kitchen available: No
Season: February–November
Office hours: Vary; call hostel for hours
Lockout: 1:00–5:00 P.M.
Curfew: 3:00 A.M.
Affiliation: None
Extras: Internet access

This smallish hostel touts itself as innovative, drug-free, and smoke-free. Dorms are actually pretty nice, almost artistic, especially the "sky room" up top. The Flying Pig chain apparently thinks enough of this place to send people here when they're overflowing with guests.

Gestalt:
Aye-Aivengo

Safety:

Hospitality:

Cleanliness:

Party index:

The Aivengo's located on a very busy and not-always-attractive street (there are prostitutes working windows on it) and they don't have lockers or a laundry or a kitchen. Stay here for the central location and the obvious change in direction. But watch yourself at night coming home.

how to get there:

By bus: Call hostel for transit route.
By car: Call hostel for directions.
By train: From Centraal Station, walk straight across bridge to Damark. Turn immediately right, walk a block or two to Spuistraat and take a left; continue to hostel on right.

bob's hostel

Nieuwezijds Voorburgwal 92, Amsterdam
Phone: 020–623–0063

Fax: 020-675-6446
Rates: €18 (about $23 US) per person; doubles €70 (about $88 US)
Credit cards: No
Beds: 150
Private/family rooms: Yes
Kitchen available: No
Season: Open year-round
Office hours: Twenty-four hours
Affiliation: None
Extras: Breakfast, dinner ($), bar, pot, lockers, TV room, games

This, quite simply, is one of the cheapest and hardest-partying hostels in town—and, since we're in Amsterdam, that's really saying something. We once heard someone describe it as "scummy," and its unclean bathrooms (just one shower per sixteen beds?) and tightly packed beds (150 in a very small facility) resemble barracks. The streetcars crank right by the window, too, reducing quiet further. Did we mention the parties?

But let's back up a bit. First off, you've got to wonder about a place when the reception is actually inside a coffee shop. Through the haze of smoke, you work your way to a huge

Best bet for a bite:
Deli next door

Insiders' tip:
You might not wanna stay here

What hostellers say:
"(inhaling joint) Aaaaahhhhh . . ."

Gestalt:
Up in smoke

Safety:

Hospitality:

Cleanliness:

Party index:

check-in line, then wait and wait while stoned Brits and Americans fumble for their wallets to pay for another night—or another baggie of grass. Meanwhile, the rave music blasts your eardrums into shrapnel.

There are both coed and female rooms (but no men's—yeah, that's fair). While the dorms here are smaller than those of some coffee shops-cum-hostels, you've really got to be the type of person who places an awful lot of value in smoking weed as a way of life—or at least tolerate it—to stay here.

And you'd better like padlocks. A'dam's liberal drug policy and the associated riffraff have created a pervasive feeling of paranoia and mistrust in the town, so much so that every hostel in this city encourages or requires the use of lockers for your stuff. When you're sleeping next to people who spend money on drugs and live so cheaply (there is a difference between living cheaply and living on a budget), you'll find they sometimes aren't the nicest people or the most trustworthy; they'll be looking to you to fund their habit. So be forewarned about places with a higher concentration of potheads than usual; it could mean safety trouble. And if you can't trust your bunkmate, who can you trust?

The ten-bedded dorms, to get back to basics, were sometimes clean and sometimes not—but a persistent smoke obviously lingers in all the rooms, and it isn't cigarettes. Check your lungs at the door. A healthful dinner is rumored to be served nightly for an extra charge, though hostellers we met were so wasted they couldn't remember if this was still an option. The hostel is well placed, at least, near the slanting buildings lining little Gravenstraat and not too far a walk from the city's best neighborhood, the Jordaan.

But let's cut the BS. Most people here have come to get stoned. And that's the only reason we could figure this place exists. It's certainly not to provide a clean or cheap bed; bathrooms are cruddy and poorly lit, dorms are too packed, and they throw extra bodies on the floor when it's busy. Goodie. You might even stumble back to discover someone crashed in your bunk by mistake, and they're not moving. Too stoned. It happens here. A lot.

key to icons

Attractive natural setting	Comfortable beds	Visual arts at hostel or nearby
Ecologically aware hostel	A particularly good value	Music at hostel or nearby
Superior kitchen facilities or cafe	Wheelchair-accessible	Great hostel for skiers
Offbeat or eccentric place	Good for business travelers	Bar or pub at hostel or nearby
Superior bathroom facilities	Especially well suited for families	Editors' Choice: Among our very favorite hostels
Romantic private rooms	Good for active travelers	

Don't even get us started about the crowd. Think spaced-out, and you're not even close. Keep going further down. Flatliners? Now you're startin' to get close.

But we have to admit, some people like it here, and we've seen far dirtier and worse in town. Just ignore the weird stuff if you're staying.

how to get there:

By bus: Call hostel for transit route.

By car: Call hostel for directions.

By train: From Centraal Station, walk straight across bridge to Damark. Turn immediately right, walk a block or two to Spuistraat and take a left; continue to hostel on right.

the bulldog hostel

Oudezijds Voorburgwal 220, 1012 GJ Amsterdam
Phone: 020–620–3822

Fax: 020–627–1612
E-mail: hotel@bulldog.nl
Rates: €17–€29 (about $21–$36 US) per person; doubles €84–€99 (about $105–$124 US)
Credit cards: Yes
Beds: 170
Private/family rooms: Yes
Kitchen available: Yes
Season: Open year-round
Affiliation: None
Extras: Meals, TV, DVD player, bar, air-conditioning, breakfast, lockers, Internet access, coffee shop, tourist information, souvenir shop

Bulldog brand founder Henk de Vries (Bulldog is also the name of his popular local energy drink and cafe) says this hostel is his "dream come true," and hostellers and our snoops all seem to agree: It's a great, casual place. (Just skip it if you're anti-drug or hate smoke: The wacky terbacky gets lit up at all hours.) Located in the heart of Amsterdam's red light district, close to Dam Square, it's filled with eight- to twelve-bedded coed dorms that share bathroom facilities, plus a selection of double, triple, and quad rooms with television and en-suite bathrooms. Free breakfast is included with all the beds, as are free lockers; the Energy bar/coffee shop stays open 'til 3:00 A.M.

What hostellers say:
"Spliffs go great with an energy drink."

Gestalt: Bulldog bunks

Safety:

Hospitality:

Cleanliness:

Party index:

most nights, serving energy drinks, coffee (and other good stuff . . .).

The surrounding neighborhood, as you might guess, is pretty sketchy—use caution. Inside the hostel, though, the twenty-four-hour front desk is equipped with video security and they won't let stragglers and marginal types get in. Management is also trying to discourage the testosterone factor by refusing to take group bookings of male sports fans and bachelor parties.

how to get there:

By bus or train: Contact hostel for transit details.
By car: Contact hostel for directions.

city hostel vondelpark

Zandpad 5, 1054 GA Amsterdam
Phone: 020–589–8996

Fax: 020–589–8955
E-mail: vondelpark@stayokay.com
Rates: €22.20–€31.40 (about $28–$39 US) per HI member; doubles €62.80–€80.40 (about $80–$100 US)
Credit cards: Yes
Beds: 536
Private/family rooms: Yes
Kitchen available: Yes
Season: Open year-round
Office hours: Twenty-four hours
Curfew: 2:00 A.M.
Affiliation: HI
Extras: Internet access, breakfast, restaurant ($), bar, bike rentals, bike storage, lockers, tourist information, discounts, TV, travel store

Inside a former schoolhouse and bordering the city's biggest and most beautiful park, this Hostelling International entry into the Amsterdam field gets points for location and good facilities.

The dorms and private rooms are somewhat newish bunks in airy schoolrooms, some with views onto the park. This is all the more surprising because, reportedly, this is one of the largest hostels in Europe, yet it doesn't feel like Sardine City. There's one really big dorm here, but that's for groups, so don't sweat it. You won't be spending much time in your room anyway. You'll be at one of the two e-mail machines or enjoying one of tons of local discounts you'll get when you flash your receipt or Hostelling International membership card.

Once you do sack out, rooms will range from about twenty four-, six-, nine-, twelve-, and fourteen-bedded ones; some doubles have views of the park. Doors are locked with electronic locks and beds come with "duvies"—thick English-style quilted blankets good for keeping out the persistent damp chill that follows you around the city in bad weather.

Best bet for a bite:
Overtoom or Leidseplein

Insiders' tip:
Kinko's on Overtoom

What hostellers say:
"Getting better."

Gestalt:
Park place

Safety:

Hospitality:

Cleanliness:

Party index:

Oh, and almost every room—from the tiniest double to the biggest group dorm—has its own bathroom, a nice plus. We met everyone from Euro-teens to Swedish families here, so obviously the word is out big-time about the place.

They serve over-heavy dinners for a fee in the ambitiously named Brasserie Backpackers; skip dinner and head there for happy hour instead, with beer on tap and always a lively crowd of Americans and Europeans with stories to share. Next morning, breakfast—served in rooms named for cities of the world and decorated in appropriate fashion—is actually quite nice: lots of fresh-baked bread, peanut butter, chocolate, cheese, and ham, plus good corn flakes. It's a good effort, especially so because they're not too clucky about your going back for seconds or thirds.

A couple of things to keep in mind: *Tons* of groups stay here (the other HI joint in town does not take groups), and you'll see them . . . at all hours. Getting stoned and giggly in the halls. Singing below your window at two in the morning. Hogging the marmalade at breakfast. So get used to it, or move along.

So, you're in for a good time as long as you can handle the constant parade of Euro-groups and the by-the-book staff. And you're just steps from both the amazing Rijksmuseum (Vermeer, van Gogh,

Rembrandt, et al.) and always-hoppin' Leidseplein, a much tamer Times Square-y alternative to the red light district. Though it's been somewhat Americanized (Micky D's, BK, Marriott, etc.) of late, this square is still the best concentration of food and safe street life in town for the money.

Just watch the park area at night; the hostel does a good job of using lots of security measures to protect the place.

how to get there:

By bus: From bus terminal, take the #12 streetcar to Van Baerlestraat stop and walk straight into park. Go down stairs to hostel on right.

By car: Call hostel for directions. (Note: there is no parking at this hostel.)

By train: From Centraal Station take #1, #2, or #5 streetcar to Leidseplein; walk up to Marriott hotel, turn left on main road and walk ¼ mile southwest to hostel sign at Zandpad; turn right and walk down walkway to hostel on right.

---

crown hotel hostel

O.Z. Voorburgwal 21, 1012 EH Amsterdam
Phone: 020–626–9664

Fax: 020–420–6473
E-mail: info@hotelthecrown.com
Web site: www.hotelthecrown.com
Rates: €40–€45 (about $50–$56 US) per person
Credit cards: No
Beds: 45
Private/family rooms: Yes
Kitchen available: No
Season: Open year-round
Office hours: 9:00 A.M.–3:00 A.M.
Affiliation: None
Extras: Bar, pool table, lockers

This place may not still be a hostel by the time this book hits your hands—and that's a damn shame, because it's one of the best in the city, run by some expatriate Englanders who really appreciate quality budget lodgings. We'd splurge here anytime for one of their great little European double rooms. Despite a terrible location near the sleaze, it's so well run that you won't care.

They now have just one dormitory here, holding only six beds in the form of three bunk-bed combos. It's a ground-floor room right behind the bar, but they've managed to keep it smoke-free and quiet despite its proximity to the action. There's one bathroom and one shower, and the beds are simple, but the position of this place is so central—and the management so friendly—that we wouldn't hesitate to sleep here. Unless five Hell's Angels had snagged the other five beds, of course . . . it being just one room, there's no escape from unpleasant bunkmates, the only minus. At least there are lockers available to hide in.

Upstairs, their no-smoking doubles are great by downtown Amsterdam standards—pine beds that smell good and feel good, terrific canal and city views, clean hall bathrooms and showers, and

Best bet for a bite:
Greenwood's, on the Singel

What hostellers say:
"Jolly good!"

Gestalt:
Great Briton

Safety:

Hospitality:

Cleanliness:

Party index:

some even coming with that hostel rarity: actual double beds. And some of the doubles include two trundle beds tucked in under two normal-sized ones free of charge. They also do triples and quads here at reasonable rates, rooms that would be just fine for a family and much preferable to many of the other hostel options in town. They're all high enough up to be quiet, and, again, some come with great views. The extremely narrow steep stairs leading up might be a problem for those with backpacks or a few beers in 'em, though.

The closest thing to do to here is just stroll. You're one minute from the sleaze of downtown A'dam (and a hundred hookers), but you can also get away from it all. In some ways this is the most central hostel in the whole city, just a couple of minutes from the train station, yet still a quiet location—worlds apart from the hostels lining tacky Warmoestraat a few blocks away.

Night security keeps the place safe in spite of yucky surrounding streets, and the British bar—with British music, British satellite TV, darts, pool, and a whole slew of great beers (instead of just the usual Dutch ones) on tap chalked up on the big board—makes this a welcome respite for Anglo-speakers. It's actually a fun place to hang out, for once, instead of just a cash-cow warehouse for tired bodies. Thumbs up for that!

how to get there:

By bus: Call hostel for transit route.

By car: Call hostel for directions.

By train: From Centraal Station, walk out front entrance and cross horizontal canal. Take second left onto Brugsteeg (just before big canal stretching away from station), and walk 2 blocks to next canal. Turn right just before water, walk along canal to first bridge, turn left and cross it; on other side, turn right and walk less than 1 block to hostel on left. Look for British flags.

croydon hostel

Warmoestraat, Amsterdam
Phone: 020–627–6065

Rates:　€35 (about $44 US) per person; doubles €70 (about $88 US)
Credit cards: Yes
Beds: 20
Private/family rooms: No
Kitchen available: No
Season: Open year-round
Office hours: Vary; call for hours
Affiliation: None
Extras: Breakfast

This place just plain sucks, set above a cheapo Indian restaurant on one of Amsterdam's suckiest streets. Sorry, but that's the truth—it's the kinda street where drug dealers solicit you in broad daylight.

There are sagging beds here in the usual sad dorms, no kitchen, no laundry, no food, no guard, no nothin'—just overpriced beds you pay for at the restaurant and then get no help with afterward. The clientele at this one must be scary indeed to take such desperate measures. We wouldn't stay here if you paid us.

So take our advice: Avoid it like the plague.

Best bet for a bite:
Elsewhere

Insiders' tip:
Avoid guys with gold teeth

What hostellers say:
"What's Dutch for 911?!"

Gestalt:
Bad trip

Safety:

Hospitality:

Cleanliness:

Party index:

how to get there:

By bus or train: Call hostel for transit route.

By car: Call hostel for directions.

durty nelly's hostel

Warmoestraat 115, Amsterdam
Phone: 020–638–0125

Fax: 020–633–4401
E-mail: nellys@xs4all.nl
Rates: €22 (about $28 US) per person
Credit cards: Yes
Beds: 42
Private/family rooms: No
Kitchen available: No
Season: Open year-round
Office hours: Twenty-four hours
Affiliation: None
Extras: Bar, breakfast, lockers, restaurant, safe

This place is set on the same sleazy Warmoestraat as two other lousy hostels (see pages 308 and 320), but it's a slight cut above one of them. Slight.

It's set above an Irish-themed bar that's heavy on cigarette smoke and English beer, a little depressing, we thought, and the staff weren't the most helpful in the world. They claim to have about forty-two beds (in mixed-sex dorms of eight, fourteen, and twenty beds) and they're supercheap beds, yeah—but this is definitely one to put in the last-resort category, especially with that smoky, loud sports bar downstairs and junkies and sex shops on all sides outdoors.

Best bet for a bite:
Supermarkets

What hostellers say:
"Let's call another hostel . . ."

Gestalt:
Durty bird

Safety:

Hospitality:

Cleanliness:

Party index:

how to get there:

By bus or train: Call hostel for transit route.
By car: Call hostel for directions.

euphemia hostel

Fokke Simonszstraat 1-9, 1017 TD Amsterdam
Phone: 020–622–9045

Fax: 020–622–9673
E-mail: euphemia-hotel@budgethotel.A2000.nl
Web site: www.euphemiahotel.com
Rates: €25–€60 (about $30–$72 US) per person; doubles €70–€120 (about $84–$144 US)
Credit cards: Yes
Beds: 76
Private/family rooms: Yes
Kitchen available: No
Season: Open year-round
Office hours: 8:00 A.M.–11:00 P.M.
Affiliation: None
Extras: Travel library, breakfast ($), TV, lockers, Internet access

The Euphemia, a former monastery, down a quiet side alley, is fairly close to Amsterdam's action without being right in the thick of it. It's also around the corner from an Internet place and a great-smelling bakery.

Best bet for a bite:
Albert Heijn Supermarket

Insiders' tip:
Boulangerie
Le Mortier bakery

What hostellers say:
"G'day!"

Gestalt:
Euphoria

Safety:

Hospitality:

Cleanliness:

Party index:

However, as it's chiefly a hotel, there are only four dorm beds available. Too bad, because it's a good place.

The wheelchair-accessible ground floor has five double rooms and a nice breakfast room with a television, closely spaced round tables, and a good little travel library where visitors swap dog-eared guidebooks.

The rest of the place is definitely not wheelchair-accessible; you have to climb a set of narrow, steep stairs to get to the upper floors and one dorm. (They discourage people with kids from lodging on upper floors because of the hazards involved. Smart.) Once up top, the lone quad dorm room is airy and nice, hotel-quality really, with lockers, a television, and a bathroom in the hall.

The other rooms are doubles, triples, and quads—some with views and all quite nice. Being mostly a hotel now, many of these double rooms come with TV and bathroom. It's not luxury, but it's a one-star hotel and that's a good budget bet for couples. Remember that the price drops in winter and goes up in summer. And in July and August, there's a minimum stay of two nights.

Run by some Dutch folks who've spent time in New Zealand, there's a friendly Down Under flavor to the proceedings—if you get the right staffer. They'll point you anywhere you need. It's a very short walk to both the popular Heineken Brewery and the Rijksmuseum and other museums in the Museumplein complex. You're also just a few steps from two well-known coffee shops (Mellow Yellow and Little Coffeeshop), as well as a natural foods store, fruit shop, and several quiet canals.

A nice pick, though it's less and less a hostel every year and more a good low-priced hotel.

how to get there:

By bus: Call hostel for transit route.
By car: Call hostel for directions.
By train: From Centraal Station, take #16, #24, or #25 tram to hostel.

flying pig downtown hostel
Nieuwendijk 100, 1012 MR Amsterdam
Phone: 020–420–6822

E-mail: downtown@flyingpig.nl
Web site: www.flyingpig.nl
Rates: €13.90–€36.90 (about $17–$43 US) per person; doubles €73.80 (about $89 US)
Credit cards: Yes
Beds: 180
Private/family rooms: Yes
Kitchen available: Yes
Season: Open year-round
Office hours: Twenty-four hours
Affiliation: None
Extras: E-mail, breakfast, bar

This huge place, a former downtown hotel marked by an unmistakable, huge pig sign on a tawdry strip, is legendary for its laid-back groove. We'll venture to say it's the best-known bunk (at least by North Americans) in the whole city. But is it the best bunk? Read on . . .

The owners came up with this concept while backpacking around Australia (their Web site tells the whole tale of the pig); this one's actually the second in the chain, begun a half year after the original Flying Pig over in the Vondelpark. But it's by far the more popular one; try to book ahead if you really wanna come.

Inside the door from the chaos on the street, you are greeted with—more chaos. A harried staff tries to work through bookings while stoned hostellers crash in a chill-out room adjacent to the very popular bar. This kiddie bar is said to be for hostellers only, not locals, and while some order beers and light up purchased-on-the-street pot, others lie in that padded front window area blissing out on the rainbow-colored pads while the world passes them by. Free pitchers of water on the bar help the weed-eaters cleanse the palate.

Best bet for a bite:
Food surrounds you

Insiders' tip:
Luggage repair place at 4 Nieuwiezijds Kolk

What hostellers say:
"Loved it/hated it."

Gestalt:
Central Pork

Safety: 🏴🏴

Hospitality: 🏴🏴

Cleanliness: 🏴🏴

Party index: 🎪🎪🎪🎪

No wonder the logo here is a pig in an aviator helmet, smoking a huge rasta spliff . . .

Upstairs, a condom machine, beer vending machine, and pinball machine greet you before you've even found your bunk . . . welcome to the dollhouse. Actually, the painted and carpeted halls, restored wooden beams, and numerous windows do display a certain attention to detail on the part of ownership; it's not just a warehouse for your wallet.

The price you pay depends heavily on the size of your room. Get a quad in this maze of a building and you'll pay a premium; camp out in the huge twenty-six-bedded room (with wilder hostellers) and it's much cheaper. Even this big room isn't too bad; it's divided into halves and looks up at a neat metal roof that used to be a hotel bar.

They also do rooms of six, eight, ten, and fourteen beds—and they've also got four rather plain doubles. These are okay, spruced up with art prints on the walls, but they're still basically two smooshed-together twin beds and a spartan bathroom; at least it's a private bathroom. This costs more, of course, but you also get wicker chairs and a bit of worn furniture. All rooms, by the way, have shower, toilet, and lockers, which is nice for a change in this city; many also come with good street views. Mattresses come on ladder-style supports, not the most comfortable.

One outstanding feature here is that this is almost the only hostel in A'dam with a kitchen, a big plus; this kitchen—open to 10:00 A.M. and noon till midnight—has two sets of electric rangetops, plenty of pots and pans, multiple fridges, and a "happy room" to dine in amid a painting of gnomes and nude women frolicking through a magical forest, dude. There's also a more conventional dining room attached to that one with perpetual TV and movies. There are strict rules, however, on how much you can eat with your breakfast; take more and you've gotta pay extra. Boo!

What else? The free e-mail in the lobby is wildly popular, although it doesn't always work properly. Reception does a brisk business selling T-shirts of the pig logo. There are few, if any, rules here; you can work to pay off your stay, and they run movies daily in the "happy room." Some 90 percent of the crowd was American when we dropped by, most of them digging the cigarette machine, video gambling, abundant pot, and beers at the bar. Few were using the piano and pool table, but maybe it was a slow night.

Problems do arise, however. A number of hostellers privately confided problems with cleanliness, comfort, retching late-night hostellers, and useless staffers. These complaints were heard repeatedly, making us think that all the amenities here might not mean much to you if you value a good night's sleep and clean bedding and bathrooms. We're giving it the thumbs-up for now, but we're keeping our eye on 'em for future developments.

The neighborhood isn't too great. There are numerous bars, souvenir shops, and crap around the area, none of it too interesting to us. If you're into the Sex Museum or Torture Museum, though, you'll love it.

how to get there:

By bus or train: From Centraal Station, walk straight out front entrance toward Damrak. Pass Victoria hotel, turn right at first alley and walk to end; look for 100 Nieuwendijk and big pig sign.
By car: Call hostel for directions.

key to icons

Attractive natural setting	Comfortable beds	Visual arts at hostel or nearby
Ecologically aware hostel	A particularly good value	Music at hostel or nearby
Superior kitchen facilities or cafe	Wheelchair-accessible	Great hostel for skiers
Offbeat or eccentric place	Good for business travelers	Bar or pub at hostel or nearby
Superior bath-room facilities	Especially well suited for families	Editors' Choice: Among our very favorite hostels
Romantic private rooms	Good for active travelers	

flying pig palace (uptown) hostel

Vossiusstraat 46–47, 1054 GA Amsterdam
Phone: 020–400–4187

E-mail: palace@flyingpig.nl
Web site: www.flyingpig.nl
Rates: €13.30–€29.90 (about $17–$37 US) per person; doubles €60 (about $75 US)
Credit cards: Yes
Beds: 130
Private/family rooms: Yes
Kitchen available: Yes
Season: Open year-round
Office hours: Twenty-four hours
Affiliation: None
Extras: E-mail, breakfast, bar

This one's basically the mirror image of its sister hostel, the Flying Pig Downtown (see previous listing): a mellower, more laid-back groove for Flying Piggies who don't want downtown's chaos or a complete party scene. More cultural travelers tend to stay at the Palace over in the Vondelpark—now officially known as the Flying Pig Uptown—while the party crowd camps out at the other one, so it all works out in the end.

Set in a town house just off the beginning of the big park that A'damers so love to bike through, it's got all the same stuff as the downtown joint—bar, free e-mail, double rooms, and huge dorms— just fewer beds, that's all. Room prices vary a lot, according strictly to size: A double or quad room is the most expensive, but six-, eight-, ten-, and twelve-bedded rooms get progressively cheaper depending on how many people you're willing to sleep with . . . er, alongside.

Best bet for a bite:
Albert Heijn on Overtoom

Insiders' tip:
Lots of car rental places around corner

What hostellers say:
"Not as crazy as the other Pig."

Gestalt:
Piggly wiggly

Safety:

Hospitality:

Cleanliness:

Party index:

If you've seen one Pig, you've seen 'em all; subtract a few stoners, add a few philosophy majors, and you've got the same picture here. A well-run place, few rules, not always spic-and-span clean but acceptable nonetheless.

how to get there:

By bus or train: From Centraal Station, take #1, #2, or #5 tram to Leidseplein stop. Walk across plaza, cross wide busy street, turn left, and walk past Hostelling International sign and park to Vossiusstraat on right. Turn right and walk down to 46 Vossiusstraat.
By car: Call hostel for directions.

globe centre hostel
Oudezijds Voorburgwal 3, Amsterdam
Phone: 020–421–7424

Fax: 020–421–7423
E-mail: info@hotel-theglobe.nl
Web site: www.hotel-theglobe.nl
Rates: €18–€20 (about $23–$25 US) per person; doubles €60 (about $75 US)
Credit cards: Yes
Beds: Number varies
Private/family rooms: Yes
Kitchen available: No
Season: Open year-round
Office hours: Twenty-four hours
Affiliation: None
Extras: Bar, restaurant

Note: Three-day minimum stay required on weekends.

Take an already bad neighborhood (the red light district), mix in a mediocre-at-best facility with rooms that seem far tinier and scrubbier than the ones depicted on the Web site, and why would you stay here? You wouldn't. (Well, we had to, but that's not the point.)

Staff are often surly and unhelpful, rooms are either too

Gestalt:
Durty bird

Safety:

Hospitality:

Cleanliness:

Party index:

pint-sized or too big. Twenty-two pairs of stoned feet in one room? C'mon, man. The cleanliness of the bunks and bathrooms varies, but it's hardly spic-and-span here.

Positives? A smokeless basement sports bar that makes for a convenient beer without setting foot outside in the dodgy streets surrounding—however, you cannot use it as the hostel common room and just hang out reading a book, which is a damned shame. They don't like that. They also serve bar food such as big burgers for low prices down there, though it ain't all that great.

The Globe's not the worst place in town, not at all—some hostels in A'dam are truly horrific. But this is hardly in even the top half of the selections available. Save yourself the trouble if you can.

how to get there:

By car: Contact hostel for directions.
By bus: Contact hostel for directions.
By train: Contact hostel for directions.

---

hans brinker hostel
Kerkstraat 136–138, Amsterdam
Phone: 020–622–0687

Fax: 020–638–2060
Rates: €21 (about $25 US) per person; doubles €70 (about $84 US)
Credit cards: Yes
Beds: 550
Private/family rooms: Yes
Kitchen available: No
Season: Open year-round
Office hours: Twenty-four hours
Affiliation: None
Extras: Bar, meals ($)

You wanna get a handle on this monster-sized, one-of-a-kind place before you show up? OK, here's what you've gotta do.

Crank up some later-period U2—you know, *Achtung Baby!* or *Zooropa,* two albums that successfully manage to encapsulate the chaotic and uncertain madness of the new Europe, the one that has torn down most of the old infrastructures and has replaced them with cultural diversity, self-expression, and global shrinkage. That, in a nutshell, describes the wild vibe at the Hans Brinker Hostel, basically a hostel on steroids; though the staff shudders at the thought of being labeled among the ranks of lowly hostels, they've got dorms, a nasty attitude, kegs of beer, and weird guests. We say: It's a hostel.

Upon arrival you're greeted by some odd posters that display the motto "Check Out" (as in "Check Out the Hans Brinker Hostel"), with a photo of some poor beat-up guy. It's hard to figure out what the message is: You'll get your butt kicked if you stay here? Possibly.

Back to the objective description. Based on a quiet street, but well within reach of the coffee-shop action, you find this one simply by following your nose to the smell of marijuana—or by following the squads of back-packs to the long check-in line.

Just inside, adjacent to reception, there's a cavernous bar with wooden floors and picnic tables, which transforms

What hostellers say:
"Tonight, the bottle let me down . . ."

Insiders' tip:
Bikes will run you down

Gestalt:
Global chillage

Safety:

Hospitality:

Cleanliness:

Party index:

at 11:00 P.M. into a free disco; here, in a dance hall adorned with psychedelic murals, resident DJs spin disco tunes while gweezy guys try out pickup lines on unsuspecting Japanese girls. All vices are catered to here: There are cigarette and beer vending machines, you can send e-mail and get plastered at the bar, and so forth.

Interestingly the population here is not the usual American college girls sprinkling every sentence with the word "like" but rather jaded Euro-types who have been around the block a few times; it's basically a combo of wastoid older guys, dudes with fly-shades strapped to their heads, girls who show a lot of navel, and lots of weird beards. A wild crowd, completely European, creating a nutso party atmosphere that goes right off the top end of our party index scale.

Yet the rooms aren't complete junk. You've got many of the amenities you'd seek in a hostel if you were young and Euro (though you can't buy pot on the premises). The six-bedded dorms are extremely tight and raucous, but they're surprisingly clean. They've also got every other size you can imagine—from single rooms to doubles, triples, quads, sevens, eights, and (hell, yes, why not) even tens.

While breakfast is included for free, other meals cost extra. You get nicked for an extra $1.50 if you're only staying one night. Yeah, that's fair. You can also blow some money buying tacky souvenirs at the front desk or save it for whatever floats your boat at the highly acclaimed "smart shop" (drug shop) Conscious Dreams or the cleverly named coffee shop Global Chillage, both just down the block.

The neighborhood is pretty happening in general, and if the hostel meals and crowd don't suit you, there are plenty of Chinese restaurants and other ethnic eateries around. A pricey but good Albert Heijn supermarket on the main street can provide picnic supplies plus a good selection of Dutch cheese, and you can wash your duds at a good laundry (The Clean Brothers) nearby. The area is overtly gay, so there are lots of, um, interesting stores, posters, and bars around.

All in all, this place manages to provide its young Euro revelers with a quiet place to chill and sleep with a place to party safely.

how to get there:

By bus: Call hostel for transit route.
By car: Call hostel for directions.
By train: From train station, take #25 or #16 tram to Kerkstraat stop; make a right and walk 1 block to hostel on left.

international budget hostel
Leidsegracht 761, 1916 CR Amsterdam
Phone: 020–624–2784

Fax: 020–772–4825
E-mail: info@internationalbudgethostel.com
Web site: www.internationalbudgethostel.com
Rates: €20–€35 (about $25–$42 US) per person; doubles €65–€80 (about $78–$96 US)
Credit cards: No
Beds: 54
Private/family rooms: No
Kitchen available: No
Season: Open year-round
Office hours: 9:00 A.M.–11:00 P.M.
Affiliation: None
Extras: Breakfast ($), TV

When one has been in the hostel-reviewing business as long as we have, one begins to immediately pick up signs that all is not really well beneath an apparently glossy surface—and that first queasy impression usually turns out to be correct.

In the case of the International Budget Hostel, at first glance it seemed like an okay enough place: decent location, clean and quiet, adequate bathroom facilities. The hostel (once a warehouse) is set several floors up nearly vertical steps from the street (dangerous for children or people loaded down with enormous backpacks) in a narrow town house with great views across a pleasant canal.

But you've got to worry when the staff immediately announce, "We're really nice people" (sure enough, they're only nice when you're doing exactly what they want you to do). They really weren't very nice; just two dudes who have a world-weary attitude and not much patience with people not involved with "the drug scene." For starters, they charged way too much for breakfast, which is included in almost all the other A'dam hostels. No wonder the hostel seemed nearly empty despite its being peak season. The rooms (which were fairly large and nice, containing four single beds each compared with other multibed army-style hostel rooms) were okay, so this seemed a mystery.

Best bet for a bite:
Nepalese

Insiders' tip:
Great beer hall around corner

What hostellers say:
"Tune in, turn on, drop out."

Gestalt:
Doobie Brothers

Safety:

Hospitality:

Cleanliness:

Party index:

Even the chill-out lounge next to reception, which has one of the best views of any hostel room in the city, was deserted. Though affiliated with the good Euphemia hostel, this one turned out to be a poorer brother in many respects, despite such a super canal-side location.

If you're still staying but want to escape the unpleasant ambience in this hostel, check out the great beer hall around the corner. On premises, there's a TV/VCR in the lounge, where movies are sometimes played along with a constant stream of music videos. You can satisfy that caffeine craving with coffee dispensed from a machine. But families beware: This hostel definitely attracts the party crowd, evidenced by the many beer bottles scattered about and a tinge of grass in the air.

Escape to the ethnic food options that abound near the Leidseplein area, or just stick to the great restaurants and bars of the hip Jordaan area you're staying in; you won't go hungry or thirsty, though you better be packing some cash—A'dam can be a bit expensive.

The nice beds and nice neighborhood weren't enough to get our blessing. But maybe someone else would like these guys better. Maybe.

how to get there:

By bus or train: From Centraal Station, take #1, #2, or #5 tram to Leidseplein. Walk back to bridge, turn left at canal, walk down to Leidsegracht, and turn left. Hostel is on right.
By car: Call hostel for directions.

---

kabul international hostel
Warmoestraat 38–42, 1012 JE Amsterdam
Phone: 020–623–7158 or 020–623–7059

Fax: 020–620–0869
Rates: €21–€50 (about $27–$62 US) per person; doubles €70–€95 (about $84–$119 US)
Credit cards: Yes
Beds: 200
Private/family rooms: Yes
Kitchen available: No
Season: Open year-round
Office hours: Twenty-four hours
Affiliation: None
Extras: Breakfast, TV, bar, pool tables

Could this be *the* worst hostel in town? Tough competition, but our snoops say yes. This is a hotel that has added hostel beds and then

Best bet for a bite:
Sandwich shops on the street

Safety:

Hospitality:

Cleanliness:

Party index:

couldn't keep the whole situation from wheeling out of control. Their motto is "a comfortable bed without unnecessary luxuries." Let's add "plus dirt" to that. Uh-huh. . . .

The modern lobby is the only common place to hang, with a couple of leatherette couches on which to watch the street circus go by. It's okay but spare. The bar is the real meeting point, with a couple inexpensive beers on tap and a few mixed drinks. A continental breakfast is included, and they also serve curry meals for lunch, though we didn't try any on this street that's full of choices in eats.

The dorms come in a variety of sizes, everything from four to sixteen beds (with differing prices to match), and tend to be plainish bunks set on sloping un-level floors. The doubles and singles cost more, obviously, and sometimes offer private bathrooms. Staff are horrifically rude, and they don't seem to care that cleanliness has really slid down the toilet (literally) in recent years. The open policy of allowing guests to smoke lots of reefer in their rooms may have something to do with that. Fire hazard? Yup.

The street outside is just nuts, a condensation of everything Amsterdam. We'd stay here only if we really, really, loved filth and drugs—and had to catch a train early in the morning (you're a two-minute stroll from Centraal Station, the main plus of staying here).

how to get there:

By bus: Call hostel for transit route.
By car: Call hostel for directions.
By train: From Centraal Station, walk straight across bridge to Damrak, continue to second street and turn left. Go 1 block and turn left onto Warmoestraat; hostel is on left.

the meeting point hostel
Warmoestraat 14, Amsterdam
Phone: 020–627–7499

Fax: 020–330–4774
E-mail: info@hostel-meetingpoint.nl
Rates: €16–€30 (about $20–$38 US) per person
Credit cards: No
Beds: 100
Private/family rooms: No
Kitchen available: No
Season: Open year-round
Office hours: Twenty-four hours
Affiliation: None
Extras: Lockers ($), bar, pool table, currency exchange, foosball

This place, which has been just around the corner from Amsterdam's Centraal Station for almost ten years now, tries hard but still hasn't quite got the hostel formula right. It's worth a shot, though, if other good hostels in town are full—we'd certainly recommend it over most of the other downtown cheapies here, which are mostly terrible and don't care at all about you except for your wallet. Here, they do appear to care.

Two-thirds of the guests are Americans or Brits, all congregating behind the locked glass door of the hostellers-only (or so claims management) bar. The bar, painted with murals and decorated with banners from European football (that's soccer to Americans) teams, offers a good beer selection, video gambling, long wooden tables, and barstools; loud rave music pumps constantly in this common room beneath a steady stream of Euro-videos. They also sell snacks and fast food here, and it's a good area for mixing. However, a number of hostellers had bought grass on the street and were smoking it in the bar, a practice clearly tolerated by management.

Upstairs, they've got several narrow floors of quite spartan dorms and family rooms, augmented by worn bathrooms. There are two kinds of dorms here, some with eight beds and the rest with eighteen beds; some coed and some for women only. Some have views—of the main canal, the train station, and downtown—while the more drab rooms contain cot-style beds. These rooms sometimes come with a bit of worn furniture, sometimes not; there are two toilets and two showers per floor, which is too few considering all the beds they've got here.

Best bet for a bite:
Chinese, maybe?

Insiders' tip:
Gollem brown cafe is cool

What hostellers say:
"I wanna get high, so high . . ."

Gestalt:
Meet 'n greet

Safety:

Hospitality:

Cleanliness:

Party index:

However, we'll give this to the staff: Those rooms on the top floors have knockout views of the main city canal and downtown Amsterdam, some of the best in the whole darned city. If you're coming for a canal view, ask for a top-floor front room and hope you get one.

The little touches here are nice—clean-smelling reception area, a buzz-in system for security, no curfew, incense in the hallways—and big points to the friendly management which offered us a "look before you pay" policy regarding rooms. Ask for the same. They also get points for a unique system of using big locked oil drum–sized barrels (they once held orange juice concentrate from South America, by the way) to store backpacks in the rooms without fear of theft.

The neighborhood is Amsterdam-crazy, with a Dutch language school around the corner for those actually here to learn something; in a month or two, they say, you can learn this hard-to-master tongue.

how to get there:

By bus: Call hostel for transit route.
By car: Call hostel for directions.
By train: From Centraal Station, walk across bridge and turn immediately left. Walk to first right, turn right, and continue to hostel on right.

shelter downtown hostel

Barndesteeg 21, 1012 BV Amsterdam
Phone: 020–625–3230

Fax: 020–623–2282
E-mail: city@shelter.nl
Rates: €16.00–€23.50 (about $20–$30 US) per person
Credit cards: No
Beds: 160
Private/family rooms: No
Kitchen available: No
Season: Open year-round
Office hours: 7:30 A.M.–2:00 A.M.
Curfew: Midnight (weekdays); 2:00 A.M. (weekends)
Affiliation: None
Extras: Breakfast, luggage storage, meals ($), lockers ($), piano, currency exchange, foosball

Tucked among red light district massage parlors and women standing in windows offering sex 'round the clock, this remarkable oasis of calm somehow offers one of the cheapest and cleanest beds in town despite its location.

There's only one catch . . . it's a Christian hostel, and though they're not pushy about the message, it's everywhere on the walls. And you may get the cold shoulder if you don't join the God Squad at (nightly) Bible time. However, as a quiet alternative to the crazed city outside, it makes a good detour for families, Bible students, or others who need some sanity.

The ground floor, behind the reception, is quite pleasant—wicker chairs, a few picnic-style tables, a pool table, and a popular piano. Oh, and religious art and messages are everywhere; note especially the

Times Square–style ticker scrolling out messages like "He gave his life for you" . . . "trust in Him" . . . and so on. You half expect stock quotes and sports scores to roll past next.

Anyway, this area leads to a snack bar serving breakfast, dinner, and snacks—nice place and good food. The real drawing card here, though, is a pretty interior courtyard with lots of lilypads—a cute place amid the squalor where you can hang out or store your bike.

Up the modern stairs, dorms are mostly twelve, sixteen, and twenty(!) bedded, but there are also some four- to eight-bedded ones—nothing special, but certainly clean and airy, if closely packed. This is by far the city's cleanest bunk. Curtains and big windows add a bit of a homey touch. Try to forget all those snoozing bodies around you.

The front desk sells shampoo, rents towels, doles out lockers for a fee, and provides the useful service of storing luggage behind the front desk during the daytime on well-organized racks. (They also host frequent Bible discussions and screen religious videos, of course.)

You'll meet supernice hostellers of all stripes here, including Americans working to pay off their stays, but you might not find the interesting characters you were seeking in crazy A'dam. One other

Best bet for a bite:
Along the main canal

Insiders' tip:
Avoid Nieumarkt subway stop

What hostellers say:
"For the Lord is my shepherd . . ."

Gestalt:
A'dam's apple

Safety:

Hospitality:

Cleanliness:

Party index:

key to icons

- Attractive natural setting
- Ecologically aware hostel
- Superior kitchen facilities or cafe
- Offbeat or eccentric place
- Superior bathroom facilities
- Romantic private rooms

- Comfortable beds
- A particularly good value
- Wheelchair-accessible
- Good for business travelers
- Especially well suited for families
- Good for active travelers

- Visual arts at hostel or nearby
- Music at hostel or nearby
- Great hostel for skiers
- Bar or pub at hostel or nearby
- Editors' Choice: Among our very favorite hostels

surprise: They allow smoking in some parts of the place, despite a general no-booze, no-drugs policy.

how to get there:

By bus: Call hostel for transit route.
By car: Call hostel for directions.
By train: From Centraal Station, walk to Nieumarkt stop, then walk across square (keep big church on your right), make a left and then an immediate right onto Barndesteeg. Hostel is on right.

shelter jordaan hostel
Bloemstraat 179, 1016 LA Amsterdam
Phone: 020–624–4717

Fax: 020–627–6137
E-mail: jordan@shelter.nl
Web site: www.shelter.nl
Rates: €16.00–€19.50 (about $20–$25 US) per person
Credit cards: No
Beds: 112
Private/family rooms: No
Kitchen available: No
Season: Open year-round
Office hours: 7:30 A.M.–1:00 A.M.
Lockout: 10:00 A.M.–12:30 P.M.
Affiliation: None
Extras: Lockers ($), currency exchange, meals ($), snack shop, breakfast, luggage storage, Bible talks

This is the other Christian hostel in Amsterdam, started over twenty years ago in a quiet canal-side neighborhood to complement the affiliated Shelter Hostel downtown. What's different about this one? Well, the location's a heck of a lot better. And the no-smoking policy (inside, that is) is probably unique in A'dam and quite welcome to nonsmoking hostellers.

The Shelter Jordaan, formerly called the Eben Haezer, touts itself as the "cheapest bed-and-breakfast in town," and they could add that they have one of the best locations in the whole city.

Granite stairs lead you up to the hostel, pretty much a no-frills affair, bed-wise—just two floors, each with big single-sex dorms packed tightly with bunks. These fourteen- to twenty-bedded rooms contain bunks set on metal frames, and the mattresses didn't look terribly comfortable; at least there are lockers in each room and huge, clean gang-style bathrooms nearby. Boys aren't allowed on the girls' floor after 10:00 P.M., which in retrospect is probably a good thing considering that some people start to wind down about that time and don't want to hear some loudmouth bragging about his great day in Amsterdam while they're saying their prayers.

Though you don't have to carry a Bible and prove you're Christian to stay the night, you do have to be able to tolerate the squeaky-clean crowd that tends to gravitate here. On the other hand, you couldn't ask for a nicer staff—they obviously care about your well-being in a way that most other hostels in town don't. For example, they sell shampoo, toothpaste, postcards, and other stuff at the front desk as well as bus, metro, and tram tickets. And they provide a well-organized info board with details on all aspects of this intriguing city.

There's been lots of work here, and it shows in the blue and red–painted bricks, the pretty patio, and a great cafeteria (which sometimes cranks Christian power pop all day long—you have been warned). Kick-start your day the right way with yogurt, muesli, etc., for breakfast. You can't use the kitchen to cook your own meals, but you can buy your own food and eat it in the dining room; dinner is served for about €4 (about $5 US). They also serve snacks like burgers. They keep an eye on your stuff for free with a locked luggage room and a video camera.

Did we describe the common areas? They have comfy couches, plants, and big windows onto the quiet streets—not to mention a suggestion box and a common room with a TV, library, and games.

Again, it's a really nice Jordaan neighborhood—a bit yuppie, but placed near veggie restaurants, great local bars, and just 300 yards from the Anne Frank House—so this is probably the best-positioned hostel in town. If you want peace, quiet, and the flavor of A'dam without any sleaze, stay here.

There is technically an age limit (you're supposed to be between fifteen and forty), but staff reportedly look the other way if you're cool or if it's the low season.

Best bet for a bite:
Vliegende Schotel (Flying Saucer) for veggie

What hostellers say:
"I was thinkin' to myself, 'This could be heaven or this could be Hell' . . . "

Gestalt:
Hostel heaven

Safety:

Hospitality:

Cleanliness:

Party index:

A night security guard keeps the riffraff out, though in the Jordaan that is hardly (if ever) a problem. The real problem here is dealing with the squeaky-cleanness of it all.

Ah, what the hell. Oops. We mean what the heck. Give it a shot.

how to get there:

By bus or train: From Centraal Station, take #13 or #17 tram to fifth stop (Marnxstraat) and cross street. Turn corner and walk to 179 Bloemstraat.

By car: Call hostel for directions.

---

stadsdoelen hostel

Kloveniersburgwal 97, 1011 KB Amsterdam
Phone: 020–624–6832

Fax: 020–639–1035
Rates: €21.40–€25.60 (about $26–$31 US) per HI member
Credit cards: Yes
Beds: 170
Private/family rooms: No
Kitchen available: Yes
Season: March 1–December 31
Office hours: 7:00 A.M.–1:00 A.M.
Curfew: 2:00 A.M.
Affiliation: HI-NJHC
Extras: Bike storage, Internet access, snacks, bar, lockers, laundry, pool table, darts, bike rentals

---

You won't believe the location of this hostel, or the groovy vibe, when you get here. It's the best backpacker-style hostel in town, no question, even more amazing because it is a Hostelling International–affiliated shop.

The bland four-floor building on a canal, a former sailors' home that became a hostel back in the 1940s—and thus predates the residential apartments that now surround it—doesn't look like much at first glance. But look again: This is the only hostel in town surrounded on both sides by canals; real estate moguls would kill for a piece of property like this today.

Inside, they really pack the beds in. But one of the interesting features about the architecture here is the way they've used minipartitions to help reduce the noise between bunks and give a little extra privacy to people in these huge rooms; it almost (but not quite) turns that twenty-six-bed behemoth into a manageable, sleepable collection of quad rooms. Neat trick.

Even neater is the laid-back management, friendly staff, and great common areas. There are two: a reception area with plenty of couches and chairs for mixin' and minglin' and playin' Monopoly and a really awesome bar out back on the second canal.

You enter the hip bar and immediately spy art on the walls, green plants hanging in pots, decorative railroad signs (who snuck into the rail yard and took those?) and assorted other cool memorabilia. It's a very colorful place with several beers on tap, a dartboard and darts, a big TV, the whole deal. So you sidle up to the big wooden bar and order a cheap, good beer. The music isn't overpoweringly loud (well, not always, anyway); they sell microwaved soups and snacks all day long here, too, at least as long as the bar is open (5:00 P.M. until midnight). Happy hour, when prices are reduced, occurs nightly between 8:00 and 9:00 P.M., too.

You get a continental breakfast for free in the morning and have access to two very important extras—the ones you want. We're talking about the kitchen and laundry. The kitchen is big, clean, and ultra-useful and serves as one of the prime mixing points for newfound friends. The laundry is right in there, too, which we actually liked—kill two tasks with one stone, you know? The staff will find you bikes to rent, then let you stash 'em in the basement for safekeeping.

The dorms? They come in male, female, and coed flavors—all of them too big, but all partitioned off as described above. Since no groups or families are allowed, you won't be awakened by crying kids at least.

Reception sells long-distance Eurolines bus tickets and keeps track of the active message board without getting preachy about anything, a welcome switch. They'll also direct you around the beautiful little neighborhood where the hostel sits, which itself is tucked just far enough away from the red light district to be comfortable and two minutes from the city's best shopping area, the Kalverstraat. (This is about a fifteen-minute walk from the train station, as well; avoid taking the Metro because the stop is kind of dangerous.)

Yeah, it seems that they've thought of everything here: big backpack-size lockers for your stuff; Internet machines to cruise and write e-mail; modern, clean bathrooms; extrasecure bike storage in the basement. (They've taken aggressive security measures in recent years to combat a dodgy neighborhood nearby.) Even the 2:00 A.M. curfew is somewhat flexible: Staff reopen the doors hourly afterward throughout the night to let in straggling hostellers.

Though the building could certainly use some upgrading after all these years, this is top-level hostelling—a lower-priced and much more laid-back alternative to the other "official" hostel in town. And a special winter deal makes it even cheaper, giving you five nights for the price of four.

Gentlepeople, start your hostelling engines . . .

how to get there:

By bus or train: Best to call hostel for directions first. From Amsterdam's Centraal Station, take #9, #16, #24, or #25 streetcar to Muntplein stop. Walk back down canal toward city center, along Nieuwe Doelenstraat; after crossing first bridge, take a right to cross another small bridge over canal. Make a left on Kloveniersburgwal; hostel is on right.

By car: Call hostel for directions.

white tulip youth hostel

Warmoestraat 87, Amsterdam
Phone: 020–625–5974

Fax: 020–420–1299
Web site: www.wittetulp.nl
Rates: €20–€40 (about $25–$53 US) per person
Credit cards: No
Beds: 72
Private/family rooms: Yes
Kitchen available: No
Season: Open year-round
Office hours: Twenty-four hours
Affiliation: None
Extras: Breakfast ($), pub, meals ($), lockers

The sweet-sounding White Tulip is actually the former Budget Hostel AVC. That place had crossed the oh-so-fine line from hostel to flop house, located above a really sleazy bar—the kind Tom Waits would write a song about. The only saving grace was its location if you wanted to party really hard and not have to go too far to reach your bed—or if you needed to make a quick getaway from the station early the next morning.

What hostellers say:
"Dirty"

Safety:

Hospitality:

Cleanliness:

Party index:

Ownership has changed; the Irish pub is still there. Now there are fourteen rooms containing a total of seventy-two beds in a series of private rooms (one to three beds), dorms with en-suite bathrooms (four to five beds), and bigger dorms (eight to ten beds). At first look, they seem quite spartan; cleanliness of the new joint has yet to improve much. And it's quite expensive for such a middling place. At least the bathrooms are OK, and the management does seem to be slightly upgrading the place, even if it's got a ways to go.

The only possible selling point is its proximity to an old church and a nice flower shop (but also the Prostitution Information Center, so there), and the Irish pub. Maybe.

how to get there:

By bus or train: Call hostel for transit route.
By car: Call hostel for directions.

norway

Norway is fjord-tough. Heh-heh. But seriously, this is some of Europe's most spectacular scenery—and if you're in the area (in other words, Denmark or Sweden), you'd be foolish not to pencil in a couple days up here. The Oslo-to-Bergen train ride has justifiably been called one of the best in the world, and several side trips off that line bring you face to face with even *more* spectacular fjord-side scenery.

Hotels are very expensive up here, though, making hostels an ever more attractive option; if you think your dorm bed costs a lot, just pick up a hotel flyer and do the conversion—you'll get down on your knees and thank us.

practical details

If you'll be traveling a great deal in Denmark, Sweden, and Norway (or even two of those three countries), get a ScanRail pass—expensive, but still one of the all-time great rail pass deals. It gets you free or discount riding on some extremely scenic routes, plus half price on some ferries to other Scandinavian countries, too.

Norway's country code is 47; Oslo's city code is 22. To dial Oslo hostels from the United States, dial 011–47 plus the number AS PRINTED. To dial Oslo hostels from within Norway, also dial the number AS PRINTED.

As we've said, things cost a lot of money. The unit of currency here is the Norwegian krone (NKr). At press time, about six kroner equaled about one U.S. dollar—so that 165-NKr dorm room costs a surprising $28 US.

oslo

Most travelers to Norway begin in Oslo; it's the biggest city, the most cultural, and the easiest to reach via overnight train or ferry from Denmark or Sweden. (You can also catch an all-day train from Copenhagen or Göteborg.) This is a place that has long benefited from its position by the water (it was founded in 1050!), but the work of being a port city has given some ground to the arts and big business. Residents zip across the water on ferries to the hidden beaches—and the Viking Ships Museum—of the Bygdøy peninsula. At night, young folks congregate in the hippest nightclubs of the moment. And you're just a short ride from the big mountains of Lillehammer, former venue for the Winter Olympics. It remains a top ski destination for Norwegians—and a great place for a hike in the meadows in summer.

If coming by train you arrive at Oslo Sentral, which faces wide Karl Johans Gate—the main street of the city, which is actually tackier and more commercial than one would hope these days, but it leads you right into the center. To get around, you can use an extensive network of streetcars, buses, or the subway (T-bana).

oslo hostels
at a glance

	RATING	PRICE	IN A WORD	PAGE
Haraldsheim Hostel		175–365 NKr	modern	p. 334
Anker Hostel		195–510 NKr	central	p. 332

anker hostel
Storgata 55, Oslo 0182
Phone: 22–99–7200 or 22–99–7210

Fax: 22–99–7220
E-mail: hostel@anker.oslo.no
Web site: www.ankerhostel.no
Rates: 195–510 NKr (about $33–$85 US) per person; doubles 510 NKr (about $85 US)
Credit cards: No
Beds: 108
Private/family rooms: Yes
Kitchen available: Yes
Office hours: Twenty-four hours (summer), 7:00 A.M. to 11:30 P.M. (September to April)
Affiliation: None
Extras: Breakfast ($), bar, laundry, Internet access, lockers

Part of the extremely bland-looking Anker Hotel, this independent hostel is very central—much more so than Oslo's other hostel, in fact, almost walking distance from its train station. Its chief redeeming value beyond location is its price: You'll find no (reputable) hotel in town to offer a cheaper double room. It is okay, not great.

It's right across the street from a clinic, too—a good thing in case the lobby bar gets you a little *too* relaxed. Inside, the place has double rooms and four- and six-bedded rooms. Dorms are equipped with handmade wooden bunks; the doubles come with little work desks and lamps. It feels a lot like our college dorm—except that all the rooms *here* have individual bathrooms, which our freshman dorms certainly *didn't*. All rooms come with duvets, but you've got to either bring your own sheet or pay big bucks to rent theirs. On the downside, the place smells vaguely redolent of curry, and security is very lax. Not good in a big-city neighborhood.

Best bet for a bite:
Kaffistova, downtown

What hostellers say:
"I guess it'll do."

Gestalt:
Phat Albertine

Safety:

Hospitality:

Cleanliness:

Party index:

There's a kitchen for hostellers to use, but as in many other Scandinavian hostels, you have to cart your own utensils; if you don't feel like doing that, a buffet lunch is served on weekdays. The hotel restaurant is also a fun place to pick up the breakfast spread and meet others doing the same. (They serve dinners only to groups, unfortunately.) A laundry, Internet access, lockers, and parking (for a fee) are also welcome additions. However, be prepared to fork over a big (about $30 US) key deposit upon check-in. Not sure why.

While seriously short on personality—the hostel and the surrounding area are Zipsville for character—this place is certainly good enough given its proximity to all the cool downtown stuff Oslo has to offer and the low price. Just don't expect a perfectly secure or social experience.

how to get there:

By bus: From bus station, take #10, #11, #12, #15, or #17 streetcar to Hausmanns Gate stop; then walk along Storgata to hostel on left.

By car: Contact hostel for directions.

By train: From train station, take #10, #11, #12, #15 or #17 streetcar to Hausmanns Gate stop; then walk along Storgata to hostel on left. Or from front station entrance, turn right and walk 2 blocks north to Storgata; turn right and continue ½ mile to hostel.

haraldsheim hostel

Haraldsheimveien 4, Grefsen (Oslo) 0409
Phone: 22–222–965 or 22–155–043

Fax: 22–221–025
E-mail: haraldsheim@haraldsheim.oslo.no
Rates: 220–425 NKr (about $37–$71 US) per person; doubles 495–575 NKr (about $83–$96 US)
Credit cards: No
Beds: 270
Private/family rooms: Yes
Kitchen available: Yes
Season: January 2–December 23
Office hours: Twenty-four hours
Affiliation: Hostelling International
Extras: Laundry, Internet access, breakfast, meals ($), parking, luggage storage, lockers, grounds, meeting rooms, TV room

Two to three miles north of Oslo's city center, the city's big "official" hostel lacks a bit of atmosphere and is far out of town. But, that said, the surrounding countryside is great looking, and this is cheaper than a hotel back in town. Just don't plan on doing much in the city.

Best bet for a bite:
Better eat here

What hostellers say:
"Nice view."

Gestalt:
Weird Haraldsheim

Safety:

Hospitality:

Cleanliness:

Party index:

Almost all the beds here come in four-bedded dorms (sixty-three of 'em), but there are eight doubles as well. Some of the newer rooms come with partial shower facilities; others share everything with everyone. There are lots of amenities that families like: a television lounge, a laundry, meals, a kitchen, Internet access, stuff like that.

Warning: Staff have been known to enforce a lockout at times.

The breakfasts here are fast becoming legend, and the good kitchen gets a workout too. A television room and Internet terminals provide distraction.

how to get there:

By bus: From Gardermoen Airport, take bus to Sinsenrysset stop;

cross field and continue uphill ½ mile to hostel. Or contact hostel for transit details.

By car: Contact hostel for directions.

By train: From train station, take #15 or #17 streetcar to Sinsenrysset stop; cross field and continue uphill ½ mile to hostel. Or take local train to Grefsen Station, then follow signs ¾ mile to hostel.

portugal

Portugal's out of the way but worth a visit if you can swing it. It's cheap, sunny, and friendly—generally speaking—if a little more challenging than, say, England.

Hostels in Lisbon are usually not the backpacker's first choice when it comes to accommodation. Why? Because hotels are really cheap compared with the rest of Europe and are more attractive because they don't have the same rules and aren't booked up with teenage school groups. That's not to say that Lisbon and Portuguese hostels are undesirable. They offer many amenities, including meals and, interestingly, almost every hostel in the country is open year-round—a mighty welcome switch from the norm. But think twice before booking a hostel over a hotel, because you won't save much dough.

practical details

Transit in Portugal is a little sketchy, though you can get to Lisbon pretty easily by long-distance or overnight train from Spain. Once you're here, you fan out into the countryside via train or, often, bus or ferry. A train pass isn't really worth buying, as the country is fairly small and tickets are cheap anyway.

Portugal's phone code is 351. To dial Portuguese hostels from the United States, dial 011–351 and DROP THE ZERO from the numbers listed. To dial Portuguese hostels from within Portugal, dial the numbers AS LISTED.

The unit of currency in Portugal is now the euro.

lisbon

Lisbon—often overlooked on quickie itineraries of Europe because of its remoteness—actually turns out to be one of the most interesting cities on the Continent. If you're coming, though, be prepared for a change: You're leaving the ordered world of a Paris or London and plunging headlong into Moorish, Spanish, and African influences. Twisting streets, weird smells, haggling over prices, and petty thieves are gonna be part of the experience. So buckle up and dive in.

If traveling by train, you'll most likely start your visit at either the Rossio or Santa Apollónia train station. From there, Lisbon's transportation system consists of buses, trams, an underground Metro, funicular stairways, and taxi-boats . . . a lot to take in! But it is economical and useful, so study a map. You buy transit tickets at *Carris* kiosks—a pass for one to seven days. These passes cover only buses and trams, however, so you might think about buying a Lisboacard, which gives you unlimited use of the Metro and other transport, plus free or discounted access to about twenty-five monuments and museums around the city.

To explore the best, start at the Baixa district—it's Portuguese for "low"—down by the water, a carefully designed grid erected in the wake of the devastating 1755 earthquake. Look here for incredibly cheap and good eats, usually some form of grilled meat, chicken, or fish. Veggie eats can be found, too. The hillside Alfama neighborhood is the Baixa's opposite, a warren of streets where you're almost certain to get mixed up. But it's mighty interesting as you pick your way among the steeper-than-steep stairways or flea market stalls that give the area so much character.

lisbon hostels
at a glance

	RATING	PRICE	IN A WORD	PAGE
Sintra Hostel	★★★	€8–€10	excellent	p. 344
Lisbon Lazy Crow	★★★	€17	tropical	p. 340
Pousada de Juventude de Catalazete	★★★	€11–€13	distant	p. 342
Pousada de Juventude Parque des Nações	★	€13	central	p. 341
Pousada de Juventude de Lisboa	★	€16	good	p. 343

Up top, finally, is Bairro Alto, with some of the best music in town and—obviously—the best views, too. The club scene is amazing, beyond belief to anyone but a Euro-clubber; come on the weekend and you'll never think your hometown's "scene" is a scene again.

To get around, use the craziest combination of trolleys, stairways, subways, and ferries you can manage; it won't be any crazier than

lisbon

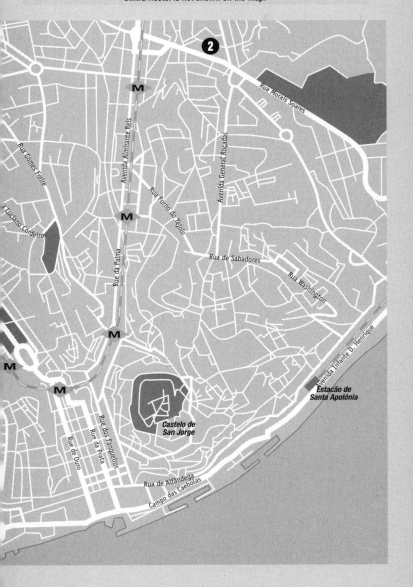

what anyone else is doing, anyway. You'd be nuts to try driving in this city, so make like the locals and do a Chutes and Ladders tour up and down the hills of this beguiling city.

Note that only two of Lisbon's hostels are central to the city; the rest are way out, though some are located in pretty countryside.

lisbon lazy crow

Santa Quitéria 12, Lisbon
Phone: 0213–909–020

Web site: www.lisbonlazycrow.com
Rates: €17 (about $21 US) per person; doubles €44 (about $55 US)
Credit cards: No
Private/family rooms: Yes
Kitchen available: Yes
Season: February to mid-December
Office hours: Vary; call for hours
Affiliation: None
Extras: Free breakfast, Internet access, TV room, patio, movies, musical events, travel information, garden, lockers, laundry

What's a lazy crow??

Anyhoo, the opening of this new place—located in the 'Rato' quarter of town but not too, too far from the Biarro Alto district—has been a great thing for Lisbon visitors so far. The top kitchen facilities, roomy dorms, and cool tropical-like garden all draw raves. There's Internet access and a free breakfast included with your stay, too. And we loved the late 11:30 checkouts, WiFi hookup, and laundry access even more!

Hospitality:
Cleanliness:
Party index:

Rooms come as dorms, doubles, and twins. The TV room gets a workout (nightly movies), and when you're not chilling out in the back patio area, you're exploring local churches, wine bars, and all the rest. Get thee here.

how to get there:

By car: Contact hostel for directions.
By bus: Contact hostel for transit route.
By train: Contact hostel for transit route.

pousada de juventude parque des nações

via de Moscavide, Lote 47101, 1998 Lisbon
Phone: 218–920–890

Fax: 218–920–891
E-mail: lisboaparque@movijovem.pt
Rates: €13 (about $17 US) per person; doubles €32 (about $40 US)
Credit cards: No
Beds: 96
Private/family rooms: Yes
Kitchen available: Yes
Season: Open year-round
Office hours: 8:00 A.M.–midnight
Affiliation: HI-MOVIJOVEM
Extras: Breakfast, meals ($), laundry, cafe, Internet access, bar, terrace

This medium-size hostel serves as a kind of nondescript overflow for the more popular central hostels. It's improving into a more fun, family-friendly place. Unfortunately, it's about 6 miles northeast of central Lisbon. Sure, it's open year-round and does have a kitchen—the main hostel in town *doesn't*—but otherwise it's not quite as good and is much farther from the action. The place consists of ten double bedrooms (two of which are handicapped-accessible) and nineteen quad rooms. If you do come, expect lotsa school groups with a minibus to get them all the way out here.

Since it's near the Plaza of Nations Park, site of the 1998 World Expo, there is a surprising amount of stuff to see, do, and eat around here. We're talking a plethora of cafes and markets where you can pick up picnic supplies or fixin's for dinner. After your little shopping trip, check out Europe's biggest oceanarium—in the park, naturally.

Best bet for a bite:
Park of Nations food court

What hostellers say:
"Obrigado!"

Gestalt:
Expo-sed

Safety:

Hospitality:

Cleanliness:

Party index:

how to get there:

By bus or train: Call hostel for transit directions.
By car: Call hostel for directions.

pousada de juventude de catalazete

Estrada Marginal (Junto ao Inatel), 2780 Oeiras (Lisbon)
Phone: 021–443–0638

Fax: 021–441–9267
E-mail: catalazete@movijovem.pt
Rates: €11–€13 (about $14–$16 US) per person; doubles €26–€70 (about $33–$88 US)
Credit cards: No
Beds: 86
Private/family rooms: Yes
Kitchen available: Yes
Season: Open year-round
Office hours: 8:00 A.M.–midnight
Lockout: 2:00–6:00 P.M.
Curfew: Midnight
Affiliation: HI-MOVIJOVEM
Extras: Meals ($), laundry, cafe, bar, TV

This pleasant midsize hostel sits pretty along its own stretch of sandy beach—a relief for those who have tired of the cacophony of the big city. Better yet, it's just a short ride by local train from the craziness of Lisbon and just beautifully run.

If it's privacy you seek, the hostel sports fourteen double rooms and one private apartment with full kitchen. Otherwise you'll be sacking out with the young'uns in one of nine six-bedded dorms. Fortunately, there's a laundry for guest use as well as a cafe and a bar serving ultrastrong coffee. Should you be sampling Lisbon's nightlife, remember that the strict curfew is at midnight and you'll have to plan on a short night. Still, the ace kitchen and clean and friendly demeanor make it well worth considering.

Best bet for a bite:
Bring your own grub

Insiders' tip:
Bring a towel

What hostellers say:
"Surf's up!"

Gestalt:
Reach the beach

Safety:

Hospitality:

Cleanliness:

Party index:

Most people staying here accept the curfew, and come for the beach. You should do the same: Leave the club scene for another night and another hostel.

how to get there:

By bus: From Lisbon's Cais do Sodré Station, take bus to Oeiras. Or contact hostel for transit route.

By car: Call hostel for directions.

By train: From Lisbon's Cais do Sodré Station, take local train to Oeiras. Walk downhill to town, underneath main road and through park; follow signs ½ mile to hostel. Or contact hostel for transit route.

---

pousada de juventude de lisboa (lisbon hostel)

Rua Andrade Corvo 46, 1050 Lisbon
Phone: 021–353–2696

Fax: 021–353–7541
E-mail: lisboa@movijovem.pt
Rates: €16 (about $20 US) per person; doubles €43 (about $52 US)
Credit cards: No
Beds: 176
Private/family rooms: Yes
Kitchen available: No
Season: Open year-round
Office hours: 8:00 A.M.–midnight
Curfew: Midnight
Affiliation: HI-MOVIJOVEM
Extras: Breakfast, meals ($), television, lockers, tourist information, conference room, disco, bar, currency exchange, laundry

With it's central location, Lisbon's only downtown hostel gets decent marks for position and upkeep. They give you a free breakfast, serve meals for very little (though we'd always eat out in this town), and have some private rooms with double beds. Amazing!

They really pile the amenities on here. Try a disco (yikes), sociable bar, television room, and tourist information desk, for starters. There are fourteen double rooms, nineteen quads, and twelve six-bedded dorms; you won't have to worry about being shoehorned into a superhuge room.

This is kind of a blah location, sure, but think of it this way: It's gonna be fairly quiet. And you're pretty close—especially by Metro subway—to the rest of the stuff you really wanna see, such as the cheap-to-eat low town or the partying high town. Some hostellers head for the nearby Eduardo Park, which is fine for a day of doing nothing much; check out the greenhouses full of exotic plants for a small charge if you like.

Best bet for a bite:
Vegetarian eatery in Saldanha

Insiders' tip:
Funiculars provide great views of city

What hostellers say:
"Duuude."

Gestalt:
Port authority

Safety:

Hospitality:

Cleanliness:

Party index:

how to get there:

By bus: Take #44, #45, or #90 bus to Picoas stop, then walk 50 yards to hostel.
By car: Call hostel for directions.
By train: From any station, walk to Rossio Metro stop and take subway to Picoas stop. Cross Avenida Augusto de Aguiar and then cross Rua Pedreira. Continue 50 yards to hostel.
By subway: Take Metro to Picoas stop, cross Avenida Augusto de Aguiar and then cross Rua Pedreira. Continue 50 yards to hostel.

sintra hostel

Parque Nacional da Pena–Santa Eufémia, 2710 Sintra (Lisbon)
Phone: 021–924–1210

Fax: 021–923–3176
E-mail: sintra@movijovem.pt
Rates: €8–€10 (about $10–$13 US) per person; doubles €18–€23 (about $23–$29 US)
Credit cards: Yes
Beds: 58
Private/family rooms: Yes
Kitchen available: No
Season: Open year-round
Office hours: 8:00 A.M.–midnight
Affiliation: HI-MOVIJOVEM

Extras: Meals ($), TV, VCR, patio, bar, meeting room

Note: **At press time this hostel was closed for renovations. Its reopening date was unknown.**

Sintra is a beautiful, hilly town where Portuguese kings took a breather from the demands of running a country. Here you'll find some of the best sightseeing opportunities in the country—palaces, castles, monasteries, and green parks all await. UNESCO has recognized Sintra as a World Heritage Site.

We'd probably give the hostel a similar designation. It's near the Pena Park, a vast greenspace full of walking trails and trees. What's best is you're paying very little to stay among such beauty: The highest rates are in effect only from July to September, and even then they're still a tremendous bargain.

A couple of cautions, though. Even though there's a bus from the train station, the hostel is still a good half-hour walk from the point at which you will get off. We would recommend a taxi—especially if you roll in after dark. Also, bring some food with you if you don't plan on paying for meals provided on site. There is no self-serve kitchen, though there is a cafeteria serving inexpensive meals.

Best bet for a bite:
Farmers' market
in Sintra-Vila

Insiders' tip:
Take a taxi

What hostellers say:
"I did it my way. . . ."

Gestalt:
Frank Sintra

Safety:

Hospitality:

Cleanliness:

Party index:

Places of interest around here include more castles, palaces, and convents than you can shake a stick at. Or just head over to Cabo da Roca, the cape that represents the westernmost point in Portugal.

how to get there:

By bus or train: From train station, take bus to São Pedro and tell driver where you're going. From bus station, make a right and follow signs 2 miles to hostel, or take taxi.

By car: Call hostel for directions.

spain

Sunny, peppy, and affordable, Spain's your place if you loathe clouds. You can lie on beaches; gawk at some of Europe's most incredible museums, castles, and historic sites; gorge yourself on fish, paella, tapas, and wine for a pittance; and dance 'til dawn—that's what the Spaniards do. We're talking about a culture where dinner happens around midnight. Really.

The hostel system in Spain is extensive, but you'll have to work to find a true bargain. That's because hotel rooms cost almost the same as a double room at a typical hostel; unless you're traveling alone, it might not make sense to find an out-of-the-way hostel.

Note that a "Hostal" in Spain is a small, European-style hotel (what other countries call a "pension"); it is NOT a hostel. Look for the words *joves* or *juvenil* (youth) or *albergue* (hostel).

practical details

It's easy to get to Spain. You can fly direct from the United States, London, Paris, and elsewhere. (See the introduction for more on European budget airlines.) Once you're here, Spain's train system is efficient if slow due to the long distances and varied terrain involved in a city-to-city trip. There are some high-speed trains between Madrid and the southern coast that can quicken the journey, but these AVE trains are quite a bit more expensive than regular trains; even Eurail Pass holders need to pay a supplemental fee.

Spain's country code is 34; there aren't any special city codes. To dial Spanish hostels from the United States, dial 011–34 plus the number AS PRINTED. To dial Spanish hostels from within Spain, dial the number AS PRINTED.

The unit of currency in Spain is now the euro.

barcelona

Located only a couple hours' train ride from the French border, Barcelona is Spain's most international and cosmopolitan city. Why do you think they got the Olympics, anyway? This is the place to see world-class art and architecture, and the food's pretty darned good, too. It's also pretty flat, making walking easy, and the transit system is top-notch—just hop the subway to get around. From Sants Station, catch a Red Line train into town (toward Fondo); from França, you can easily walk to the action.

While here, you'll want to see the Modernist architecture of such stars as Gaudí. If you're not into that, check out the amazing nightlife; this city rocks all night. Las Ramblas is the main drag, connecting most of the downtown parts; the elevated Montjuïc (Jewish Mountain) is the location of the Olympic Stadium and palaces. L'Eixample is probably the most interesting neighborhood.

There is one "official" hostel in the city, but it's a pretty hefty trek from the action.

barcelona hostels
at a glance

	RATING	PRICE	IN A WORD	PAGE
Itaca Hostel	◣	€20	best	p. 353
Albergue Mere de Déu	◣	€13.35–€23.45	faraway	p. 347
Angie's	◣◣	€15–€18	friendly	p. 350
Gothic Point	◣◣	€17–€23	unusual	p. 352
Kabul Hostel	◣◣	€19.50–€31.00	social	p. 354

albergue mere de déu ◣
Passeig de la Mare de Déu del Coll 41–51, 08023 Barcelona
Phone: 93–210–5151

Fax: 93–210–0798
E-mail: alberg-barcelona@tujuca.com
Rates: €13.35–€23.45 (about $17–$30 US) per person
Credit cards: Yes
Beds: 220
Private/family rooms: Yes
Kitchen available: No
Season: Closed December 24–December 26
Office hours: Twenty-four hours

barcelona

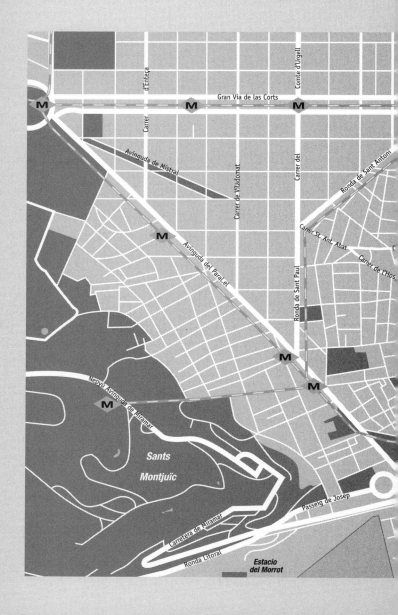

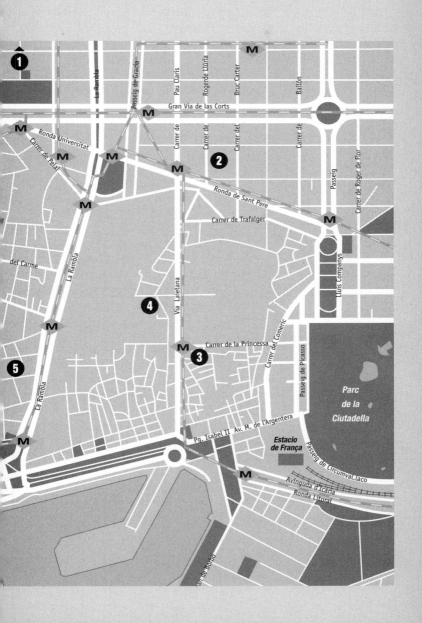

Affiliation: HI
Extras: Breakfast, luggage storage, lockers, playground, laundry, information desk, parking, TV room, Internet access, meals ($)

Staff here must be pretty overworked. The first time we called to reserve a room, we were told that they were full up. (Click.) The next time we called, still full—and less than gracious.

To be fair, though, the place is gorgeous once you get here (and finish dealing with the staff)—nicely designed, with homier-than-you'd-expect touches. Rooms are pretty decent, too: There are five doubles for couples, two quad rooms, twenty-five six-bedded dorms, and six larger dorms. It's all supplemented by tons of amenities, everything from Internet access to a TV room to meals, lockers, a luggage room, and grounds. Needless to say, Spanish school groups love the place.

Best bet for a bite:
Back in the city

What hostellers say:
"Nice place; too distant."

Gestalt:
Far out

Safety: N

Hospitality: N

Cleanliness: N

Party index: 🎉🎉🎉

Drawbacks? It's kind of remote—you're far north of the central city, several miles away, in fact, and though there are certainly some eateries and other distractions, it's really not where you wanna be. Thank goodness for Metro access.

how to get there:

By bus: Take #28 bus from Plaça de Catalunya to hostel.
By car: Contact hostel for directions.
By train: From Sants Station, take Metro Blue Line (#5) toward Horta to Provença Station. Walk through concourse to Diagonal Station, change to Green Line (#3), and continue toward Montbau three stops to Vallcarca Station. Walk through Plaça Mons down Avenida Rep. Argentina; cross over Avenida Hospital Hilitar and bear left to hostel.

angie's hostel N

Roger de Llúria 10 (first floor), Barcelona
Phone: 93–411–2137

Fax: 93–491–1942

E-mail: angies@angies.f2s.com
Web site: www.angies.f2s.com
Rates: €15–€18 (about $18–$23 US) per person; doubles €40–€46 (about $50–$58 US)
Credit cards: No
Beds: 29
Private/family rooms: Yes
Kitchen available: Yes
Season: Open year-round
Office hours: Twenty-four hours
Affiliation: None
Extras: CD player, TV room, free Internet access, bar

Note: At press time, this hostel was closed for renovations. Check ahead before arrival.

Rather expensive for Spain, but on the other hand located right in the thick of some of Barcelona's action, Angie's is an OK bunk for the night—it takes most of its charm (and sometimes lack of it) from the spunky eponymous owner who whirls around cleaning, chastising, collecting rent, advising, and the like. It's a two-story hostel inside a handsome old building.

Dorms here are split into doubles, two-bunked rooms, and a series of tightly packed four-, five-, six-, eight-, ten-, and twelve-bedded dorms as well. Bathrooms are kept clean, though they could use a bit of renovation. There's also a common room with TV lounge and CD player and two kitchens in which to cook. The free Internet access is a great bonus,

What hostellers say:
"Angie's a hoot."

Gestalt:
Ramblas man

Safety:

Hospitality:

Cleanliness:

Party index:

too, and Angie will even do your laundry for about six bucks a load. (She's *quite* a character, by the way.) But the most obvious draw here is the hoppin' "saloon" room with its beer dispenser (bring your Euro coins!), free-flowing talk, and wine.

On the downside, the tiny rooms get mighty hot in summer (no, there's no AC here, baby). Those pricier doubles are truly postage-stamp size, possibly not worth the additional cost. And they're a little too (make that very) laissez faire on the security. At least it's all just a two-minute walk from the big thoroughfare known as the Ramblas and the busy Plaza de Catalunya. All in all, not bad.

how to get there:

By bus: Contact hostel for transit details.
By car: Contact hostel for directions.
By train: From Sants Station, take Metro Green Line (#3) toward Canyelles seven stops to Catalunya Station, then walk 1 block down Fontanella Street to Urquinaona Square; cross square to 7-11 store and continue to hostel. From Passeig de Gracia Station, walk 5 blocks to Plaza de Catalunya, turn left, and continue 2 blocks to 7-11; turn left and continue to hostel at #10.

gothic point hostel

Carrer dels Vigatans 5, 08003 Barcelona
Phone: 93–268–7808

Fax: 93–310–7755
E-mail: info@gothicpoint.com
Web site: www.gothicpoint.com
Rates: €17–€23 (about $21–$29 US) per person
Credit cards: Yes
Beds: 145
Private/family rooms: Yes
Kitchen available: No
Season: Open year-round
Office hours: Twenty-four hours
Affiliation: None
Extras: Free Internet access, breakfast, bar, tours

This newish place with the spaceship theme has its ups and its downs. For starters the bunks are a little strange and quite hard to get into if you're put on a top level—you've got to see what we mean. They're enclosed, which is good, but it's all a bit claustrophobic. However, the biggest drawback is the lack of air circulation here. As a result, the dorm rooms can get very hot in summer (not to mention noisy). We also noted that the hostel didn't always deliver all the amenities promised online . . . a trap to beware of when booking that way.

Gestalt:
Visigothic

Safety:

Hospitality:

Cleanliness:

Party index:

The location is ace, though, and the bathrooms are surprisingly good for such a busy hostel; the lounge is fun; and they do serve up a kind of (not very nutritious) breakfast. Thanks for trying, guys. Fun can be had here, and often is. And the "nodules" get generally good reviews—again, see what we mean. There's also a good attempt to clamp down on security.

It'll do in a pinch, but there are better places in town.

how to get there:

By car: Contact hostel for directions.

By train: From Sants Station, take Metro Blue Line (#2) to Verdaguer Station; change to Yellow Line (#4), continuing to Jaume I Station. From Catalunya Station, take Red Line (#1) to Urquinaona Station, then change to Yellow Line (#4) and continue to Jaume I Station.

itaca hostel
Carrer de Ripoll 21, Barcelona 08002
Phone: 93-301-9751

E-mail: pilimili@itacahostel.com
Web site: www.itacahostel.com
Rates: €20 (about $25 US) per person, doubles €50–55 (about $63–$69 US)
Credit cards: No
Beds: 30
Private/family rooms: Yes
Kitchen available: Yes
Season: Open year-round
Office hours: Twenty-four hours
Lockout: Yes
Curfew: 4:00 A.M.
Affiliation: None
Extras: Lockers, breakfast

This nice-looking place in the city's so-called Gothic neighborhood, small (and a bit hard to find) but very well kept, has great positioning working for it: just a short stroll from the Picasso Museum, the Ramblas, the Cathedral, and tons o' Gaudi. Couldn't pick a better spot to build a hostel if you tried.

Rooms here are broken out into six-, eight-, and twelve-bedded dorms, and they've also got some private rooms with their own en-suite bathrooms. Amazingly, each room has a balcony, and pastel colors predominate rather than a party ethos. It scores high in all categories with us: friendly, hip, kept clean, and reasonable. A few folks quibbled with the 4:00 A.M. curfew since Barca's a late-night town, but, hey. That's a small quibble. All in all, this is an excellent choice.

What hostellers say:
"Amazingly good!"

Safety:

Hospitality:

Cleanliness:

Yes, there is a kitchen here, as well as a breakfast (you have to pay a little for that) and storage lockers with keys; if you're traveling with a family or small group, inquire about the more expensive private apartment.

how to get there:

By bus: From bus station, take Metro line 1 from Arc de Triomf to Urquinaona station. Walk along Via Laietana to Avenida de la Catedral, then follow Carrer del Dr. Joaquím Pou to hostel.

By car: Contact hostel for directions.

By train: From train station, walk along Via Laietana to Avenida de la Catedral, then follow Carrer del Dr. Joaquím Pou to hostel. Or take Metro Line 3 to Plaça Catalunya and walk along Portal del l'Angel to Avenida de la Catedral; follow Avenida de la Catedral to Carrer del Dr. Joaquím Pou, then continue to hostel.

By subway: Take Metro line 1 to Urquinaona station, then walk along Via Laietana to Avenida de la Catedral, then follow Carrer del Dr. Joaquím Pou to hostel.

kabul hostel

Plaça Reial 17, 08002 Barcelona
Phone: 93–318–5190

Fax: 93–301–4034
E-mail: info@kabul.es
Web site: www.kabul.es
Rates: €19.50–€31.00 (about $25–$39 US) per person
Credit cards: No
Beds: 200
Private/family rooms: No
Kitchen available: No
Season: Open year-round
Office hours: Twenty-four hours
Affiliation: None

Extras: Breakfast, bar, restaurant ($), laundry, TV room, Internet access, pool tables

This place is good for one thing, one thing only: drinking. You come for a party, not for clean beds, friendly management, or anything else pleasant. Of course, if you're looking to meet fellow travelers it's great for that . . . provided you want to meet them when they're completely inebriated.

The dorm facilities here—with rooms of four, six, eight, ten, twelve, and twenty beds—are, frankly, kinda beat-up and flimsy. Sure, they've got a laundry, serve meals, run an Internet terminal, and maintain a television lounge; but the main draw at the Kabul is the bar, and that's where everyone eventually gravitates. Management encourages drinking, drinking, drinking. Heck, there's even a *beer vending machine.* There's so much merriment here that things can get out of hand . . .

Best bet for a bite:
Juicy Jones

What hostellers say:
"Anotherrrrr roundd pleeez, bendtender . . ."

Gestalt:
Kabulship

Safety:

Hospitality:

Cleanliness:

Party index:

people crashing all over the floor and such. And, ya know what? When we showed up staff weren't even friendly, either. They bordered

key to icons

Attractive natural setting	Comfortable beds	Visual arts at hostel or nearby
Ecologically aware hostel	A particularly good value	Music at hostel or nearby
Superior kitchen facilities or cafe	Wheelchair-accessible	Great hostel for skiers
Offbeat or eccentric place	Good for business travelers	Bar or pub at hostel or nearby
Superior bathroom facilities	Especially well suited for families	Editors' Choice: Among our very favorite hostels
Romantic private rooms	Good for active travelers	

on nasty, in fact, which is odd considering that hostellers are forking over cash to stay here.

At least the location is decent, on the central Plaça Reial, and we liked the funny murals—but take care at night, as this isn't the city's safest neighborhood.

how to get there:

By bus: Contact hostel for transit route.
By car: Call hostel for directions.
By train: Take Metro Green Line (#3) to Liceo stop.

madrid

Stuck right in the middle of Spain, the nation's capital takes a lot of traveling to get to from just about anywhere. It's a heavy seven-hour slog from Barcelona, for example, and the scenery along the way isn't all that impressive. It's probably best to take an overnight train from somewhere like Paris, though that option certainly isn't cheap if you want to sleep lying down as opposed to sitting upright.

madrid hostels at a glance

	RATING	PRICE	IN A WORD	PAGE
Barbieri Hostel	◪	€14.50–€16.00	colorful	p. 360
Los Amigos	◪	€19–€22	good	p. 361
A.J. Santa Cruz de Marcenado	◪	€8.50–€12.00	fine	p. 357
A.J. Richard Schirmann	◪	€7.80–€10.80	marooned	p. 359
Ole International Hostel	◪◪	€16–€18	okay	p. 362

You'll probably arrive at Chamartín Station, far north of the city center, so you'll need to take the good and cheap Metro subway into town. Once downtown (they call it El Centro), just wander around, checking out all the squares, cathedrals, and museums you'd expect of a capital. Plenty of parks, palaces, and gardens can be found nearby, as well; consult a good map to find them. The Huertas neighborhood is one of the hippest for eating and drinking. The Metro is incredibly cheap (costing €1.00/about $1.20 US per ride, or roughly €6.40/$8.00 US for a book of ten tickets). Study the system first to figure out where you're going, though, as the network can be a little confusing with all those lines.

The city's hostels suffer the same problems experienced by those all over Spain: They're not always centrally located and don't necessarily provide the best possible deals for budget travelers, especially for those over age twenty-six or those traveling alone. They're also prone to being block-booked by school groups during the school year. Staff can seem indifferent at best and downright snippy at worst. Still, they present a good alternative for diehard hostel fans, and each has enough good points to merit a stay—especially for disabled travelers (whose needs aren't necessarily met by other budget options). Just remember that they're quite popular, so you should make bookings at least two weeks in advance. And there's a strict limit of three consecutive nights' stay and six nights' stay in any six-month period as well.

albergue juvenil
santa cruz de marcenado

Santa Cruz de Marcenado 28, 28012 Madrid
Phone: 91–547–4532

Fax: 91–548–1196
E-Mail: alb.juv.marcenado@madrid.org
Rates: €8.50–€12.00 (about $11–$15 US) per person
Credit cards: No
Beds: 44
Private/family rooms: No
Kitchen available: No
Season: Open year-round
Office hours: 8:00 A.M.–10:00 P.M.
Curfew: 1:30 A.M.
Affiliation: HI
Extras: Laundry, TV lounge, breakfast, luggage storage, lockers, information desk

Of Madrid's two "official" hostels, this one is more centrally located—about 2 miles north of the Centro—and thus a better choice for party animals. And it's so cheap. Located in the studenty Argüelles neighborhood, the modern, well-equipped facility is easily accessible by Metro or bus. The decor isn't exactly outstanding, but most hostellers who choose to stay here don't bother sticking around much, since the area offers a lot to do.

Insiders' tip:
Clamores Jazz Club for jazz

What hostellers say:
"Great area!"

Gestalt:
Mambo No. 5

Safety:

Hospitality:

Cleanliness:

Party index:

Inside, they've got two double rooms, six quads, two six-bedded dorms, and four larger dorms. The place isn't exactly teeming with facilities, but it's clinically and decently run. (Staff could be more tolerant of us non-Español speakers, though.) There is a laundry, lounge with a TV, and a luggage room, and the location more than makes up for anything else it lacks. Fall out of bed one way and you're on the doorstep of the Centro Cultural Conde Duque, a converted seventeenth-century barracks that hosts concerts and art expositions. Roll a little farther east and you're in the Plaza Dos de Mayo, filled with wonderful cafes and kids by day, the epicenter of student life by night.

This proximity to the activity—and the fact that Argüelles is linked to the rest of the city by three efficient Metro lines—means this place scores pretty high on the convenience meter. And if you can't find someone in the hostel who wants to do something, you shouldn't have far to go outside before you find something to do by yourself.

So bring on the Mambo Taxi—Madrid awaits.

how to get there:

By bus: Take #2, #21, #44, or #133 bus. Contact hostel for further details.

By car: Contact hostel for directions.

By train: From the Centro, find Sol, Callao, or Lavapiés Station and take #3 Line north (toward Moncloa) to Argüelles Station. Exit station at Camino Alberto Aguilera exit (on south side) and walk east for 1 block; turn right onto Camino Serrano Jove, then make an immediate left onto Camino Santa Cruz de Marcenado.

From Chamartín Station, take Metro Line #10 toward city center (toward Aluche) six stops to Alonso Martínez Station, then change to Line #4 and continue to last station at Argüelles. Exit station at Camino Alberto Aguilera exit (on south side) and walk east for 1 block; turn right onto Camino Serrano Jove, then make an immediate left onto Camino Santa Cruz de Marcenado.

albergue juvenil
richard schirmann
Casa de Campo, s/n, 28011 Madrid
Phone: 91–463–5699 or 91–463–5697

Fax: 91–464–4685
Rates: €7.80–€10.80 (about $10–$14 US) per person
Credit cards: No
Beds: 134
Private/family rooms: Yes
Kitchen available: Yes
Season: Open year-round
Office hours: 9:00 A.M.–10:00 P.M.
Affiliation: HI
Extras: Laundry, kitchen, TV room, bar, library, parking, meals ($)

Close to a park with facilities for children, plus a swimming pool and jogging areas, this hostel *might* fill the bill if you're wanting a little less action in a bucolic (though somewhat dodgy) area.

Located in the gigantic Casa de Campo park, west of the downtown core, this place is certainly attractive. Decorations show a detectable IKEA influence, and the place is fabulously equipped (there's both a bar *and* a library, and how's that for covering all the bases?). It's quiet and bright throughout. Although it's a bit of a ways from downtown, you can be downtown in under half an hour if you time your transit connections right. The Teleférico (sky-ride) near the lake is kind of cheesy, but views of the Guadarrama mountains to the north are well worth the *fromage* factor. At least it's something to write home about.

That being said, it has a number of considerable disadvantages. Number one, it's not at all easy to reach. Number two, personal safety is something worth being paranoid about. The Madrid City Council has been encouraging prostitutes and their johns to vacate the city center, and guess where they've ended up? Here. The problem is tolerable during the day, but at night it's downright creepy: Curb-crawling cars

Best bet for a bite:
Casa Mingo

What hostellers say:
"No, I *don't* want a date . . ."

Gestalt:
Schir thing

Safety:

Hospitality:

Cleanliness:

Party index:

can be a pain in the ass, and solo women may not feel comfortable or safe in the area. You'd be well advised to either take a taxi or ask staff about the best way to get back after dark. Number three, unlike the Santa Cruz hostel, individual hostellers can't book beds in advance. You just have to show up or give a call that day.

Still, in the frying-pan heat of a Madrid summer, it may be the best call you make. Just watch out for those school groups and hookers.

how to get there:

By bus: Take #31, #33, #39, or #45 bus to Casa de Campo, then walk along Paseo de las Castañas, away from the lake.
By car: Contact hostel for directions.
By train: Contact hostel for transit details.

barbieri international hostel
Calle Barbieri 15, 28004 Madrid
Phone: 91–531–0258

Fax: 91–531–0262
Web site: www.barbierihostel.com
Rates: €14.50–€16.00 (about $17–$20 US) per person
Credit cards: Yes
Beds: 38
Private/family rooms: No
Kitchen available: Yes
Season: Open year-round
Office hours: Twenty-four hours
Affiliation: None
Extras: Lockers, breakfast, laundry, TV room, air-conditioning, Internet access, reading room, meals

Yes another newish backpackers-style fun spot in Spain, this one gets nods from hostellers far and near for its hospitality, amenities, and amazingly clean rooms and bathrooms. It's not perfect—staff make mistakes, it gets crowded—but it's very good and fun.

The Barbieri's located in the center of the city, near the famous Puerta del Sol. Inside, the dorms are two- to eight-bedded—a little tight, but quite clean and well-cooled by the all-important air-conditioning that ought to be mandatory in a Spanish summer hostel, if you're unaccustomed to the weather. The lounge bops with TV viewers, Internet cruisers, and wine drinkers (they'll sell you a bottle at the desk), while a separate reading room area is better for bookworms.

What hostellers say:
"A breath of fresh air."

Gestalt:
Madrid about you

Safety: ◧

Hospitality: ◧

Cleanliness: ◧

Party index: 🍕🍕🍕🍕

Great feel, decent management, central location. What else do you want?

how to get there:

By bus: From depot, take Metro Light Blue Line (#1) to Gran Via Station, turn left on Hortaleza Street and make second right onto Infantas Street; take next left onto Calle Barbieri. Hostel is at #15, on second floor.

By car: Contact hostel for directions.

By train: From Chamartín Station, take Metro Blue Line (#10) to Chueca Station; turn right and continue down Calle Barbieri. Hostel is at #15, on second floor.

los amigos hostel ◧

Campomanes 6 (fourth floor), 28013 Madrid
Phone: 91–547–1707

Fax: 91–559–9745
E-mail: info@losamigoshostel.com
Web site: www.losamigoshostel.com
Rates: €19–€20 (about $24–$27 US) per person; doubles €48 (about $60 US)
Credit cards: Yes
Beds: Number varies
Private/family rooms: Yes
Kitchen available: Yes
Season: Open year-round
Office hours: Twenty-four hours

Affiliation: None
Extras: Lockers, Internet access, TV room, VCR, games, mail storage, breakfast, bar

On a calm side street (which is an important late-night consideration in Spain), yet quite close to some old neighborhoods and plazas, Los Amigos is hot. Hostellers are gushing about the friendly staff, clean digs, and goodies like cheap Internet access and a kitchen.

Gestalt:
See Amigos

Safety:

Hospitality:

Cleanliness:

Party index:

The furniture in the six- to eight-bedded dorms has simple lines, and rooms are spacious enough and well-kept; big lockers are available in each one for your stuff. The common lounge—where you'll spend most of your time, probably—rocks with its TV, VCR, and games, and the bar kicks in additional cheery atmo. They also serve a very basic breakfast here. There's even an unusual half-day rate if you just need to crash for a bit. Note that front desk security does give you the once-over—and that's a good thing. Again, the vibe here is just so happy that you can't help but leave with new friends (including some of the staff). The central nabe doesn't hurt a bit, either.

My tip? Book a few days ahead; it's getting a lot of buzz—and deservedly so.

how to get there:

By bus: Contact hostel for transit details.
By car: Contact hostel for directions.
By train: From Atocha Station, take Metro Light Blue Line (#1) to Sol Station; change to Red Line (#2) to Opera Station. From Chamartín Station, take #10 Line to Alonso Martínez Station; change to Green Line (#5) and continue to Opera Station.

ole international hostel
Manuela Malasaña 23, 28004 Madrid
Phone: 91–446–5165

Fax: 91–446–5165
E-mail: reservas@olehostel.com

Web site: www.olehostel.com
Rates: €16–€18 (about $20–$23 US) per person
Credit cards: Yes
Beds: Number varies
Private/family rooms: No
Kitchen available: Yes
Season: Open year-round
Office hours: Twenty-four hours
Affiliation: None
Extras: Breakfast, meals, Internet access, laundry, lockers, bar

Not exactly clean, not exactly sweet-smelling . . . this place is only so-so at best. Sure, they offer an Internet terminal, minuscule lockers, a piddling breakfast, a pricey laundry service, a good kitchen, and the option of meals at night. You get your choice of four- and twelve-bedded coed dorms. But it's just not as well kept or thrilling as some other joints around the city. And those rooms . . . *too small.* And that receptionist. *So rude.* We could go on.

What hostellers say:
"Coulda done better . . ."

Gestalt:
Holy Ole

Safety:

Hospitality:

Cleanliness:

Party index:

The only redeeming virtue here is (once again) the bar area, where hostellers bond together with each other and their vino.

how to get there:

By bus or train: Contact hostel for transit details.
By car: Contact hostel for directions.

seville (sevilla)

The city that gave its name to a type of orange remains one of Spain's prettiest draws. The center is compact enough that you might not need to use the local bus system. While wandering, you'll soon enough find the city's amazing (and amazingly big) cathedral, plus plenty of other wonders—castles, museums, and Barrio Santa Cruz, an attractive warren of tiny streets.

albergue juvenil sevilla

Camino Isaac Peral 2, 41012 Sevilla
Phone: 95–505–6500

Fax: 95–505–6508
E-mail: sevilla.itj@juntadeandalucia.es
Rates: €7–€12 (about $9–$15 US) per person
Credit cards: Yes
Beds: 294
Private/family rooms: Yes
Kitchen available: Yes
Season: Open year-round
Office hours: Twenty-four hours
Affiliation: HI
Extras: Cafe ($), laundry, meeting rooms, Internet access, TV room, store, luggage storage, game room, breakfast, garden

In recent years, the regional governments of many Spanish provinces have started to fund and run the hostel networks in their area. Andalusia is one example of an area where they got it right: InturJoven, the organization that oversees the hostels in this southern province, has recently streamlined its operations. It now has about twenty hostels in towns, cities, and near beaches, and the Seville youth hostel is one of the better places it runs.

Best bet for a bite:
Tapas and paella in the Centro

What hostellers say:
"Very nice."

Gestalt:
Orange you glad you came?

Safety:

Hospitality:

Cleanliness:

Party index:

The hostel is located in the southern part of town, near Reina Mercedes University. When you approach the hostel, you see that there are actually two buildings; one of the university residences is right next door. (Unfortunately, hostel residents don't get to use the basketball or tennis courts that separate the two buildings.) Inside the clean and spacious hostel building, the vast majority of rooms are triples, with en-suite bathrooms that take a little getting used to: A strange combination of doors and shower curtains means that you've got to be veeeeery careful your shower doesn't end up submerging the whole floor. If you've forgotten your towel, you can rent one for about a dollar. There are also plenty of doubles, a good bonus for couples or families. All the beds include linens, and energetic central heating means no freezing your butt off—if it's working properly.

Management has thoughtfully equipped the place with a number of amenities, including a laundry, kitchen, conference rooms, a game room, a TV lounge, and a cafeteria that serves included breakfast and lunch and dinner for a charge (making up for the strange lack of eateries in the surrounding area). Internet access is available at the hostel, too, though it costs six bucks an hour; you're definitely better off checking out some of Seville's excellent Internet cafes, which normally cost less.

A taxi from the center will cost about €4 (about $5 US), or you can walk the distance in about half an hour, enjoying the older, more historic areas of the city—including Plaza de España and Maria Luisa Park. The park, built for the 1929 Ibero-American Exposition (which didn't end up happening) is worth a look just for the insanely ornate architecture and tile work on its buildings. Otherwise, this hostel isn't close enough to the city center that a party vibe ever really catches on. Most nights it's pretty tame, making this a good place for those who need to get up early for travel or sightseeing.

how to get there:

By bus: Take #34 bus from Plaza Nueva or #6 bus from front of the Plaza de Armas bus station.
By car: Contact hostel for directions.
By train: From Seville Station, take C2 or #27 bus to hostel, or walk 1 mile.

sweden

From Malmö to Lappland, Sweden is a big country and takes in a little bit of everything. Mostly it's woods and lakes punctuated by small towns of beautiful, healthy people tooling around in their Volvos. Stockholm, the capital, is the buttoned-down business center where most of the heavy lifting gets done. Over on the other coast, Gøteborg faces off against Denmark with a salty mixture of port activity, university life, and a bustling arts and music scene.

practical details

Sweden's trains are super clean and efficient, but the long travel distances over flat terrain mean you'll spend a lot of time staring out the window at . . . well, Sweden. If you'll be traveling a great deal in Denmark and Norway as well (or even two of the three countries), get a ScanRail pass. Expensive but still one of the all-time great rail pass deals, it gets you free riding on almost all Swedish trains, plus half-price discounts on most ferries.

Things are expensive here. The unit of currency is the Swedish krona (SEK); at this writing there were approximately seven kronor to one U.S. dollar, a good rate—but that still means your 210 SEK dorm room costs a whopping $30.

Sweden's phone code is 46; Stockholm's city code is 08. To dial Stockholm hostels from the United States, dial 011–46, then DROP THE ZERO from the number listed. To dial Stockholm hostels from Sweden, dial the number exactly AS LISTED. To dial Stockholm hostels from within Stockholm, DROP THE 08 and dial the number exactly as printed.

"Vandrarhem" means hostel in Swedish. Hostels here are uniformly clean and cheaper than the exorbitant hotels—Swedish families think nothing of staying at a hostel when on vacation (and kids get deep discounts). But remember to join HI before coming: The official hostels charge a stiff 50 SEK surcharge (about $7 US) per nonmember per night.

stockholm

Among Europe's most beautiful cities—especially when you consider the gorgeous oceanside setting—Stockholm simply must be seen on a Scandinavian tour, though it's quite far from most anywhere else and quite hard on your wallet, too. Another interesting fact about this city: A number of its hostels are located on boats floating in the harbor—a novel way to get to know the city.

Gamla Stan (the Old Town) is the central and logical starting point for a tour. This area is jam-packed with palaces, churches, squares, and statues, not to mention chic restaurants, jazz bars, shops, and the like. The real up-and-coming district, though, is Södermalm, just south of here; this is where the beautiful people bop all night long.

You'll get around best by using the subway, known here as the T-bana; all lines conveniently converge at the station known as T-Centralen, right next to the train station. Subway rides cost around $3 US, so to save dough think about buying an SL Travelcard from the transit authority. It costs about $13 US for one day, but only about $27 US for three days.

Also take the time at some point to hop a ferry to one of the out-lying islands of the Stockholm archipelago—they're very quiet and pretty, and most ferries are discounted or free with ScanRail or Eurail passes.

stockholm hostels
at a glance

	RATING	PRICE	IN A WORD	PAGE
Långholmen	★★★	210–400 SEK	quiet	p. 375
Zinkensdamm	★★★	200–390 SEK	green	p. 380
City Backpackers	★★★	230–520 SEK	homey	p. 372
Red Boat Mälarens	★	210–430 SEK	salty	p. 378
M/S Rygerfjord	★	210–225 SEK	cruisin'	p. 377
af Chapman/ Skeppsholmen	★	165–210 SEK	interesting	p. 370
Backpackers Inn	★	140–195 SEK	bland	p. 371
Gustaf af Klint	★½	160–195 SEK	iffy	p. 374

stockholm

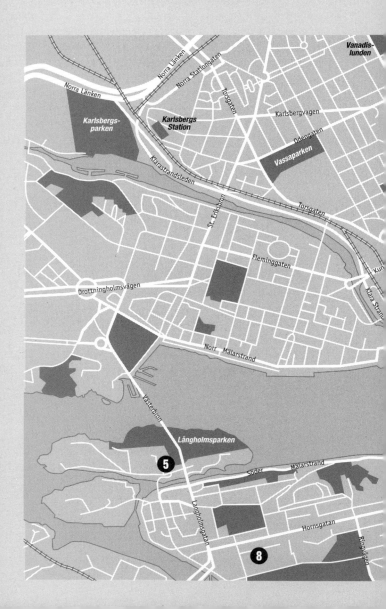

af chapman/skeppsholmen hostels

Västra Brobänken, 111 49 Stockholm
Phone: 08–463–2266

Fax: 08–611–7155
E-mail: chapman@stfturist.se
Rates: 165–210 SEK (about $27–$30 US) per HI member; doubles 490–590 SEK (about $70–$84 US)
Credit cards: Yes
Beds: 285
Private/family rooms: Yes
Kitchen available: Yes
Season: Open January 1–January 7 and January 12–December 31
Office hours: Twenty-four hours
Lockout: 11:00 A.M.–3:00 P.M. (af Chapman only)
Curfew: 2:00 A.M. (af Chapman only)
Affiliation: HI-STF
Extras: TV room, laundry, luggage storage, lockers, meals ($), parking

This double-barreled hostel covers all the bases, from land to sea, and must be seen to be believed. Both are as central to Stockholm's downtown as a hostel could ever be, too, making them a real steal since you won't need public transit once you're here.

Half the hostel actually floats, like several other hostels in the city: It's an eighteenth-century sailboat moored in the water. Rooms are very tight, but the place nevertheless fills up months in advance; you'd better call way ahead if you want a bunk. "Skeppsholmen's Vandrarhem," the sister hostel sitting up on the dock, is a little roomier and nicer, a very good place to meet fellow travelers. It used to be a workshop, however, so it's not exactly plush either.

The crowd here ranges from Euro-teenyboppers to Swedish families and even elderly folk day-tripping around the country. Together, the two hostels consist of twenty double rooms, thirteen triples, twenty-two quads, one five-bedded dormitory,

Best bet for a bite:
Here and now

What hostellers say:
"This is wild . . ."

Gestalt:
Ship ahoy

Safety:

Hospitality:

Cleanliness:

Party index:

eight six-bedded dorms, and eight even larger dorms. The boat rooms are, just as you'd expect, pretty cramped and uninspiring (and the bathrooms are frankly horrible)—but some come with water views. In the bigger, landside wing there's a laundry, kitchen, and meal service; the dry hostel is wheelchair-accessible, too. But if you've gotta pick, why not try both? Sleeping on water is a unique experience, that's for sure.

Views of Stockholm, on all sides of you, are splendid. What's really amazing about this location, though, is the clutch of cool sights in the area. You're closer to the Modern and National museums than anyone sleeping in the city's $500-a-night digs, and you're within walking distance from both the Royal Castle and Parliament. You can catch a ferry to another cool island right from here, walk back into town for upscale shopping and clubbing, or just hang out on the dock or boat when the weather's good. About the only thing lacking is a subway stop, but that's a minor complaint. This is a good place, efficiently run, and so popular that you will want to book *miles* in advance to stay.

how to get there:

By bus or train: From Central Station, take #65 bus to Skeppsholmen Island and walk 100 yards to hostel.

By car: Contact hostel for directions.

---

backpackers inn
Banérgatan 56, 102 72 Stockholm
Phone: 08–660–7515

Fax: 08–665–4039
E-mail: info@backpackersinn.se
Rates: 140–195 SEK (about $20–$28 US) per HI member; doubles 460 SEK (about $66 US)
Credit cards: No
Beds: 300
Private/family rooms: Yes
Kitchen available: No
Season: Open June 23–August 10
Office hours: Twenty-four hours
Affiliation: HI-STF
Extras: Parking, meals ($), laundry

Not to be confused with the independently run City Backpackers (see page 372), this huge hosteller-warehouse—okay, it's actually a school—takes in overflow hostellers from other city HI-affiliated hostels. As you might expect of a school, it's utterly lacking in character,

Best bet for a bite:
Glass och Pastahus

What hostellers say:
"Kinda bland."

Gestalt:
Cash cow

Safety: 🗲

Hospitality: 🗲

Cleanliness: 🗲

Party index: 🎉🎉🎉

sometimes cramped, but at least they serve meals, maintain a few family rooms, and have parking. Dorms contain three to fourteen beds each, and they're nothing spectacular at all. Pretty uninspiring, actually. At least the staff were nice when we were there.

Though the Karlaplan neighborhood isn't the city's most exciting, the huge traffic circle has plenty to offer, and the whole area is surprisingly close to the action—only two short hops via the T-bana from the central train station. There are a number of vegetarian restaurants around here, for some reason, so take that into account if you're trying to stay pork-free in honor of your pet piggy.

how to get there:

By bus: From city bus terminal, take T-bana to Karlaplan stop; exit at signs for Vallhallavägen, walk 1 block north to Vallhallavägen, then turn right and continue approximately 2 short blocks to Banérgatan. Turn left and cross street to hostel.

By car: Contact hotel for directions.

By train: From train station, take T-bana to Karlaplan stop; walk 1 block north to Vallhallavägen, then turn right and continue approximately 2 short blocks to Banérgatan. Turn left and cross street to hostel.

city backpackers hostel 🗲🗲
Upplandsgatan 2a, 111 23 Stockholm
Phone: 08–206–920

Fax: 08–100–464
E-mail: city.backpackers@swipnet.se
Rates: 230–520 SEK (about $33–$75 US) per person; doubles 590–1,120 SEK (about $85–$160 US)
Credit cards: Yes

Beds: 65
Private/family rooms: Yes
Kitchen available: Yes
Season: Open year-round
Office hours: 7:30 A.M.–noon; 2:00–7:00 P.M.
Affiliation: None
Extras: Laundry, sauna ($), Internet access, TV room, games

This hostel—a big apartment with wooden stairs and wooden doors—has a great location within walking distance of the city's central train station, and you can walk to the Old Town, museums, and lots of shops, theaters, and cinemas. It's also quite friendly, despite a number of rules. In short, fun!

Door security consists of a key-code. You walk in between houses in a small backyard; inside, it's all very quiet despite the street traffic. They ask you to take off your shoes, which keeps things clean; then you enter through a sort of reading room decorated with pictures of movie stars and pictures of ABBA and Björn Borg. A big map of the world on the wall reminds you of why you're here: to mix and mingle with others from different places. Staff are thoughtful and have carefully arranged bus timetables and ideas for things to do in the city in the same room. There's a book exchange for free, too, culled from other travelers' leavings.

What hostellers say:
"So central."

Gestalt:
Stockholm sweet Stockholm

Safety:

Hospitality:

Cleanliness:

Party index:

Rooms consist of five doubles, six three-to-four-bedded dorms, and four eight-bedded dorms. It's not the biggest place, not the most hard-rocking, but it's adequate and central. The kitchen downstairs sure is tiny, but to compensate there's a television room with tables beside it where eating is allowed. The bathrooms are also tucked down here, all kept spic-and-span, and you can rent games like Trivial Pursuit for the night. There's also a laundry and—check this out!—a sauna, though both cost extra. Internet access costs about $3 a day, a great deal if it keeps up.

They don't serve breakfast on site and don't have a bar, but there's a good buffet place within a half mile. In fact, since this is the very heart of Stockholm, there are tons of coffee shops and restaurants of all price ranges. And if you're just falling-down-tired after a long flight or train ride, this is perfect—only five minutes' walk from the main station. With all those ABBA posters, you'll be humming "Dancing Queen" or "Fernando" in no time: a sure sleeping pill.

how to get there:

By bus: Contact hostel for transit details.
By car: Contact hostel for directions.
By train: From Central Station, walk ¼ mile to hostel.

gustaf af klint hostel

Stadsgårdskajen 153, 116 30 Stockholm
Phone: 08–640–4077 or 08–640–4078

Fax: 08–640–6416
Web site: www.gustafafklint.se
Rates: 180–195 SEK (about $26–$28 US) per person; doubles 440 SEK (about $63 US)
Credit cards: Yes
Beds: 152 (summer), 130 (winter)
Private/family rooms: Yes
Kitchen available: No
Season: Open year-round
Office hours: Twenty-four hours
Affiliation: None
Extras: Bar, coffee shop, laundry, breakfast ($), TV, restaurant, Internet access

The first thing we noticed, climbing aboard this hostel, was the "boat smell"—a strong odor of oil and boat polish, great if you're planning on joining the merchant marine but not so great if you've got allergies. We felt a little queasy, frankly.

But we soldiered on, heading through an entryway room that has been restyled to look very much like an English pub—an English pub with wooden couches, that is. Music was blaring on the radio, and the receptionist immediately copped a snooty 'tude. Again, we soldiered on.

The boat is very small inside, and dark; even in those rooms with great views of the city through portholes or windows, lighting is a definite problem. But we're getting ahead of ourselves. You climb down into the hostel deck on tiny stairs to find eight double rooms, seventeen four-bedded cabins, and a huge fourteen-bedded dormitory that gets used only during the summer. All of 'em rock a little, even though the boat's tied up, and we didn't find this a problem with other boat hostels in town. (Maybe they should spring for a new rope? Just wondering . . .) Rooms were tiny, and very tall or claustrophobic people should probably sleep elsewhere in the city. In spite of all that, the boat was pretty clean at least—even the bathrooms, located in the narrow hallways. Somehow they've also squeezed in a bar (where you can drink wine) and a laundry in the place.

Best bet for a bite:
Fried-fish stands

What hostellers say:
"Shiver me timbers . . ."

Gestalt:
Overboard

Safety: ◩

Hospitality: ◩◩

Cleanliness: ◩

Party index: 🎉🎉🎉

There are a few pictures on the walls, but otherwise you won't get much to cheer about here. They don't do any tours or activities, and the information about what you can do in Stockholm was, frankly, lame and outdated. Maybe that's because they want you to stay here: During the summer you can sit out on the deck, and they run a combination restaurant/snack bar year-round (the room with the English-pub decor), which also doubles as the TV room. The breakfast is actually pretty nice—lots to eat, with great views while you do.

The *Gustaf af Klint*'s tied up in the middle of the city, surrounded by restaurants, bars, coffee shops, museums, and parks, but the proximity to busy streets and subway lines could mean that nights get noisy.

how to get there:

By bus: Contact hostel for transit details.
By car: Contact hostel for directions.
By train: From Central Station, take T-bana subway to Slussen Station; take lower exit and walk 200 yards east to hostel on water.

långholmen vandrarhem ◩◩
Långholmsmuren 20, Kronhäktet, 11733 Stockholm
Phone: 08–720–8500

Fax: 08–720–8575
E-mail: vandrarhem@langholmen.com
Rates: 210–400 SEK (about $30–$57 US) per HI member; doubles 520 SEK (about $75 US)
Credit cards: Yes

Beds: 254 (summer), 26 (winter)
Private/family rooms: Yes
Kitchen available: Yes
Season: Open year-round
Office hours: Twenty-four hours
Affiliation: HI-STF
Extras: Bar, breakfast ($), TV room, laundry, store, museum, restaurant ($)

Note: Discounts for children.

This hostel, hidden in a leafy park on a small island off the beaten path, was a prison until 1975—but you'd hardly know it (if not for the surveillance cameras scanning the grounds). This is now Stockholm's quietest hostel, and one where you've got a decent shot at actually securing a bed.

The hostel's close to town, but you've got to stroll a ways from the subway station. At least the walk's pleasant, with birds singing and water and greenery all around you. Eventually you come to a stone wall, follow it, and then come to the big blond stone structure. The former guard station is now the reception, where friendly staff check in hostellers and sell T-shirts and postcards (in Swedish, of course).

Best bet for a bite:
Back in Södermalm

What hostellers say:
"Tonight there's gonna be a jailbreak . . ."

Gestalt:
Soft cell

Safety: 🔧

Hospitality: 🔧

Cleanliness: 🔧

Party index: 🎉🎉

You sleep in the old cells, which occupy the bottom floor: There are quad rooms, three-bedded rooms, and a mess of doubles down here, though in winter they scale back drastically from more than 250 beds to just 26! Must be the weather. Anyway, many hostellers share bathrooms in the hallway, but you can pay more for a double room—er, cell—with its own bathroom and telephone. There's a small museum in the big hallway, with exhibits describing the former life of the building; up big stone stairs, you'll find a small but good (and clean) eat-in kitchen. They also serve dinner and breakfast ($7, yikes!) here, both for an extra charge. Other amenities are good as well—a laundry (about $4 US), a bar, and city information.

They claim not to accept group bookings, and that's a huge bonus if you're sick of school kiddies roaming the halls having food fights and such. On the other hand, there's zero party action, and this is one of the most inconvenient hostels to reach . . . if only they rented bikes, it would be among our top picks in this part of Europe. Take note of a few rules, though: There's no smoking in the rooms, and you can stay only a maximum of five nights in a row. You also have to pay a $3 cleaning charge when you check out.

how to get there:

By bus: Contact hostel for transit details.
By car: Contact hostel for directions.
By train: From Central Station, take T-bana subway to Hornstull Station; walk ½ mile north up Vasterbbron and cross bridge onto island. Continue to hostel.

---

m/s rygerfjord hostel
Södermälarstrand Kajplats 12, 118 25 Stockholm
Phone: 08–840–830

Fax: 08–840–730
E-mail: hotell@rygerfjord.se
Rates: 210–225 SEK (about $30–$32 US) per person; doubles 590 SEK (about $63 US)
Credit cards: Yes
Beds: 240
Private/family rooms: Yes
Kitchen available: No
Season: Open year-round
Office hours: 8:00 A.M.–midnight
Affiliation: None
Extras: Restaurant ($), breakfast ($), TV, musical performances

---

Yep, there's one more boat to be covered; you're gonna be seasick by the time you finish touring Stockholm. No, actually this one's very nice—and a little bigger and more party-hardy than the others in town. The first things you see in the entryway, after all, are a cigarette machine and then a gambling machine, just like on a cruise boat. That's the feel: fun. A big map of Stockholm hangs on the wall, and red carpets welcome the bedraggled hosteller.

As with other boats, you descend a stairway to the rooms belowdeck—in this case, though, stairs aren't so small that you'll break your legs in the process. Rooms are small, but they're brightened by small round windows; in all, there are twelve quad rooms, a twelve-bedded dorm, and tons of single and double rooms. Bathrooms are all in the hallways, and there are sinks with hot and cold water—oh, the luxury—in each dorm as well. All in all, the whole place is quite well lit and bright feeling.

The hostel restaurant is big, too, with great views through portholes of Stockholm day or night; they serve meals and breakfast here, and it's one of the few areas where smoking's allowed. (The television lounge is the other.) They also maintain a bar, and during the summer hostellers sit outside on the deck and watch the city. Sometimes live bands get things rocking.

We'd be remiss if we didn't mention the staff. The owner/manager who gave us the tour is the "captain" of the operation, and he hailed everyone with a friendly hello. He really seems to care about his passengers' well-being, and they felt taken care of in kind. Other staff were middling, however, and we have one more complaint: Noise *really* carries here.

how to get there:

By bus: Contact hostel for transit details.
By car: Contact hostel for directions.
By train: From Central Station, take T-bana subway to Mariatorget. Walk to shore, following signs.

red boat mälarens hostel
Södermälarstrand, Kajplats 6, 117 20 Stockholm
Phone: 08–644–4385

E-mail: info@theredboat.com
Rates: 210–430 SEK (about $30–$61 US) per person; doubles 530–630 SEK (about $76–$90 US)
Credit cards: Yes
Beds: 90
Private/family rooms: Yes
Kitchen available: No
Season: Open year-round

Office hours: Twenty-four hours
Affiliation: None
Extras: Bar, restaurant, laundry service, breakfast ($), televisions

---

Double your pleasure: This hostel consists not of one boat in the water, but two! It's locally known as "the red boat," so you should have absolutely no trouble finding it, and it gets our vote for coolest decor in Stockholm. The one next door is "the white boat."

The entrance is small, with a wooden couch you can sit on. Inside, everything is made of wood, and decorations run to the nautical—lamps, ropes, fishing nets, and so forth. Then you climb down very narrow stairs to the rooms. There are ninety beds between the two ships, split up into thirty-two double rooms (some of which can be converted into very expensive singles), seven three- or four-bedded dorms, and a bigger ten-bedded cabin—though nothing is all *that* big when you're talking about boats; narrow (and also stuffy) is again the rule.

What hostellers say:
"Call me Cap'n."

Gestalt:
Shipshape

Safety:

Hospitality:

Cleanliness:

Party index:

Showers and bathrooms are located in the hallways; showers are clean and spacious, though the hallway is narrow indeed. All the doors are red, by the way, just like the ship's exterior.

There's no smoking in the rooms, but you can smoke in the lounge or in part of the restaurant, which has more wooden tables with red-and-white tablecloths on them—like a small (floating) Italian restaurant—and more wall hangings: Bits of rope, paintings, buoys; you get the picture. They run this eatery from spring through fall, it doubles as the TV room, and there are both smoking and nonsmoking sections; each has its own television set.

Staff are extremely helpful and will dispense info or send your laundry out to a nearby service (though it costs about $7 US); they run a bar as well. Breakfast costs about $8 extra.

how to get there:

By bus: Contact hostel for transit details.
By car: Contact hostel for directions.
By train: From Central Station, take T-bana subway to Slussen Station; exit via lower exit and walk 300 yards west to hostel.

zinkensdamm vandrarhem

Zinkens väg 20, 117 41 Stockholm
Phone: 08–616–8120

Fax: 08–616–8120
Web site: www.zinkensdamm.com
Rates: 200–390 SEK (about $29–$56 US) per HI member; doubles 490 SEK (about $70 US)
Credit cards: Yes
Beds: 490
Private/family rooms: Yes
Kitchen available: Yes
Season: Open year-round
Office hours: Twenty-four hours
Affiliation: HI-STF
Extras: Laundry, bike rentals, solarium ($), store, TV room, breakfast ($), sauna ($), grounds

Another great family-friendly hostel in a leafy locale, this one's a little far from Södermalm's nighttime action—but excellent if you're bringing a family and/or a car in tow. It's also spotless, perhaps the cleanest joint in a clean city when we visited.

What hostellers say:
"Quiet as a mouse."

Gestalt:
Green machine

Safety:

Hospitality:

Cleanliness:

Party index:

The big yellow structure has been designed on a small-town theme: The reception area is big and something like a train station, and this is where you check in, purchase postcards and snacks, book tickets, mail letters, and pick up city info. Moving along, each spacious hallway has its own Swedish street name plus street signs directing you around the complex. (It's harder to get lost that way.) Dorm and corridor walls and floors are painted yellow, light blue, and light pink—all kept absolutely clean throughout, with a mirror and small table in each room. Paintings on the walls enliven the atmosphere further.

Room sizes vary, as usual, with most rooms containing four beds each; there's also one section containing larger dorms of eight beds apiece and a wing of doubles. You can choose from rooms with en-suite bathrooms or those with shared bathrooms, paying less for the latter. The kitchen's clean and bright, with light-blue walls and prominent recycling bins. Even the television lounge is friendly and happy, its '50s furniture contrasting with more pastel walls, and they have installed a restaurant with bar as well. The big backyard is a great spot to hang out on sunny days—or rent a bicycle from reception. The sauna and solarium are also quite popular, as is the laundry.

Of all the city's hostels, this might be the best-kept, most family-friendly place. But partying types won't like it at all: It's a bit too quiet and remote.

how to get there:

By bus: Contact hostel for transit details.
By car: Contact hostel for directions.
By train: From Central Station, take T-bana subway to Zinkensdamm Station. Walk down Ringvagen and make a right at STF signs; continue to hostel.

switzerland

Switzerland is, quite simply, an amazing travel experience. Just don't come expecting warm fuzzies; the notoriously efficient Swiss hostel managers are hardworking, focused on cleanliness, and not really inclined to yuk it up or even show lots of emotion.

But the hostels are almost all decent, if similarly devoid of character. The independent hostels of Switzerland are a happy exception—homey, fun, laid-back, and tucked in quiet scenery.

practical details

Swissair is the national airline, but it's pretty expensive; better to fly into Germany, France, or England instead, then take a train.

Once you're here, SBB—Switzerland's rail company—is as efficient as a Swiss watch; its trains and tracks are world renowned for their comfort and scenery. While these rail systems cross an incredible variety of landscapes, even the iron horse can't get everywhere. It's likely that at some point you will need to supplement your train travel with some form of gondola, lift, bus, cog railway, steam train . . . something. It's all part of the fun.

Swiss Railpasses are one of the best deals in the world. They come in bunches of four, eight, fifteen, and thirty days; like other country railpasses, they confer free passage on all state railroads and most private ones, too. They get you free passage on terrifically scenic rides like the Glacier Express, Bernina Express, Panorama Express, and more; you pay only for a seat reservation. As a great bonus, they're also good on the postbus system (see bus section below) and ferryboats that ply Swiss lakes. As if that weren't enough, many mountain railways and gondolas—which are not covered by this otherwise amazing pass—will still give you a 25 percent discount for holding one.

Other options include a Half-Fare Travel Card, which gets you half off all train tickets for a month, a Swiss Flexipass, a Swiss Card, a Rail 'n' Drive Pass, and a Family Card. Contact the tourism offices or travel offices listed in this book for the latest pricing info, or just stand in line at any Swiss train station ticket office; the staff are exceptionally knowledgeable about this stuff.

Austrian railpasses are also available in various changing packages, which a travel agent can better fill you in on.

Always remember to punch your train ticket before you get on the train; there will be a machine in every station that stamps the current date and time on the ticket, showing the conductor that it has been "used up."

Oh, and let's not forget this important side note: Train station toilets—marked with a WC—almost always require you to cough up something like 1.50 Swiss francs (that's about $1.25 US!). As a bonus (we guess), these same joints sell shampoo, shaving kits, and what have you; use one of the nice sinks and you could even spruce up in one of these places before a big meeting or date. Suddenly that buck isn't hurting quite so much. (Some Swiss train stations even offer inexpensive pay showers.)

Finally, the Swiss have an interesting system of getting you to the sticks while delivering mail at the same time: a postbus, which carries you up mountain passes and into tiny hamlets where no train would dare venture. They're cheap, too. Always remember to punch your ticket for local bus rides; there will be a machine either at the bus stop or on the bus. Most are good for one hour. Longer-distance tickets don't need to be punched, just shown to the driver when you get on.

Switzerland's country code is 41. To call Swiss hostels from North America, dial 011–41 and DROP THE ZERO from the numbers printed in this book. To call Swiss hostels from Europe, dial 0041 and DROP THE ZERO. To dial Swiss hostels from within Switzerland, dial the numbers just AS PRINTED. Also remember that it's cheaper to make coin calls at night and that directory assistance is invariably expensive (dial 111).

You'll need money, that's for sure—this is one of the most expensive countries in Europe, and that means everything from your hostel bed to your train ticket to your groceries. Don't even think about eating out on the cheap. Swiss money consists of solid, heavy change—just as you'd expect from such a prosperous and efficient land—plus a selection of paper bills. The change weighs a ton when you're traveling, so get in the habit of paying for purchases with the coins whenever possible; save a few for lockers at train stations, too, which take only coins. At press time there were about 1.25 Swiss francs (CHF) to the U.S. dollar (the rate fluctuates, of course). Here's a quick primer:

- Five-franc coins are enormous barbells; they're worth about $4.00 US.
- Two-franc coins are smaller but also weighty and are worth something like $1.60 US.
- One-franc coins are thinner than the twos and are worth perhaps 80 cents US.
- The half-franc is a tiny oddball, yet worth about 40 cents US.

Swiss francs get split up into 100 centimes (or *rappen,* in German) for the purposes of making change. The twenty-centime pieces are solid but not worth much, just 25 cents each or so. And the skinny five- and ten-centime coins aren't worth your time of day; though they're light, give 'em to street musicians—or else be stuck with an ever-growing pocket of souvenirs.

The paper is easier to carry, obviously, and to keep straight in your head. That's because you'll normally be dealing only with the four kinds of bills noted below; ATMs give only the first two. That long blue 100-franc note is worth about $80 US—enough for a hostel night and a dinner, about what you'd probably spend in a typical day on the road. The slightly shorter 50-franc note is worth half as much, about $40 US. Twenty-franc notes—shorter again, and pinkish—are worth about $16 US, and the yellowish-orange ten-franc notes, really short, are worth about $8 US.

No sweat, right? The real challenge, as we've said, is to keep your balance with all that really heavy change weighing down your pockets.

geneva

Set beside a pretty lake, with a decent climate and views of the Alps on a very clear day, Geneva's got some serious advantages when you're considering a travel itinerary. It's very close to France if you're going to or coming from that way. And this city lets its hair down in a way that no other place in Switzerland quite does; that alone makes it worth a stop.

Superb transportation connections mean that you can be in Paris, Zürich, or Italy within a little more than half a day. Once here, getting around is very easy, thanks to a comprehensive network of buses and, especially, streetcars (also called trams) that wind through the alleys, boulevards, hills, and streets. As a bonus, a Swiss Pass will get you free rides on all of 'em. Clear maps of all routes are posted at each stand, and you're never far from one.

Eating and going out to clubs at night are two of the joys of being here. Some tourists want to catch boats and cruise around the lake; that's fine, particularly on a sunny day, but we found the mélange of cultures that have gathered here—most of them speaking French—so interesting that we never got far away. Clubs and bars are numerous, ranging from Anglo to African to Euro-pop in feel. Restaurants, well, there are so many that we can't begin to describe the options. Just know that most are good; the French insistence on quality eats has shaped the town's culinary habits.

An expensive city to eat and play in, sure, but so's all of Switzerland—and this is probably the best food town in the country. So enjoy yourself.

geneva hostels at a glance

	RATING	PRICE	IN A WORD	PAGE
City Hostel Geneva	⬥⬥	31–63 CHF	central	p. 385
Nouvelle Auberge de Jeunesse	⬥	28 CHF	ethical	p. 388

city hostel geneva ⬥⬥
2 rue Ferrier, CH-1202 Geneva
Phone: 022–901–1500

Fax: 022–901–1560
E-mail: info@cityhostel.ch
Web site: www.cityhostel.ch
Rates: 31–63 CHF (about $25–$50 US) per person; doubles 72–86 CHF (about $57–$69 US)
Credit cards: No
Beds: 98
Private/family rooms: Yes
Kitchen available: Yes
Season: Open year-round
Office hours: 7:45 A.M. to noon; 1:00 to 11:00 P.M.
Affiliation: Swiss Backpackers
Extras: Internet access, parking ($), currency exchange, lockers, TV, book exchange, laundry, shop, transit cards

This newest entry in the Geneva hostelling sweepstakes is already getting great reviews for friendly management, a good location, and affordable pricing.

geneva

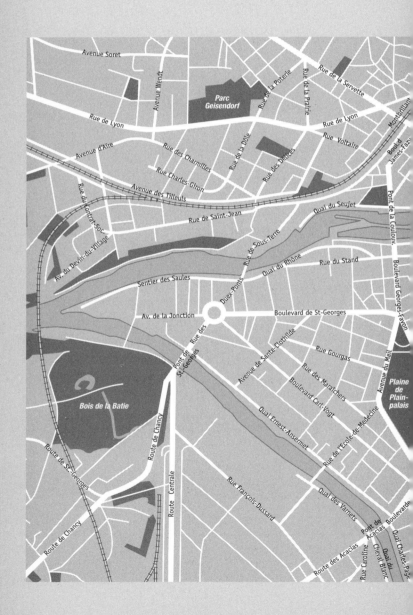

❶

❷

Gare de Cornavin

Rue de Paquis

Rue des Alps

Quai du Mont-Blanc

ntons de Chantepoulet

Lac de Genéve

Quai des Bergues

Pont du Mont-Blanc

St. Gervais

Quai du Générat- Guisan

Rue du Rhone

Quai Gustave-Ador

Rue de Eaux-Vives

Rue de la Corraterie

*Temple
de la
Madeline*

Rue Ferd-Holler

Versonnex Pictet-de-Rochemont

Avenue de Frontenex

Rue du Conseil-Général

Rue de la Croix-Rouge

Rue de la Terrassiere

Villereuse

Av. Th. Weber

Prom. des Bastions

Boulevard Jaques-Dalcroze

Boulevarde Helvetique

Route de Malagnou

Boulevarde de des Philosophes

Boulevarde des Tranchees

Route

u de Carouge

Boulevarde des Philosophes

Avenue de Chaampel

Route de Contamines

Rue de

Florissant

u Pont d'Arve

Rue

Avenue de Chaampel

*Parc
Alfred-
Bertrand*

Avenue Peschler

The place is open twenty-four hours, with no curfew or lockout, yet it doesn't party all night like many independent big-city hostels do.

Best bet for a bite:
Any produce market (ask the staff)

What hostellers say:
"Good new place."

Gestalt:
Swiss please

Safety: ◧

Hospitality: ◧

Cleanliness: ◧

Party index: ▨▨

Dormitories here come in various sizes, but none is too, too big; they range from a cheaper three- or four-bedded room to shared doubles, private doubles (more expensive ones have private bathrooms and television sets in them), and even some single rooms. No matter what you pay, there are always sinks in the rooms and lockers in the halls. They're surprisingly spacious, and cleaner than most any other hostel around.

There's no included breakfast at the hostel, but there is a coin-op laundry—and tons of eating options almost right outside your door in an interesting ethnic neighborhood. Some are described on the hostel's comprehensive bulletin board guide to local eats. We also liked the fact that the place claims to invest a small percentage of its profits in a local nonprofit that brings disadvantaged youth to the city. The non-smoking policy (inside) was even better. Other extras include a currency exchange at the front desk, parking in a private lot, *a free city transit card to get you around town (!),* and Internet terminals for e-mailing the latest on Switzerland back home.

how to get there:

By bus: Contact hostel for transit details.
By car: Contact hostel for directions.
By train: From Cornavin Station, exit and make an immediate left onto big rue de Lausanne. Walk ¼ mile to rue Prieure, turn left, and continue to rue Ferrier on right.

nouvelle auberge de ◧ jeunesse (new geneva hostel)
28–30 rue Rothschild, CH–1202 Geneva
Phone: 022–732–6260

Fax: 022–738–3987
E-mail: geneve@youthhostel.ch

Rates: 28 CHF (about $20 US) per HI member
Credit cards: Yes
Beds: 334
Private/family rooms: Yes
Kitchen available: Yes
Season: Open year-round
Office hours: 7:00–10:00 A.M.; 2:00 P.M.–midnight
Lockout: 10:00 A.M.–4:00 P.M.
Affiliation: HI
Extras: Breakfast, meals ($), TV, laundry, Internet access, pool table, games, free transit card

This hostel's entrance area is typical of French-style hostelling—it's cavernous and dedicated to a variety of activities. One part's been sectioned off to form a "bistro" (read: cafeteria); another, the laundry room; there's a television somewhere in there and, finally, the hosteller kitchen. Though you have to figure out the weird system for using these things—it costs a "token" to cook for forty-five minutes and three tokens to do laundry, which you buy from the front desk—it all actually works quite well once you deduce that you're supposed to put tokens and not money into the machines. Lots of people had trouble with this operation, not surprising since instructions were variously printed in German, French, Italian, or English.

It's a six-stage building, which actually means eight floors in American terms: a ground floor, six floors above that, and a basement. The rooms are upstairs, and the doubles here are real stunners—two single bunks, a bathroom, a closet, and a concrete balcony overlooking the lake and mountains. Whoever designed these was really thinking.

Dorm rooms aren't great and they aren't bad, divided mostly into six-bedded rooms with bathrooms and sinks. The laundry is good, containing multiple washers and dryers, and the kitchen has a long table and enough burners to accommodate four or five folks at once. A free city transportation card is an amazing bonus. Reception staff

Best bet for a bite:
Public Market, rue de Coutance

Insiders' tip:
Free bikes available on waterfront

What hostellers say:
"C'est beau!"

Gestalt:
Geneva pool

Safety:

Hospitality:

Cleanliness:

Party index:

get very busy but somehow usually manage to keep any cynicism in check and get the job done. Overall, the place is uneven—sometimes fun, sometimes boring; sometimes great, sometimes too basic—but it'll certainly do.

The hostel neighborhood is ethnically diverse, meaning that you can nibble kebabs, cruise the Internet, and buy great French bread—all within half a block. You can also walk a block and sun by huge Lake Leman, one of the prettiest we've seen; that's big Mont Blanc looming way off in the distance, while vineyards and France cover the opposite shore. On the way, stroll past the UN's European headquarters, just a stone's throw away in Wilson Palace. (The guy with the Uzi and the earpiece guarding the entrance won't joke around with you. Don't even try.)

For eats you've got a wealth of choices. Back toward the station, in just ten minutes we found a superific Swiss grocery store, a daily produce market, an Italian grocer, and a hole-in-the-wall veggie joint. (Since this is basically France, people were smoking inside while they ate the health food!) Penetrating farther into the old city, we located lots of cafes where people sipped coffee or mineral water and ate pastries, a popular pastime around here.

how to get there:

By bus: Take #1 bus to Wilson Palace, then walk less than 50 yards to hostel.

By car: Call hostel for directions.

By train: From front of Geneva Station, turn left and walk down rue de Lausanne less than ½ mile. Turn right at hostel sign down AMAT street, then left at next sign to hostel, on corner of rue Rothschild.

zürich

Zürich gets a bad rap from some, but our feeling was that young travelers who want to experience a hip city should come here. Along with Geneva—a very different place, by the way—this town's got the most vibrant nightlife in all Switzerland, one part Berlin/Zoo Station/fly shades and one part Teutonic cool.

The two hostels here are total opposites in character: One's strict, hygienic, pastoral, and staid; the other's central, hopping, noisy, young, and fun. Take your pick.

Zürich's public transit is decent, not great—a network of buses and trams fans out from the train station into the commercial, tourist, and residential areas.

One option, if you think you're going to be hopping around the city doing a lot of sightseeing, is the "9 o'clock Travelcard" (in German, *9-Uhr-Tagespass*). It gets you free public transit within city limits on weekdays from 9:00 in the morning until the time when everything stops running (around 1:00 A.M. for most lines) and all day long on weekends. It's not cheap, and you'd have to ride a whole lot to make it worth your while. Still, it's something to think about.

There's obviously lots to do around town, including several theater companies, a variety of cruises on Lake Zürich, and huge and impressive department stores right on Bahnhofstrasse outside the train station. If you like movies, the city has an interesting promotion each Monday: big reductions on tickets. The theaters are packed! So get in line early.

The Swiss National Museum, directly behind the train station (and pretty close to the independent hostel), showcases Swiss history— old stoves, weapons, artifacts, and lots of other stuff that traces the story of this fascinating mountain-rimmed land. The Kunsthaus museum downtown exhibits modern art; the Fraumunster church's Chagall stained-glass work is also worth a look.

Mid-August is a good time to come—the city hosts its biggest party, the annual Lake Parade. Begun in 1991, the parade now throws a half-million crazed Germans, locals, traveling Americans, and other visitors into one heaving stewpot. It's a lot of fun as the normally reserved Swiss let loose for a day.

zürich hostels
at a glance

	RATING	PRICE	IN A WORD	PAGE
City Backpacker Hotel Biber	◪	33–69 CHF	social	p. 392
Zürich Hostel	◪	37.50–109.00 CHF	strict	p. 393

the city backpacker
hotel biber

Niederdorfstrasse 5, CH–8001 Zürich
Phone: 044–251–9015

Fax: 044–251–9024
E-mail: sleep@city-backpacker.ch
Rates: 33–69 CHF (about $26–$55 US) per person; doubles 98 CHF (about $78 US)
Credit cards: Yes
Beds: 65
Private/family rooms: Yes
Kitchen available: Yes
Season: Open year-round
Office hours: 8:00 A.M.–noon; 3:00–10:00 P.M.
Affiliation: Swiss Backpackers
Extras: Laundry, lockers, travel store, Internet access

This is the better bet of Zürich's two hostels, mostly because it's quite central to Zürich's considerable action—but also because it is looser and more laid-back than its HI counterpart, while being kept decently clean and fun at the same time.

Best bet for a bite:
All along Niederdorfstrasse

What hostellers say:
"Couldn't be more central—this rocks!"

Gestalt:
Zürich man, poor man

Safety:
Hospitality:
Cleanliness:
Party index:

Its location is smack in the Niederdorf, the city's really fun old town—think dance clubs, cafes, souvenir shops, and poseurs, all crammed into every available square inch of the winding lanes, avenues, and very old town houses that make up the area.

Don't be discouraged when you arrive and are faced with a steep climb up winding stairs to reception. There's no elevator, but the hostel is worth it. Don't duck into the restaurant kitchen on the first couple of floors; the cooks might come at you with cutlery. (Just kidding.)

There are four or five doubles here, plus fifty other beds, most of those in six-bedded rooms; there are also some quads. Rooms are nice and airy, with lockers and a little furniture—well done, we say. And clean! Each floor comes with relatively clean bathrooms, and—this is the real reason for coming here—its own little kitchen featuring fridges, rangetops, a nice little table, plus a window onto Zürich. Breaking up the kitchen space this way, by floor, avoids the dinnertime crush that often plagues bigger hostels.

As we said, there are few rules here: No lockout, no curfew; you come and go as desired. They've got a laundry downstairs and have added an Internet station for e-mail–happy hostellers. The little front desk shop sells Swiss army knives and other souvenirs at reasonable (not rip-off) prices. One more bonus: The manager is one of the cofounders of Switzerland's independent association, Swiss Backpackers, so he can brief you (well, in addition to this book) on other backpacker-style digs around the country.

This place is incredibly convenient to Zürich's main train station—it's a five- to ten-minute walk away—and that means you can day-trip just about anywhere in Switzerland: Geneva, the Alps, even Italy are only a three- to four-hour ride. But more likely, you'll be hanging out in the place that calls itself "little big city" and does indeed pack a lot of nightlife and fun into the old core.

You can stay right in this neighborhood and get the best of the bars, discos, and other nightlife. Or walk around the area, checking out the city's numerous clock towers.

how to get there:

By bus: Call hostel for transit route.
By car: Call hostel for directions.
By train: From Zürich Station, walk out front entrance and turn immediately left. Walk to river and cross little bridge, then turn right on Limmatquai. Go ½ block, turn left up alley, then turn right onto Niederdorfstrasse. Hostel is on right, above Spaghetti Factory restaurant. Climb stairs up and up to reception.

---

zürich hostel

Mutschellenstrasse 114, CH–8038 Zürich
Phone: 043–399–7800

Fax: 043–399–7801
E-mail: zuerich@youthhostel.ch
Rates: 37.50–109.00 CHF (about $30–$87 US) per HI member
Credit cards: Yes
Beds: 281
Private/family rooms: Yes

Kitchen available: Sometimes
Season: Open year-round
Office hours: Twenty-four hours
Affiliation: HI
Extras: Breakfast ($), meals ($), information desk, laundry, meeting rooms, TV, lockers, garden, table tennis, bike storage, pool table, jukebox, fireplace, snack bar, Internet access

This hostel—in an institutional set of bunkerlike, five-story buildings that could probably withstand a bomb blast—delivers the goods in some ways. It's not convenient to town at all; it's not fun or spic-and-span, but it has enough services for families or backpackers who have cars to survive the night. And it was recently reconfigured to increase privacy. Good thing, 'cuz it's soooo expensive.

Yeah, you heard right. You've got to get wayyyy out of town to get to this place. The entrance area features the usual hanging-out lounge, in this case a huge one with a TV that even has an English-language channel. That room's adjacent to the dining area, where they serve the daily, included, breakfast buffet starting at the ungodly hour of 6:00 A.M. They did serve a good breakfast, we'll give 'em that.

Snacks are served throughout the day, and dinner can be purchased at night in the hostel restaurant; the kitchen claims to be renowned for its Asian buffet, but we wouldn't traipse all the way out here just to eat. Our feeling is that the hostel food and drink are overpriced, especially since you're so far from town that you'll be forced to eat their dinners.

Best bet for a bite:
Not around here

What hostellers say:
"Overpriced and disappointing."

Gestalt:
Far and away

Safety:

Hospitality:

Cleanliness:

Party index:

Inside, all dorms contain no more than six beds, which is a nice switch from the usual sardine job. In addition to the five six-bedded rooms with sinks, there are sixteen doubles with their own bathrooms and thirty-one quad rooms (only ten have en-suite bathroom facilities) that are good for families, couples, or buddies traveling together. Each dorm comes with lockers and one desk. Though staff are as Swissly efficient and impersonal as ever, we were surprised to find the place not all that clean.

Showers, toilets, and hair dryers are available on each floor and sometimes in rooms, too. Other amenities include a courtyard, giant chess board outside, bike shed, and lots more services—almost like a rustic hotel, really, except with much less charm or attention.

You can tell they're really geared to groups at this place when you stumble across the huge, 200-seat auditorium; the rec room—yeah, that's a big-screen TV in there, along with foosball, a pool table, and a jukebox—or one of the two seminar rooms. Don't even think about cleaning your bike in there or taking a nap or eating a picnic. They won't like it.

The hostel's far from town but close to Lake Zürich, which is one possible trip. But you didn't come here to see that, did you? Yes? Well, then this hostel is perfect for you. The only other interesting option around here is the Rote Fabrik cultural centre, a showplace for avant-garde art, music, dance, and the like. It's practically next door, lending some much-needed culture to this too-remote place.

how to get there:

By bus: From Zürich Station, take #7 streetcar to Morgental stop and walk ¼ mile north to hostel. Or take #66 bus to hostel.

By car: Call hostel for directions.

By subway: Take #8 S-Bahn (suburban train) to Wollishofen stop, then walk 3 blocks to Mutschellenstrasse; turn right and continue 2 more blocks to hostel, following signs.

By train: From Zürich Station, take #7 streetcar to Morgental stop and walk ¼ mile north to hostel. Or take #8 S-Bahn (suburban train) to Wollishofen stop, then walk 3 blocks to Mutschellenstrasse; turn right and continue 2 more blocks to hostel, following signs.

united kingdom
(england, scotland, & wales)

Once a great empire, now a fairly small group of islands, the United Kingdom (U.K.) still casts a huge cultural shadow.

England is the land of pubs, banks, rolling countryside, and (of course) London—which believes itself to be capital of the world, if there can be such a thing. Wales is the most mysterious, wildest part of the U.K.; people speak Welsh, the identity is distinct, and the combination of farms, quarries, mountains, and fewer people make this a great place to hike by yourself. Welsh hostels also seem to be among the friendliest in the U.K. Scotland can be summarized pretty quickly: bagpipes and beer. Stir in bags of rain, iffy food, and a measured dose of friendliness, and you've pretty much captured the essential Scottish experience. The hostels here are spare and less friendly, but they're beautifully located—some in old stone houses.

practical details

Getting There and Getting Around

There are oodles of flights from the United States (and everywhere else) to London. In a sea of competitors, shop around vigorously, but we've found that the following are especially worth checking out:

British Airways (www.britishairways.com) runs the most flights to the States, and outside the summer season these are often the cheapest as BA scrambles to fill nearly empty planes. In high summer, though, prices escalate.

Virgin Atlantic (www.virgin-atlantic.com) is often just as cheap, with lots better service and food. Their Web site has a good online booking engine, and it has a fun personality (for an airline). Its European short-hop carrier is called Virgin Express (www.virgin-express.com).

British Midland (www.flybmi.com) flies to the UK from Newark, Chicago, and Phoenix, among other airports, adding to its good and cheap inter-Europe service.

From Europe, **Ryanair's** (www.ryanair.com) fares out of Ireland and London are almost always unbeatably low, though heavy airport taxes can add to the price you're quoted online.

EasyJet (www.easyjet.com) flies to Luton airport north of London from Europe at competitively low prices.

British trains—overseen by British Rail (www.britrail.com)—are a traditional way to travel in the U.K., though quality varies a lot and the trains don't go everywhere. Remember that the U.K. is NOT covered by Eurail passes; you'll need to either buy expensive point-to-point tickets or else invest in a BritRail pass before you get there. (Occasionally you can find one at a train station, but don't risk it.) This pass isn't cheap, but it does include free passage on the Heathrow Express, a handy commuter train that zips from Heathrow airport to a Tube stop in downtown London three times hourly. Other passes in the U.K. include combination passes URL Ireland; London-only passes; Scottish passes; and more.

Finally, train schedules can be accessed anywhere in the U.K. by calling the national info number (08457–484–950). It's a toll call, however. From the Untied States, contact the rail company by simply dialing 1–866–BRITRAIL.

Buses are by far a cheaper ride than trains, and they're a fine way to go—in fact, they're probably going to be your main mode of transport in the U.K., so get used to riding and waiting. The main problem: figuring out what seem like hundreds of local bus lines and their changing schedules. The good news is that there's usually a bus going wherever you're going in England, as long as you don't travel on Sunday or certain Mondays, when some lines run less frequently. It might take you all day to make connections, but most bus drivers in the U.K. are helpful, so you'll get there eventually.

Between-city buses run constantly, too, and even in the sticks you'll be amazed when a double-decker pulls up in the middle of nowhere to whisk you away to East Twee or somewhere. Look for "coach" in the phone directories.

National Express (08705–808–080; www.nationalexpress.co .uk) is England's huge, Greyhound-like company; it runs tons of scheduled daily lines along major routes and some weird ones too. If you're seriously wanting to get from Aberdeen to, say, Stratford-upon-Avon, give 'em a call to see if they go there. They well might. Buses are less expensive than the train, but not a lot cheaper with the Express. In return you get a few perks like on-time buses, helpful drivers, toilets, and, sometimes, an attendant walking down the aisle with snacks for sale.

Local buses fill the rest of the gaps, and these can range from incredibly efficient lines to laughable ones. There are literally hundreds of small bus companies in England, sometimes a half-dozen in one town or city, so there's no central way to contact them. Just ask at the hostel or bus station when you arrive, or study the posted schedules at the bus stop where you're dropped off.

In Scotland, **Scottish Citylink** (08705–505050, www.citylink.co .uk) brings you from big city to big city efficiently; it now also covers the Isle of Skye as well. To get to really remote places in Scotland, the postbus system is one more potential ally. These buses or station wagons, which really do carry the mail, will carry you, too, for a slight charge. However, they sometimes run as infrequently as once a day or week, so be sure you know the return schedule before you commit. (They don't run at night.) Usually it's no trouble.

The most popular kind of backpacker travel these days, however, is none of the above; it's the **"JOJO"** (jump on, jump off) minibus service that circles the British Isles like sharks, scooping up backpackers in faraway train stations and depositing them safely in remote, beautiful places. It's also known as "HOHO," which is hop on and hop off.

MacBackpackers (0131–558–9900; www.macbackpackers.com), a company started by an independent hostel chain, offers six-leg tours for about £75 ($150 US). You've gotta stay in their hostels, like 'em or not. But their drivers are pretty knowledgeable.

You probably won't be using ferries much, unless you're visiting Scotland—in which case you almost certainly will, to see the islands. **Caledonian MacBrayne** (08705–650–000; www.calmac .co.uk) runs most of the ferries in Scotland; **P&O** (www.poferries.com; 08705–980–333 in the U.K.) runs most of the rest. Other ferries in England, Wales, and Scotland are locally run; consult the local tourism office for information on getting to places like the Orkneys and such.

Money

You'll need money, as everything in the U.K. is expensive. One English pound equals, at this writing, about $2 US. (Check the current exchange rates before your departure for the U.K.) To get a rough idea of what something in English pounds would cost you in the United States, take the English price and add almost double of it to itself. Ouch! Yeah, you just paid forty bucks for that £20 pub meal purchased in that oh-so-cute little seaside village.

Look over the change, because bigger isn't always better. A copper pence is just like an American penny. Two-pence coins are also copper but bigger. Ten-pence coins are like dimes, except larger. Twenty-pence coins look funny, like small stop signs; fifty-pence coins look like bigger stop signs. A pound is a very small but thick coin that's worth a lot—don't tip people with them unless you mean to tip $2 US each time you toss one down. Two-pound coins are kind of rare; they're two-colored, a gold outside and a silver inside. Bills (or "notes") are more obvious, but look sharp: The number of pounds is printed lightly in the upper-left-hand corner. A five-pound bill is worth about $10 US, a ten-pound bill is worth about $20 US, and so on. In Scotland you'll sometimes get unusual one-pound bills. Exchange them for coins or larger bills before you get to France because they might be suspicious of these. Yes, really.

In Northern Ireland you'll get a slightly different kind of cash: still British pounds sterling (known simply as pounds), but a little different because they're printed by banks in Northern Ireland. They're worth exactly the same as pounds in England and a little more than Irish pounds. If you're going to England afterward, note that you can't spend Northern Ireland–printed pounds there, so change them all before you leave, if possible. (You can use British or even Scottish pound notes in Northern Ireland with no trouble at all, however.)

Phones

All phone and fax numbers listed in the book are written as dialed from within the U.K. itself. To call hostels in the U.K. from North America, dial 011–44 and then DROP THE ZERO from the numbers printed here. To call U.K. hostels from elsewhere in Europe, dial the long-distance code (usually 00), then 44, then drop the zero. To call them from within the U.K., as we've said, dial them just AS PRINTED. To call the hostels from within their home cities, you usually DROP THE CITY CODE (the first part; 0131 for Edinburgh, for example).

BT (British Telecom) pay phones almost always accept phone cards, which can be bought at any post office in £5 to £10 increments. Hostel pay phones require you to dial the number first and insert a coin when the phone is answered. Be sure to use something small like a 10-pence coin in case you get a wrong number. The phone won't give you change. You will be unable to use a phone card from home at one of these phones; they block the toll-free codes required to access your phone card, forcing you to make an expensive call with the assistance of a telephone operator.

However, some phone booths *don't* block the toll-free access codes. You'll find that many pubs and independent hostels have installed touch-tone pay phones that allow you to use your phone card, as well.

cardiff

Cardiff, largest city in Wales, is the exception to the rule that Wales is a quiet and somewhat traditional place. This city possesses a thriving (though hardly huge) metropolis with youthful energy, helpful tourist officials, decent food, and one heckuva castle. Try to get away from London, even for a day-trip—which is possible, given the fast direct trains from England—to see it.

cardiff hostels at a glance

	RATING	PRICE	IN A WORD	PAGE
Cardiff Backpacker		£16.50	funky	p. 400
Cardiff Ty Croeso		£13.95–£17.50	okay	p. 401

cardiff backpacker
98 Neville Street, Riverside, Cardiff CF1 8LS
Phone: 029–2034–5577

Fax: 029–2023–0404
E-mail: info@cardiffbackpacker.com
Rates: £16.50 (about $33 US) per person; doubles £42.50 (about $85 US)
Credit cards: Yes
Beds: 84
Private/family rooms: Yes
Kitchen available: Yes
Season: Open year-round
Office hours: Call hostel for hours
Affiliation: None
Extras: Pub, TV, fax, breakfast, travel agency, terrace, pool table, free pickups, Internet access, bike rentals

Note: Children not allowed.
 By far the more central of Cardiff's two hostels, this one's placed

smack downtown—well, close enough, anyhow. It's housed in a hip purple building very close to the little Taff River that divides the city, and it's attached to a bar where most of the hostellers do their socializing. It didn't disappoint. Good thing—it costs a mint, just like lots of things in the U.K.

Tremendous work seems to have gone into the facilities here, which include a fax, double and single rooms, newspaper subscriptions, a rooftop terrace, game room, and more. Recently added: a budget travel agency.

You're not far from Cardiff's splendiferous castle, tons of pubs, and a big riverside park. A big thumbs-up from us for the nonsmoking policy, too. Only concern? This neighborhood isn't the safest. Be careful.

Best bet for a bite:
Celtic Cauldron

Insiders' tip:
Castle is worth it

What hostellers say:
"Works for me, dude."

Gestalt:
Cardifferent

Safety:

Hospitality:

Cleanliness:

Party index:

how to get there:

By bus: From Cardiff bus station walk out to Wood Street and turn left. Cross river (street becomes Tudor) and turn right at Clare Street. Continue to corner of Neville Street; hostel is on left.

By car: Call hostel for directions.

By train: From Cardiff Central Station walk out to Wood Street and turn left. Cross river (street becomes Tudor) and turn right at Clare Street. Continue to corner of Neville Street; hostel is on left.

cardiff ty croeso (welcome house) hostel
2 Wedal Road, Roath Park, Cardiff CF2 5PG
Phone: 0292–046–2303 or 0870–770–5750

Fax: 0292–046–4571
E-mail: cardiff@yha.org.uk
Rates: £13.95–£17.50 (about $24–$31 US) per HI member
Credit cards: Yes
Beds: 66
Private/family rooms: Yes
Kitchen available: Yes
Season: Open year-round

Office hours: 7:00 A.M.–11:00 P.M.
Lockout: 10:00 A.M.–3:00 P.M.
Curfew: 11:00 P.M.
Affiliation: HI-YHA
Extras: TV, laundry, bicycle shop, dinner ($), bar

It's a couple miles outside the central city, yet Cardiff's hostel is still plagued by extremely busy surroundings. Bring some earplugs if you want some rest. Otherwise, it's a decent enough place, serving up good meals—and a beer on the side, if you like—to go with its plain dorm rooms, which consist of six quad rooms, an eight-bedded dorm, and two monster dorms averaging seventeen beds each. There are two lounges and a telly to occupy the little ones, plus a laundry to occupy the big ones. That early curfew, though, is a killer.

Best bet for a bite:
Bella Pasta

What hostellers say:
"More fun than I expected."

Gestalt:
Score Cardiff

Safety:
Hospitality:
Cleanliness:
Party index:

While in town most visitors suck down a couple beers before quickly heading out for this beautiful country's rural parks. Cardiff's more interesting than you think, though. For one thing, there's a giant castle perched right at the head of downtown. Eyeball that baby while you're drinking a pint. (Pubs are scattered about.) Second, cheap and surprisingly diverse food options are everywhere. There's a bay. And you can get a bus or train from here to just about anywhere else in Wales, it seems.

Need directions? The local tourist office (located in the Cardiff Central train station) is great. We know. They once sent a free taxi to fetch our wayward credit card as we were waiting for a train to leave. Honest.

how to get there:

By bus: From downtown take #78, #80, or #82 bus to hostel.
By car: From M4 take A48M to roundabout; exit first left off roundabout, follow Whitchurch Road to Fairoak Road, and make a left. Continue to smaller roundabout; hostel is at corner of Wedal Road and Fairoak.
By train: From Cardiff Central Station walk 2½ miles, or take #78, #80, or #82 bus to hostel.

edinburgh

You can't believe just how striking Edinburgh is until you've actually gotten here. Hop off the train and walk up the grueling Waverley Steps . . . hmm. A busy street, no big deal.

But then you turn around and see the castle up on its rock, symbol of Scotland, explore the Royal Mile's pubs and shops, check out how the other half lives in tony but nice New Town, and go for a long walk in the free and beautiful Botanic Gardens. If only the weather would cooperate more often.

Hostels here are generally decent, and most are concentrated close to downtown; all can be reached by a bus ride of up to half an hour. City buses, in fact, are generally excellent, though they do shut down late at night and run less frequently on Sunday. The bus and train stations are very convenient and close together.

edinburgh hostels
at a glance

	RATING	PRICE	IN A WORD	PAGE
Edinburgh Central		£15–£25	modern	p. 410
Edinburgh Metro		£18.50–£23.50	nice	p. 411
High Street Hostel/ Royal Mile Backpackers		£13–£15	social	p. 412
Castle Rock Hostel		£12.50–£14.00	good	p. 408
Brodie's Backpackers Hostel		£11–£22	fun	p. 407
Princes Street Backpackers		£11–£15	social	p. 413
Belford Hostel		£12.50–£18.00	funkorama	p. 406
Edinburgh Backpackers		£14.00–£18.50	big	p. 409

edinburgh

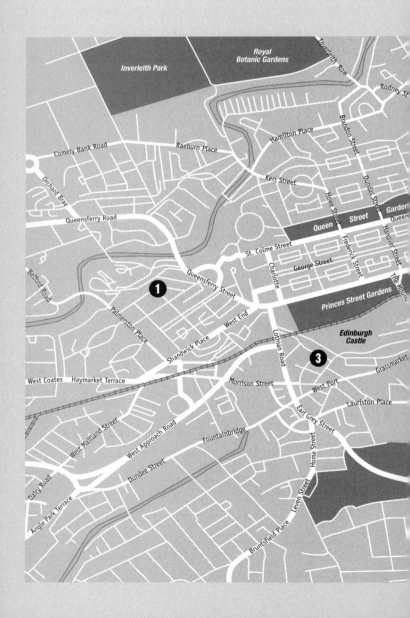

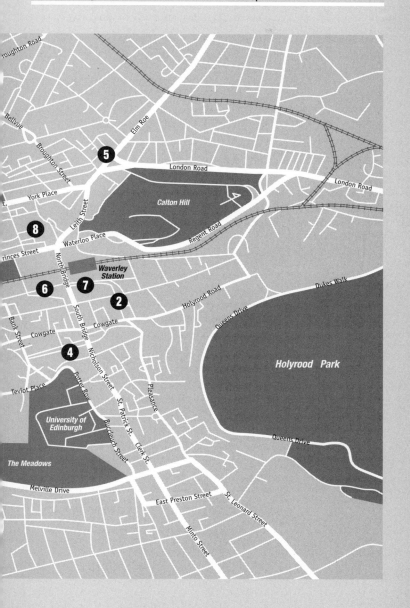

Note that there are two train stations here; for downtown hostels, get off at Waverley. For suburban joints, hop off a stop earlier at Haymarket.

belford hostel

6–8 Douglas Gardens, Edinburgh EH4 3DA
Phone: 0131–220–2200

E-mail: info@hoppo.com
Web site: www.hoppo.com
Rates: £12.50–£18.00 (about $25.00–$36.00 US) per person; doubles £42.50–£65.00 (about $85–$130 US)
Credit Cards: Yes
Beds: 100
Private/family rooms: Yes
Kitchen available: Yes
Season: Open year-round
Office hours: 7:00 A.M.–3:00 A.M.
Affiliation: IBHS
Extras: Laundry, pool table, bar, barbecue, Internet access, TV room, bike rentals

We've heard pretty mixed reports about this funky place housed in a former church: some good, some not so good.

Gestalt:
Holy smokes

Hospitality:

Cleanliness:

Party index:

Yeah, it's a church. The windows still contain stained glass, and it's a bit of a creepy feeling if you're a heathen and you awaken to the sight of it. (Religious hostellers will probably faint with happiness, believing they've gone to heaven.)

Things are pretty noisy and lively here, and the pool table and bar keep it that way much of the time. There are five family rooms for those who seek a bit of extra quiet, and the location's good and central.

how to get there:
Call hostel for directions.

brodie's backpackers hostel

12 High Street, Edinburgh
Phone: 0131–556–2223

Fax: 0131–556–6697
Web site: www.brodieshostels.co.uk
Rates: £11–£22 (about $22–$44 US) per person; doubles £44–£62 (about $88–$124 US)
Credit Cards: Yes
Beds: 50
Private/family rooms: No
Kitchen available: Yes
Season: Open year-round
Office hours: 7:00 A.M.–midnight
Affiliation: None
Extras: Laundry, stereo

Incredibly central, pretty happenin' and good, this hostel is well managed as far as we can tell, supplying spacious bunks in mixed and coed dorm rooms. Bathrooms are a bit in short supply, and not always clean, but otherwise this is a fun place to hang your hat for a night or two.

Dorms are large, with three fourteen-bedded rooms and a single eight-bedded room. (Three of them are coed.) The big size is offset by cleanliness (usually) and wide spacing from neighbors. Also, they use hotel bunks here, a big plus. They do laundry for a small fee and will play your tapes on the hostel stereo if they like 'em.

It seemed much more fun than some of the other hostels (we're talking SYHA here) in town: People

Best bet for a bite:
Tempting Tatties

Insiders' tip:
Hit the Tass (pub)

Gestalt:
Jekyll & Hide

Hospitality:

Cleanliness:

Party index:

like playing music, hanging out in the small common room around the ying-yang table, and ducking out for a pint of ale or a stuffed baked potato around the corner.

But a warning: Some guests may be the dreaded "long-termers," folk who think the hostel is their home and pay by the month. Shame on management for allowing that. Otherwise, no complaints.

how to get there:

By bus: From bus station walk to Princes Street and turn left onto it after crossing to the other side; turn right at North Bridge, cross the bridge, then turn immediately left onto High Street (Royal Mile). Continue a few blocks to hostel on right.
By car: Call hostel for directions.
By train: From Waverley Station, exit onto Princes Street; turn right, then right again to North Bridge and cross the bridge to High Street (Royal Mile). Turn left and continue a few blocks to hostel on right.

---

castle rock hostel
15 Johnston Terrace, Edinburgh EH1 2PW
Phone: 0131–225–9666

Rates: £12.50–£14.00 (about $25–$28 US) per person
Credit Cards: Yes
Beds: 220
Private/family rooms: No
Kitchen available: No
Season: Open year-round
Office hours: Twenty-four hours
Affiliation: None
Extras: Internet access, breakfast ($), laundry, bar, pool table, movies, TV

A big hostel opened by the folks in the Scotland's Top Hostels chain, this place is really good and getting better—and dig the location! You're literally right beneath the famous castle that symbolizes all things Scottish, so start right here. Take a snapshot and send it home to your buds.

Best bet for a bite:
Helios Fountain

Gestalt:
No-hassle castle

Hospitality:

Cleanliness:

Party index:

Just down a long set of stairs from the hostel, you're deep in the heart of student heaven. The University of Edinburgh and an art school make their homes around here, and the Grassmarket area is home to many a cool restaurant or other diversion. So, although this hostel is not on the main drag (i.e., Royal Tourist Trap), that means it's actually mostly immune to the hordes of wide-eyed American tourists dying to get their pictures taken next to the guy wheezing away on his bagpipes up on the Mile.

Nice view of that castle, plus Internet access and a fun crowd. Not bad. Just don't expect quiet or smoke-free environs.

how to get there:

By bus: From bus station, turn left and walk down to Princes Street; cross street, turn right, and walk to Waverley Bridge; turn left and cross bridge. Climb up to Royal Mile (High Street), then turn right and walk uphill to Johnson Terrace on left. Bear left and walk downhill to hostel on left.

By car: Call hostel for directions.

By train: From Haymarket Station walk up ramp to Waverley Bridge and turn left; cross bridge, climb up to Royal Mile (High Street). Turn right on High Street and walk uphill to Johnson Terrace on left; bear left and walk downhill to hostel on left.

---

edinburgh backpackers hostel
65 Cockburn Street, Edinburgh EH1 1BU
Phone: 0131–220–2200

Fax: 0131–477–4636
Web site: www.hoppo.com
Rates: £14.00–£18.50 (about $28–$37 US) per person; doubles £45–£65 (about $90–$130 US)
Credit Cards: Yes
Beds: 110
Private/family rooms: Yes
Kitchen available: Yes
Season: Open year-round
Office hours: Twenty-four hours
Affiliation: IBHS
Extras: Meals ($), Internet access, pub crawls, TV, storage

This big hostel's located on too-hip-for-its-own-good Cockburn Street, which winds downhill from the famous Royal Mile. From the main train station, it's much easier to access from a ramp that ends at the Waverley Bridge than by the tortuous Waverley Steps.

Again, location is everything here if you're looking to get pierced or tattooed. The drill's the same as at the other indie hostels—a more lax attitude toward cleanliness and an emphasis on having a good time. It's very noisy here, and bunks are kinda flimsy, but it's hardly a terrible place.

Gestalt: Hipper than thou

Hospitality:

Cleanliness:

Party index:

For all of you who thrive on the famous SYHA sterility, you'll not appreciate the vibes here. The building is standardly Victorian in architecture but wedged near the aforementioned tattoo parlor as well as an S&M shop, a hemp shop, and a half dozen pubs in which to wet your whistle.

how to get there:

By bus: Exit terminal and turn left. Walk downhill to Princes Street; cross over and walk toward Waverley Bridge. Turn left and cross bridge, then cross Market Street and walk uphill. Hostel is near top of the hill on left.

By car: Call hostel for directions.

By train: From Waverley Station follow signs uphill to Waverley Bridge. Follow ramp to bridge; turn left and walk to the end of the bridge. Cross Royal Mile at Market Street and walk uphill. Hostel is near top of street on left.

edinburgh central hostel
9 Haddington Place, Edinburgh EH7 4AL
Phone: 0131–524–2090

E-mail: edinburgh.central@syha.org.uk
Web site: www.edinburghcentral.org
Rates: £15–£25 (about $30-$50 US) per HI member; doubles £74 (about $148 US)
Credit cards: Yes
Beds: 302
Private/family rooms: Yes
Kitchen available: Yes
Season: January 7–October 31
Office hours: Twenty-four hours
Affiliation: SYHA
Extras: TV room, DVD, Internet access, cafe ($), lockers ($), laundry, conference room

Incredibly modern and nice despite the uninspiring, warehouse/slash/French train station-like exterior, this new "official" Edinburgh entry is a winner and it's open almost year-round. Rooms are entered with a key card (welcome to the modern age—finally—hostels). Rooms range from single and double up to airy eight-bedded dorms, all with lockers and their own bathrooms. It's pretty close to both Waverley Station (Edinburgh's central hub) and famous Princes Street.

What hostellers say:
"Good deal."

Gestalt:
Central park

Safety:

Hospitality:

Cleanliness:

Party index:

Like all SYHA hostels, this one has a hostel kitchen for your own cooking pleasure—but it also has got a little cafe. Both continental and Scottish-style (heartier) breakfasts can be purchased, as well as lunches and dinners.

Large plasma-TV screens are scattered about the lobbies, and yeah, they've got Wi-Fi throughout (natch). Pay Internet terminals are also set up near the lobby, and a handy laundry is also a boon.

how to get there:

By bus: Contact hostel for transit route.
By car: Contact hostel for directions.
By train: Contact hostel for transit route.

edinburgh metro hostel
**Robertson's Close, Cowgate,
Edinburgh EH1 1LY
Phone: 0870–004–1115**

Rates: £18.50–£23.50 (about $37–$47 US) per HI member
Beds: 285
Credit Cards: Yes
Private/family rooms: Yes
Kitchen available: Yes
Season: July 13–August 27
Office hours: Open twenty-four hours
Affiliation: HI-SYHA
Extras: Laundry

Gestalt:
Hipper than thou

Hospitality:

Cleanliness:

Party index:

Believe it or not, this overflow annex to the HI hostels consists entirely of private rooms! That's great if you're traveling with a family. Not too hot if you want atmosphere or lotsa friends, 'cause you won't find them. At least you're in atmospheric digs, and the price is wayyy less than you'd pay at a B&B or hotel in town. But 285 single bunks?? Hmm. Seems more like a capsule hotel.

Oh yeah, one more thing. It's open only for six weeks in summer.

how to get there:

Call hostel for directions.

high street hostel/royal mile backpackers

8 Blackfriars Street or 105 High Street, Edinburgh EH1 1SG
Phone: 0135–557–3984

Fax: 0131–556–2981
Rates: £13–£15 (about $26–$30 US) per person; doubles (High Street only) £40–£50 (about $80–$100 US)
Credit cards: Yes
Beds: 175
Private/family rooms: None
Kitchen available: Yes
Season: Open year-round
Office hours: Twenty-four hours
Affiliation: IBHS
Extras: Breakfast ($), laundry, TV, pool table, VCR

Gestalt: High times

Safety:

Hospitality:

Cleanliness:

Party index:

This related pair of hostels is superbly placed—right on the Royal Mile, for gosh sakes.

Inside most dorms contain six beds each. People seem to have a really good time here, which is a good sign, and you're within a mile of more than a hundred pubs, we'd guess. It's also nice to be able to shuttle back and forth between the two places and check out their different vibes—though "fun" is the operative word at both. Just be aware that cleanliness and order slide a lot. If you can handle a little chaos, though, go for it!

how to get there:

By bus: From bus station walk to Princes Street; cross street and turn right down South Bridge. Cross bridge and continue to High Street (Royal Mile). Turn left and walk down High Street. Hostel is on left, above cafe.

By car: Call hostel for directions.

By train: From Waverley Station walk to Princes Street; turn right, then right again on South Bridge and cross bridge to High Street (Royal Mile). Turn left and walk down High Street. Hostel is on left, above cafe.

princes street backpackers

5 West Register Street, Edinburgh EH2 2AA
Phone: 0131–556–6894

Fax: 0131–557–3236
Rates: £11–£15 (about $22–$30 US) per person; doubles £30 (about $60 US)
Credit cards: Yes
Beds: 120
Private/family rooms: No
Kitchen available: Yes
Season: May 1–September 30
Office hours: Twenty-four hours
Affiliation: None
Extras: Laundry, TV, VCR, Internet access, meals ($), pool table, game room, shop

This hostel's tucked in a decidedly unhip part of town. Still, it's not far from the pub action on Rose Street. In fact, there's a pub just beneath it.

Dorms run from four to twelve beds, and rates include sheets. Facilities aren't terrific—even bordering on the grubby—but it's fun, at least. Staff are so amazingly helpful, and there are two kitchens.

Gestalt:
Beer blast

Hospitality:

Cleanliness:

Party index:

Check out the interesting room-numbering (actually lettering) system, too. It is almost impossible to *not* have a good time here . . . unless you're a clean freak.

how to get there:

By bus: From bus station, walk down to Princes Street and make a right, then another immediate right onto West Register Street. Hostel is on right, above pub.

By car: Call hostel for directions.

By train: From Waverley Station, walk across Princes Street to West Register and turn onto it. Hostel is on right, above pub.

glasgow

Definitely Scotland's second city, Glasgow is experiencing an arts boom of late: Filmmakers, musicians, and the like are pouring in, and this place now knows an energy that it hadn't felt in decades. Make that centuries. Once denizens of an industrial town, today Glaswegians live in one of the most exciting, changing scenes that Scotland has to offer.

glasgow hostel

8 Park Terrace, Glasgow G3 6BY
Phone: 0870–004–1119 or 0141–332–3004

Rates: £10–£16 (about $20–$32 US) per HI member
Credit cards: Yes
Beds: 149
Private/family rooms: Yes
Kitchen available: Yes
Season: Open year-round
Office hours: Twenty-four hours
Affiliation: HI-SYHA
Extras: Store, laundry, meals ($), TV room

A nice facility close to a green park, Glasgow's official Hostelling International joint is improving. This historic building was recently renovated and features meals, a laundry, and even a kitchen now. It's still showing a lot of wear and tear, though. The television lounge is a hit. Dorms consist mostly of four- and six-bedded rooms, with a few smaller and a few bigger.

This university-area neighborhood's attractive and safe, a far cry from Glasgow's more industrial areas, and this working-class city is also enjoying a renaissance as a of hotbed the arts.

Gestalt:
Great Scot

Hospitality: ◣

Cleanliness: ◣

Party index: 🎉🎉

how to get there:

By bus: Bus station is 1 mile from hostel; walk to Cathedral Street, take #11 bus to Woodlands Road, and walk to hostel. Local buses are also available; call hostel for transit details.

By car: Call hostel for directions.

By train: From Queen Street Station, walk to Cathedral Street and take #11 bus to Woodlands Road; walk to hostel. From Central Station, take #44 or #59 bus to Woodlands Road and walk to hostel.

london

London's one happenin' place these days. A melting pot since forever, it seems, the city has only improved in recent years. The incredible selection of ethnic food options, the all-night dance scene, the history staring you in the face everywhere you go—it's almost enough to make you forget the dreary weather and air pollution so bad that it still leaves you coughing up black stuff.

The hostels here are strange—some come and go each summer (mostly run by skanky hotels trying to make a fast buck off desperate budget travelers), but the legitimate ones are pretty good. Especially considering the way student types storm London by force so reliably each summer that hostels could charge fifty bucks for a sleeping bag on the floor and probably get away with it. Instead, most of them pass the minimum test for cleanliness, friendliness, and fun. They're also mostly well located, almost all close to some cool neighborhood or a train station. The exceptions are some of Hostelling International's seven London joints (they run more here than they do in any other city in the world); some of them are quite a long way from the center of London, though they can be nice as green suburban getaways. YHA's hostels are as humdrum here as they are elsewhere, but the Oxford Street and Earl's Court joints are two very welcome exceptions to the usual rule.

Subway rides on the Tube are expensive; get a pass. For maximum transit value, order a London Visitor Travelcard ahead of time. This

london

handy-dandy pass—good for a number of consecutive days—gets you unlimited travel on the Tube, the city bus system, most regional British Rail trains, and the Docklands Light Railway (as if you needed that).

Just remember that you've gotta buy the pass *before* you get to England. Call BritRail at (866) BRITRAIL for more information.

If you forget, buy regular Travelcards in London at any Tube station as soon as you get to town. A one-day pass costs about $14 US for four zones, quite a bit less if you're staying downtown and don't need to get out to the burbs. Weekend passes are even cheaper, about $10 US for four zones, less for a central pass. A weekly pass is cheaper still; all quickly pay for themselves if you make at least three hops per day, which you're guaranteed to do unless you're a total couch potato.

london hostels
at a glance

	RATING	PRICE	IN A WORD	PAGE
St. Pancras	◤◤◤	£21–£25	great	p. 432
International Student House	◤◤◤	£15–£33	popular	p. 426
City of London St. Paul's Hostel	◤◤◤	£21–£25	downtown	p. 419
Thameside Hostel	◤	£19.50–£24.00	remote	p. 433
Earl's Court Hostel	◤	£20.50–£24.50	okay	p. 422
Oxford Street Hostel	◤	£19.50–£23.00	central	p. 427
Holland Park Hostel	◤	£19.50–£22.50	quiet	p. 424
Generator Hostel	◤◣	£10–£35	hip	p. 423
St. Christopher's Village	◤◣	£12.00–£17.50	hoppin'	p. 430
Curzon House Hotel	◣	£15–£35	unkempt	p. 421
Piccadilly Backpackers	◣	£12.00–£50.50	iffy	p. 429

YHA London hostels include linen in the price of your stay. You are required to have an HI membership card, best purchased through your home organization. You can book London hostels through their central reservations line at 0870–770–8868 (from inside the UK) or (+44) 1629–592–700 from outside the country (Monday to Saturday 9:00 A.M.–5:00 P.M.) by calling the hostel direct or by e-mailing the hostel.

Though England is generally quite safe, certain parts of London—such as the King's Cross/St. Pancras area, the docks, and Brixton—need to be treated with caution. Really, so does anywhere that's deserted at night. So be careful, especially if you're traveling alone or venturing out after dark.

All phone numbers in London have been changed to reflect the new area code system—020 precedes the new phone number, taking the place of 0171 or 0181. The new phone number now starts with either 7 or 8 (7 meaning downtown and 8 referring to the burbs), followed by the rest of the number. (Some hostels have toll-free numbers, which in England start with 0870. These numbers can't be dialed from the U.S.)

city of london st. paul's hostel
36–38 Carter Lane, London EC4V 5AD
Phone: 0207–236–4965 or 0870–770–5764

Fax: 0207–236–7681
E-mail: stpauls@yha.org.uk
Rates: £21–£25 (about $42–$50 US) per HI member; private rooms £53.50 (about $107 US)
Credit cards: Yes
Beds: 190
Single rooms: Yes
Private/family rooms: Yes
Kitchen available: No
Season: Open year-round
Office hours: 7:00 A.M.–11:00 P.M.
Affiliation: HI-YHA
Extras: TV, laundry, breakfast, meals ($), bureau de change, shop, video games, Internet access, luggage storage

Once a choir school for beautiful St. Paul's Cathedral, this place would seem to have the best location of any hostel in London Town—it's right smack in the financial district, and the high prices (for a hostel)

reflect the high-rent district. During the daytime this area hops with bankers, museum-goers, and bridge-gawkers, plus people looking up at tremendously inspiring St. Paul's Cathedral. (That's where Charles and Di got married, in case you've been living under a rock for the past hundred years.)

However, keep in mind that this part of town becomes a ghost town at night because nobody actually lives here; everyone heads home or to Bloomsbury or the West End, so you'll be hard pressed to find excitement after hours.

Not surprisingly, the place tends to draw families and elderly travelers, who pile into dorm rooms that range from four to fifteen beds. Quad rooms are slightly more expensive; "economy dorms," with fifteen beds, are cheaper. There's the usual kitchen and TV lounge—heck, some rooms even have TVs! No breakfast is included with your night's sleep, but upper-floor rooms are blessed with great views of downtown London. There's a decent restaurant here, plus video games and a friendly, fairly hip front desk staff.

Best bet for a bite:
The Rising Sun (Thai)

Insiders' tip:
St. Paul's dome climb (375 steps)

What hostellers say:
"London bridge is falling down . . . ."

Gestalt:
Saint in the city

Safety:

Hospitality:

Cleanliness:

Party index:

key to icons

Attractive natural setting

Ecologically aware hostel

Superior kitchen facilities or cafe

Offbeat or eccentric place

Superior bathroom facilities

Romantic private rooms

Comfortable beds

A particularly good value

Wheelchair-accessible

Good for business travelers

Especially well suited for families

Good for active travelers

Visual arts at hostel or nearby

Music at hostel or nearby

Great hostel for skiers

Bar or pub at hostel or nearby

Editors' Choice: Among our very favorite hostels

All in all, this hostel grades out as decent and quiet, if boring. Hey, at least you're almost on top of that cathedral and a few pubs.

how to get there:

By Tube: Take Central Line to St. Paul's or Circle and District Lines to Blackfriars stop. From Blackfriars, walk 2 blocks north on New Bridge, then make a right onto Carter Lane; from St. Paul's, walk down Godliman Street, then right onto Carter Lane.

curzon house hotel
58 Courtfield Gardens, London SW5 0NF
Phone: 0207–581–2116

Fax: 0207–835–1319
E-mail: info@curzonhousehotel.co.uk
Web site: www.curzonhousehotel.co.uk
Rates: £15–£35 (about $30–$70 US) per person; doubles £44–£48 (about $88–$96 US)
Credit cards: Yes
Beds: 88
Private/family rooms: Yes
Kitchen available: Yes
Season: Open year-round
Office hours: Vary; call for hours
Affiliation: None
Extras: Breakfast, TV

Good views and decent atmospherics characterize this place, which is pretty popular with your rucksacking set—those types who blow into London with a smile and not much else, fresh from a junket to Tasmania.

Rooms have windows and just four to six beds—that's beds, not bunks—each. Some have views of a local church; some look out onto the quiet square known as Courtfield Gardens. Continental breakfast is also included here, plus access to a small kitchen.

Gestalt:
Courtfield of dreams

Safety:

Hospitality:

Cleanliness:

Party index:

However, the upkeep has seriously slid downhill in recent visits—expect dirt and creeping critters. Too bad, 'cause the staff are really cool. But we can't put this on our "to stay" list any more.

how to get there:

By Tube: Take Tube to Gloucester Road stop. From station, turn right onto Courtfield Road, then right again on Courtfield Gardens.

---

earl's court hostel

38 Bolton Gardens, London SW5 0AQ
Phone: 0207–373–7083

Fax: 0207–835–2034
E-mail: earlscourt@yha.org.uk
Rates: £20.50–£24.50 (about $41–$49 US) per HI member; doubles £50 (about $100 US)
Credit cards: Yes
Beds: 186
Private/family rooms: Yes
Kitchen available: Yes
Season: Open year-round
Office hours: Twenty-four hours
Affiliation: HI-YHA
Extras: Breakfast, laundry, bureau de change, TV, garden, bike storage, video games, kitchen, Internet access

---

Best bet for a bite:
Shish kebab stands

What hostellers say:
"Cool, man."

Gestalt:
Duke of Earl's

Safety:

Hospitality:

Cleanliness:

Party index:

Handy and well placed, this handsome Earl's Court joint looks like a good deal to us, if plain—and predictably stuffed to the gills in high summer season. It's a town house located in a quiet and pretty neighborhood, safe and very near all sorts of other good things—nightlife, sights, and so forth.

Dorms come with four to six beds per bunkroom, with a few in the seven-to-ten-bed range. Things get tight as a tick sometimes, as this is a pretty popular location. They've even resorted to using triple bunk beds—three bunks on one frame!

Needless to say, this can be a major pain if you're on the bottom and one or two inebriated bunkmates show up late-night. The crowding takes a slight toll on the cleanliness and general condition of the bathrooms and kitchen.

Still, we liked the exceptionally nice kitchen and courtyard garden, not to mention the access to airport buses and great Kensington museums. (Lots of new twin rooms add an escape valve for couples.)

how to get there:

By Tube: Take Tube to Earl's Court stop; exit right onto Earl's Court and make a left onto Bolton Gardens.

generator hostel
37 Tavistock Place, London WC1H 9SE
Phone: 0207–388–7666

Rates: £10–£35 (about $20–$70 US) per person; doubles £40–£60 (about $80–$120 US)
Credit cards: Yes
Beds: 844
Private/family rooms: Yes
Kitchen available: No
Season: Open year-round
Office hours: Twenty-four hours
Affiliation: None
Extras: Restaurant ($), bar, Internet access

This party place is definitely one of the weirder joints in England. It's a huge, monstrous brick building on a side street just off Russell Square—which, itself, is practically on top of the world-famous (and free!) British Museum—in a quiet neighborhood of Camden. The hostel logo is a guy with a cyberhelmet on. Or is that a cyberface? Who knows?

Anyway, this enormous hostel packs in more than 800 beds. Yes, 800. Some are occupied by long-termers—you know, people living here while they look for a job—and others are taken up by huge tour groups. More and more regular hostellers are beginning to show up, too. It's a basic place, to be sure, but for drunken debauchery and not much else. It is what it is, a place to get hip with Generation X'ers from all over Europe.

Definitely not the place to choose if you don't like dyed hair, rave clothing, tattoos, piercings, trust-fund hippies, guys with ties . . . hey, who let them in here?

On the other hand, if you don't feel comfortable with all that other stuff, we've got just one question: Why the heck are you in London in the first place?

The bar and cafeteria here seem to focus the socializing, and rooms are decently maintained. There's a serious herd feeling and loads o' dirt, but if you can stand that, it's an okay bunk.

Best bet for a bite:
Safeway

Insiders' tip:
Nice park nearby

What hostellers say:
"Moooo."

Gestalt:
Big Generator

Safety:

Hospitality:

Cleanliness:

Party index:

how to get there:

By Tube: Take Tube to Russell Square stop, then walk down Bernard Street to Marchmont; turn left and continue to Tavistock Place. Turn left at Compton Place shortly afterward; hostel is at end of short street.

---

holland park hostel
Holland Walk, Kensington, London W8 7QU
Phone: 0207–937–0748

Fax: 0207–376–0667
E-mail: hollandpark@yha.org.uk
Rates: £19.50–£22.00 (about $39.00–$44.00 US) per HI member
Credit cards: Yes
Beds: 200
Private/family rooms: No
Kitchen available: Yes
Season: Open year-round
Office hours: 7:00 A.M.–11:30 P.M.
Affiliation: HI-YHA
Extras: Laundry, lockers, breakfast, TV, bureau de change, dinner ($), kitchen, games, bike rentals

Note: **You must be a member of HI to stay here.**

The biggest advantage to this Hostelling International joint is its very quiet location: It's stuck smack in the middle of gorgeous Holland Park and not too far from Kensington's artsy offerings and upscale shopping. We liked that, but some hostellers didn't like having to hike to the fun stuff—and noticed that some guests tend to stay here a looooong time. Ah, well. It's still just fine, and there's no lockout either.

Half the place is a roomy Jacobean mansion (as YHA will remind you again and again), though take note: When you get there, you could well get put in the newer concrete annex across the outdoor walkway instead—and that's more like a barracks than a palace, definitely a little less glamorous than what you might have been expecting. Dorms vary wildly in size, from four to twenty beds per room (be forewarned that most contain at least a dozen bunks), and they can be a tight squeeze; that's one drawback here. A handful of private rooms are possible but almost never available, as group leaders get first dibs on 'em.

Best bet for a bite:
Marks & Spencer

What hostellers say:
"Zzzzzz."

Insiders' tip:
Beware of pigeons; keep windows closed always!

Gestalt:
Goin' Dutch

Safety: 🔪🔪

Hospitality: 🔪

Cleanliness: 🔪

Party index: 🎉

The kitchen here is good, dinners aren't bad at all, and they give you a sizable breakfast, too. Front desk staff are super at orienting you; they will also sell guidebooks (though not this one for some reason!), useful Travelcards for the Tube, and other stuff. A separate laundry building is also a bonus.

While we didn't have any problems, the friendly staff recommend that you be careful walking through the park if you're arriving by night. There are two ways to come by Tube. At night, get off at the High Street Kensington stop. In daytime, use the Holland Park stop instead, though you'll need to look sharp for the sign marking the entrance to the park on your right.

A good security system requires everyone to be buzzed in by a security guard after 4:30 in the afternoon—a bit annoying, but a good idea nevertheless. Why so early? It's already dark by then in winter, that's why.

how to get there:

By Tube: At night, take Tube to High Street Kensington. Exit station, cross street, and turn left. Walk several blocks to Holland Park entrance on right. Turn right onto Holland Walk, pass field, enter park on left, then take a right to hostel. In daytime, you can take the Tube to Holland Park. Exit station, cross street, and turn left. Walk down street away from convenience store; turn right into park entrance, and walk down pathway to hostel entrance on right.

international student house
229 Great Portland Street, London W1 5HD
Phone: 0207–631–8310

Fax: 0207–636–5565
E-mail: accom@ish.org.uk
Web site: ish.org.uk
Rates: £15–£33 (about $30–$66 US) per person; private rooms £50–£72 (about $100–$144 US)
Credit cards: Yes
Beds: 550
Private/family rooms: Yes
Kitchen available: Yes
Season: Open year-round
Office hours: 8:00 A.M.–10:30 P.M.
Affiliation: None
Extras: Laundry, breakfast, restaurant ($), bar, gym, Internet access, bureau de change, events, TV, jukebox

Best bet for a bite:
Covent Garden area

What hostellers say:
"Bonjour!"

Gestalt:
International house of pots
and pancakes

Hospitality:

Cleanliness:

Party index:

Note: Discounts given to ISIC cardholders.

This hostel's well equipped and caters to students (duh), hence it's very, very popular—full, in other words—most of the time. You'll certainly need to book in advance, especially during summer.

The hostel actually consists of three separate facilities: two buildings here on Great Portland Street, a university residence hall that opens its door to travelers during the summer, and a nearby annex. Among the recently added goodies are an Internet cafe, a gym/fitness center, a bar, a restaurant, and a laundry. Breakfast comes with your bed almost all the time, and the staff run a potpourri of activities and events.

Only drawback? All this luxury costs a lot of quid: This is one of the most expensive hostels in London, unless you're an ISIC cardholder (a student, in other words), and then you get a discount.

how to get there:

By bus or train: Call hostel for transit route.
By car: Call hostel for directions.
By plane: Two airports are outside London; take A2 airbus to hostel.
By Tube: Take Tube to Great Portland Street stop; walk across street to hostel.

---

oxford street hostel
14–18 Noel Street, London W1 1PD
Phone: 0207–734–1618

Fax: 0207–734–1657
E-mail: oxfordst@yha.org.uk
Rates: £19.50–£23.00 (about $39–$46 US) per HI member; doubles £49 (about $98 US)
Credit cards: Yes
Beds: 75
Private/family rooms: Yes
Kitchen available: Yes
Season: Open year-round
Office hours: 7:00 A.M.–11:00 A.M.
Affiliation: HI-YHA
Extras: TV, lockers, bureau de change, breakfast ($), laundry, kitchen, Internet access

---

Note: No children allowed.

How on Earth did YHA snag such a primo hostel location? You're smack in the heart of London's hippest addresses, SoHo and Covent Garden and the West End—incredible. The pub, club, and schmooze scene here rivals any in the world.

And the hostel's okay, considering how many folk want to squeeze in here. Not great. Be forewarned that this is a really small hostel (in a bland building) with smallish dorm rooms; expect a bit of a squeeze plus lots of stairs to hike up first. Cleaning also suffers—more and more over time, we've noticed. Your reward for the hike? Rooms that mostly contain just two to four beds each.

Best bet for a bite:
Mildred's

Insiders' tip:
Hostel pay phones are useless

What hostellers say:
"This neighborhood is *so* cool."

Gestalt:
West End Girls

Safety: ◣

Hospitality: ◣◢

Cleanliness: ◣◢

Party index: 🎿🎿🎿

Management and staff are sometimes friendly (lots of Aussies during our visits); if not, tell us and we'll fix 'em up good. The kitchen's small but pretty good and clean, actually. And the laundry is an extremely welcome addition in a town where just finding a place to wash your clothes can be a chore.

Hostellers come here for the extremely hip location, so you've got to book very early. Some hostellers hang out in the enormous television room. One thing this place ain't is quiet—with all the clubbing at hand, you're sure to be sandwiched between an Aussie and a brewski, but that's all right.

key to icons

◆ Attractive natural setting	▣ Comfortable beds	◉ Visual arts at hostel or nearby
◆ Ecologically aware hostel	Ⓢ A particularly good value	♬ Music at hostel or nearby
✗ Superior kitchen facilities or cafe	▲ Wheelchair-accessible	🎿 Great hostel for skiers
◆ Offbeat or eccentric place	▢ Good for business travelers	▯ Bar or pub at hostel or nearby
▲ Superior bathroom facilities	▟ Especially well suited for families	◈ Editors' Choice: Among our very favorite hostels
♡ Romantic private rooms	◉ Good for active travelers	

how to get there:

By Tube: Take Tube to Oxford Circus. Walk east on Oxford Street, turn right on Poland and then turn left on Noel.

---

piccadilly backpackers
12 Sherwood Street, Piccadilly, London W1F 7BR
Phone: 0207–434–9009

Fax: 0207–434–9010
E-mail: bookings@piccadillybackpackers.com
Rates: £12.00–£50.50 (about $24–$101 US) per person; doubles £53.00–£67.50 (about $106–$135 US)
Credit cards: Yes
Beds: 700
Private/family rooms: Sometimes
Kitchen available: No
Season: Open year-round
Office hours: Twenty-four hours
Affiliation: None
Extras: Ticket office, laundry, travel store, breakfast ($), bar, lockers, Internet access ($), fax, TV, activities

---

Just a minute (literally) from Piccadilly Circus, this newish and huge (700 beds) hostel is already securing a reputation as a place promising a pretty cool design and an ace location . . . but then delivering only half of that promise (the location part).

Doubtless this is one of the best-situated hostels in the city: Leicester Square (the theater district), Trafalgar Square, Big Ben, hip Soho, and the London Eye are all within ten minutes' walk. Nobody's arguing that.

But once you step inside, things begin to diverge from the Web hype. Staff are standoffish. The elevator takes forever, forcing you to possibly walk up five flights of stairs with your pack. The 'net connections are frequently on the blink. And so on. Rooms range from small to biggish, with some wooden bunks and some odd "pod" bunks that feel a little too cozy; it can get drafty, and cleanliness is not great at all. Also, be aware that most of the dorms here are coed—that means guys 'n gals bunking together—though there are a few single-sex dorms, as well.

There isn't a full kitchen, so be prepared to go out scavenging for takeout. They do allow twenty-four-hour access to microwave ovens here—better than nothing, for sure, but still not the same thing as having a proper stovetop. The free lockers (bring your own padlock or buy one at the desk) are pretty small, although the chill-out hosteller bar has to be counted as a positive. There's no smoking throughout this hostel, not even in the Moroccan-themed lounge, but there's also no curfew; if you're a late-nighter intent on raving it up in Soho, that's a good thing.

Best bet for a bite:
Chip shop across street

What hostellers say:
"Not what I expected..."

Gestalt:
Picked clean

Safety: ◣◣

Hospitality: ◣

Cleanliness: ◣

Party index: ◣◣

By the way, while you're out there in the city, stock up on chow—breakfast here is a big disappointment. As was this hostel. It's not the worst we've seen, but we'd stay in a lot of other places first.

how to get there:

By Tube: From Piccadilly station, take Exit 1 up to Glasshouse Street; cross onto Sherwood Street, and walk to yellow entrance of hostel.

st. christopher's ◣◣
village hostel

161–165 Borough High Street, London SE1 1HR
Phone: 0207–407–1856

Fax: 0207–403–7715
E-mail: st.christophers@interpub.co.uk
Web site: interpub.co.uk/st.christophers
Rates: £12.00–£17.50 (about $24–$35 US) per person
Credit cards: Yes
Beds: 165
Private/family rooms: Yes
Kitchen available: No
Season: Open year-round
Office hours: Twenty-four hours
Affiliation: None
Extras: Laundry, bar, TV, roof patio, job board, breakfast, meals ($), pinball, hot tub, sauna

The name on the Web page says it all: The Hostel With Attitude. And let's face it: The reason most hostellers rolled in here was (a) the cheap price and (b) the attached pub.

Yes, a smoky, typical Brit pub. And what a deal! For half what some hostels in London charge, you get a free continental breakfast, meal discounts, and access to a good private lounge.

Dorms come two to fourteen beds per room, but you won't spend much time there. You'll likely be in the pub, shooting free pool on Monday or trying out your karaoke. Noise can be a problem when rock bands play late in the club, though; best to bring your earplugs. Also, smoke from the bar curls upward inevitably to the dorm rooms. If it bugs you, this might not be the place to stay. On the other hand, the rooftop hot tub and sauna just might keep you here.

Best bet for a bite:
On-site pub grub

What hostellers say:
"Fill 'er up!"

Gestalt:
Brew hotel

Safety:

Hospitality:

Cleanliness:

Party index:

The staff here seem to go the extra mile, with advice on getting through the hoops of money changing, visas, and so forth—it seems to attract people who've landed in London to work for a while. They also do wake-up calls. Other amenities include a laundry; that private hostellers' lounge with bar, pinball machine, and forty-channel TV (yippee); a job board; and a mail-forwarding service. We were also impressed with security measures: Each room here is accessed with a key-card. However, we can't recommend the dirty bathrooms, useless storage facilities, and Lilliputian beds.

Just 200 yards from London Bridge, the hostel straddles a blue-collar area and sparkly sights. Keep in mind that it's on the much-less-nice South Bank of the Thames, but there are fewer crowds here. Try a dance club like The Ministry of Sound for something different.

Note that several annexes of this hostel have opened around town in Camden, Greenwich, Shepherd's Bush, and near this one.

how to get there:

By Tube: Call hostel for directions.

st. pancras international hostel

79–81 Euston Road, London NW1 2QS
Phone: 0207–388–9998

Fax: 0207–388–6766
E-mail: stpancras@yha.org.uk
Rates: £21–£25 (about $42–$50 US) per HI member; private rooms £56 (about $112 US)
Credit cards: Yes
Beds: 152
Private/family rooms: Yes
Kitchen available: Yes
Season: Open year-round
Office hours: 7:00 A.M.–11:00 P.M.
Affiliation: HI-YHA
Extras: TV, bike storage, laundry, dinner ($), breakfast, kitchen

London's newest Hostelling International joint isn't in the greatest neighborhood, but it's close to a number of fine attractions and extremely well equipped.

Best bet for a bite:

Drummond Street, near Euston Square

What hostellers say:

"No, I don't wanna buy any drugs."

Gestalt:

Saint in the city

Safety:

Hospitality:

Cleanliness:

Party index:

Placed near St. Pancras train station, it gets seedy at night and isn't recommended for the solitary female traveler. On the other hand, facilities are pretty nice. Dorm rooms contain just two to five beds, and everything's new, of course. The outside and inside are decked out in modern touches like chrome trim.

The train station couldn't be closer, and you're an incredibly short walk from the British Library as well as several Tube stops. The Camden Town area hops despite the sleaze factor, offering bargain shops by day and lots of live music and pubbing by night.

how to get there:

By train: From St. Pancras Station, turn right onto Euston Road, cross Judd Street; hostel is second building on right after crossroad.

By Tube: Take Tube to King's Cross Station. Turn right onto Euston Road and cross Judd Street; hostel is second building on right after crossroad.

thameside hostel
20 Salter Road, London SE16 5PR
Phone: 0870–770–6010

Fax: 0207–237–2919
E-mail: thameside@yha.org.uk
Rates: £19.50–£24.00 (about $39–$48 US) per HI member; doubles £51.50 (about $103 US)
Credit cards: Yes
Beds: 320
Private/family rooms: Yes
Kitchen available: Yes
Season: Open year-round
Office hours: 7:00 A.M.–11:00 P.M.
Affiliation: HI-YHA
Extras: Laundry, bureau de change, breakfast ($), travel shop, TV, dinner ($), Internet access, bar

You'll hear this well-equipped place touted as being just a mile from the Tower Bridge, but truth be told we're a bit skeptical about the location. It's in the Docklands, distant from most attractions—and not heavily foot-trafficked at night, either. The twenty-four-hour desk security made us feel better once we'd arrived, though. Atmosphere is absolutely lacking and you'll likely spend very little time here doing anything other than sleeping.

Otherwise, this purpose-built hostel is great. Rooms are nice and small—lots of doubles here—and all contain en-suite bathrooms. The private rooms reminded us of a hotel, and there's a travel shop for stocking up on supplies. Staff are straightforward, rather than peppy,

Best bet for a bite:
Elsewhere

What hostellers say:
"Pass the Geritol."

Gestalt:
Dry dock

Safety:

Hospitality:

Cleanliness:

Party index:

but everything's kept quite clean. Just allow lots of time to get to this not-exactly-perfect location, which isn't so much seedy as blah.

how to get there:

By bus: Take East London Tube line to Rotherhithe. From station, walk along Brunel Road to Salter or take taxi to hostel. From Waterloo Station, take P11 bus to hostel.

By Tube: Take East London Tube line to Rotherhithe. From station, walk along Brunel Road to Salter or take taxi to hostel.

manchester

All right, we'll go ahead and confess to it: Manchester surprised the heck out of us. Sure, it's got a rap as a grimy, industrial place—and that's true—but there's a lot of cultural life here in the North. We came away feeling like this was one of our favorite cities, and not just because The Stone Roses and other seminal Brit-pop bands formed here.

manchester hostels
at a glance

	RATING	PRICE	IN A WORD	PAGE
Manchester Hostel	▨▨	£15.50–£30.00	plush	p. 435
The Hatters	▨	£15–£30	heady	p. 434

the hatters ▨

50 Newton Street, Manchester M1 2EA
Phone: 0161–236–9500

Web site: www.hattersgroup.com
Rates: £15.50–£30.00 (about $31–$60 US) per person; doubles £50–£55 (about $100–$110 US)

Credit cards: Yes
Beds: 200
Private/family rooms: Yes
Kitchen available: Yes
Season: Open year-round
Office hours: Twenty-four hours
Affiliation: None
Extras: Free light breakfast, storage, Internet access, bike storage, tourism information, TV, free popcorn, pool table

This newish indy hostel opened in a former Manchester hat factory in 2003, and it has been really nicely renovated inside. A big brick building with arched windows, it seems to have gotten a complete once-over. Dorm rooms contain two to ten beds, and they've got singles as well.

Gestalt:	Hats off
Safety:	
Hospitality:	
Cleanliness:	
Party index:	

The location is fairly central, a little north of town but not too too far, and they've equipped the place with amenities such as a pool table and Internet access.

Staff makes free popcorn to accompany movie viewing in the TV lounge, and a key-card system ensures better security. Staff are cool. So far, so good.

how to get there:

By car: Contact hostel for directions.
By bus: Contact hostel for transit route.
By train: Contact hostel for transit route.

manchester hostel

Potato Wharf, Castlefield, Greater Manchester M3 4NB
Phone: 0161–839–9960

Fax: 0161–835–2054
E-mail: manchester@yha.org.uk
Rates: £16–£21 (about $32–$42 US) per HI member
Credit cards: Yes
Beds: 136
Private/family rooms: Yes
Kitchen available: Yes
Season: Open year-round

manchester

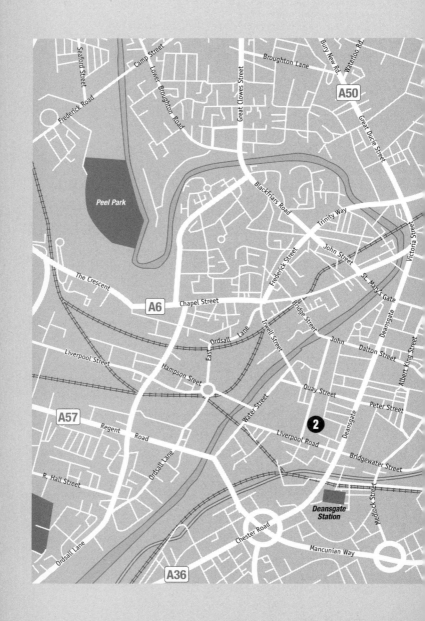

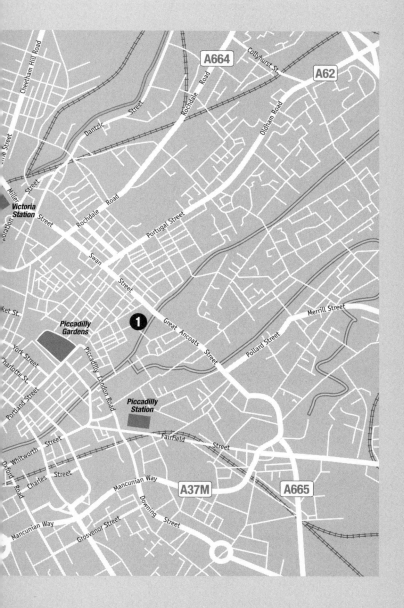

Office hours: Twenty-four hours
Affiliation: HI-YHA
Extras: TV, game room, laundry, meals ($), lockers, conference rooms

Some call this the best hostel in the world. And we've got to agree that it certainly deserves all the thumbs up we can muster. It remains as perfect (or nearly so) as ever, even upon repeat viewings-and-bunkings.

Lots of thought seems to have gone into the joint, which is almost like a sleek modern hotel. There are plenty of private rooms, for starters, and even the dorms never have more than six beds. Every room has its own en-suite bathroom, a rarity in the world of Eurohostelling. Some of the rooms are wheelchair-accessible, too, and some have televisions. Staff are incredibly friendly, the place is spotless, good meals are served— and you can actually have fun here in the common rooms talking with people! It's so unlike a YHA hostel we almost fell over in surprise.

Best bet for a bite:
Rusholme neighborhood
(Indian)

Insiders' tip:
Hacienda dance club
nearby

Gestalt:
Manchester United

Safety: [symbol]

Hospitality: [symbol]

Cleanliness: [symbol]

Party index: [symbols]

As a bonus, it's right across the road from the good Museum of Science and Industry, which charts the Industrial Revolution and central England's crucial role in it.

As a city, Manchester's definitely on the comeback trail after years of industrial gray. Despite the smog and bricks, you can find tons of veggie eats, pubs, gay culture, bars, and a pumpin' music scene. Raves that the likes of Madonna might drop in for (at the Hacienda dance club), beers at any of a hundred pubs (the Ox Noble and the White Lion next door are great), gardens, universities, a Roman fort . . . the list goes on and on.

Tack on Europe's best Indian food—a mile-long strip of curry houses—and you'll be sticking around at least a night or two. This place is getting fun.

how to get there:

By bus: From Piccadilly Gardens, take #33 bus to hostel. From main bus station, walk 1 mile to hostel, behind Castlefield Hotel. Or take

Metro to G-Mex Centre and walk along Liverpool Road to Potato Wharf on left; turn left and walk to hostel on left. Take cab at night. **By car:** Call hostel for directions.

By train: From Deansgate Station, walk to Chester Road then turn left at Liverpool Road; take next left. Hostel is on left, behind Castlefield Hotel. From Piccadilly Station, walk 1 mile through city center, following signs to Castlefield/Museum of Science and Industry. Or take Metrolink to G-Mex Station and walk 2 blocks up Bridgewater and Liverpool to hostel. Hostel is behind Castlefield Hotel. Take cab at night.

paul's picks*

(*with the help of hundreds of others)

12 GREAT EUROPEAN CITY HOSTELS

10 HARD-ROCKIN' EUROPEAN PARTY HOSTELS

about the author

Paul Karr is an award-winning writer, writing coach, and the author or co-author of more than twenty-five books. He contributes regularly to magazines and writes and records music when he's not traveling. He has twice been named a writer-in-residence by the National Parks Service. You can e-mail him directly at:

Paulkarr@aol.com